Who Really Made Your Car?

Who Really Made Your Car?

Restructuring and Geographic Change in the Auto Industry

Thomas Klier
James Rubenstein

2008

W.E. Upjohn Institute for Employment Research
Kalamazoo, Michigan

Library of Congress Cataloging-in-Publication Data

Klier, Thomas H.
  Who really made your car? : restructuring and geographic change in the auto
industry / Thomas Klier and James Rubenstein
      p. cm.
  Includes bibliographical references and index.
  ISBN-13: 978-0-88099-333-3 (pbk. : alk. paper)
  ISBN-10: 0-88099-333-2 (pbk. : alk. paper)
  ISBN-13: 978-0-88099-334-0 (hardcover : alk. paper)
  ISBN-10: 0-88099-334-0 (hardcover : alk. paper)
  1. Automobile supplies industry—United States. 2. Automobiles—Parts.
3. Automobile industry—United States. I. Rubenstein, James M. II. Title.
  HD9710.3.U52K55 2008
  338.4'762920973—dc22

                          2008017763

The facts presented in this study and the observations and viewpoints expressed are
the sole responsibility of the authors. They do not necessarily represent positions of
the W.E. Upjohn Institute for Employment Research.

Cover design by Alcorn Publication Design.
Index prepared by Nancy Humphreys.
Printed in the United States of America.
Printed on recycled paper.

Contents

Figures

Tables

Acknowledgments

The work on this book started a number of years ago when we both recognized we were independently working on understanding the changing geography of the U.S. auto supplier industry. We subsequently undertook a series of joint projects, resulting in publications and conferences on the auto industry. This book represents the culmination of that joint research.

Along the way, many individuals contributed. At the Federal Reserve Bank of Chicago, we would like to thank the current and immediate past bank presidents, Charlie Evans and Michael Moskow, and Dan Sullivan, director of research, for encouraging and supporting the work on this book. We especially thank Bill Testa, vice president and director of regional programs, for providing invaluable support and advice throughout the entire process. Glenn Hansen, senior vice president and manager of the Detroit branch, was always enthusiastic about our project and provided help in getting in touch with some of our interviewees. We would also like to thank Loretta Ardaugh, assistant vice president, research support; Kathy Schrepfer, vice president, administration; and Ella Dukes, senior administrative assistant, for their contributions.

As with any data-intensive research project, the compilation of the database underlying the analysis for this book represents the work of many talented individuals. We extend our thanks for assistance with research to Cole Bolton, Taft Foster, Anna Gacia, Joanna Karasewicz, Paul Ma, Vanessa Haleco-Meyer, Neil Murphy, Mike Rorke, Tommy Scheiding, George Simler, and Alexei Zelenev, who have all worked on data preparation and support at one point or another during this project. Special thanks to Vanessa and Cole for producing extraordinary maps. As they say, a picture is worth a thousand words; a good picture is worth even more.

We would also like to extend our thanks to many individuals in the auto industry, representing carmakers, suppliers, analysts, observers, and economic developers, who indulged in early versions of our analysis as well as provided useful insights through conversation and discussion. We would especially like to thank David Andrea, vice president, industry analysis and economics, Original Equipment Suppliers Organization; and Sean McAlinden, chief economist and vice president, research, Center for Automotive Research, for offering encouragement and suggestions from the early days of this project.

The staff at the W.E. Upjohn Institute for Employment Research was very helpful in publishing the results. We would like to thank Randall Eberts, Allison Hewitt Colosky, Bob Wathen, and Richard Wyrwa for their comments throughout the publication process. We also extend our thanks to an anonymous referee whose comments greatly improved the book.

Thomas Klier would like to thank his family, Teresa and the boys, Alex and Josh, for putting up with book-related disruptions to the finely tuned family schedule. Jim Rubenstein would like to thank his wife Bernadette Unger, who has been by his side through his two-decade auto journey.

We dedicate this book to our respective spouses. And, no, neither one of us knows how to actually fix a car.

1
The Parts of Your Vehicle

In an operation like ours, the suppliers will make you or break you.[1]

Motor vehicle producers are among the world's most recognizable brands. Thanks to elaborate marketing, nameplates like Ford, Toyota, and Volkswagen are familiar to consumers around the world. Consumers are attracted to the ruggedness of Ford, the reliability of Toyota, or the style of Volkswagen. Yet the driving experience—comfort, performance, and reliability—primarily is not set by the company whose name is on the dashboard, but by the hundreds of suppliers of the vehicle's parts.

Think about the radio in the center console of your vehicle. A vehicle is put together from hundreds of components like the radio. These components range from pistons and cylinders to door handles and steering wheels. And a radio, in turn, consists of many individual parts, such as knobs and wires and sensors, not to mention nuts and bolts and screws. Disaggregating a vehicle in this fashion reveals a highly complex supply chain involving thousands of parts and almost as many individual companies.

The motor vehicle industry is composed of two types of manufacturers: assemblers and parts makers. First, a handful of assemblers, usually referred to in this book as *carmakers*, put together vehicles at several dozen final assembly plants in the United States. Second, several thousand parts makers, usually referred to in this book as *suppliers*, produce the roughly 15,000 parts that go into the vehicles (Australia Department for Environment and Heritage 2002).

Until the late twentieth century, U.S. carmakers produced most of their own parts themselves and dominated the suppliers of the parts that they did purchase (see Chapter 2). In the twenty-first century, responsibility for making many parts has been passed to independently owned suppliers. Several thousand companies, employing more than 670,000 workers, produce several hundred billion dollars worth of parts every year for new vehicles assembled in the United States.

"The motor vehicle supplier sector has become the backbone of the motor vehicle assembly industry, employing . . . substantially more than the number of people employed by the assemblers" (Hill, Menk, and Szakaly 2007). About 186,000 workers were employed in U.S. final assembly plants in 2007, compared to approximately 673,000 in parts supplier plants (Table 1.1). The true ratio of parts to assembly employment was even higher than three to one because more than one-fourth of the parts purchased in 2006 came from overseas factories, and those workers were not included in the comparison.

The total value of all of the parts delivered by Tier 1 suppliers to final assembly plants averaged $13,600 per vehicle in 2006, compared to $11,100 in 2000, an increase of 22.5 percent over six years (Merrill Lynch 2007). In comparison, the average expenditure on a new car increased only 10.0 percent during that period, from $20,600 in 2000 to $22,650 in 2006 (Ward's Automotive Group 2007).

PRINCIPAL OBJECTIVES OF THE BOOK

The motor vehicle parts industry has been changing geographically as well as functionally. This book analyzes the linkages between changes in the auto industry's geography and structure. It raises the level of understanding of how the industry is organized by providing analysis at a much richer level of detail than has been provided in previous studies.

This book has two major purposes. The first is to describe the key characteristics of parts suppliers, which account for the largest and increasing share of the value added in manufacturing motor vehicles. The analysis relies heavily on data collected concerning several thousand parts plants in the United States, Canada, and Mexico. The second principal purpose is to describe the changing geography of U.S. motor vehicle production at local, regional, national, and international scales. The book explains that these spatial changes have resulted from changing relationships between carmakers and their suppliers.

An industry that was once heavily clustered in Michigan has been dispersing to other states, as well as to other countries. In the mid-twentieth century, three-quarters of all parts were made in or near Michigan;

Table 1.1 U.S. Assembly and Parts Employment, 2007

	Employment (000)	Share (%)
Carmakers		
Total light vehicle assembly	185.5	21.6
Parts suppliers		
Chassis	73.5	8.6
Electronics	79.5	9.3
Exterior	154.0	17.9
Interior	63.5	7.4
Powertrain	141.7	16.5
Other	160.3	18.7
Total parts suppliers	672.5	78.4

SOURCE: Bureau of Labor Statistics (n.d.).

in the twenty-first century, only one-quarter come from there. Between 2000 and 2007 alone, Michigan's employment in the motor vehicle parts industry fell by 43 percent, from 227,000 to 129,000. Yet, at a regional scale, the U.S. motor vehicle industry is still heavily clustered, in a region—known as Auto Alley—that lies in a north–south corridor between the Great Lakes and the Gulf of Mexico.

Parts are made by two kinds of companies, original equipment manufacturers (OEMs) and aftermarket suppliers. Original equipment manufacturers make parts for new vehicles, and aftermarket suppliers make replacement parts for older vehicles. Original equipment accounts for about 70 percent of total parts sales and the aftermarket about 30 percent (Office of Aerospace and Automotive Industries 2007). The distinction between the two groups is not always clear-cut because more than one-third of the 100 largest OEM suppliers also rank among the 100 largest aftermarket suppliers, but for the most part, the two sectors of the motor vehicle industry remain distinct (Automotive Aftermarket Suppliers Association 2007; *Automotive News* 2007a).

This book is concerned with OEM suppliers, which have varying characteristics. Some of them are multibillion-dollar enterprises, whereas others are very small. Some have been around for more than a century, whereas others were created in the twenty-first century. Some are family owned, and others are controlled by venture capital.

What nearly all parts makers share in the eyes of the motorist is invisibility. If consumers like a vehicle, the carmaker gets the credit. If it is disliked, the carmaker is blamed. Even auto industry insiders know little about most of the parts makers. Numerous histories have been written about carmakers, as well as about their founders and leaders. A search of any good-sized library or online retailer will turn up hundreds of books just on Henry Ford and the Ford Motor Co. A similar search will reveal that little if anything has been written about the vast majority of the parts companies discussed in this book.

Consider, for example, the best-selling car in the United States in 2007, the Toyota Camry. Two-thirds of the value of the Camry was added not by Toyota but by independent suppliers. The motor vehicle industry's principal newspaper, *Automotive News*, depicted some of Toyota's several hundred Camry suppliers (Figure 1.1). Several were Japanese-owned companies with close historical links to Toyota, such as the wire harness supplier Yazaki and the spring supplier NHK. But consumers attracted to a Japanese car with a well-earned reputation for high quality may be surprised to see how few of the parts were actually made in Japan or by Japanese companies.

The parts in a 2007 Camry represent a veritable United Nations of ownership, including British-based shaft supplier GKN, Canadian-based hinge supplier Cosma (now Magna), German-based ABS brake supplier Robert Bosch, and Swedish-based airbag supplier Autoliv. Venerable U.S.-owned corporations were major contributors as well, including hose supplier Dana, valve supplier Eaton, interior supplier Lear, and paint supplier PPG. Other parts makers highlighted in Figure 1.1 are themselves multinational joint ventures, such as American–Japanese exhaust supplier Arvin Sango and seat supplier Trim Masters, and German–Japanese sealing supplier Freudenberg-NOK.

The suppliers mentioned in the two previous paragraphs all are ranked among the largest in the motor vehicle industry, each with annual sales in the billions of dollars. Other Camry suppliers are more modestly sized, generating revenues only in the tens of millions of dollars, for example, stabilizer bar supplier Brewer Automotive Components, headrest supplier Gill, and oil filler cap supplier Miniature Precision.

When the Ford F-150, the best-selling truck model in the United States, was redesigned in 2004, it too had a mix of large and small domestic- and foreign-owned suppliers (Figure 1.2). Although the F-150

Figure 1.1 Major Suppliers to the Toyota Camry

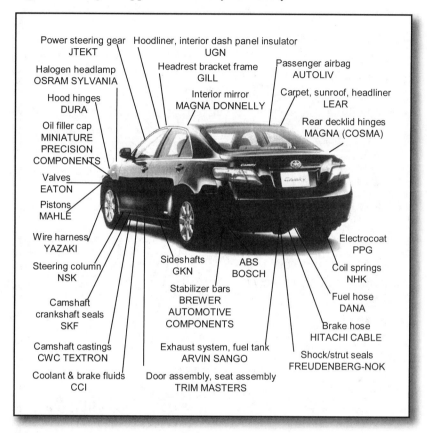

Power steering gear
JTEKT

Hoodliner, interior dash panel insulator
UGN

Halogen headlamp
OSRAM SYLVANIA

Headrest bracket frame
GILL

Passenger airbag
AUTOLIV

Hood hinges
DURA

Interior mirror
MAGNA DONNELLY

Carpet, sunroof, headliner
LEAR

Oil filler cap
MINIATURE
PRECISION
COMPONENTS

Rear decklid hinges
MAGNA (COSMA)

Valves
EATON

Pistons
MAHLE

Wire harness
YAZAKI

Electrocoat
PPG

Steering column
NSK

Sideshafts
GKN

ABS
BOSCH

Coil springs
NHK

Camshaft
crankshaft seals
SKF

Stabilizer bars
BREWER
AUTOMOTIVE
COMPONENTS

Fuel hose
DANA

Brake hose
HITACHI CABLE

Camshaft castings
CWC TEXTRON

Exhaust system, fuel tank
ARVIN SANGO

Shock/strut seals
FREUDENBERG-NOK

Coolant & brake fluids
CCI

Door assembly, seat assembly
TRIM MASTERS

SOURCE: Adapted by the authors from *Automotive News* (2006).

was a truck made by a U.S.-owned company and the Camry a car made by a Japanese-owned company, the two models had some of the same suppliers. Not only did the "Japanese" Camry and the "American" F-150 share leading U.S.-owned suppliers such as Dana, Dura, and Lear, they both had brakes and lights supplied by leading German suppliers Robert Bosch and Osram Sylvania, respectively.

Suppliers to these two best-selling vehicles differed in two key aspects. The leading F-150 supplier by far, Visteon Corp., was not a major Camry supplier. Among Visteon's many contributions to the F-150 were alternators, antitheft devices, axles, fuel tanks, headlamps,

Figure 1.2 Major Suppliers to the Ford F-150

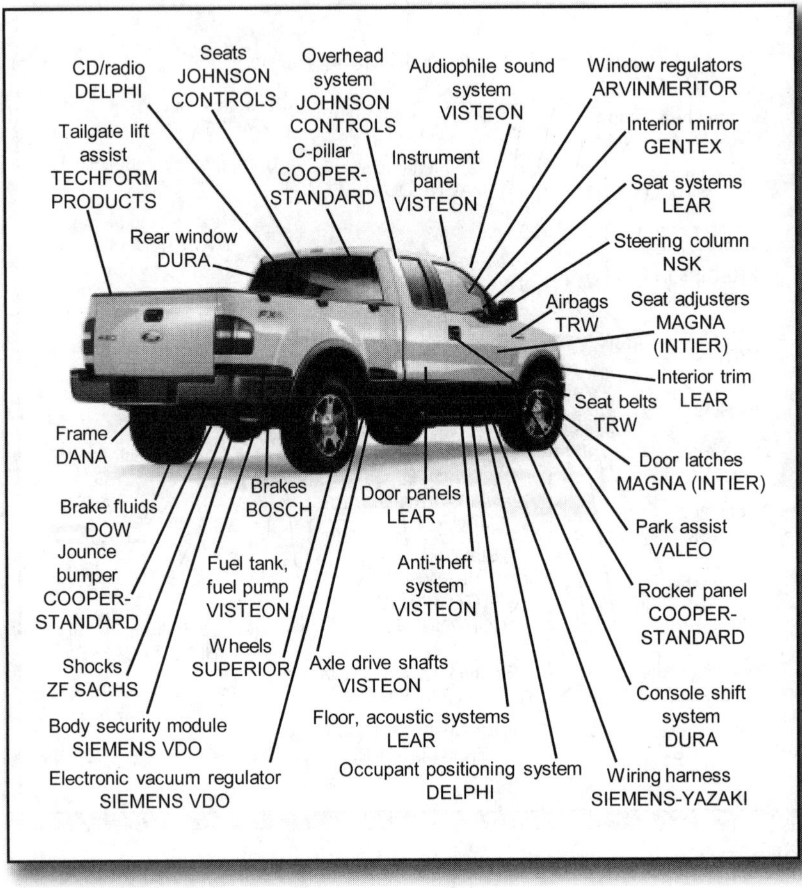

CD/radio
DELPHI

Seats
JOHNSON
CONTROLS

Overhead
system
JOHNSON
CONTROLS

Audiophile sound
system
VISTEON

Window regulators
ARVINMERITOR

Tailgate lift
assist
TECHFORM
PRODUCTS

C-pillar
COOPER-
STANDARD

Instrument
panel
VISTEON

Interior mirror
GENTEX

Seat systems
LEAR

Rear window
DURA

Steering column
NSK

Airbags
TRW

Seat adjusters
MAGNA
(INTIER)

Interior trim

Seat belts   LEAR
TRW

Frame
DANA

Door latches
MAGNA (INTIER)

Brake fluids
DOW

Brakes
BOSCH

Door panels
LEAR

Park assist
VALEO

Jounce
bumper
COOPER-
STANDARD

Fuel tank,
fuel pump
VISTEON

Anti-theft
system
VISTEON

Rocker panel
COOPER-
STANDARD

Shocks
ZF SACHS

Wheels
SUPERIOR

Axle drive shafts
VISTEON

Console shift
system
DURA

Body security module
SIEMENS VDO

Floor, acoustic systems
LEAR

Electronic vacuum regulator
SIEMENS VDO

Occupant positioning system
DELPHI

Wiring harness
SIEMENS-YAZAKI

instrument panels, pumps, radiators, sound systems, and windshields. In 2004, Visteon was the second-largest parts maker in North America, with $11 billion in sales for new vehicles. Visteon was not the F-150's leading supplier by accident. Until 2000, when it was spun off as an independent company, Visteon was Ford Motor Company's parts-making operation.

The other major difference concerns geography. The F-150 was put together at arguably the most venerable assembly plant in the country, Ford's Rouge complex in Dearborn, Michigan. At its height of importance between the two world wars, the Rouge complex employed more

Figure 1.2 (continued)

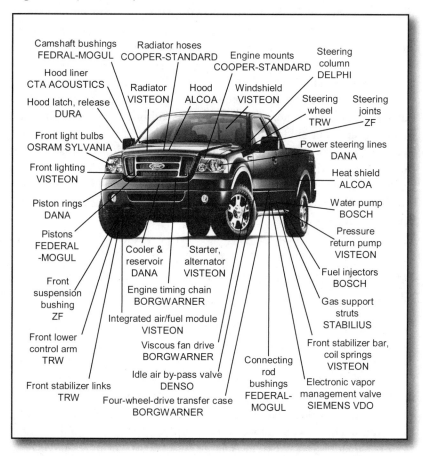

SOURCE: Adapted by the authors from *Automotive News* (2006).

than 100,000 workers in more than 100 buildings. Raw materials famously arrived at one end and finished vehicles rolled out at the other. Ford's twenty-first-century Rouge assembly plant bears little physical resemblance to the mid-twentieth-century version. A display in the Rouge visitor center illustrates how much the complex had changed. Yet the plant continued to be a major reason why Michigan was still the leading car-producing state in the early twenty-first century.

Meanwhile, 300 miles south, Toyota was assembling most of its Camrys in Georgetown, Kentucky, previously best known for a small college that hosted the Cincinnati Bengals preseason camp. Toyota deliberately chose to build a campus with nearly 10,000 employees in a small town with little tradition in the motor vehicle industry. Ironically, Toyota's current Georgetown complex comes closer to the organizational spirit of the mid-twentieth-century Rouge than does Ford's twenty-first-century assembly plant on the Rouge site.

Where vehicles are assembled affects where parts are made. Some parts are made right next door to the assembly plants, and some are made on the other side of the world. In the context of just-in-time production, however, we show that most parts are made within a several-hundred-mile radius of the assembly plant in which they are used. Thus, most of the F-150 parts are made within several hundred miles of the Rouge, and most of the Camry parts are made within several hundred miles of Georgetown.

DATA FOR THIS BOOK

The first challenge in writing about parts suppliers is actually finding them. Other empirical studies have relied on government summary data and interviews with selected industry officials and observers (e.g., Cooney 2005; Cooney and Yacobucci 2005; Dyer 2000; Office of Aerospace and Automotive Industries 2007; Van Biesebroeck 2006).

This study's database, in contrast, has been built by aggregating observations from several thousand individual parts plants in the United States, Canada, and Mexico. A large number of variables have been collected for every factory operated by the 150 largest North American suppliers, as well as more than a thousand smaller companies. Together, these plants account for the overwhelming majority of parts production in North America, probably well over 90 percent.

One hundred percent coverage cannot be claimed for the database. Information may be incorrect for particular plants, and some plants undoubtedly have been missed altogether. But this is by far the most comprehensive and detailed compilation of data on parts suppliers in North America, making it possible to identify trends and draw conclusions at a higher level of detail than is possible with summary data.[2]

Government Data Sources

The primary government data source is the U.S. Census of Manufactures, collected every five years, including 1997 and 2002. The Census of Manufactures provides information about both the value of shipments originating from manufacturing establishments and the value added at manufacturing establishments in each sector of the economy. The census also provides information on employees, payroll, production workers, wages, cost of materials, and capital expenditures.

Motor vehicle assembly operations are allocated to North American Industrial Classification System (NAICS) code 3361. NAICS 3361 is divided into three six-digit codes: NAICS 336111 for automobile manufacturing (i.e., final assembly), NAICS 336112 for light truck manufacturing, and NAICS 336120 for heavy truck manufacturing. The value of parts delivered to automobile and light truck final assembly plants in the United States was $156.2 billion according to the 2002 census (Table 1.2).

The manufacture of many motor vehicle parts is assigned to NAICS 3363, which is divided into eight six-digit codes: engines, electrical, steering & suspension, brakes, transmissions, fabrics & seats, metal stampings, and other. We also include NAICS 336211, motor vehicle

Table 1.2 Value of Shipments and Receipts of Motor Vehicle Parts (NAICS 3363)

NAICS	Parts	Shipments from suppliers ($, billions)	Received by assemblers ($, billions)
336330, 336340	Chassis	23.6	9.5
336320	Electronics	25.7	4.0
336370, 336211	Exterior	32.9	11.9
336360	Interior	17.2	19.1
336310, 336350	Powertrain	70.5	42.9
336390	Other	41.4	6.6
	Total	211.3	Unknown
—	Other NAICS codes	Unknown	Unknown
—	Total value of parts	Unknown	156.2

SOURCE: U.S. Census Bureau, 2002 Census of Manufactures.

bodies, in our definition of motor vehicle parts. The value of shipments for NAICS codes 3363 and 336211, motor vehicle parts and motor vehicle bodies, in 2002 was $211.3 billion. The six-digit NAICS codes are subdivided into more detailed eight- and 10-digit codes. For example, transmissions (NAICS 336350) is divided into transmissions for new vehicles (NAICS 33635011), transmissions for heavy trucks and buses (NAICS 33635012), transmission parts (NAICS 33635013), axles (NAICS 33635014), and other drivetrain parts (NAICS 33635015). NAICS 33635015 in turn is divided into seven 10-digit codes, such as clutches (NAICS 3363501522) and drive shafts (NAICS 3363501528).

The large discrepancy between the value of deliveries and the value of shipments, as well as the large size of "other" categories, points to three serious limitations of NAICS data. First, shipments include both original equipment and aftermarket sales. As mentioned earlier in this chapter, an estimated 30 percent of shipments go to the aftermarket, although precise figures are not available from the census and percentages are likely to vary among NAICS codes. Second, deliveries include both domestic-made and foreign-made parts. As discussed in more detail in Chapter 13, at the time of the 2002 census, roughly one-fourth of parts arriving at U.S. assembly plants were produced in other countries.

The third critical limitation, affecting both shipments and deliveries, is that some key parts, including tires, glass, and paint, have been placed in NAICS codes other than 3363 if their primary customers are outside the motor vehicle industry. Consequently, it is not possible, using census data, to break out values on the shipments of these parts to vehicle assembly plants.

This Study's Database

Rather than relying predominantly on aggregated government data, research for this book included creating a database of several thousand parts plants by name and address. The starting point for the plant-level database was information acquired from ELM International, Inc., a Michigan-based vendor of information about automotive suppliers.[3]

Although it was not designed with research applications in mind, the ELM International database purports to offer exhaustive coverage, with 4,268 plant-level records in 2006, covering the United States, Canada, and Mexico. Additional records are continuously added. Information about individual plants includes name, address, products made at the plant, names of customers, number of employees, and name of the union if present.

We made five types of substantial revisions to the ELM International database. First, the names of companies and unions were corrected to reflect the many mergers, acquisitions, and other changes affecting the industry in recent years.

The second revision concerned employment level. Plants shown by ELM International to have more than 2,000 employees were checked either by phone or a review of the company Web site. Employment figures reported in the ELM International database for 2006 averaged about one-fourth higher than the field-checked employment figures. Consequently, employment figures based on ELM International data were not used in this study unless they were found to be in substantial agreement with other sources.

We also added plants that should have been included by ELM International to the database and removed others that had closed. Every plant operated in the United States in 2006 by the 150 largest parts suppliers, according to *Automotive News* (2007a), was identified, representing a total of approximately 1,600 plants. There was a net of 335 plants added to the ELM International database, approximately a 20 percent increase.

Fourth, we collected additional information about the 4,268 plants in the database beyond that provided by ELM International. The age of the plant and the nationality of the owner were found for most of the plants through contacting the companies or reviewing state industrial directories, press reports, and trade associations (e.g., the Japan Auto Parts Industries Association). The latitude and longitude of each plant location was geocoded to facilitate mapping of plant distributions, which was especially important for the geographic analysis found throughout this book.

The final significant revision was to identify one primary type of part for each of the 4,268 plants. The ELM International database listed up to 13 distinct parts being made at a particular plant; only 1,551 plants had only 1 parts code, 37 had at least 10 parts codes, and 4 plants had the maximum 13. The mean number of parts codes per plant was about 2.4. For this book, we assigned each plant one of six codes: chassis, electronic, exterior, interior, generic, and powertrain.

The principal limitation of the database that could not be overcome concerned the customers for each plant. The database showed the names of the carmakers to which the parts were ultimately attached, but it rarely listed the name of the immediate customer, which in many cases would be another supplier. In other words, most suppliers of seat parts, for example, reported their customer to be a carmaker even though the seat parts were actually shipped to a seat assembler.

Key findings of the database included:

- Number of plants: 3,179 plants were located in the United States, plus 416 in Canada and 673 in Mexico (see Figure 1.3).

- Type of owner: 3 percent of the U.S. parts plants were owned by carmakers; 42 percent by the 150 largest suppliers, each with annual North American original equipment sales of more than $200 million; and 55 percent by 1,000 other suppliers.

- Plant size: Median plant employment was 220, mean was 350, and 6 percent had more than 1,000 employees.

- Nationality of owner: 77 percent were owned by companies with U.S. headquarters and 23 percent by companies with foreign headquarters.

- Date of opening: 55 percent were opened before 1980 and 45 percent between 1980 and 2006.

- Location: 25 percent were located in Michigan, 36 percent in other Great Lakes states, 28 percent in the South, and 11 percent in the rest of the country.

- Union: 85 percent of the plants reported on their union status: 30 percent had a union and 70 percent did not.

- Type of part: 22 percent of plants made parts for the powertrain, including the engine and transmission; 19 percent of plants made parts for the chassis, including tires, wheels, brakes, steering, and suspension; 15 percent of plants made parts for the exterior, including bodies, bumpers, glass, and paint; 14 percent of plants made parts for the interior, including seats, instrument panels, doors, headliners, and carpeting; 15 percent of plants made parts for the electronic systems, including engine management, passenger convenience, and safety; and 16 percent of plants made generic parts, including bearings, brackets, and hinges.

Figure 1.3 Parts and Assembly Plants in North America

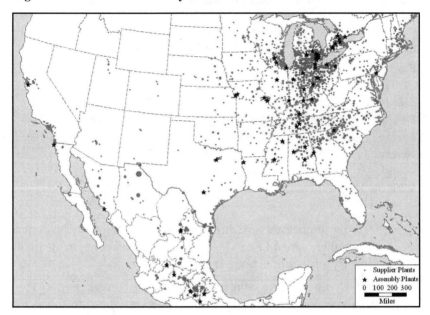

SOURCE: Adapted by the authors from *Ward's Automotive Yearbook*, ELM International, and other sources.

Compared with supplier studies by the U.S. Census Bureau, the Center for Automotive Research (CAR), and Merrill Lynch, this study has found a smaller percentage of powertrain plants and a larger percentage of chassis plants (Table 1.3). The difference can most likely be attributed to differences in allocating parts among systems. For example, should the axle be considered part of the powertrain or part of the chassis?

BOOK OUTLINE

The book is divided into four sections, based on impacts of changing carmaker–supplier relationships at various geographic scales:

- Part I: The motor vehicle industry's traditional core region cen-

Table 1.3 Percent Vehicle Content by System

| System | This study | | Census | | | Merrill |
	With generic	Without generic	With generic	Without generic	CAR	Lynch
Powertrain	22	26	27	33	40	36
Chassis	19	22	9	11	15	18
Electronics	15	17	21	25	11	18
Exterior	15	18	19	23	16	19
Interior	14	17	6	8	18	10
Generic	16		18			

NOTE: Columns may not sum to 100 due to rounding.
SOURCE: McAlinden and Andrea (2002); Merrill Lynch (2007).

tered on southeastern Michigan and adjacent Midwest states near the southern Great Lakes. Which parts are still being made in the industry's traditional home and why?

- Part II: Local-scale connections between carmakers and their suppliers. Which parts are being made very close to their customer—a final assembly plant—and how are the rest of the parts being moved from supplier to customer?

- Part III: Clustering of motor vehicle production at the regional scale, known as Auto Alley. Why have most suppliers located in Auto Alley, and what factors account for choice of location within Auto Alley?

- Part IV: International shifts in production of parts for the U.S. motor vehicle industry. What is the magnitude and rate of growth of the outsourcing of parts to other countries, and which of the many parts in a motor vehicle are the ones being sourced overseas?

CARMAKER–SUPPLIER RELATIONS

Manufacture of original equipment parts constitutes an intermediate step in the process of producing motor vehicles. As a result, the fortunes of the producers of the parts depend to a large extent on their ultimate customers, the carmakers. A book on motor vehicle parts suppliers therefore must acknowledge the perspective of carmakers. In this section, we briefly review changes in the role of parts makers from the carmaker's perspective, as well as the literature on relationships between carmakers and parts suppliers.

The "Big 3" carmakers (GM, Ford, and Chrysler) dominated twentieth-century production, but they entered the twenty-first century on very shaky ground. Their U.S. market share plunged from 95 percent in the mid-twentieth century to 75 percent in the late twentieth century to 50 percent in the first decade of the twenty-first century. Ford and GM faced their most serious financial challenges since the Great Depression, and Chrysler was first sold to German carmaker Daimler-Benz, then to private equity firm Cerberus. Reflecting the declining market share, the "Big 3" were more accurately known in the twenty-first century as the "Detroit 3."

As the Detroit 3 struggled, Japanese-based companies led by Toyota were raking in record profits and market share. Foreign-owned carmakers accounted for more than one-third of motor vehicle production in the United States during the first decade of the twenty-first century (Andrea 2007). Toyota passed Ford as the world's second-largest producer in 2004 and GM as the world's largest producer in 2007 (Child 2008). When it overtook GM, Toyota became the first non-American company to lead world production since the nineteenth century.

Toyota's success was based on its distinctive production system that efficiently turned out vehicles nearly free of defects. The Toyota Production System has many key elements, and often underappreciated among them is a distinctive relationship between the carmaker and its suppliers. "At least part of Toyota's success is because of its harmonious relationship with supplier companies."[4]

In a fiercely cutthroat market, the relationship with suppliers has become a key source of competitive advantage for some carmakers. As Toyota passed Ford and then GM as the world's largest carmaker, favorable supplier relations contributed to its success. "The automaker thinks it can gain a competitive advantage in North America if suppliers are satisfied by their relationship with the automaker" (Chappell 2005b).

Benefits of Good Carmaker–Supplier Relations

Researchers have been especially interested in documenting and explaining the competitive advantage accruing to carmakers as a result of good supplier relations. The seminal study *The Machine That Changed the World* by the International Motor Vehicle Program based at the Massachusetts Institute of Technology introduced many in the U.S. auto industry to the successes of Japanese-inspired lean production, including the different relationships between carmakers and suppliers as compared with the U.S. model (Womack, Jones, and Roos 1990).

Research on changing relations between carmakers and their suppliers has emanated from two types of scholars. Analysts in nonacademic settings have measured the magnitude of the parts industry and have documented the enhanced role of suppliers in the production process. Academic researchers have emphasized the underlying meaning and significance of changing carmaker–supplier relations and the comparative advantage that accrues to some carmakers through enhanced supplier relations.

Most of the recent studies on the motor vehicle parts sector have come from analysts in nonacademic settings. Researchers are based in three types of organizations: auto industry specialists, financial services firms, and government agencies. Described below are some of the studies that industry specialists have released to the public.

The CAR Economics and Business Group has addressed changing relationships between carmakers and suppliers in numerous studies. CAR researchers have estimated the total number of jobs generated by the auto industry in the United States and in selected states (Hill 2005; Hill, Menk, and Szakaly 2007), the future size of union membership and the Detroit 3 workforce (McAlinden 2007), and a "stay/go" index to forecast the likelihood that production of particular types of parts will abandon Michigan (McAlinden 2006).

DesRosiers Automotive Consultants has estimated the magnitude of the supplier sector in North America and the likelihood of increased overseas outsourcing (DesRosiers 2005, 2006). The firm is Canadian based, so it breaks out U.S. and Canadian data.

The Original Equipment Suppliers Association (OESA), representing the perspective of the leading parts makers in North America, has documented the difficulties faced by suppliers, especially in the context of the global economy. OESA has also described the increasing role of equity investment firms in the parts supplier industry (De Koker 2006; Motor & Equipment Manufacturers Association 2007; Original Equipment Suppliers Association 2006).

CSM Worldwide has specialized in forecasting future demand for vehicles and parts, with a worldwide focus (Robinet 2005). Roland Berger Strategy Consultants has also concentrated on future worldwide trends in demand for different parts, especially in view of technology changes (Maj, Benecchi, and van Acker 2004). The McKinsey Global Institute within McKinsey & Company has documented productivity improvements in the motor vehicle industry (Baily et al. 2005). IRN, a Michigan-based consultancy, focuses on auto supplier issues (Korth 2007).

Studies on the motor vehicle parts sector have also been produced by agencies of the federal government. The U.S. Department of Commerce Office of Aerospace and Automotive Industries publishes an annual assessment of the parts industry.[5] Reports on aspects of the auto industry of particular interest to Members of Congress are published by the Congressional Research Service (Cooney 2005). The Government of Canada has also commissioned studies of its automotive market (Van Biesebroeck 2006).

Analysts based in financial services firms have been primarily concerned with the financial challenges facing motor vehicle suppliers as a result of changing relations with carmakers (see, for example, Steinmetz 2006). Merrill Lynch has monitored the supplier sector with an eye to recommending companies for investment (Merrill Lynch 2007); the firm has also looked at future energy technology (Merrill Lynch 2006).

Elements of Changing Carmaker–Supplier Relations

The shift from parts and components to modules and systems has fundamentally changed the role of parts suppliers in the development and production of cars. Analysts agree on the following basic dimensions of change (Wasti and Liker 1999).

Fewer parts and more modules

What goes into a vehicle can be sorted into the following hierarchy:

- Parts are typically small, individual pieces of metal, rubber, or plastic stamped, cut, or molded into distinctive shapes, such as knobs and levers.

- Components are several parts put together into recognizable features, such as radios and seat covers.

- Modules are several components combined to make functional portions of a motor vehicle, such as instrument panels and seats.

- Systems are groups of components that are linked by function into major units of motor vehicles, such as interiors and engines.

In the past at their final assembly plants, carmakers gathered together thousands of individual parts and components purchased either from independent suppliers or made by their own parts divisions. Now, suppliers are being asked to deliver large modules and systems ready to be installed on the final assembly line. "A modular system is composed of subsystems (or modules) that are designed independently but still function as an integrated whole" (Dyer 2000, p. 171). Modularization was described by GM vice president Bob Lutz as "like the definition of a Lego set" (Mackintosh 2004).

"What was once a highly vertically integrated industry has become ever more dependent on supplier companies to fulfill increasingly complex piece and module design and production" (Hill, Menk, and Szakaly 2007, p. 9). As a result, some analysts speculate that "[m]odularization may remove the nameplate assembler from directly manufacturing much of the product; it becomes rather the marketer, coordinator and distributor of the final vehicle" (Cooney and Yacobucci 2005, p. 41).

SupplierBusiness.com (2004) described the difference between a module and a system this way: "[T]he different parts of a safety system or a braking and traction control system are located in separate areas of the vehicle and incorporated into several different modules, but they will have been designed to work together as a complete system . . . [M]odules are being designed as complex units, which incorporate multiple functions. Examples of modules include seats, doors, cockpits, front-ends and suspension corner modules. Each of these can include components from two or more major vehicle systems."

A parts producer stated the difference more flippantly: "Two parts bolted together is a module. Three parts bolted together is a system."[6]

Larger contracts to fewer suppliers

Instead of buying from thousands of suppliers, carmakers are offering large contracts to only a handful of suppliers, which are consolidating into fewer larger firms and driving smaller firms out of the industry.

"Productivity improvements and the declining market share of domestic OEMs have led to considerable consolidation among motor vehicle parts suppliers" (Hill, Menk, and Szakaly 2007, p. 10). "Since the early 1990s . . . the largest 20–30 suppliers in the industry have taken on a much larger role in the areas of design, production, and foreign investment, shifting the balance of power in some small measure away from lead firms towards suppliers" (Sturgeon, Van Biesebroeck, and Gereffi 2007, p. 3). As a result, "[w]hile the total number of vehicles produced in North America grew by 40 percent between 1991 and 2005—from 11.6 million to 16.3 million—the combined sales of the largest 150 suppliers in North America almost tripled over the same time period . . ." (Hill, Menk, and Szakaly 2007, p. 24).

Longer relationships between suppliers and carmakers

Instead of awarding contracts annually to the lowest price bidders, carmakers are developing long-term relationships with suppliers, at least for the several-year life of specific vehicle models, if not longer.

"The continued efforts by original equipment manufacturers (OEMs) to reduce costs has led to an ever-increasing amount of manufacturing, sub-assembly, and R&D work being shifted to suppliers . . . The supplier companies design, engineer and manufacture the vast majority of the parts that go into a modern-day motor vehicle" (Hill, Menk, and Szakaly 2007, pp. 1, 9). "For niche vehicles or low-volume cars the entire assembly is sometimes turned over to an outside contractor. The practice allows OEMs to assemble vehicles locally without large capital investments or to increase production capacity when their own assembly plants cannot satisfy demand for an unexpectedly successful model" (Van Biesebroeck 2006, p. 210).

More research and development by suppliers

Instead of providing detailed specifications, carmakers are giving suppliers responsibility for research and development to design and build innovative modules and systems.

In 2000, suppliers spent $6.6 billion on research and product development, accounting for 36 percent of total automotive-related spending on research and development; this increased to $6.8 billion in 2003, or 40 percent of all research and product development spending (Hill, Menk, and Szakaly 2007). "Most innovations in safety, emissions, and entertainment come from Tier 1 suppliers."[7] "Some suppliers are willingly taking on the new responsibilities offered to them by the OEMs, transforming themselves into 'Tier One-Half systems integrators,' that engineer and build complete modules (for example, an entire interior, 4-corner suspension sets, or an entire rolling chassis) and assume both product design and development responsibilities and down stream supply chain management functions previously undertaken by the OEMs" (Office of Aerospace and Automotive Industries 2007, p. 6).

Smaller parts inventory and more just-in-time delivery

Instead of maintaining a large inventory of parts, carmakers are requiring suppliers to deliver modules and systems on a just-in-time (JIT) basis, often within only a few minutes before needed on the final assembly line.

"Because there is no built up inventory, JIT allows the firms to correct quality problems as they are discovered, and to make running changes in product specifications or volume requirements when needed" (Office of Aerospace and Automotive Industries 2007, p. 5).

Two Paradigms for Carmaker–Supplier Relations

Researchers argue that an automaker's strong relationships to its supply base can be a valuable strategic capability that is difficult and time-consuming for competitors to imitate. According to Jeffrey Dyer (2000, p. 169), "competitive advantage will increasingly be jointly created, and shared, by teams of firms within a value chain."

Analysts' perspectives on Japanese carmaker–supplier relations

Japanese carmakers have established constructive partnerships with their suppliers. A key to better supplier relations is trust. The three leading Japanese carmakers, Toyota, Honda, and Nissan, are seen as legitimate semi-insiders by supplier companies (Sako 2004, p. 301): "Suppliers' trust of (Japanese carmakers) lay in the latter's competence as teachers, but also in devising a clear set of rules for sharing specific gains from short-term intervention, and for letting suppliers appropriate wider gains from long-term capability enhancement."

According to Wasti and Liker (1999), positive supplier relationships are achieved by following six steps: 1) understand how suppliers work, 2) turn supplier rivalry into opportunity, 3) supervise vendors, 4) develop supplier technical capabilities, 5) share information intensively but selectively, and 6) conduct joint improvement activities.

From interviews with nearly 100 managers at Honda and Toyota as well as their suppliers, Liker and Choi ([2004]; see also Dyer and Nobeoka [2000]) concluded that these two carmakers "have struck remarkable partnerships with some of the same suppliers that are at loggerheads with the Big Three and have created latter-day *keiretsu* across Canada, the United States, and Mexico . . . Toyota and Honda have managed to replicate in an alien Western culture the same kind of supplier webs they built in Japan." (*Keiretsu* is defined on p. 22.)

It is no coincidence that many of today's fastest growing and most financially stable suppliers set up shop in the United States at the behest of Japanese carmakers. "For Toyota and Honda, making sure their suppliers earn a profit is a key part of their formula for success. Profitable suppliers are able to develop technologies that give their customers an advantage" (*Automotive News* 2005a). Japanese carmakers have nursed their suppliers, and suppliers like doing business with them. In addition, supplier networks incorporate a complex system of incentives.

The three leading Japanese carmakers do not have identical supplier relations (Sako 2004). Although all three transfer knowledge to suppliers through a variety of development activities and management control systems, Toyota shares more information with suppliers and has more separation between purchasing and engineering development. "[Each of the three Japanese carmakers] clearly distinguishes between the inner core of suppliers to which processes for 'capability enhancement' are taught in a hands-on manner, and the rest, who are mainly given incentives to make improvements through long-term customer commitment. This distinction ensures that tacit knowledge is shared only with the inner core. This inner core ranges from 25 companies at Nissan and 52 at Toyota, and up to 63 at Honda" (Sako 2004, p. 302).

Analysts' perspectives on Detroit 3–supplier relations

In contrast, Sako and Helper surveyed 675 Tier 1 suppliers in the United States and 472 in Japan during the 1990s and found that "[t]he U.S. auto industry has been characterized by decades of adversarial buyer-supplier relations" (Mudambi and Helper 1998, p. 789). They also state that "suppliers to the U.S. automobile industry have little expectation of being treated fairly by their customers" (p. 776). Table 1.4 summarizes the contrast between the two models of supplier relations.

"Experts agree that American corporations, like their Japanese rivals, should build supplier keiretsu: close-knit networks of vendors

Table 1.4 Relationships between Suppliers and U.S. and Japanese Carmakers

Criteria	Detroit 3[a]	Japanese 3[b]
Relationship orientation	Adversarial; focus is on cost and OEMs' short-term gain	Strategically integrate suppliers into partnership-like relationship
Open, honest communication	Indifference; incomplete and late information	High level and timely
Protect confidential information	Little regard for suppliers' proprietary information or intellectual property	High regard
Importance of cost vs. quality and technology	By far, primary focus is on cost	Also seek low cost but balance it with quality improvements and technology
Supplier survival	Little regard	Concern for long-term success and stability

[a] GM, Ford, and Chrysler.
[b] Toyota, Honda, and Nissan.
SOURCE: PPI (2005).

that continuously learn, improve, and prosper along with their parent companies" (Liker and Choi 2004, p. 106). The key word in the previous sentence is *should*, because the reality is that "current attempts to increase informal commitment and trust are constrained by the existence of adversarial buyer-supplier relations in the past" (Mudambi and Helper 1998, p. 776).

U.S. carmakers have tried going down the path of cooperation. During the early 1990s, for example, Chrysler implemented a more cooperative way of doing business with its suppliers that showed almost immediate improvements in its supplier relationships. In the wake of its merger with Daimler, however, that approach was abandoned in favor of the traditional way of doing business.[8]

Mudambi and Helper (1998, p. 789) concluded that relationships between U.S. carmakers and suppliers are close even though they are adversarial: "[T]he close but adversarial model represents the current state of buyer-supplier relations in the majority of cases." U.S. carmakers have created a framework of formal cooperation with their suppliers, but it is accompanied by uncooperative behavior. U.S. carmakers take advantage of the competitive weaknesses of suppliers to reap short-term gain (Mudambi and Helper 1998). Especially damning was the perspective of U.S. suppliers, which were less trusting than Japanese suppliers, except when they had Japanese carmakers as customers (Sako and Helper 1998).

Liker and Choi (2004) show that U.S. carmakers have adopted all of the Japanese-inspired organizational strategies, including slashing the number of suppliers, awarding long-term contracts to the survivors, encouraging Tier 1 suppliers to set up lower-tier networks, ordering systems and modules instead of parts and components, receiving deliveries on a just-in-time basis, and giving suppliers responsibility for quality and costs. "However, while these American companies created supply chains that superficially resembled those of their Japanese competitors, they didn't alter the fundamental nature of their relationships with suppliers. It wasn't long into the partnering movement before manufacturers and suppliers were fighting bitterly over the implementation of best practices, like continuous quality improvement and annual price reductions" (Liker and Choi 2004, p. 106).

Carmaker–Supplier Relations: Converging or Diverging?

Helper and Sako (1995) did detect some convergence in the way U.S. and Japanese carmakers work with suppliers.

- **Information disclosure.** The percentage of suppliers reporting an increase in information disclosed by U.S. carmakers rose from 38 percent in 1984 and 50 percent in 1989 to 80 percent in 1993; the percentage of suppliers reporting an increase in information disclosed by Japanese carmakers declined from 80 percent in 1989 to 77 percent in 1993.

- **Joint problem-solving.** The percentage of suppliers reporting that U.S. carmakers helped them match efforts by competing suppliers increased from 32 percent in 1989 to 51 percent in 1993; the percentage of suppliers reporting that Japanese carmakers helped them match competitors declined from 45 percent in 1989 to 40 percent in 1993.

- **Contract length.** Suppliers to U.S. carmakers reported that the average contract increased from 1.2 years in 1984 to 2.3 years in 1989 and 2.4 years in 1993; two-thirds of suppliers to Japanese carmakers reported no time-specific contracts.

The immense cost pressures faced by the Detroit 3 have since pushed the pendulum in the other direction and again made cost the main criterion in supplier selection. First, the Detroit 3 carmakers have been more easily able to source globally, notably from China. As a result, many North American suppliers now have to compete with the "landed costs" of parts produced in China and other low-wage countries. Second, Internet-based technologies have allowed the Detroit 3 to get suppliers to compete on cost more efficiently—and more brutally—than they used to. Confrontational tactics of Detroit 3 purchasers include "beat[ing] down prices with electronic auctions or rebidding work to a competitor. Japanese are equally tough on price but are committed to maintaining supplier continuity" (Chappell 2004a; Sherefkin and Wilson 2003). Consequently, the relations between carmakers and suppliers in America have deteriorated even as the quality of vehicles has improved (Liker and Choi 2004). According to Stallkamp (2005b), "Typically, in any one of the Big Three automakers there might be more than 250 to 300 buyers working at one time, each responsible for managing a small aspect of the parts or services that go into the vehicle." Isolated from engineering, manufacturing, and marketing people, these buyers have been motivated primarily by the desire to reduce the piece or unit price. A penny per part adds up to big savings for a buyer.

Detroit 3 financial monitors have further increased pressure on suppliers through "open book pricing," such as auditing quotes and reviewing overhead expenses. "What happens is the big guys, major OEMs, keep putting more and more requirements on the supplier that are non-negotiable. They simply say, 'This is the way it is going to be done as of this date, and next year we want another 5 percent price reduction.'"[9]

In response, Stallkamp (2005b) suggests that suppliers have engaged in an elaborate game:

> The supply base participants quickly figured out that a low quote was the major deciding factor and often bid at cost or even below cost to secure the business. They recovered their profits over time because the development process each of the U.S. companies used was so lengthy and convoluted that each part was changed several times, each time providing a chance for the supplier to increase its price for the design change. Suppliers often padded these design changes, but because the business was based on the initial quote, little was done to move to another supplier because switching would cost time, cause disruption and possibly produce quality issues.

OUTLOOK AND UNCERTAINTIES

"Industry surveys consistently have shown the U.S. component supplier segment to be mistrustful, resentful and rebellious against their Big 3 customers, while favorable to the Japanese transplants such as Toyota and Honda" (Chappell 2005b). One such survey of carmaker–supplier relationships has been conducted annually since 2000 by Planning Perspectives Inc. (PPI). From the responses of more than 200 suppliers, PPI (2005) constructed a Working Relations Index to measure how carmakers treat their suppliers on the basis of 17 business practices. According to a 2007 PPI survey of 308 North American parts makers, including 69 of the 150 largest, Toyota was ranked highest in

Table 1.5 Planning Perspectives Inc.'s Working Relations Index 2002–2007

Carmaker	Year						2006–07 % change	2002–07 % change
	2002	2003	2004	2005	2006	2007		
Toyota	314	334	399	415	407	415	2.0	32.2
Honda	297	316	384	375	368	380	3.3	27.9
Nissan	227	259	294	298	300	289	−3.7	27.3
Chrysler	175	177	183	196	218	199	−8.7	13.7
Ford	167	161	160	157	174	162	−6.9	−3.0
GM	161	156	144	114	131	174	32.8	8.1
Industry mean	224	234	261	259	266	270	1.3	20.7

NOTE: The index ranks OEMs based on 17 criteria across five broad areas: relationship, communication, help, hindrance, and profit opportunity.
SOURCE: PPI (2007).

fostering positive business relationships, followed by Honda, Nissan, Chrysler, GM, and Ford (PPI 2007; Table 1.5).

Why do supplier relations matter? Because good relationships to the supply base have become a key element of some carmakers' business strategies. "For the Big 3, the danger is that suppliers may stop offering them their best technology" (*Automotive News* 2005b). Suppliers say they have reduced spending on research and development for the Detroit 3 and increased it for Japanese carmakers. More mistrustful of Detroit 3 business methods, suppliers have been less willing to share technology with them or invest in their products as compared with Japanese carmakers (Chappell 2004b).

Larry Denton, CEO of Dura Automotive Systems, summarized the situation in Sherefkin and Wilson (2003): "Catalytic converters, ABS, airbags, automatic transmissions, safety belts—those were all innovations that came from the traditional Big 3. We can't name anything like that that has come in the last five years because if I look at iDrive, advanced diesel engines, hybrids, CVT—where did they come from? There's something broke here. Innovation isn't getting through the old domestics . . . Even though we're all suppliers to all of them, technology is headed in one direction because of the business model, and it needs to be fixed."

Notes

1. Bill Taylor, Mercedes-Benz U.S. CEO, quoted in Chappell (2005a).
2. Research for this book also benefited from a dozen strategic interviews with carmakers as well as parts makers, both large and small.
3. The ELM International, Inc. Web site can be accessed at http://www.elm-intl.com.
4. Lars Holmqvist, CEO of the European Association of Automotive Suppliers (CLEPA), quoted in Wernle (2005a).
5. The "U.S. Automotive Parts Industry Annual Assessment" is published annually.
6. Sam Licavoli, president of Textron Automotive Co. Trim Operations, quoted in *Automotive News* (1997).
7. Andrew Brown, Delphi executive director of engineering, 2003, quoted in Van Biesebroeck (2006, p. 209).
8. For an enlightening description of that episode, see Stallkamp (2005a).
9. Ken Rice, manager of manufacturing the engineering-commercial division at IMMI, Westfield, Indiana, provider of seat belt assemblies, quoted in Murphy (2004).

Part 1

Detroit: Heart of the Auto Industry

To assert that Detroit and the auto industry have long been synonymous may seem either unnecessary or anachronistic. For most of the twentieth century, the city's central position in the auto industry was so obvious as to need no elucidation. As recently as the mid-twentieth century, two-thirds of the nation's auto industry jobs were in Michigan.

Detroit's preeminence in the auto industry derived from the emergence of the Big 3 carmakers. The clustering of Big 3 management and technical operations contributed heavily to the Detroit area's auto employment during the twentieth century, and they continue to do so in the twenty-first century. However, the preponderance of Michigan's Big 3 auto jobs historically was actually in parts-making facilities. In the mid-twentieth century, the Big 3 assembled most of their vehicles outside Michigan, but they made nearly all of their parts inside Michigan.

Since the late twentieth century, the declining fortunes of the Big 3 have caused declining fortunes for Detroit. Michigan's job loss in the auto industry in the early twenty-first century averaged 6 percent per year. Having lost their status as the three largest carmakers, the Big 3 are now being referred to as the Detroit 3, even more closely linking a struggling city with the struggling companies. Derelict factories and empty office towers gave mute testimony to the collapse of Detroit's auto industry.

"Detroit's long reign as the dominant force in the American car industry is over," proclaimed auto analyst Micheline Maynard on the first page of her 2003 book, and just to make sure, she repeated on the second page, "Detroit's single-handed control of the American automobile industry has been lost forever" (Maynard 2003). Although its auto employment has declined sharply, Michigan remains the leading parts-making state. This section discusses how the Detroit 3 parts-making operations came to be clustered in that state. It then examines the three leading types of parts made in Michigan: engines, bodies, and "bin" or generic parts.

2
Rise and Fall of Vertical Integration in the Midwest

[Hyundai officials] know that the Detroit area is the brain center of not only the global automobile industry, but particularly the North American automobile industry.[1]

Thousands of companies were established to build cars in the United States in the first years of the twentieth century. At the end of the first decade of the twenty-first century, there were only three American-owned carmakers—Chrysler LLC, Ford Motor Co., and General Motors Corp. By 1910 Ford and GM had emerged as the two top-selling carmakers in the United States and worldwide, and they remained so until they were passed by Toyota in the first decade of the twenty-first century.

Many reasons accounted for the success of Ford and GM, but arguably the most important was the ability of the two companies to make most of their own parts instead of buying them. Ford and GM both regarded the strategy, known as "vertical integration," as an important competitive advantage. Chrysler, the third of the Detroit-based Big 3 carmakers, was somewhat weaker in large measure because it was less vertically integrated than its two larger competitors. Unable to compete with the Big 3 on price and quality, other carmakers were driven out of business, and independent suppliers were relegated to a marginal role in the production process.

Vertical integration was also the basis for the dominance of motor vehicle production in the Midwest, especially in southeastern Michigan. At the height of vertical integration, parts-making was more highly clustered in southeastern Michigan than was final assembly. Parts produced in southeastern Michigan were shipped to final assembly plants located near big cities around the country, like New York and Los Angeles.

After nearly a century of making most of their own parts, GM and Ford both exited the parts-making business within a year of each other, in 1999 and 2000, respectively. Making their own parts had become a liability rather than an asset for GM and Ford because other carmakers were buying better quality parts from independent suppliers at lower prices.

Just as the rise of vertical integration underlay southeastern Michigan's dominance of the motor vehicle industry for much of the twentieth century, so has the end of vertical integration triggered hard times in Michigan. At the height of vertical integration, immediately before and after World War II, Ford and GM together made about 60 percent of their parts in Michigan but assembled only about 15 percent of their vehicles there. At the beginning of the twenty-first century, Michigan's share of Ford and GM's North American final assembly operations had increased to 20 percent, but the state's share of parts production had fallen to about 25 percent.

BENEFITS OF VERTICAL INTEGRATION

Every manufacturer needs inputs into its production process and ways to get its goods to customers. Vertical integration measures the extent to which a firm is integrated with its "upstream" sources of inputs and its "downstream" distribution to customers.

A firm must either procure inputs from other firms or control the input sources itself. A firm that is relatively integrated upstream produces most of its raw materials and semifabricated inputs itself. Similarly, a firm either turns over its output to other firms or controls the sources of distribution itself. A firm that is relatively integrated downstream controls most of its own distribution activities instead of turning over its goods to independent wholesalers and retailers.

The benefits of vertical integration were recognized by economists long before the establishment of the motor vehicle industry. Industrial organization textbooks (e.g., Scherer and Ross 1990) distinguish several motives for vertically integrating a business activity. Vertical integration can have the following benefits:

- **Reducing costs.** According to Nobel Laureate Ronald Coase, who proposed a transaction cost theory of firms, activities will be collected in a firm when the cost of using the price mechanism (procuring across markets) exceeds the cost of organizing those same activities through direct managerial control. Several empirical studies have shown that auto manufacturers tend to integrate the production of a component if the production process generates very specialized and nonpatentable know-how (Masten, Mehan, and Snyder 1989; Monteverde and Teece 1982).

- **Enhancing control.** Producers have more control over their economic environment; for example, they are provided with immunity from total interruption in the supply of a part.

- **Optimizing scale.** Various production operations with different optimal scales can be combined in one corporate structure if markets are prone to a breakdown of competitive supply conditions. At the height of vertical integration in the motor vehicle industry, for example, the most efficient assembly plants produced about 200,000 vehicles per year on two shifts. Stamping body parts and machining automotive transmissions are characterized by much higher minimum annual volumes, up to 400,000 units each (White 1971). The much larger scale of stamping operations limited the number of possible independent stamping companies. Carmakers therefore protected themselves by integrating the stamping operation.

Carmakers have shown little interest in "downstream" vertical integration. Frustrated with the inexperience of early dealers, Ford did set up company-owned stores called branch houses during the first decade of the twentieth century (Rubenstein 2001). Located in major cities, branch houses were staffed by Ford employees who received a salary plus a bonus based on sales (Parlin and Youker 1914).

By the 1910s, though, Ford had abandoned direct selling. Ford could not open branch houses fast enough to meet demand, nor could it find enough qualified people to staff the branches (Epstein 1928; Knudsen 1926). More crucially, Ford officials concluded that salaried employees were not sufficiently motivated to sell cars. According to an industry analyst writing in the 1920s (Epstein 1928, pp. 135–136), "If a dealer has a financial interest in his own company, he is found to be much more satisfactory than a branch manager, who has practically no financial interest in the branch."

Although they abandoned downstream vertical integration, the Big 3 remained vertically integrated upstream until the end of the twentieth century. As recently as the 1980s, GM produced more than 70 percent of its own parts and Ford 54 percent. Chrysler, which then had just emerged from a near-brush with bankruptcy, produced only 39 percent of its own parts (Andrea, Everett, and Luria 1988).

PIONEERING PARTS PRODUCERS

The question, "Which came first—parts makers or carmakers?" is not a chicken-and-egg puzzle. The parts makers came first. Early carmakers were primarily assemblers and distributors, and they were capable of producing few if any of their own parts. Experimental vehicles in the 1890s were put together by adapting parts that were being made for other purposes.

In Chapter 1, we identified six major vehicle systems: body, chassis, electronics, interior, generics, and powertrain. Early vehicles did not have electronics or an interior, but they did have the other four systems. A powertrain was needed to propel the vehicle, a body to contain people and equipment, a chassis to carry the weight without bogging down, and generic parts like nuts and bolts to put the other pieces together.

Carmakers had to rely on already established companies to obtain these parts. Detroit and nearby communities attracted carmakers because the principal sources of parts were already there. To supply industries that existed before motor vehicles, nineteenth-century firms that would later prove to be expert parts makers had settled in a region that centered on southeastern Michigan and extended along the southern Great Lakes between Buffalo and Milwaukee.

Of the 50 largest suppliers in the United States in 2007, 20 predated the establishment of the motor vehicle industry in the 1890s. The list includes some of America's most venerable manufacturers, such as DuPont, established in 1802 to make gunpowder, and Navistar, established in 1831 to make McCormick reapers. Several of the older firms began in the nineteenth century as suppliers of parts such as bearings, frames, springs, and tires for carriages and bicycles. Others making a successful transition to motor vehicle parts started out producing metal, glass, and textile products for household use; some even began as retailers or service providers rather than manufacturers.

Leading Suppliers in 1900

As commercial production of motor vehicles soared in the first few years of the twentieth century, two Detroit-area machine shops emerged as the industry's leading parts suppliers: Leland & Faulconer Manufacturing Co. and Dodge Brothers. The two firms supplied parts for a high percentage of vehicles produced during the first years of the twentieth century and were responsible for a high share of the value added in the manufacturing process.

Leland & Faulconer

At the top of the list of needs for the early carmakers was a reliable engine. In 1900, southeastern Michigan was the leading center for supplying gasoline engines. Once gasoline defeated steam and electricity as the preferred power source for car engines during the first years of the twentieth century, Detroit was the unrivaled leader in supplying motor vehicle parts.

There were two principal markets for Detroit's gasoline engines before motor vehicles. First, small stationary gasoline engines were sold to generate power on farms and in other rural settings that lacked access to electricity. The nation's leading supplier of small stationary gasoline engines during the 1890s was Lansing-based Ransom E. Olds. He then turned to motor vehicle production and became the best-selling carmaker during the first three years of the twentieth century.

Gasoline engines were also used to power boats. The leading supplier of marine gasoline engines during the 1890s was Leland & Faulconer, founded in Detroit in 1890 by skilled machinist Henry M. Leland and lumber magnate Robert C. Faulconer. Leland & Faulconer first worked with Olds in 1899 to correct problems with noisy transmissions, then supplied transmissions beginning in 1900 and engines in 1901. The Leland & Faulconer engine quickly established a reputation for delivering more horsepower than its competitors because it was built to more exacting manufacturing standards (Hyde 2005, p. 30). Henry Leland became president of the Cadillac Automotive Co. in 1903, and Leland & Faulconer merged with Cadillac in 1905.

Dodge Brothers

Founded by John and Horace Dodge in 1900, Dodge Brothers initially designed and built steam engines for yachts, repaired typesetting and typography machines, and made replacement parts for them. Beginning in 1886, the brothers worked in several machine shops in southeastern Michigan and Windsor, Ontario. They patented an improved bicycle bearing in 1895 and started making the E. & D. Bicycle a year later, with partner Fred S. Evans (the "E" in the name), as a subsidiary of the Canadian Typograph Co. When U.S. and Canadian bicycle firms consolidated into a monopoly in the late 1890s, the Dodge brothers sold their interest and used the capital to open their own machine shop in Detroit.

The Dodge Brothers' first large motor vehicle contract was to make engines for Olds Motor Works after a fire destroyed the Olds factory in Detroit on March 9, 1901. After Olds switched its engine contract to Leland & Faulconer, Dodge Brothers started supplying Ford. Over the next decade, the fate of Ford and Dodge became intertwined—Ford assembled half the world's cars, and Dodge made most of Ford's parts. Dodge Brothers worked exclusively for Ford and became the world's leading parts maker by a wide margin.

When Ford was unable to pay for the initial parts contracted in 1903, John and Horace Dodge agreed to accept 50 shares each of Ford Motor Co. in exchange for their notes of $5,000 each. Had Ford failed, so would have Dodge Brothers. But when Ford became the world's dominant carmaker, the Dodges became wealthy. The brothers used their wealth to switch from making parts to making their own cars in 1914. The Dodge car quickly gained a reputation for good value and reliability without flashiness, suitable for doctors and other professionals.

Henry Ford bought the Dodge Brothers' shares of Ford Motor Co. in 1919 for $25 million. John and Horace Dodge died within months of each other in 1920. Their widows sold the car company to investment firm Dillon, Read in 1924, and Chrysler Corp. acquired Dodge Brothers in 1928.

Early Ford Suppliers

The importance of suppliers in the early years of motor vehicle production is especially well documented in the archives of Ford Motor

Co. In its first year of production (1903), Ford spent $404 to make each vehicle. Of this, $384, or 95 percent, came from the cost of buying parts, and only $20 of value was added during final assembly (Table 2.1).

The 1903 Ford sold for $750. Included in the 86 percent markup from production cost to selling price were $150 for advertising, sales force salaries, and other costs of selling the vehicle and $46 for a contingency fund to finance legal battles. That left a handsome profit of $150 per vehicle or 20 percent of gross revenue. Henry Ford reinvested most of the profits back into company expansion.

Ford's financial records show that most of the manufacturing costs were allocated to purchasing three types of parts: running gear, body, and tires. The most important of these by far was running gear, which consisted of the engine, transmission, and axles mounted on a frame. Ford contracted with Dodge Brothers in 1903 to supply 650 sets of running gear for $250 each, accounting for 62 percent of manufacturing cost (Hyde 2005, p. 31).

Ford's second-leading supplier in its first year of production, behind Dodge Brothers, was C.R. Wilson Carriage Co. Ford bought bod-

Table 2.1 Ford Production Costs in 1903

Item	Cost ($)
Running gear[a]	250
Body	52
4 tires	40
4 wheels	26
Seat cushions	16
Cost of assembling[b]	20
Production cost	404
Cost of selling[c]	150
Contingencies	46
Profit	150
Selling price	750

[a] Includes engine, transmission, axles, and frame.
[b] Includes wages, rent, insurance, and factory incidentals.
[c] Includes advertising, salaries, and commissions.
SOURCE: Based on Quaife (1950) as quoted in Hyde (2005, p. 36) and Model T Ford Club of America (2007).

ies from Wilson for $52 each and seat cushions for $16 each. Charles R. Wilson had established a blacksmith and wagon repair shop in Detroit in 1870 and a carriage maker (C.R. & J.C. Wilson Carriage Co.) with his brother three years later. The brothers split the company during the 1890s. J.C. Wilson Co. manufactured horse-drawn trucks and wagons, and it produced the Wilson Truck between 1915 and 1925. C.R. Wilson Carriage Co. concentrated on horse-drawn buggies and carriages and was reorganized as the C.R. Wilson Body Co. in 1897.

As Ford sales increased rapidly after introduction of the Model T in 1908, Wilson was no longer the exclusive body supplier. After Charles Wilson died in 1924, the body company was merged with several competitors into the Murray Body Co., which survived as an independent body supplier until World War II (Theobald 2004).

Ford's third largest supplier in 1903 was the Hartford Rubber Works Co., which provided tires for $10 each. Even when carmakers started to make most of their own parts, they continued to purchase tires from independent suppliers. Hartford became part of the United States Rubber Co., the leading tire supplier in the early years of the industry. U.S. Rubber merged with B.F. Goodrich Co. in 1986 to form Uniroyal, which was acquired by Michelin in 1990.

VERTICAL INTEGRATION AT FORD AND GM

Vertical integration at Ford and GM began with production of the mechanical portion of the vehicle, that is, the powertrain and chassis. As electrical components and interiors were added to vehicles, they were also integrated into the core competency of the two carmakers. The body was last to be added. By the 1920s, Ford and GM were highly integrated with most of their upstream inputs.

Yet the two companies approached vertical integration differently:

- Ford set up most of its own parts-making operations, whereas GM acquired them.

- Ford clustered most parts production in one complex in the Detroit area, whereas GM's was spread throughout southeastern Michigan.

- Ford integrated the production of inputs such as steel, glass, and wood into its corporate empire, whereas GM procured them through market relationships.

With the Big 3 carmakers firmly established, the sequence of location decisions characteristic of the pioneering years of the motor vehicle industry was reversed. Early carmakers had located in southeastern Michigan primarily to be near suppliers. Now independent suppliers began to cluster in southeastern Michigan to be near the Big 3 carmakers.

Ford Clusters Parts Production

Dependency on others—be they associations, financiers, service providers, or parts makers—rankled Henry Ford from the outset. Associations protected monopolies, financiers cared about the bottom line, service providers were unreliable, and parts makers could not meet Ford's demanding production schedule. Through the first two decades of the twentieth century, Henry Ford defied trade associations, eliminated financial backers, bought out suppliers, and made his own parts.

Conventional wisdom in 1900 was that cars were toys for the rich, and profit would be maximized by building a small number of expensive models that could be sold at a high per-unit markup. In contrast, Ford believed that demand for cars was universal, and he set about meeting that demand by building a high volume of low-priced vehicles. When his competitors, financial backers, service providers, and parts suppliers did not share his vision, Ford decided to go it alone. Once the validity of his approach was proved, Ford felt he no longer needed the others.

Ford starts making parts

Shortly after the Ford Motor Co. was incorporated in June 1903, Henry Ford met with Fred L. Smith, treasurer of Oldsmobile and acting president of the Association of Licensed Automobile Manufacturers (ALAM), a trade association formed earlier that year. The purpose of the meeting was to discuss Ford's prospects for obtaining an ALAM license. Smith told Ford that the ALAM would likely reject the application because the Ford Motor Co. did not make its own engines and other parts, and it was therefore "a mere assemblage place." Ironically, within a decade Ford would be making more of its own parts than any other car-maker. And a century later, Ford—as well as other carmakers—would head back in the direction of being "a mere assemblage place."

To make parts for his "mere assemblage place," Henry Ford set up a parts-making operation in 1905 called the Ford Manufacturing Co. Ford Manufacturing made engines, gears, and other parts for Ford Motor's low-priced cars, while Dodge Brothers continued to supply most of the key parts for Ford's higher priced models. Henry Ford's motivation for setting up a separate parts-making subsidiary was largely driven by a dispute with his principal financial backer. Unable to borrow money from Detroit's banks after two earlier attempts to set up a company had failed, Ford turned to the city's leading coal dealer, Alexander Y. Malcomson, who had sold coal to Edison Illuminating Company when Ford worked there during the 1890s. Most of Ford's other investors in 1903 were either relatives or business associates of Malcomson.

Henry Ford financed Ford Manufacturing Co. by reducing Ford Motor Co. dividends in 1906, against the wishes of Malcomson. After Malcomson reacted to the dividend cut by investing in a competitor (Aerocar), Ford Motor's board of directors asked him to resign as treasurer and director. With Malcomson out of the picture, Henry Ford merged Ford Motor and Ford Manufacturing and consolidated operations in the Piquette Ave. assembly plant. Heavy equipment, suitable for machining the engine and axles, was placed on the first floor. Other light machining and subassembly were done on the second floor. Chassis assembly took place on the third floor (Model T Automotive Heritage Complex 2007; Rubenstein 2001, p. 15).

Logical sequencing of parts

Ford pioneered one of the principal innovations of vertical integration at the Piquette plant: logical sequencing. Three elements of logical sequencing were noteworthy in the Piquette plant. First, appropriate tools were placed next to each workstation. Traditionally, machine tools were kept in one place; a worker needing a particular tool would retrieve it, bring it to the workstation, do the work, and return the tool to storage.

Second, workstations were arranged in the building so that parts would not have to travel far from one operation to the next. According to Ford's chief tool designer, Oscar C. Bornholdt, logical sequencing avoided "a lot of handling and trucking and saved lots of floor space . . . Under this method of operation the company did not have to pile up parts between machines in the aisles, and it also was able to reduce inventory greatly" (Bornholdt 1926, pp. 2–3).

Third, the specific number of machines and workers allocated for each workstation was appropriate for maintaining even production through the factory. According to Bornholdt, "one type of machine would produce exactly the number of parts necessary for 100 percent production by the next type of machine, the production of all being so synchronized that there was no excess or shortages anywhere" (Bornholdt 1926, pp. 2–3).

When Ford transferred production from Piquette to Highland Park in 1910, logical sequencing was incorporated from the beginning. Sequencing began at the top floor and flowed downward. Body parts were fashioned on the fourth floor, painted on the third floor, assembled on the second floor, and dropped on top of the chassis on the first floor. As at Piquette, engines, transmissions, and other powertrain components were made on the first floor of Highland Park because they required the heaviest machinery (Arnold and Faurote 1919).

Highland Park became famous as the home of the moving assembly line, first installed in 1913. Starting as an extension of the logical sequencing that had been used for several years at Piquette, the moving assembly line became the revolutionary centerpiece of the company's approach to vertical integration, overshadowing Ford's other innovations in materials handling.

Vertical integration at the Rouge

Within a decade of moving into Highland Park, Ford started constructing a much larger facility along the banks of the River Rouge in Dearborn. The Rouge would be the most vertically integrated complex in the auto industry. At its peak around 1940, the Rouge employed 110,000 workers in 127 structures totaling 11 million square feet spread out over 2,000 acres.

At the center of the Rouge complex was a canal slip along the River Rouge, enabling large ships to arrive from the Great Lakes by way of the Detroit River. Raw materials, such as coal and iron ore, were unloaded into large storage bins along the east side of a canal slip that cut through the center of the complex. East of the canal slip was a power plant that produced electricity for the complex. Parts operations were clustered in three areas of the Rouge complex:

1) The engine block and other iron components were cast in buildings to the north of the canal slip from pig iron smelted in Rouge blast furnaces and shaped in the Rouge foundry, the world's largest.

2) A steel-making complex on the west side of the canal slip stamped bodies and powertrain components.

3) Glass, tires, and other nonmetal parts were made in buildings situated to the northwest of the canal slip.

Though the Rouge included a final assembly plant—raw materials were said to arrive at one end and finished vehicles to depart at the other end—most of the parts made at the Rouge, as well as at Highland Park before it, were actually shipped in knocked-down form to other final assembly plants. A railroad boxcar could be filled with enough parts to assemble 26 cars, compared to only seven or eight fully assembled cars, thereby dramatically reducing the company's freight bill.

Ford's board of directors authorized construction of a branch plant in Kansas City, which opened in 1912. By 1917, Ford was assembling cars in 30 U.S. cities, using parts made in Michigan.

GM Acquires Parts Producers

GM founder William C. Durant was a strong advocate of vertical integration. Prior to organizing GM in 1908, Durant had made Durant-Dort Carriage Co. the country's largest carriage maker through vertical integration. Durant believed that parts-making was the key to minimizing production costs and achieving economies of scale (Epstein 1928, pp. 50–53; Pound 1934, p. 88). While competitors assembled carriages with parts bought from independent suppliers, Durant-Dort made its own bodies, wheels, axles, upholstery, springs, varnish, and whip sockets (Rubenstein 1992, p. 33). "We started out [in the carriage industry] as assemblers with no advantage over our competitors," Durant reminisced. "We paid about the same prices for everything we purchased. We realized that we were making no progress and would not unless and until we manufactured practically every important part that we used" (Durant n.d., p. 12).

Durant entered the motor vehicle business in 1904, when he was asked to reorganize the foundering Buick Motor Co., which was based in his hometown of Flint, Michigan. Buick founder David Dunbar Buick "was an innovative fellow who had made a fortune in the plumbing business . . . He began to manufacture gasoline engines in 1900 and decided to design an automobile. But his business foundered. He tinkered a lot, but he did not produce cars commercially" (Wright 1996). Under Durant, Buick became the best-selling carmaker in the United States and formed the "foundation stone" of General Motors in 1908 (Pound 1934, p. 68).

As Durant moved from making carriages to cars, he continued to make vertical integration a key element in his competitive strategy. Unlike Ford, which had Dodge Brothers supply its first engine, Buick could produce an engine in-house from the start. Although automotive historians disagree on allocating credit for the engine among Buick's first chief engineer Walter L. Marr, his successor Eugene C. Richard, and David Buick himself (Gustin 1993), Buick developed and patented the first overhead valve engine for motor vehicles, and "in 1915 Buick began to advertise and promote its patented engine as the 'valve-in-head'" (Buick Club of America 2007).

Bringing parts makers to Flint

Durant needed sources of other parts. What he couldn't find already in Flint, he worked hard to bring to Flint. Durant's chief asset in attracting suppliers to Flint was his personal charm. Walter Chrysler, president and general manager of Buick from 1916 to 1920, later described Durant's charm particularly well: "I cannot hope to find words to express the charm of the man. He has the most winning personality of anyone I've ever known. He could coax a bird right down out of a tree" (Chrysler 1937, p. 143).

Among the parts makers Durant coaxed to Michigan were Albert Champion and Charles Stewart Mott. When Durant was in Boston to open a Buick showroom, Champion, a French-born race-car driver, showed him a magneto he had designed. Durant did not need a magneto, but he was interested to learn that Champion also made spark plugs. At Durant's invitation, Champion moved to Flint in 1905 and manufactured spark plugs in a corner of the Buick factory. AC Spark Plugs moved to a separate building in Flint in 1917.

Durant had difficulty securing suitable axles from his carriage-making operations, so he wooed Charles Mott, president and general manager of Weston-Mott Company, a leading axle supplier, to relocate from Utica, New York, to Flint in 1906. Mott was a descendant of a prominent upstate New York family that included his grandfather Samuel Mott, who had founded Motts Apple Sauce in 1842. Reluctantly Mott moved the company and eventually sold it to GM. He later became mayor of Flint and a prominent philanthropist in his adopted hometown.

Republic Motors

During his two years in control of GM between 1908 and 1910, Durant bought 30 firms, including Cartercar Co., Dow Rim Co., Elmore Manufacturing Co., Jackson-Church-Wilcox Co., Michigan Auto Parts Co., and Michigan Motor Castings Co. These companies made useful parts, but acquiring so many proved to be a financial drain on a fledgling GM.

Particularly disastrous to GM's financial health was Durant's acquisition of Heany Electric Co., whose founder, John Heany, claimed to hold a valid patent on the electric light bulb. General Electric sued, and Heany's lawyer and a patent office clerk were convicted and jailed for falsifying the patent application. Support for Heany drained GM's scarce financial reserves, and the company was saved by Eastern bankers, who replaced Durant with new management, although Durant was permitted to remain on GM's Board of Trustees.

Ousted from GM, Durant decided to replicate his strategy of building cars with an eye for vertical integration. He organized three new companies in 1911: Little Motor Car Company, Mason Motor Company, and Chevrolet Motor Company. Little produced a small car, Mason a four-cylinder engine, and Chevrolet a model based on a prototype developed by the well-known Swiss race-car driver Louis Chevrolet. Republic Motors was created a year later to market and distribute Chevrolet and Little cars.

The Little was a well-designed but underpowered car, whereas the Chevrolet was a high-priced, high-performance vehicle with limited appeal. To increase Republic's overall sales, Durant put the Chevrolet name on the Little. Louis Chevrolet, furious at having his name associated with the aptly named Little, left the company, but Chevrolet (i.e., the rebadged Little) sales soared.

Durant then had enough capital for his next move, which was to convince enough GM shareholders into swapping their GM stock for Republic Motors stock (at the attractive rate of one GM share for 10 shares of Republic) that he was able to regain control of GM in 1916. "Upon regaining control of General Motors, Durant's first act was to fire [GM general manager Charles] Nash . . . 'Well, Charlie, you're through,' he told his former employee who he felt had thrown in his lot with the bankers" (Wright 1996).

United Motors

Back at the helm of GM, Durant resumed his pursuit of vertical integration. A key acquisition was United Motors, a holding company for several parts makers Durant had created in 1916. Durant also consolidated United Motors, as well as Republic Motors (including Chevrolet), into General Motors in 1918.

Major additions to GM through the United Motors acquisition included Dayton Engineering Laboratories Company, Harrison Radiator Corporation, Hyatt Roller Bearing Company, New Departure Manufacturing Company, and Remy Electric Company.

Dayton Engineering Laboratories Company. Later known by the acronym Delco, the Dayton Engineering Laboratories Company was founded in 1909 and invented an electric self-starting ignition, which was first installed as standard equipment on GM's Cadillac in 1912. Delco's director Charles F. Kettering, appointed head of GM's newly created Research Laboratories in 1920, was instrumental in making Dayton, Ohio, GM's largest parts-making center outside Michigan.

Harrison Radiator Corporation. Founded in 1910 by Herbert C. Harrison in Lockport, New York, the Harrison Radiator Corporation produced honeycomb-shaped radiators that helped reduce overheating (a common problem of early car engines). Although Harrison is credited by some with its invention, German automotive pioneer Wilhelm Maybach held a patent on it.

Hyatt Roller Bearing Company. Founded by John Wesley Hyatt in 1892 in Harrison, New York, the Hyatt Roller Bearing Company started producing roller bearings for cars in 1896. Because a roller bearing, which consists of a cylinder sandwiched between two races, can withstand a relatively heavy load, it is commonly used in transmissions and wheels.

New Departure Manufacturing Company. Brothers Edward D. and Albert F. Rockwell founded New Departure in Bristol, Connecticut, in 1888 to make doorbells. The company started producing ball bearings for car axles in 1907.

Remy Electric Company. The Remy Electric Company was founded by brothers Frank and Perry Remy in 1896 to make magnetos for a number of early cars, including Buick. After joining GM, Remy was merged with Delco into a single electrical parts-making division. Remy's hometown of Anderson, Indiana, became GM's second-largest parts-making center outside Michigan.

Fisher Body and Packard Electric

Outside United Motors, Durant's most significant contribution to GM's vertical integration was acquiring a controlling interest in Fisher Body. Founded in Detroit in 1908 by the Fisher brothers, the company became GM's leading supplier of bodies during the 1910s. GM acquired 60 percent of the company in 1919 and the remainder in 1926. GM heavily advertised "Body by Fisher" and attached a plate with the phrase on all of its vehicles.

After Durant was ousted for a second and final time in 1920, GM continued to acquire a few other key parts makers, notably Packard Electric in 1932. Packard Electric, established by brothers James W. and William D. Packard, first made incandescent lamps and transformers and then assembled luxury cars beginning in 1899. Packard's carmaking operations were sold to Detroit investors and its lamp operations to General Electric, leaving Packard Electric to concentrate on wiring.

VERTICAL DISINTEGRATION AT FORD AND GM

Market-based transactions increasingly dominated carmaker relations with their parts suppliers in the late twentieth century. "A dominant trend in the organization of production (in both the automotive industry and elsewhere) during the past decade [1990s] has been the shift away from vertical integration as manufacturers have increasingly outsourced parts to their suppliers" (Dyer 2000). The share of a vehicle's value added in the production process by parts makers rose rapidly, from approximately 40 percent in 1990 to approximately 60 percent in 2000. Suppliers were anticipated to add 80 percent to the value of a new vehicle by 2010.[2]

The impetus for changing carmaker–supplier relations was the diffusion of lean production into the U.S. manufacturing sector (Milgrom and Roberts 1990; Womack, Jones, and Roos 1990). Starting in the early 1980s, the arrival of Japanese-owned carmakers in North America illuminated a different approach to supplier relations. After World War II, resource-constrained Japanese carmakers had fostered partnerships and alliances with a small number of suppliers, in the process building long-term relationships with them. When they came to the United States, Japanese carmakers brought some of these key suppliers with them.

Reacting to these changes, GM spun off most of its parts-making plants into an independent company called Delphi Corporation in 1999. A year later, Ford spun off most of its parts-making plants into Visteon Corporation. Armed with contracts to supply parts to what were still the world's two largest carmakers, Delphi and Visteon immediately became North America's two largest parts makers.

Delphi and Visteon each reported initial quarterly profits between 0.5 and 1 percent of sales, which was not bad for the troubled auto parts sector and better than forecast. But those bright prospects soon faded. Within a half-dozen years, Delphi would seek bankruptcy protection, and Visteon would not be in much better shape.

Delphi and Visteon had problems with both revenues and expenses. Revenues were overstated due to transfer costs from one division to another. As independent companies, Delphi and Visteon were pressured by GM and Ford to charge prices that were competitive with independent suppliers. GM and Ford moved business away from Delphi and Visteon if independent suppliers could provide parts at lower prices. At the same time, Delphi and Visteon faced higher expenses than independent suppliers. As former divisions of GM and Ford, the two parts makers were paying wages comparable to those that GM and Ford paid for final assembly work, rather than the lower wages prevailing in the motor vehicle parts industry.

From GM to Delphi

GM consolidated most of its parts plants into a division called Delphi Automotive Systems in 1995. Delphi Corp. became an independent company four years later when shares were sold to the public or turned over to GM stockholders. Delphi immediately became the largest U.S.-based parts producer by a wide margin, with North American sales of $21 billion.

As an independent company, Delphi initially had seven divisions:

1) Delphi Energy & Engine Management Systems, primarily plants from AC, Delco-Remy, and Rochester Products that made fuel lines, ignitions, and other engine parts.

2) Delphi Steering Systems, primarily plants in Saginaw, Michigan, that made crankshafts, steering gears, and other cast parts.

3) Delphi Chassis Systems, primarily Delco, Hyatt, and New Departure plants that made brakes, bearings, shock absorbers, and other chassis parts.

4) Delphi Harrison Thermal Systems, primarily Harrison Radiator plants that made heating and cooling parts.

5) Delphi Interior Systems, primarily Fisher Body, Inland Manufacturing, and Guide Lamp plants that made seats, steering wheels, and other interior parts.

6) Delphi Packard Electric Systems, primarily Packard plants that made wiring.

7) Delphi Delco Electronics Systems, primarily Delco plants that made radios.

During its first six years of independence, Delphi set out to reduce dependency on sales to its largest customer, GM. According to Delphi chairman and CEO Robert S. "Steve" Miller (*Detroit News* 2005), "[t]he basic idea was for Delphi to outrun the legacy problem of its inherited labor costs by diversifying its customer base and global footprint." Success came quickly: sales of parts to carmakers other than GM more than doubled from $4 billion in 1999 to $9 billion in 2005. Carmakers other than GM accounted for half of Delphi's revenue in 2005, compared to only one-fifth in 1999.

Taken in isolation, this would have constituted remarkable growth in both percentage and dollar terms—only three other suppliers even totaled $5 billion in revenues, let alone increased sales by that amount or percentage. But, during the same time period, Delphi's sales to GM fell from $17 billion in 1999 to $9 billion in 2005. As GM's North American production declined from 5.7 million vehicles in 1999 to 4.6 million in 2005, so did its purchases from its largest supplier—and one-fourth of GM's total parts buy was from Delphi.

As a result of the GM cuts, Delphi's total North American revenues declined from $21 billion in 1999 to $18 billion in 2005. Only six years after it was created, Delphi filed for Chapter 11 protection, the largest bankruptcy in motor vehicle industry history. Steve Miller, who placed Delphi in bankruptcy three months after being hired, gave reporters his perspective on what went wrong. He focused on three things:

1) The spread between automaker labor costs and competitive supplier labor costs has widened sharply over the past decade, driven by globalization and by rising health care and pension costs.

2) Given Delphi's high fixed costs and inflexible labor rates, the recent sharp declines in Delphi's shipments to GM due to their market share losses have been devastating.

3) The game plan for Delphi included "flow-backs" to GM of excess Delphi workers. But GM has had no room to accept Delphi employees, resulting in a $100 million penalty last quarter (Q3 2005) alone for 4,000 idled workers in Delphi's jobs bank, drawing full pay and benefits (*Detroit News* 2005).

Emerging from bankruptcy protection would make Delphi a drastically different company than the one spun off by GM in 1999. It was going to be:

- **A much smaller company.** The number of U.S. plants was to be cut from 29 to 8. The jettisoned plants would be sold if a buyer could be found, otherwise they would be closed. Hourly employment was cut from 33,000 in 2005 to 6,000 in January 2008 (*Clarion Ledger* 2008).

- **A more Mexican-oriented company.** Delphi had more employ-
  ment and plants in Mexico than in the United States.
- **A lower-wage company.** Average hourly wages were reduced
  from about $28 to about $15.
- **A more specialized company.** Most of the remaining operations
  in North America concentrated on electronics, based on the old
  Packard division's wiring production that had grown rapidly in
  Mexico during the 1980s.

Concentrating on electronics was a fortuitous choice for Delphi
because that was the most rapidly growing sector of the industry (see
Chapter 14). But emerging as an electronics specialist was a far cry
from the 1999 company that seemed to have the capability of supplying
nearly any type of part.

From Ford to Visteon

Visteon was incorporated in 2000, for six months as a wholly owned
subsidiary of Ford, then as an independent company with stock distributed to Ford shareholders.

Visteon was initially organized into seven business units:

1) Chassis Products, including axles, catalytic converters, shafts,
   steering, and suspension.
2) Climate Control Products, including air conditioning and engine cooling.
3) Electronic Products, including audio and driver information.
4) Exterior Products, including bumpers and headlamps.
5) Glass Operations, including windows and windshields.
6) Interior Products, including consoles, doors, and instrument
   panels.
7) Powertrain Products, including alternators, fuel lines, intake
   manifolds, and wipers.

Ford spun off Visteon at the end of an extended period of unusually
harmonious labor relations. The top negotiators—Ford executive vice
president for corporate relations Peter J. Pestillo and UAW vice president and director of the Ford Department Ernest Lofton—were golfing

partners who had both held their positions for more than two decades. Ford agreed to "look to Visteon first" as its supplier of choice when making sourcing decisions.

Visteon workers actually remained employees of Ford "on assignment" to the parts maker. Visteon workers would continue to draw the relatively high wages paid to Ford employees and to participate in Ford's relatively generous health care and pension plans. Ford issued checks to the workers, and Visteon reimbursed Ford for a percentage of the wages and benefits. Only the workforce hired after the spin-off actually became Visteon employees. The "assigned" Ford employees, reluctant to join an untested parts maker, were assured that they would still be on the Ford payroll should Visteon fail.

Ford and Visteon both paid a heavy price for this "sweetheart" deal. As Ford vehicle sales sagged, it spent $3 billion less on parts from Visteon in 2004 than in 2001. Visteon offset the decline with an increase in sales of parts to other carmakers by $3 billion in North America and by $2 billion in the rest of the world. But Visteon failed to make a profit and ran up $3 billion in debt.

The original spin-off agreement was renegotiated in 2003. Ford released Visteon from more than half of its $3 billion retirement benefit obligations, assumed half of the costs for Visteon's information technology, and accelerated payment for components. In return, Visteon agreed to reduce prices. Still, losses mounted at both companies.

As Visteon neared bankruptcy in 2005, a more drastic deal was struck. All 17,700 Ford employees still assigned to Visteon were returned to Ford. Ford offered buyouts to 5,000 and reabsorbed the remainder. Visteon was relieved of a $2 billion liability in health care and life insurance benefits for Ford employees and retirees. Visteon also returned to Ford 24 unprofitable plants, one of which was closed, two were reabsorbed into Ford, 11 were put up for sale, and the remaining 10 were left with an unclear future. Visteon's total worldwide employment, which was at 82,000 at the time of the spin-off from Ford, was reduced to 43,000 in January 2008 (Sherefkin 2008).

The last restructuring radically altered the makeup of Visteon's North American labor force. With Mexican workers far outnumbering UAW members at Visteon, "they have become largely a foreign supplier" (Wernle 2005b).

Chassis, climate control, and interior each accounted for 22 percent of Visteon's sales in 2004. Powertrain sales accounted for 17 percent, electronics for 10 percent, exterior for 4 percent, and glass for 3 percent. After restructuring, climate control had increased to 34 percent of Visteon revenues in 2005, electronics to 26 percent, and interiors to 24 percent. The other four areas had declined from a combined total of 46 percent to 16 percent.

Underlying the restructuring was the recognition that Visteon had cut back to a single core competency—cockpits—which combined instrument panels (interiors) with climate control, tied together by electronics. Visteon had become the North American market leader in cockpits (Chappell 2005c). But this was a far cry from Ford's full-service parts maker—the $11 billion supplier in 2000 had been reduced to $4 billion in 2007, and sales were still falling.

OUTLOOK AND UNCERTAINTIES

The spin-offs of Delphi and Visteon were the most visible evidence that vertical integration as a dominant business strategy had ended in the motor vehicle industry along with the old millennium. In the twenty-first century the strongest carmakers were not the vertically integrated ones; rather, they were the ones working best with independent parts suppliers.

The Delphi and Visteon spin-offs were also emblematic of uncertainties facing the suppliers in the new millennium. Set adrift as independent companies, neither company was able to survive simply as principal parts supplier for its former boss. Nor could either survive as a one-stop shopping center for every sort of part, be it large or small, expensive or cheap, high-tech or generic.

Once the second-largest supplier in the United States, Visteon fell to ninth place in 2007 and was set to decline further in subsequent years. Shed of its highest-cost workers and unprofitable plants, Visteon became primarily an overseas producer, with more employees in Mexico than in the United States. Like Visteon, Delphi was likely to survive primarily as a foreign-based company. Wiring, audio equipment, and other electronics would be produced in low-wage countries for insertion into vehicles assembled in the United States.

As Visteon struggled to survive, its corporate offices moved in 2004 to Visteon Village, a 256-acre, nine-building complex, in Van Buren Township, Michigan, 10 miles southwest of Detroit Metro airport, near the junction of I-94 and I-275. Occupying much of Visteon Village's street-front space were retailers, such as a bank, café, dry cleaner, fitness center, hair salon, and Starbucks. Offices were on the upper floors. An office tower straddled the middle of Main Street. Behind the southern tier of buildings was 15-hectare (37-acre) Grace Lake, where local residents walked their dogs and office workers ate their lunch in summer. Cars—the business of the company—were banished to peripheral lots, leaving employees with a shuttle bus commute or a lengthy hike—a somewhat arduous prospect during Michigan's long, cold winters.

A visitor couldn't help but wonder whether Visteon Village was a make-believe place, like Disneyland or Colonial Williamsburg. How could Visteon plan such an elaborate and costly campus in the face of financial crisis? Was Visteon Village destined to join southeastern Michigan's already unmatched collection of industrial archaeology?

Notes

1. Delphi chairman and CEO Robert S. Miller, quoted in *The Washington Post* (2005).
2. Management consultant Roland Berger made this estimate in 2002, as quoted in Ziebart (2002).

3
Supplying the Power

*I'm not sure the buyer of a Buick LaCrosse would know or
care if the engine was multivalve or pushrod. I don't think a
Camry buyer would know either, for that matter.*[1]

"Powertrain" is the term the motor vehicle industry uses to encompass the systems responsible for providing power. The two principal powertrain systems are the engine and drivetrain. Components attached to the engine and drivetrain, as well as others closely related to the provision of power, can also be included in the powertrain designation.

All but a handful of the world's one billion motor vehicles produced during the twentieth century were powered by a four-stroke gasoline-burning internal combustion engine. The heart of the engine is a piston moving back and forth inside a cylinder in four cycles or "strokes."

- On the first stroke—called the intake stroke—the piston descends, filling the cylinder with a mixture of gasoline and air drawn through an open intake valve.

- On the second stroke—compression—the piston rises as the intake valve is closed, compressing the mixture.

- On the third stroke—power—the piston descends again, driven down as the mixture is ignited and explodes.

- On the fourth stroke—exhaust—the piston rises again, pushing the spent gases out through an open exhaust valve.

Most gasoline engines have had four to eight cylinders. An eight-cylinder engine typically had two rows of four cylinders set at a 90 degree angle to each other. Thus it was V-shaped and known as a V-8; if there were fewer than eight cylinders, they were more likely to be bored in a straight line.

Displacement is the total volume displaced by all of the pistons in the engine block. *Horsepower* measures the rate at which the engine performs work. Before the motor vehicle age, one horsepower had been defined as the amount of power needed to lift 33,000 pounds one foot in one minute. U.S. engines have typically displaced three to five liters and achieved 150 to 300 horsepower. Engines built elsewhere in the world have generally been smaller.

The heart of the drivetrain is the transmission, which contains gears that are connected to the engine by means of an input shaft and to the axles by means of an output shaft. The purpose of the transmission gears is to adjust the input shaft to turn faster or slower than the output shaft, depending on conditions.

The number of revolutions per minute that the input shaft—as well as the engine's crankshaft to which it is attached—rotates is a factor of what is known as torque. Torque is a measure of force that produces rotation. At a high speed, the engine is capable of turning the crankshaft and input shaft more rapidly than is needed to keep the vehicle moving. In contrast, at a low speed the engine does not generate enough torque to move the vehicle except with some assistance. The transmission gears provide that assistance by increasing the torque delivered by the engine at low speed and decreasing it at high speed.

The transmission adjusts torque by means of gears that mesh with each other. To move the vehicle at low speed or up a hill, the transmission increases torque by connecting the input shaft to a smaller gear and the output shaft to a larger gear. As a result, the input shaft turns several times before the output shaft makes one complete revolution. On the other hand, at high-speed driving or going downhill, gears are engaged to slow the rotation of the input shaft.

Carmakers consider the powertrain to be one of their core competencies because it is vital to vehicle performance and character. A principal in-house activity is the assembly of engines and transmissions. Although carmakers put together most of their powertrains in-house, they purchase most of the parts from independent suppliers. Powertrain components add more value than any other system, an estimated $2,750 per vehicle in 2004, but only one-fifth of the value of the powertrain is estimated to be added by independent suppliers (Tomkins plc 2004, p. 4).

Powertrain production is heavily clustered in the Midwest. Central to this distribution is the long-standing regional concentration of nearly all of the Detroit 3 facilities for assembling engines and transmissions. For manufacturers of powertrain components, a location in the Midwest has traditionally offered a compelling combination of proximity to skilled labor, their Detroit 3 customers, and their main sources of inputs (such as steel mills that are also clustered in the region).

The dominance of the Midwest in powertrain production has been eroded under the influence of the leading Japanese-owned carmakers, which have sited their powertrain plants farther south. Suppliers of some powertrain components have also opened facilities in the South. Nonetheless, the preponderance of powertrain facilities remain in the Midwest because the region's geographic assets listed in the previous paragraph remain important.

POWERTRAIN ASSEMBLY IN THE MIDWEST

In 2008 the Detroit 3 built the vast majority of their engines and transmissions themselves at 13 engine plants, 8 engine parts plants, and 10 transmission plants that were heavily clustered in the Midwest. Carmakers also outsourced entire engines and transmissions that they could not cost-effectively produce themselves. In most cases, outsourcing was designed to capture new technology or items with sales potential too low to recoup developmental expenses.

Detroit 3 Powertrain Plants

Seven of the 13 Detroit 3 U.S. engine plants were in Michigan, 3 in Ohio, and 1 each in New York, Tennessee, and Wisconsin (Figure 3.1). The Detroit 3 carmakers also made engines in 2008 at 4 plants in Mexico and 2 in Canada.

All of the Detroit 3 transmission plants were located in the Midwest. Five transmission plants were in Michigan, three in Ohio, and two in Indiana (Figure 3.2). The Detroit 3 also built transmissions at one plant each in Canada and Mexico.

Ford powertrain production

Ford had six North American engine plants as of 2008, one each in Dearborn and Romeo, Michigan; Brook Park and Lima, Ohio; Windsor, Ontario; and Chihuahua, Mexico. Ford also produced engine parts (crankshafts) in Woodhaven, Michigan, and operated casting plants in

Figure 3.1   Location of Carmakers' Engine Plants

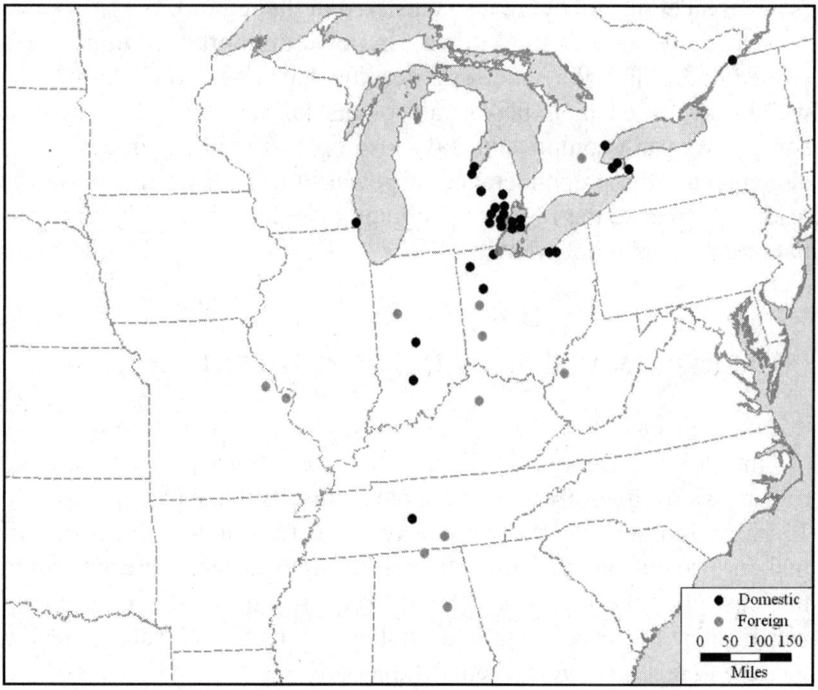

SOURCE: Adapted by the authors from the ELM International database and other sources.

Brook Park, Ohio, and Windsor, Ontario. It made transmissions at two Michigan locations, in Livonia and Sterling Heights, as well as in Sharonville, Ohio.

Until the 1950s, Ford manufactured all of its engines at its home plant in the Detroit area—first at Highland Park and then at the Rouge. Both complexes had foundries to cast engine blocks and shops to machine pistons and cylinders. Finished engines were shipped by rail to Ford's branch assembly plants around the country for installation in finished vehicles. To serve the then-separate Canadian market, Ford opened an engine plant in Windsor in 1923.

Ford subsequently opened several powertrain parts and assembly plants in Ohio during the 1950s, enticed by lower taxes and a desire to counter what came to be seen as excessive centralization of its opera-

Figure 3.2 Location of Carmakers' Transmission Plants

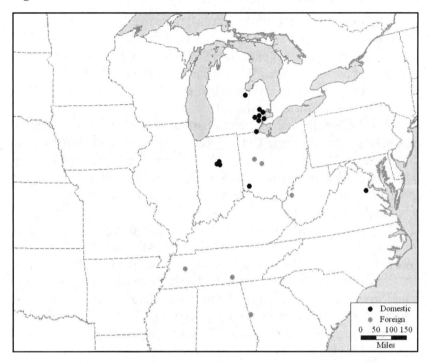

SOURCE: Adapted by the authors from the ELM International database and other sources.

tions at the Rouge. Much of Ford's engine production was relocated to northern Ohio during the 1950s, including several facilities in the Cleveland suburb of Brook Park, plus one in Lima. Transmission production went to the other end of the state, at a plant in the Cincinnati suburb of Sharonville.

After the burst of investment in Ohio during the 1950s, Ford added powertrain facilities in the Detroit area, including Livonia in 1952, Sterling Heights in 1968, Essex, Ontario, in 1981, and Romeo in 1990. Another Cincinnati suburb, Batavia, received a Ford transmission plant in 1980 as front-wheel-drive transaxles became more popular. The Batavia plant, situated on a street named "Front Wheel Drive," was turned over to supplier ZF in 1999 and subsequently closed seven years later.

GM powertrain production

GM operated nine North American engine plants as of 2008, located in Flint, Livonia, and Romulus, Michigan; Tonawanda, New York; Moraine, Ohio; Spring Hill, Tennessee; St. Catharines, Ontario; and Ramos Arizpe and Silao, Mexico. GM also had engine parts plants in Bedford, Indiana; Bay City and Saginaw, Michigan; Massena, New York; Defiance, Ohio; and Toluca, Mexico.

GM Powertrain produced transmissions in 2007 at six North American plants. Five were near Detroit: Romulus, Warren, and Willow Run, Michigan; Toledo, Ohio; and Windsor, Ontario. GM also made transmissions in Ramos Arizpe, Mexico. The plant in Spring Hill stopped producing transmissions in 2006. Transmission parts were made in Fredericksburg, Virginia.

The opening dates of GM's powertrain plants were spread evenly through the decades. The Tonawanda plant was the oldest, built in 1938. Warren and Willow Run dated from the 1940s; Toledo from the 1950s; St. Catharines and Windsor from the 1960s; Livonia and Romulus (engine) from the 1970s; Muncie, Ramos, and Silao from the 1980s; and Moraine, Romulus (transmission), and Spring Hill from the 1990s. The Flint engine plant was opened in 2001 as a replacement for facilities that dated back a century.

Each of GM's major car brands had traditionally been responsible for producing its own powertrain. Individual responsibility was primarily a legacy of each division's origin as an independent company. Once swallowed up by GM in the early twentieth century, each brand was encouraged by the corporation's decentralized decision-making structure to develop its own powertrain. When GM controlled half the U.S. market, GM brands often regarded their principal competitors to be other GM brands rather than other companies. Therefore, unique engines and transmissions for its brands were seen as a way to enhance differentiation within the corporation.

GM broke down much of its traditional brand distinctiveness during the 1960s when it introduced additional size categories of vehicles, such as compacts and intermediates. Chevrolet and Pontiac compacts shared key components, as did Oldsmobile and Buick intermediates, and so on through the product lineup.

Several decades later, GM's various engine plants were combined into an Engine Division in 1990. In addition, the increasing importance of electronic controls made close integration of engineering, design, and production for engines and transmissions essential. GM therefore combined its Hydra-Matic transmission division with its Engine and Central Foundry divisions as well as its Advanced Engineering Staff into a Powertrain division in 1991.

Chrysler powertrain production

Chrysler had three U.S. engine plants in 2008, including two in Michigan and one in Wisconsin. Chrysler made all of its North American transmissions in Indiana. The company also had an engine plant in Ramos Arizpe, Mexico, and was a partner in the GEMA joint venture engine plant in Dundee, Michigan.

Like Ford, Chrysler produced nearly all of its components in Michigan prior to World War II. Chrysler's largest parts facility was the Dodge Main complex in the Detroit suburb of Hamtramck, where Dodge vehicles were also assembled. Components produced at Dodge Main were also trucked to other Chrysler assembly plants clustered in the Detroit area. Dodge Main was closed in the early 1980s.

Chrysler opened two other Detroit-area engine plants during the 1960s, in Trenton on the south side and Warren on the north side. The Warren facility on Mound Road was closed in 2002, three years after another engine plant was opened in Detroit on the site of a demolished stamping facility at Mack Avenue. The Saltillo complex, opened in Ramos Arizpe in 1981, included an engine plant as well as final assembly and stamping operations. From its American Motors acquisition, Chrysler also inherited an engine plant in Kenosha, Wisconsin, dating back to 1917.

Chrysler also had two engine parts plants in North America. Engine blocks were cast at a foundry in Indianapolis, acquired by Chrysler from the American Foundry Co. in 1946. Aluminum engine components were cast at a plant in Etobicoke near Toronto, Ontario, which opened in 1942 and was acquired by Chrysler in 1964.

Chrysler clustered all of its transmission production in Kokomo, Indiana. The company did not produce a fully automatic transmission until 1953, 13 years after GM began producing the Hydra-Matic. Production of automatic transmissions was placed at a plant on the south side of Kokomo in 1956. After it was acquired by Daimler-Benz, Chrysler opened two more transmission plants in Kokomo, in 1998 and 2003.

Transmission parts (e.g., torque converters) were machined at a plant that opened in 1966 in Perrysburg, Ohio, a suburb of Toledo.

After its separation from Daimler, Chrysler was expected to sharply increase its powertrain outsourcing between 2007 and 2013 from 42 percent to 77 percent of engines and from 35 percent to 68 percent of transmissions, according to CSM Worldwide (Phillips and Wernle 2007). The first step in Chrysler's outsourcing was a transmission plant being built near Kokomo. Chrysler was to pay only 43 percent of construction costs and hold only a 15 percent equity stake in the plant. Remaining costs, as well as management control of the plant, were the responsibility of the German supplier, Getrag Corp (Phillips 2007).

Outsourced Diesel Engines

The most common outsourcing of entire engines by the Detroit 3 has been for diesels. The diesel engine was developed by Rudolph Diesel during the 1890s. It differs from the more common gasoline engine because it takes only air into the cylinder on the first intake stroke, rather than a mixture of air and fuel. Instead, fuel is injected only after the air has been compressed on the second stroke. The heat of the compressed air rather than a spark ignites the fuel. Compared to a regular gasoline engine, a diesel engine can operate more efficiently because it compresses air at a higher ratio.

In Europe, where diesel engines now account for more than half of new car sales, the major vehicle manufacturers build their own. In the United States, 1.5 million diesels were manufactured in 2005; two-thirds were destined for heavy trucks and one-third for light vehicles. The major challenge in expanding the market for diesel engines in the United States has been emission standards. Under the Clean Air Act Amendments (CAAA) of 1990, Tier 1 emission standards were adopted in 1991 and phased-in between 1994 and 1997. Tougher Tier 2 standards were adopted in 1999 and phased-in between 2004 and 2009. Tier 2 standards required light-duty diesel engines to emit no more than 0.07 grams per mile of NO_x (oxides of nitrogen). In comparison, Volkswagen cars—the only cars with diesel engines sold in the United States in 2005—emitted about 1.25 grams. Companies such as Daimler and Robert Bosch were in the process of developing the technology that would enable diesel engines to continue to be sold in the United States starting in 2008.

The location of diesel engine manufacturing plants reinforces the clustering of powertrain production in the Midwest. The leading U.S. suppliers of diesel engines for light vehicles have been International and Cummins. A GM-Isuzu joint venture, Dmax, was also a major supplier.

International/Navistar

The largest supplier of diesel engines in the United States for both heavy-duty trucks and light vehicles has been International/Navistar. Navistar has also been the third-leading producer of heavy-duty trucks in the United States, behind Freightliner and Paccar. International started manufacturing diesel engines in Indianapolis in 1937. That facility has produced engines for Ford heavy-duty vehicles. International also produced diesel engines in Huntsville, Alabama (for Ford), and in Melrose Park, Illinois (for other companies). Its casting plants for engine components were located at Waukesha, Wisconsin, and Indianapolis, Indiana.

International has venerable roots as a successor to the McCormick Harvesting Machine Co., founded by Cyrus McCormick to produce the first successful reaper, which he invented in 1831, as well as other machinery that revolutionized American agriculture in the late nineteenth century. J.P. Morgan formed the International Harvester Co. (IHC) in 1902 by merging McCormick with other firms, including its principal competitor, Deering Harvester Co. IHC dominated agricultural equipment production for much of the early twentieth century.

IHC was acquired in 1985 by J.I. Case Co., another venerable nineteenth-century agricultural equipment manufacturer. At the time, Case was a subsidiary of Tenneco Inc., which had acquired it in 1967. Founded by Jerome I. Case in 1842, Case was the world's largest producer of steam engines in the nineteenth century, and it was the first to build a practical stationary steam engine marketed for agricultural use. "International Harvester" and "IHC" remained Case brand names, while IHC's truck and diesel engine division was split off as a separate company, called Navistar.

Cummins

Cummins has been the second-largest supplier of diesel engines in the United States. It was founded in 1919 in Columbus, Indiana, by auto mechanic Clessie Lyle Cummins. Financial backing came from Columbus banker William Glanton Irwin, who had originally hired Cummins in 1908 to drive and maintain his car. Irwin's great-nephew J. Irwin Miller became general manager in 1934 and led the company for four decades.

Clessie Cummins built what the company claims was the first diesel-powered car in the United States by placing a diesel engine in Irwin's Packard. Backed by Irwin's money, Cummins raced diesel-powered vehicles, setting speed and endurance records that attracted truck manufacturers. Attracted by the diesel's economy and durability, Cummins secured the rights to manufacture a Dutch truck known as the Hvid. After making significant improvements to the Hvid engine, Cummins started selling his own diesel engines, primarily for boats, as well as stationary ones for farm use.

As diesel engines became common in trucks, manufacturers of trucks merged with engine suppliers, much as manufacturers of cars made their own engines. But in the case of Cummins, a merger with White Motors in 1963 failed, so Cummins remained an independent engine supplier. Cummins's market was almost exclusively engines for medium- and heavy-duty trucks until 1989, when Chrysler offered a Dodge Ram pickup truck with a Cummins diesel engine. In addition to operations in its hometown, Cummins produced diesel engines in Jamestown, New York, and participates in two joint ventures: Consolidated Diesel Co., in Rocky Mount, North Carolina, opened in 1980 with J.I. Case Corp., and Cummins Komatsu Engine Co. in Seymour, Indiana, opened in 1993 with Komatsu, Ltd. One-half of Cummins's $6.3 billion sales in 2003 were overseas.

Dmax and Detroit Diesel

Dmax, the third-leading producer of diesel engines in the United States, was owned 40 percent by GM and 60 percent by Isuzu. Isuzu has been responsible for design and engineering, and GM for finance, public relations, and support activities. The joint venture produced diesel engines for GM pickups and sport utility vehicles beginning in 2000 in a plant built by GM in Moraine, Ohio. The Moraine plant replaced an older GM diesel engine plant nearby.

General Motors has a long history of producing diesel engines in the United States. The company owned the world's largest builder of diesel-powered locomotives, Electro-Motive, until it was sold in 2005 to Greenbrier Equity Group and Berkshire Partners. To produce diesels for motor vehicles, primarily heavy-duty trucks and off-road machines, GM established the GM Diesel Division in Detroit in 1938. It was turned into an independent company, the Detroit Diesel Corp., in 1988 as a joint venture with Penske Corp. and was acquired by DaimlerChrysler in 2000.

POWERTRAIN COMPONENTS IN THE MIDWEST

Powertrain-related parts can be divided into four main subsystems: 1) the engine block, including cylinders, pistons, and valves; 2) the thermal system, including cooling and climate control; 3) the exhaust system, including pipes and mufflers; and 4) the drivetrain, including clutches and torque converters.

About 46 percent of plants that make a powertrain part produce engine block components, 25 percent produce thermal components, 20 percent make drivetrain components, and 9 percent make exhaust components. These subsystems are discussed in the next four sections. Some plants also specialize in generic powertrain parts (e.g., bearings and mounts), which are discussed in Chapter 5 along with other generic parts.

The production of all four of the principal powertrain subsystems has been concentrated in the Midwest, with the percentages of parts made in the Midwest ranging from 59 percent for exhaust components to 64 percent for the drivetrain (see Table 3.1). Figure 3.3 illustrates the clustering of powertrain plants in the Midwest. It includes three concentric circles drawn around Detroit. These circles represented quartiles of the distance from the suppliers to Detroit, which serves as the reference point for the center of this industry. The closest one-fourth of all exterior parts suppliers are located within the inner circle, the next closest fourth were between the inner and middle circle, the third closest quartile were

Table 3.1 Powertrain Parts Plants in the Midwest

Powertrain system	Number of plants	% in Midwest
Engine block subsystem	849	61.8
Engine bearings and cylinder blocks	44	70.5
Pistons	70	68.6
Crankshafts and balance shafts	37	75.7
Cylinder heads and liners	45	57.8
Valvetrain	146	60.3
Intake and exhaust manifolds	90	72.2
Vibration dampeners	63	74.6
Oil pumps, pans, and filters	65	60.0
Belts, pulleys, flywheels, and dipsticks	58	55.2
Timing gears and chains	17	52.9
Sensors	24	29.2
Other engine parts	190	55.3
Thermal subsystem	463	60.4
Air conditioning	110	61.8
Fans	30	56.7
Radiators	27	29.6
Engine cooling sensors	15	60.0
Thermostats, water pumps, and coolant reservoirs	45	75.6
Heating	21	57.1
Ducts, hoses, and tubes	128	66.4
Other cooling and climate control	87	54.0
Exhaust subsystem	167	59.3
Pipes and tailpipes	21	47.6
Catalytic converters	18	27.8
Mufflers and resonators	32	50.0
Heat shields	15	73.3
Emission controls	26	69.2
Other exhaust parts	55	70.9
Drivetrain subsystem	379	63.9
Transmission parts	121	68.0
Clutch parts	64	71.9
Differential parts	25	60.0
Gearshift parts	25	68.0
Other drivetrain parts	144	63.9
Total powertrain	1,858	61.7

SOURCE: Adapted by the authors from the ELM International database and other sources.

Figure 3.3 Location of Powertrain Plants

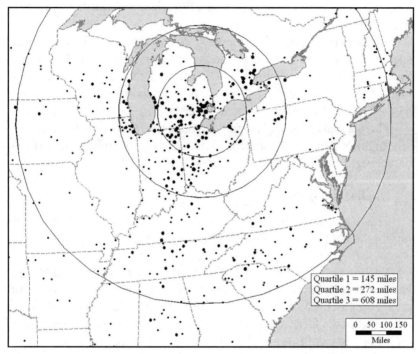

| Quartile 1 = 145 miles |
| Quartile 2 = 272 miles |
| Quartile 3 = 608 miles |

0   50 100 150

Miles

NOTE: Circles are drawn around Detroit and envelop plants producing powertrain parts by quartile. In other words, the tightest circle around Detroit envelops a quarter of the powertrain auto parts plants in North America.

SOURCE: Adapted by the authors from the ELM International database and other sources.

between the middle and the outer circle, and the final quartile is beyond the outer circle. In other words, one-half of powertrain parts producers were located within the middle circle, 272 miles from Detroit, and three-fourths were within the outer circle, 608 miles from Detroit.

Engine Block

The primary engine block parts include pistons, cylinders, and valves, as well as rods and shafts. The Detroit 3 have cast most of their engine blocks at in-house casting plants, although some outsourcing has begun. Blocks were traditionally made of iron, but aluminum has become increasingly common, so carmakers typically maintain both iron and aluminum casting facilities, though some iron facilities have been closed.

A scattering of other engine parts continued to be made in-house, such as crankshafts at Ford's Woodhaven plant, pistons at GM's Bedford and Saginaw foundries, and shafts and rods at GM's Bay City plant. Most other mechanical parts for engines have been outsourced by the Detroit 3 to independent suppliers.

The percentage of engine parts made in the Midwest was exceptionally high, exceeding 70 percent in many cases, including crankshafts, dampeners, manifolds, and the blocks themselves.

Domestic suppliers

The two leading engine parts suppliers in the early twenty-first century in the United States were Eaton and Federal-Mogul.

Eaton. Eaton, founded in 1911 to make truck axles, has been a valve specialist and major supplier of other engine parts. Its first chairman, Joseph O. Eaton, bought the company in 1922, changed its name from Torbensen Gear & Axle (named for its first president), and moved the company from Bloomfield, New Jersey, to Cleveland to be closer to the center of motor vehicle production. Eaton has been closely associated with the city of Cleveland since then. A large number of acquisitions and divestitures during the 1990s left Eaton with a very different profile than the original axle supplier. Two-thirds of company revenues were generated by nonautomotive products, especially hydraulics and electrical controls.

Federal-Mogul. Federal-Mogul has become the other large U.S.-owned supplier of engine parts, including engine bearings, pistons, piston pins, piston rings, cylinder liners, valve seats and guides, transmission products, and connecting rods. Federal-Mogul was created from the 1924 merger of two pioneering U.S. engine bearings companies, Federal Bearing and Bushings Co. and Mogul Metal Co.

- "Mogul" was a trademarked secret process for making engine bearings used by the Muzzy-Lyon Co., founded in Detroit in 1899 by Edward F. Lyon and J. Howard Muzzy. Muzzy-Lyon made bearings from an alloy of tin, antimony, and copper based on a process that was patented by Isaac Babbitt in 1839 to prevent rotating metallic shafts from overheating and wearing out.

- Federal was founded in 1915 by a group of Detroit businessmen who took over the assets of a defunct brass and aluminum foundry to make bronze bearings, castings, and bushings.

Federal and Mogul made a logical merger, according to the company Web site, because Federal did bronze foundry work but lacked the capacity to produce Babbitt metal, whereas Muzzy-Lyon operated a Babbitt foundry but had to purchase bronze.

Acquisitions during the 1990s, especially of the British firm T&N plc in 1997, gave Federal-Mogul a dominant position as the supplier of more than 90 percent of engine bearings in North America and 50 percent worldwide. The T&N acquisition was especially important in Federal-Mogul's goal of becoming a "one-stop" source for engine parts. It was also instrumental in forcing Federal-Mogul to file for Chapter 11 bankruptcy protection in 2001. Inherited from T&N was a massive legal liability stemming from claims that asbestos in its products made 360,000 victims ill.

> Federal-Mogul may be the best example of a supplier gone awry. It grew quickly between 1996 and 1998, following the industry trend. It took on more responsibility for engineering and design work, got bigger to lower costs through economies of scale and diversified its product offerings.
>
> One of the problems suppliers have faced is too much seat-of-the pants planning. In Federal-Mogul's case, the company knew it had to get bigger to keep up with demand but has had no time to decide how to wring efficiencies from the acquisitions.
>
> The frenetic pace of the industry, while a boon to revenue streams, hasn't been as kind to the bottom line, and suppliers are beginning to feel it. (Strong 2000)

Federal-Mogul emerged from Chapter 11 at the end of 2007.

Foreign-owned suppliers

Other leading suppliers of powertrain parts in the United States have been foreign-owned firms, including Linamar Corp., Mahle Inc., Nemak SA., and Teksid Aluminum North America Inc.

Linamar Corp. Linamar Corp. was a Canadian company founded in 1965 by Frank Hasenfratz. Most of its production facilities were located in Guelph, Ontario.

Mahle Inc. Mahle Inc. was a German pioneer in piston production during the 1920s and had two dozen U.S. engine parts facilities in 2007. The company opened its first plants in the United States in the 1970s primarily in the South and expanded rapidly through a 2007 acquisition of Dana Corporation's engine parts plants, many of which were in Michigan.

Nemak SA. Nemak SA was a joint venture that was established in 1979 between Ford and the Mexican company Alfa. Alfa was one of Mexico's largest industrial conglomerates, founded in 1974 through combining steel manufacturer Hojalata y Lamina, packaging manufacturer Empaques de Cartón Titán, mining company Draco, and a minority interest in the television broadcaster Televisa. Nemak operated no plants in the United States, although Ford transferred control of two aluminum parts plants in Windsor and Essex, Ontario, to Nemak in 2000.

Teksid Aluminum North America Inc. Originally Italian carmaker Fiat's parts-making operations, Teksid Aluminum North America Inc. was spun off in 1978. Teksid opened what it claimed to be the world's largest aluminum foundry in Dickson, Tennessee, in 1987 to produce cylinder heads and blocks for GM and Ford engines. It was acquired in 2002 by TK Aluminum Ltd., a holding company based in Bermuda and owned by equity investors led by Questor Management.

Thermal Systems Suppliers

An engine normally operates at a temperature of about 2,000°F, although much higher temperatures can be reached. In the absence of cooling devices, parts would melt or expand to the point that they would seize up and be unable to move.

The principal purpose of the thermal system is to remove the engine's excess heat. The thermal system also heats up the engine to operating temperature as rapidly as possible and maintains the engine at a constant temperature because a cold engine is less efficient, emits more pollutants, and causes parts to wear out faster.

Most motor vehicle engines are cooled with water, which circulates through pipes and passageways. As the water passes through the hot engine, it absorbs heat from the combustion chamber and cools the engine. After the water leaves the engine, it passes through a radiator, which consists of a core made of finned tubes surrounded by coolant tanks. The radiator transfers the heat from the water to air blowing through it. To help cool the water, air is pulled in through a grille with the help of a fan.

The radiator also supplies heat to the passenger compartment. A fan blows air from the radiator core through a heater core into the passenger compartment. Alternatively, to cool the passenger compartment, the air conditioning system removes excess heat as well as moisture. A fan pulls the hot, humid air through an evaporator and a condenser, where a liquid refrigerant condenses water from the hot air and discharges it from the vehicle before returning the "cooled" air through the evaporator back to the passenger compartment.

Cooling and climate control modules have attracted several of the largest foreign-owned suppliers to the United States, and they control the largest share of the market. Nonetheless, most thermal parts are still made in the Midwest, including the air conditioners and hoses. Leading suppliers have included Valeo, Denso, CalsonicKansei, and Behr.

Valeo Inc.

Valeo Inc., the leading thermal systems supplier in the United States, began making heat exchangers in the United States in 1981 in Greensburg, Indiana, and Jamestown, New York. Climate control components were made beginning in 1988 in Hamilton, Ohio, initially as a joint venture with Chrysler's Acustar division. Valeo took over several GM plants in Rochester, New York, that made motors for climate control, engine cooling, interior components, and wipers.

Valeo, originally known as Société Anonyme Française du Ferodo (SAFF), was established in France in 1921 to distribute and then manufacture brake linings pioneered by British firm Ferodo Ltd, established in 1897. The name "Valeo," came from the Latin "to be strong, able, vigorous, and in good health."

Denso Corp.

Denso Corp. was Toyota's in-house electrical and radiator maker until 1949. Known as Nippondenso until 1996, Denso became Japan's largest supplier and third-largest supplier worldwide (after Robert Bosch and Delphi) in the first decade of the twenty-first century. Toyota still owned one-fourth of Denso and accounted for one-half of sales in 2007 (Denso Corporation 2007).

Denso entered the U.S. auto parts industry in 1971 to sell after-market air conditioners for Japanese cars. Its first U.S. manufacturing facility, which opened in 1984 in Battle Creek, Michigan, made air conditioners. It has since become the largest supplier of original equipment air conditioners worldwide and has held a leading position in engine cooling.

CalsonicKansei North America Inc.

Nissan's former in-house thermal system supplier, CalsonicKansei, was the third-largest thermal system supplier in North America, behind Valeo and Denso (CalsonicKansei 2004). CalsonicKansei was formed in 2001 through the merger of Calsonic Corp. and Kantus Corp. Calsonic, known until 1988 as Nihon Radiator Manufacturing Co., produced radiators beginning in 1938, and added mufflers in 1954, heaters in 1955, and air conditioners in 1966. Kantus, originally Kanto Seiki Co., was established in 1956 to make speedometers licensed from the German company VDO and the British company Smiths. The company claimed to be Japan's first modular supplier—a front-end module that combined the radiator, condensers, grille, and other heat-exchange components with headlights.

Behr GmbH.

Europe's second-leading European thermal systems supplier behind Valeo, Behr supplied most German carmakers with radiators from the first decade of the twentieth century onward. Car heaters were added in 1949 and air conditioners in 1957. Behr started producing air conditioners in the United States in 1974 in what was then a remote location of Fort Worth, Texas. Engine cooling was added in North America in 1993 through a joint venture with Cummins Engine. Acquisition of DaimlerChrysler's Dayton, Ohio, Thermal Products plant in 2002 tripled

Behr's U.S. presence and gave it 10 percent of the U.S. engine cooling and climate control market.

Exhaust Module Suppliers

The exhaust module carries gases through pipes from the engine to the rear of the vehicle, where they are discharged into the air. At the engine end, the exhaust gases are carried from the combustion chambers through the exhaust manifold, a pipe usually made of cast iron bolted to the cylinder head.

Before being discharged through the tailpipe, the exhaust gases pass through a muffler, which deadens the loud noise that would result from the escape of the gases by reducing the otherwise very high pressure level. A catalytic converter, which reduces pollutants in the exhaust gases, is attached to the exhaust line between the exhaust manifold and muffler.

The distinctive challenge of shipping exhaust modules is readily visible in a final assembly plant. Whereas most parts arrive in tightly packed crates, exhaust pipes arrive delicately hung on racks or laid-out in large coffins. As a result, the distribution of exhaust module production has been similar to that for final assembly plants. Production of the individual exhaust-related parts has been clustered in the Midwest.

The largest suppliers of exhaust modules in the United States into the twenty-first century included ArvinMeritor, Tenneco Automotive, Faurecia, and Benteler Automotive.

ArvinMeritor

One of the largest U.S.-owned suppliers, ArvinMeritor Inc., formed by merger of Arvin Industries Inc. and Meritor Automotive Inc. in 2000. Meritor, spun off from Rockwell International in 1997, was a leading manufacturer of axles and other chassis components (see Chapter 11). Arvin's predecessor, Indianapolis Air Pump Co., founded in 1919 by Q. G. Noblitt, started making what would become its core product (mufflers) in 1927. Richard Arvin patented the company's first successful product, a car heater, in 1920. ArvinMeritor cobbled together "a collection of assets without many compelling synergies," according to UBS analyst Robert Hinchliffe (Sherefkin 2004).

Tenneco Automotive

Tenneco Automotive was spun off in 1999 from Tenneco Inc. Its primary automotive parts activity derived from a 1967 acquisition of Walker Manufacturing, a major supplier of exhaust and emissions control devices founded in 1888 in Racine, Wisconsin, originally to make springs for horse-drawn wagons. Tenneco Inc., formed in 1943 to build a natural-gas pipeline from Texas to West Virginia, was a conglomerate that also included the manufacturer of Hefty trash bags and the first TV dinner.

Faurecia

Europe's leading exhaust components supplier, Faurecia, moved into third place in the United States after it acquired AP Automotive Systems Inc. in 1999. GM played a central role in nursing Faurecia to the front ranks of U.S. suppliers, primarily in seating (see Chapter 7). "In what analysts say was an unusual move, GM (in 1998) passed over industry exhaust system giants Tenneco and Arvin and asked a consortium of three suppliers (Faurecia, AP Automotive, and Magneti Marelli) to make exhausts." Faurecia gave GM "another supplier in North America and GM wants more competition," according to industry analyst Craig Cather (Sherefkin 1999a). Similarly, GM added Faurecia as a seat supplier in 1999 in order to add competition (see Chapter 7).

Benteler Automotive

Benteler Automotive has claimed to be the world's largest family-owned supplier. Founded as an ironmonger shop in Germany in 1876 by Carl Benteler, three generations of the family have followed in management. Benteler produces an eclectic mix of metal components, including exhaust manifolds and other exhaust components at two plants in the United States. The company also produces chassis and body structural components in the United States.

Transmission Parts Suppliers

Transmission parts suppliers are also clustered in the Midwest. Like engine parts, drivetrain parts have been made in the Midwest in part because of the combination of historical proximity to inputs and customers.

Most drivetrain suppliers have been small companies not included in the Automotive News list of the top 150 suppliers. The leading U.S. supplier of transmission parts historically was BorgWarner Automotive.

BorgWarner Automotive

BorgWarner Automotive was founded in 1928 through the merger of the leading clutch producer Borg & Beck with the leading independent transmission supplier Warner Gear. When manual transmissions predominated in the United States, into the 1950s, BorgWarner supplied 75 percent of the U.S. clutch market. As automatic transmissions took over in the 1950s, BorgWarner was the leading supplier of torque converters. The company also supplied complete automatic transmissions to Ford, Studebaker, and London's famous black taxis.

Into the twenty-first century, the company has shifted its focus from transmissions to engine components. Its largest product segment has become the turbocharger, which increases the amount of air and fuel injected into the engine. Early in the twenty-first century, components such as the turbocharger started to receive increasing attention from automakers in North America because they were expected to produce cleaner and more fuel efficient vehicles.

INTERNATIONAL CARMAKERS POWERTRAIN

International carmakers that assemble vehicles in North America have begun to produce some of their engines and transmissions in North America. However, many also continue to be imported from Japan (see Chapter 13). In addition, Toyota and Nissan have outsourced many of their transmissions.

International Carmakers Powertrain Plants

Most vehicles assembled in North America by Toyota, Honda, Nissan, and Subaru have been equipped with engines produced in North

America. A smaller share of transmissions has been made in the United States. The international carmakers, especially Honda, have added to the clustering of powertrain plants in the southern part of the Midwest. However, much of international powertrain production has been located in the South, especially Kentucky and Tennessee (see Figures 3.1 and 3.2).

Japanese-owned engine plants

Toyota's initial North American production facilities that opened during the 1980s in Georgetown, Kentucky, and Cambridge, Ontario, were designed as relatively self-contained campuses, including engine plants adjacent to final assembly plants. Georgetown produced major powertrain components and assembled the best-selling Camry models, and Cambridge was similarly set up for the Corolla model.

As Toyota began to assemble a wider variety of models in North America, new engine plants were added in Buffalo, West Virginia, in 1998 and in Huntsville, Alabama, in 2003. Neither engine plant was adjacent to a final assembly plant. Huntsville supplied truck engines to Toyota's truck assembly plant in Princeton, Indiana, whereas the Buffalo plant produced engines primarily for Toyota's widening array of lower volume car models that were assembled at Georgetown. The distance from the engine plant to the nearest assembly plant was virtually identical in both cases, approximately 280 miles, or about a half-day's drive.

Toyota's strategy of sprinkling engine and assembly plants across the southern United States was heavily influenced by labor availability concerns. Difficulties with finding a sufficiently large pool of skilled labor within commuting distance of its Georgetown complex induced Toyota to disperse its powertrain and assembly operations several hundred miles east to West Virginia, west to southern Indiana, and south to Alabama, well beyond the central Kentucky labor market area—although they did not go north to Ohio or Michigan.

Honda tied its engine plant locations more closely to its assembly plants. The company's initial North American final assembly complex opened during the 1980s in Marysville and East Liberty, Ohio, and received its engines from a facility that opened in 1985 in Anna, Ohio, 40 miles northwest. (That facility is Honda's largest auto engine plant worldwide, producing nearly 1.2 million engines annually.) Similarly, Honda's assembly plant that opened in Lincoln, Alabama, in 2003 receives its engines from a nearby facility that opened at about the same time.

Nissan's Powertrain Assembly Plant in Decherd, Tennessee, produced engines for its two U.S. assembly plants in Smyrna, Tennessee (70 miles to the north), and Canton, Mississippi (400 miles to the southwest). Subaru started building engines at its Lafayette, Indiana, complex in 2002, 13 years after assembly operations began in the same complex. Mazda did not operate a U.S. engine plant, but it did assemble some vehicles in the United States with engines produced by Ford.

Mitsubishi and Hyundai did not produce their own engines in the United States, but both were being supplied by the Global Engine Manufacturing Alliance (GEMA), a joint venture of the two companies as well as Chrysler. The GEMA plant, which opened in 2005 in Dundee, Michigan, located in southeastern Michigan, has been a prominent example of the continued viability of the Midwest for powertrain production. GEMA's Web site offered the following reason for the site selection: "It is located near several large industrial-based manufacturing centers with thousands of tech-savvy workers to choose from. The region boasts many technological resources. It has easily accessible transportation routes. And it's a family-friendly community, offering a full array of lifestyle enhancing experiences" (GEMA 2007).

The GEMA plant in Michigan, currently one of five plants among the three partners, was built to specialize in the production of four-cylinder engines for entry-level and lower value models sold by the three carmakers. Highly capital intensive and lean, the plant did quickly go to the top of the list of most productive powertrain plants in the United States (Barkholz 2006). The alliance has also opened plants in Japan and South Korea.

A key to the high productivity at GEMA was flexible work rules. Production workers were placed in only one job classification and organized into teams. Three sets of teams work four 10-hour shifts per week, for a total of 120 hours of production per week, compared to a total of 80 hours per week generated in the traditional scheduling of two sets of five 8-hour shifts per week.

Japanese-owned transmission plants

Of the three leading Japanese-owned carmakers, only Honda has produced nearly all of its own transmissions. Moreover, Honda has been largely able to meet demand for transmissions at its U.S. assembly plants and has imported relatively little from Japan.

Honda Transmission Manufacturing of America (HTM) has produced transmissions in Bellefontaine and Russells Point, Ohio, and in Tallapoosa, Georgia. The Ohio plants were originally opened in 1982 by the Honda-controlled Bellemar Parts Industries to supply Honda's nearby Marysville and East Liberty final assembly plants with a variety of parts, including seats, tire assemblies, exhaust systems, catalytic converters, and brake and fuel lines. Honda's U.S. transmission production was initially in its Anna, Ohio, engine plant. Bellemar became a subsidiary of American Honda and shifted production to transmissions in 1996. Transmission components were made at Bellefontaine, and transmissions were assembled at Russells Point. The components formerly made there were subsequently sourced to other suppliers. In 2006 Honda opened a plant in Georgia to supply transmissions to its Lincoln, Alabama, assembly plant, 60 miles west.

Toyota and Nissan joined Honda in opening transmission production facilities in the United States during the late 1990s, Toyota in Buffalo, West Virginia, and Nissan in Decherd, Tennessee. Toyota and Nissan both combined transmission with engine production in the same facility.

Transmissions Outsourced by Japanese Carmakers

Toyota and Nissan, in contrast to the other leading carmakers, have met much of their transmission needs from independent suppliers. Not surprisingly, the world's two largest independent transmission producers, Aisin World and Jatco, have become the principal suppliers for Toyota and Nissan.

Aisin

One of the world's 10 largest suppliers, Aisin is the second-largest Japanese-owned supplier after Denso in both worldwide and North American sales. Aisin is 24.5 percent owned by Toyota Motor Corp. and is closely tied to Toyota's keiretsu network. Two-thirds of Aisin's sales are to Toyota. Aisin is one of the most diversified of the world's very large suppliers. Powertrain components have accounted for about half of Aisin's sales. Body and chassis components make up most of the other half.

The relationship between Toyota and Aisin is typical in that neither does the carmaker totally control its supplier, nor is the supplier completely independent of the carmaker. "Consequently, the Toyota suppliers were independent companies, with completely separate books. They were real profit centers, rather than the sham profit centers of many vertically integrated mass-production firms. Moreover, Toyota encouraged them to perform considerable work for other assemblers and for firms in other industries because outside business almost always generated higher profit margins" (Womack, Jones, and Roos 1990).

Aisin supplied transmissions to Toyota primarily from a facility in Durham, North Carolina. Other transmissions were imported from Japan. Aisin also produced a wide variety of other parts in the United States, primarily for Toyota, including brakes, body parts, and sensors. Its 17 U.S. automotive parts production facilities in 2007 included six in Indiana and three in Illinois.

Jatco

Challenging Aisin as the world's leading independent producer of complete transmissions was Jatco. It may be the largest supplier and should have been included in the *Automotive News* rankings of top 150 North American and top 100 world suppliers, but it is not. This exclusion may result from Jatco being regarded as a Nissan captive rather than truly independent.

Jatco was created in 1970 jointly by Nissan and Mazda, but Mazda sold its stake in 1999 to Nissan, which in turn combined it with its own transmission unit. Mitsubishi Motors turned over its transmission operations to Jatco in 2002, in exchange for a minority ownership in the supplier. Nissan accounted for 59 percent of Jatco sales in 2005 and Mitsubishi for 14 percent (Treece 2005). In addition to Nissan, Mazda, and Mitsubishi, Jatco also supplied complete transmissions to BMW, Isuzu, Jaguar, Subaru, Suzuki, and Volkswagen (Treece 2001). Jatco operated a transmissions plant in Aguascalientes, Mexico. Rather than produce transmissions in the United States, Jatco has imported them from Japan.

OUTLOOK AND UNCERTAINTIES

The future health of powertrain suppliers in southeastern Michigan and throughout the Midwest depends, like much of the motor vehicle industry, on the future health of the Detroit 3 carmakers. However, powertrain production in the region may more easily weather market shifts among carmakers. Powertrain production has been strongly embedded in the Midwest, as firms depend on proximity to iron and steel inputs, powertrain assembly customers, and skilled labor.

In the longer run, carmakers and parts suppliers have been scrambling to produce viable alternatives to the internal combustion engine. Hybrid electric vehicles rapidly gained market share during the first decade of the twenty-first century, and fuel cell vehicles were lurking around the corner.[2]

A fuel cell produces electricity by separating a hydrogen molecule into a positively charged proton and a negatively charged electron. The proton flows through a membrane while the electron flows through an external circuit from an anode to a cathode, creating electricity. A catalyst on the cathode side of the membrane facilitates recombining of the hydrogen ions with oxygen to form water.

The principal challenge with fuel cell technology has been storage and delivery of the hydrogen. "[Y]ou don't have a hydrogen pipeline coming to your house, and you can't pull up to a hydrogen pump at your local gas station" (Nice and Strickland 2007). A further difficulty has been dependency on platinum, a costly and finite resource, to coat the membrane. A key hurdle on the path to mass production has been the development of a supply base. "Manufacturing capacity for the batteries is limited because the technology required is relatively new. There are very few suppliers in the world that not only know how to put battery cells together but also how to manufacture them."[3]

GM and Toyota have backed away from fuel cells, expressing "doubts about the viability of hydrogen fuel cells for mass production in the near term . . . Daimler AG [however] expects to begin producing fuel-cell cars in limited quantities in 2010," according to its chief executive Dieter Zetsche (Taylor and Spector 2008). Because fuel cell vehicles were not ready for mass production in the early twenty-first century, carmakers needed an immediate strategy to reduce fuel consumption and lower emissions. Hybrid electric vehicles, combining a gasoline engine with an electric motor, moved into the lead as the quickest and least expensive way to make progress. Consumer-oriented publications like *Consumer Reports* and *Car & Driver* warned their readers that hybrids were unlikely to achieve advertised fuel efficiency under most driving conditions, and higher purchasing and operating costs were not likely to be recouped during the life of the vehicle. Nonetheless, sales of hybrids increased in the United States from 85,000 in 2004 to 338,851 in 2007; 50 hybrid models were expected to account for 1 million sales in the United States in 2010 (Chew 2005; Truett 2005).

Much of the success at pushing hybrids in the United States came from Toyota. Competitors charged that Toyota was selling hybrids at a loss to tout itself as an environmentally friendly company. But this was exactly the point for Toyota: when consumers demanded more fuel-efficient and environmentally friendly vehicles, they would look first at Toyota's products. As a result, other carmakers were forced to allocate scarce resources to developing their own hybrids instead of developing possibly more viable long-term solutions like fuel cells.

During 2007, when it decided on the major engineering issues for the third generation of the Prius, its best-selling hybrid car, Toyota took a more cautious approach than other carmakers regarding the feasibility of using lithium ion batteries and producing a plug-in version (White 2007). Toyota's cautiousness despite being the market leader in hybrid vehicles illustrated the uncertainties associated with a technology widely considered as transitional.

Fuel cell, hybrid, and other alternative fuel technologies are destined to shake up the motor vehicle industry in the long run. In the first decade of the twenty-first century, the large powertrain and electronics suppliers were jockeying to obtain leading roles in supplying hybrid components in the short term and fuel cell components in the long run. Suppliers of components such as alternators were scrambling to cope with obsolescence of their products in an alternative fuel world. As is often the case with new technologies, small start-up companies were positioned to be early innovators in producing alternative fuel components.

Then there was the question of who would take the lead in hybrid technology R&D. To advance its Chevrolet Volt hybrid, GM awarded two battery development contracts to independent suppliers in 2007:

- A joint venture between Cobasys LLC, a suburban Detroit maker of nickel-metal hydride batteries, and its partner, A123 Systems of Watertown, Massachusetts.

- A joint venture between two large auto parts makers, Johnson Controls and French battery-maker Saft Group SA (LaReau 2007).

On the other hand, when it failed to find reliable suppliers of hybrid technology, Toyota gained leadership by investing in its own research efforts and obtained several patents on key hybrid technology.

In the early twenty-first century, it was uncertain whether carmakers like Toyota would continue to design and produce most of their engines with new technologies or whether suppliers would be the principal source. And if the responsibility were outsourced, would new companies evolve into major powertrain suppliers or would already-existing large Tier 1 suppliers prevail either through in-house creation of technology or acquisition of the upstart companies?

Notes

1. Gordon Wangers, managing partner, Automotive Marketing Consultants, quoted in Guilford (2004).
2. For a more detailed analysis of the challenges of creating automobiles that will run on cleaner energy sources, see Carson and Vaitheeswaran (2007).
3. Jim Queen, GM group vice president of global engineering, quoted in LaReau (2007).

4

The Body Builders

For two executives whose life-blood is engineering and, of course, the bottom line, [Martinrea Chief Executive Officer] Fred Jaekel and [President] Nick Orlando have a keen eye on another science—geography. "We get plants in Mississippi, Tennessee, Kentucky; it allows us to get to the south," Mr. Orlando says. (Keenan 2006)

The system of the motor vehicle most responsible for the Midwest's continued—if diminished—leadership in parts production is the exterior. Major exterior modules include the body, frame, and bumpers.

More than two-thirds of all exterior parts were made in the Midwest (Figure 4.1). Especially likely to be made in the Midwest were the bulkiest exterior modules, notably bodies and bumpers (Table 4.1). Even manufacturers of small exterior parts, such as grilles and hardware, were overwhelmingly clustered in the Midwest.

Proximity to both raw materials and customers explained the Midwest's attraction for suppliers of the bulkier stamped exterior parts. The principal input into stamping exterior parts was steel, which was produced primarily at Midwestern mills. Suppliers also sought to minimize the cost and distance of shipping stamped exterior parts to the final assembly plants because they are relatively bulky and fragile, and of relatively low value.

STAMPING OF BODY PARTS

The body drop is perhaps the most entertaining station at a final assembly plant. Stamped, welded, and painted bodies are finally married to the powertrain. To casual visitors, the bewildering complexity of motor vehicle assembly finally starts to make sense when the vehicle takes shape at the body drop.

Figure 4.1 Location of Exterior Supplier Plants

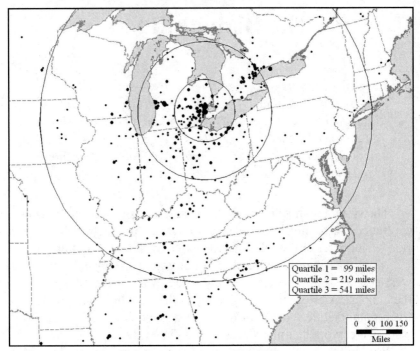

Quartile 1 = 99 miles
Quartile 2 = 219 miles
Quartile 3 = 541 miles

0   50 100 150
Miles

SOURCE: Adapted by the authors from ELM International database and other
sources.

The body drop was the most widely photographed and filmed feature of Ford's revolutionary moving assembly line at Highland Park a
century ago. The attraction then as now was partly the dramatic visual
image. At Highland Park, the body drop had the added value of taking
place along an exterior wall of the plant, where early twentieth-century
cameras could obtain much better quality images than possible inside.
Bodies built on the upper floors at Highland Park were slid down an
outside chute and attached to chassis built on the first floor and rolled
outside under the chute.

Some bodies are still dropped onto chassis, but these are confined to
larger trucks. Most light vehicles are now built through so-called unitized construction, which involves welding the frame of front, rear, and
side rails into an underbody. Top and side frames are then welded to the
underbody to form a shell. This is one of the most automated steps in

Table 4.1 Exterior Parts Plants in the Midwest

Exterior part	Number of plants	% in Midwest
Body	260	75.0
Body molding	57	75.4
Roofs and body panels	127	76.4
Doors	76	72.4
Frame	70	62.9
Bumpers and fascia	79	72.2
Exterior trim	286	64.9
Door hardware	108	65.7
Labels and exterior decals	37	64.9
Grills and luggage racks	35	74.3
Windshield washers	35	54.3
Mirrors	32	59.4
Hardware	21	71.4
Other body parts	479	62.8
Total exterior	1,156	66.7

SOURCE: Adapted by the authors from the ELM International database and other sources.

final assembly, with most welding done by robots. Hood, trunk, door, and fender panels arrive at the body build-up area ready for hanging on the shell. Panels are stamped or pressed from sheets of steel, aluminum, or plastic at stamping facilities operated by the carmakers or by independent suppliers. The built-up body, known as "body-in-white," subsequently goes to the paint shop.

Carmakers have been more reluctant to outsource body build-up and painting stampings than other components because of the high capital cost associated with these two operations. Stamping operations, especially purchase of stamping dies, have represented 10 percent of the cost of a new vehicle program (Child 1996). The paint shop has been even more expensive, accounting for one-third of the cost of a final assembly plant. Stamping has been kept in-house because accurate stamping of large panels has been critical to meet the tight tolerance required in today's assembly of vehicles, and therefore to vehicle quality.

Outsourcing of exterior components has been increasing in the twenty-first century. The chief reason has been a proliferation of body styles, many designed for low-volume models. Because carmakers cannot justify the high cost of dies to produce body panels for limited production models, they have turned to independent suppliers.

Exterior parts other than body panels are also more likely to be outsourced. The bumper, once stamped in-house or purchased as a stand-alone part, is now outsourced as part of a larger front-end or rear-end module called a fascia. Glass and coatings have always been a principal responsibility of independent suppliers.

In-House Stamping

The Detroit 3 operated 27 stamping plants in the United States in 2008, including 13 by GM, 10 by Ford, and 4 by Chrysler. These facilities have a contemporary layout and modern equipment, but beneath the surface are remnants of their heritage from the era of vertical integration. Many of them are "full-sized" free-standing body stamping plants, but some are integrated with an assembly plant. The Detroit 3 also operated two stamping facilities in Ontario and five in Mexico.

The Detroit 3 stamping plants are clustered along the southern Great Lakes (Figure 4.2). Twelve of the 27 are located in southeastern Michigan, six in northern Ohio, and two in central Indiana. Three others are not all that far away in Buffalo, New York, and Belvidere and Chicago Heights, Illinois. Outliers are the GM facilities in Fairfax, Kansas; Spring Hill, Tennessee; and Wentzville, Missouri; and a Ford stamping plant in Louisville, Kentucky. Most stamping plants were built shortly after World War II, including eight in the 1950s; four in the 1960s; and three each in the 1930s, 1940s, and 1980s. One plant each was also built in the 1920s, 1960s, and 1970s. Plants typically occupied roughly 2 million square feet and employed 1,000 to 2,500 workers.

Historically, a stamping plant was dedicated to meeting the need for bodies at a nearby final assembly plant. At Ford's Rouge complex, for example, bodies were stamped in one building and dropped on the chassis in the adjacent final assembly building. Cadillac bodies were trucked through the streets of Detroit from the Fort Street Fleetwood stamping plant to the Clark Avenue final assembly plant two miles away. Chevrolet bodies were stamped at a plant in Fairfield, Ohio, and shipped by rail 15 miles south to a final assembly plant in Norwood, Ohio. Bodies were painted in the final assembly plant.

Figure 4.2 Location of Stamping Plants Owned by Carmakers

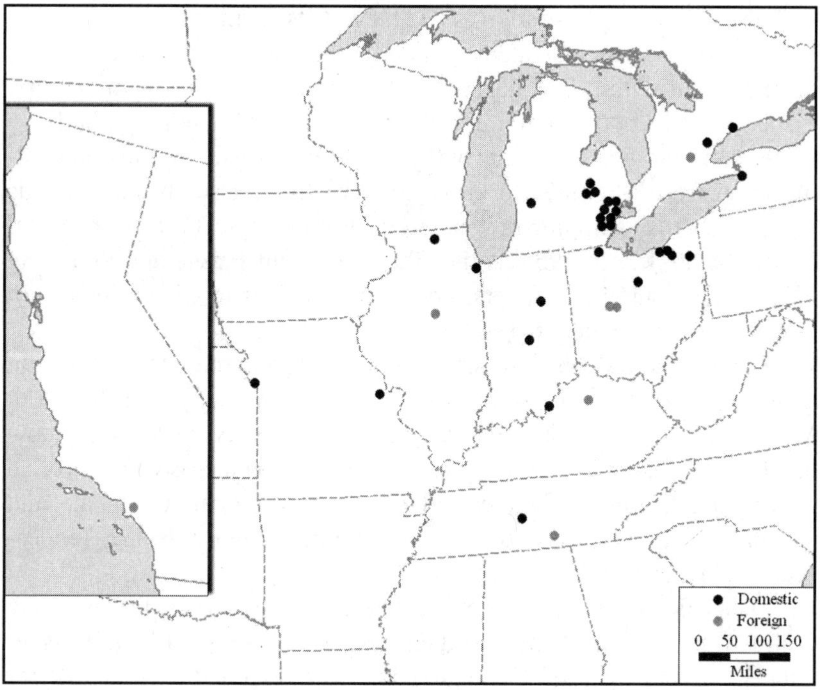

SOURCE: Adapted by the authors from the ELM International database and other sources.

Most Detroit 3 stamping plants are now "stand-alone" facilities rather than tied to supplying a specific assembly plant. Consequently, they now compete with each other to obtain the right to make particular body parts and ship them to multiple assembly plants. Division of responsibility among Detroit 3 stamping plants is thus by type of part rather than by model or platform. For example, among Chrysler facilities in 2004, truck hoods and fenders were stamped at the Warren plant, truck roofs and floor pans at the Twinsburg plant, and car panels at the Sterling Heights plant. In the early twenty-first century, Ford's Torrence Avenue assembly plant received front and rear doors from both Chicago Heights and Buffalo.

GM stamping

GM's stamping operation is a legacy of its relationship with Fisher Body, first as an independent company, then as a highly autonomous business unit within GM during the first half of the twentieth century. Fisher placed a body stamping plant near each GM assembly plant.

Because bodies were very bulky and fragile, Fisher found that hauling them from Michigan to GM's then far-flung assembly plants was more costly than shipping raw materials. For example, GM's Flint Metal Center began life in 1954 as the Chevrolet Flint Frame and Stamping Plant, which supplied fenders, hoods, and frames to Chevrolet's Flint assembly plant opened in 1947.

Fisher generated its own set of suppliers during the 1920s. It bought controlling interest in National Plate Glass Company and Ternstedt Manufacturing Company, which made body parts such as window cranks. Because early bodies were made of wood, Fisher controlled nearly 250,000 acres of timberland, mostly in Michigan, Louisiana, and Arkansas, and sawmills and woodworking plants in Louisiana, Tennessee, and Washington.

Fisher Body lost its distinct identity during the 1980s, first merging with Guide Lamp in 1986 and then with Inland to form Inland Fisher Guide Division in 1990. The division was renamed Delphi Interior and Lighting Systems in 1994, and then Delphi Interior Systems when GM spun off much of its parts operations in 1999. GM consolidated 13 Fisher stamping facilities into the Metal Fabricating Division in 1994. Even that faint vestige of Fisher's one-time autonomy was extinguished when Metal Fabricating was folded into GM's North American manufacturing operations in 2005.

Five of the surviving Fisher facilities (located in Indianapolis; Flint; Lordstown and Parma, Ohio; and Spring Hill, Tennessee) did stamping, one (in Flint) made dies, and five (in Marion, Indiana; Grand Blanc, Grand Rapids, and Pontiac, Michigan; and Mansfield, Ohio) did both stamping and die-making. Stamping plants in Lansing, Michigan, and Pittsburgh, Pennsylvania, were closed in 2006 and 2007. Stamping plants are adjacent to assembly plants at Fairfax, Kansas; Oshawa, Ontario; and Wentzville, Missouri. GM's two stamping facilities in Mexico, at Ramos Arizpe and Silao, are inside assembly plants.

Ford stamping

Ford characteristically concentrated nearly all stamping operations at the Rouge complex during the 1930s. Bodies were stamped in what was then called the Pressed Steel Building and either sent next door to the final assembly plant or shipped to branch assembly plants around the country.

Ford later broke up the extreme concentration of production at the Rouge after World War II. Stamping facilities were placed near long-standing final assembly plants in Buffalo and Chicago, as well as in Walton Hills, part of Ford's emerging postwar components production center in the Cleveland area. Two other stamping plants were added in the 1960s and 1970s in Woodhaven in the Detroit–Toledo corridor, as well as adjacent to assembly plants in Dearborn, Louisville, and Wayne.

Ford's substantially downsized Rouge complex still includes a stamping plant. Though a modernized operation, the Dearborn stamping plant is one of the Rouge's clearest relics of an earlier era because steel comes in at one end from the adjacent, independently owned steel mill, and doors and hoods come out at the other end destined for the adjacent final assembly plant. Ford's stamping facility in Hermosillo, Mexico, was part of an assembly plant.

Chrysler stamping

Chrysler did not own a car body stamping facility until 1953, when it purchased its principal supplier Briggs Manufacturing Co. Established in 1908 by Walter Owen Briggs, the body maker emerged as the largest surviving independent supplier during the 1920s once Ford and GM started making their own.

Briggs survived by selling to the smaller carmakers that lacked in-house body-making capabilities, including Chrysler. Briggs's Mack Avenue stamping plant in Detroit, originally built in 1916 by the Michigan Stamping Co., produced bodies for Chrysler's Plymouth division, which had a final assembly plant two miles west on Mt. Elliott Avenue. In 1926 Briggs acquired LeBaron Carrossiers Inc., which became the source of bodies for Chrysler's luxury cars.

Walter Briggs was well-known in Detroit after he purchased the Detroit Tigers baseball team in 1935. The team's ballpark was known as Briggs Field between 1938 and 1961, when the name was changed to Tiger Stadium.

Meanwhile, Chrysler opened stamping plants adjacent to its truck assembly plant in Warren in 1949 and its car assembly plants in Sterling Heights and Belvidere, Illinois, in the 1960s. The company also opened a stamping plant in Twinsburg, outside Toledo, in 1957 and continued to make bodies at Briggs's Mack Stamping plant until closing it in 1979 during its near brush with bankruptcy.[1] Briggs remained in business manufacturing plumbing supplies until it was sold to Cerámicas Industriales in 1997. Chrysler also operated two stamping plants in Mexico (Toluca and Saltillo) and one in Canada (Brampton).

Japanese stamping facilities

Japanese-owned carmakers had six stamping facilities in the United States and one in Canada in 2008. Toyota had two stamping plants at its Georgetown, Kentucky, complex, as well as one in Long Beach, California. Honda had two stamping facilities adjacent to its two Ohio assembly plants. Mitsubishi had one adjacent to its Normal, Illinois, assembly plant. Nissan operated a stamping plant along with powertrain facilities in Decherd, Tennessee, an hour from its Smyrna final assembly plant.

Outsourced Exterior Systems

The leading independent suppliers of exterior modules, including stamped body parts, were two Canadian companies, Magna and Martinrea, and the U.S. frame-making firm Tower. Magna International was the second-largest supplier in the United States during the first decade of the twenty-first century, and it generated by far the largest amount of revenue from exterior components of any supplier.

Magna International

Canada's largest parts maker has become the only supplier to be a major player in as many as four of the five main parts systems (all but electronics). It has also been a pioneer in providing integrated modules, as well as in assembling entire vehicles on behalf of carmakers. Magna is a technology leader in the body segment. It has pioneered hydroform technology, which is effective in shaping vehicle frames and bodies as well as making them lighter. For example, hydroformed Magna frames have been used in GM's large trucks.

Frank Stronach, a 25-year-old tool and die engineer who had immigrated to Canada from Austria in 1954, founded Magna's predecessor, Multimatic Investments Limited, in 1957. Multimatic's first automotive contract was to supply GM with metal brackets for sun visors. Multimatic merged with defense contractor Magna Electronics Corporation in 1969 and adopted the Magna International name four years later. Aerospace and defense operations were sold in 1981, leaving Magna as an automotive specialist.

Stronach imposed a strong personality on Magna. The centerpiece was what he called a "Corporate Constitution," which he announced in 1971, based on what he called a "Fair Enterprise" management philosophy. The "Corporate Constitution" specified the distribution of profits among employees, management, charities, and research and development. For example, "ten percent of Magna's profit before tax will be allocated to employees. These funds will be used for the purchase of Magna shares in trust for employees and for cash distributions to employees, recognizing length of service" (Magna International 2007). Shareholders would get 20 percent, management 6 percent, charities 2 percent, and research and development 7 percent of the profits.

In order to concentrate on his love for horse racing, Stronach turned over control of Magna International to his daughter, Belinda Stronach, who became CEO in 2001 and president in 2002. She left the company in 2002 to pursue political ambitions but returned in 2007. Stronach adopted decentralized management for Magna, including so-called groups for each of the major systems. An Executive Strategy Committee coordinated the groups. Decentralization was pushed further in the late 1990s by spinning off groups into independently traded public companies. Magna wanted to avoid becoming one of what it called the "lumbering dinosaurs" by creating "a smaller, more focused and more entrepreneurial company," according to Don Walker, CEO of Intier (Armstrong 2004a). Top managers were considered more likely to remain with the company if they received ownership stakes in the new pieces, although Magna retained ultimate financial control.

The arrangement proved short-lived, and Magna reacquired the three spun-off companies in 2005 because it discovered that Japanese carmakers preferred dealing with a single supplier. Magna president Mark Hogan said, "It got a little confusing as to who to deal with" (Armstrong 2004a).

Magna has a reputation for being perhaps the most publicity-shy of all of the major suppliers. Seemingly straightforward information, such as the address of its plants, is difficult to extract from the company. Even Ontario government officials have difficulty getting a handle on the company's operations.

The company had 236 manufacturing facilities worldwide in 2007, including 52 in the United States and 61 in Canada. Eighteen of the U.S. facilities were in Michigan, primarily those producing interior parts. Body stamping facilities were more likely to be outside the Midwest.

Martinrea (Budd)

In the early 1900s, bodies were made primarily of wood. White ash was most preferred, with oak, beech, teak, pine, and elm also common. Timber took 10 years to properly season, and it took many weeks for skilled craft workers to fashion coaches. "[By the late 1930s,] there were only a few sticks of wood left in the passenger job. To all intents and purposes, you might say that wood, as far as passenger jobs were concerned, was discontinued."[2]

Philadelphia furniture maker Hale & Kilburn, then the dominant producer of steel seats for trains, was credited with producing the first steel car body, for the 1912 Hupmobile. Hale & Kilburn's general manager Edward Budd set up his own firm in 1912 to produce steel car bodies. "[T]rue revolution came with Edward G. Budd, founder of The Budd Co., who invented and patented the all-steel car body in 1912" (Winter 1996).

To prove that steel bodies were stronger and therefore safer than wood ones, Budd staged outrageous publicity stunts during the 1910s. An elephant sitting on top of a Budd body did not crush it, even when the doors were opened and closed. Probably the most spectacular stunt was driving a Dodge with a Budd steel body off a cliff. After rolling over several times, the car was still drivable, and the driver emerged uninjured.

Low-volume luxury brands such as Packard and Peerless were early adopters of Budd's steel body. The first large order came in 1914 from Dodge Brothers, which was then in the process of converting from the

nation's largest parts supplier to a high-volume carmaker. Dodge paid
Budd $42 per body and $2 for each set of fenders (Hyde 2005, p. 81).

Ford's decision to purchase Budd steel bodies in 1917 was a critical step in speeding up Model T production. The principal constraint in
increasing assembly speed had been the time needed to paint the body.
Paint applied to a steel body at a high temperature dried in a few hours,
whereas varnish took two weeks to dry on a wood body.

Edward Budd (1870–1946) and Henry Ford (1870–1947) were con-
temporaries and allegedly developed a personal relationship through
the years, and Ford wrote in his newspaper, *The Dearborn Independent*,
that Budd was "a high-class, Christian gentleman. Just the type of man
I would like to see in the manufacturing world. There are too few men
like Budd to me." However, Budd (the man or the company) is never
mentioned in Allan Nevins's exhaustive history of Henry Ford and the
first half-century of the Ford Motor Company (Nevins 1954; Nevins
and Hill 1957, 1962).

More generous in citing Budd is the most authoritative history
of Dodge (the brothers and the company; Hyde [2005], p. 79): "The
Dodge Brothers automobile was not merely another mid-range offering
on the market but an innovative product because it incorporated all-
steel bodies supplied by the Edward G. Budd Manufacturing Company
of Philadelphia. Dodge Brothers developed an innovative, cooperative
relationship with Budd in the process."

Budd was also credited with developing unitized body construction during the 1930s, three decades before it was widely adopted. By
then, though, the car body business had declined sharply, as a result
of Depression-era cutbacks and in-house body-making. Beginning in
1934, Budd devoted its attention to what became its best-known product, stainless steel passenger railroad cars, especially the Pennsylvania
Railroad's streamliner trains.

Much later, faced with collapse of the U.S. railroad car market, the
struggling Budd Company was acquired in 1978 by German steel manufacturer Thyssen AG, which merged in 1999 with another venerable
German steelmaker, Krupp AG.

ThyssenKrupp sold its U.S. stamping operations in 2006 to the little-
known Canadian company Martinrea International Inc. Martinrea was
formed in 2002 by former leaders of Magna's metal-forming unit Cosma International. Not coincidentally, Martinrea's corporate philosophy

was modeled on Magna, including an Employee Bill of Rights. Martin-rea CEO Fred Jaekel said "[I]t would be an honour to be called 'Magna Jr.'" (Keenan 2006).

Before the ThyssenKrupp Budd acquisition, Martinrea was a company with 3,000 employees and $500 million in revenues worldwide. It had one U.S. stamping facility, in Corydon, Indiana, which had opened in 2005. The addition of the ThyssenKrupp stamping facilities tripled revenues, doubled the number of employees worldwide, and increased the number of U.S. plants from 1 to 14.

Tower

The starting point for putting together a body is the frame, constructed of steel members welded or riveted together, usually in the shape of a rectangle with crosspieces, sometimes in an X-shape. Front and rear portions of the rectangle are rounded up to provide clearance over axles and suspension. The frame must be very rigid, in order to provide support and alignment for the body and powertrain, which are bolted to it.

A.O. Smith was the dominant frame supplier for much of the twentieth century. As with a number of leading chassis suppliers, Milwaukee-based A.O. Smith predated the motor vehicle industry by producing wood frames for carriages beginning in 1874. Through such innovations as using pressed steel and automatic riveting, A.O. Smith captured two-thirds of the market in 1901 and produced 10,000 frames a day.

A.O. Smith's dominance as a frame supplier diminished after carmakers adopted unibody construction for cars and some trucks beginning in the 1960s. Unibody construction involved welding a frame to a body shell. Welding the two together gave a vehicle greater structural rigidity and made it less likely to shake and rattle. As a frame specialist, A.O. Smith found itself competing with systems integrators (e.g., Magna) who could provide an entire unibody. By 1997 A.O. Smith had diversified into nonautomotive sectors, including water heaters, electric motors, fiberglass pipe and fittings, and glass-lined storage tanks, which generated higher returns on investment, so it sold its Automotive Division to Tower Automotive.

Tower Automotive was formed in 1993 when Minneapolis-based holding company Hidden Creek Industries spent $83 million for R.J.

Tower Co., a small machine shop that had started in 1874 to repair metal farm implements. As a result of acquisitions like A.O. Smith, Tower was able to offer a wide variety of structural body components made of stamped and pressed steel, including body pillars, top cross frames, lower side sills, rails, fender reinforcements, and floor pans.

In 2004, Tower became one of the first suppliers to operate a facility inside a U.S. final assembly plant at Nissan's Smyrna facility. Tower provided Nissan with fully assembled frames for Nissan's pickup trucks, while Nissan continued to assemble frames itself for its sport utility vehicles with rails supplied by Tower. The relationship deepened at Nissan's second U.S. assembly plant in Canton, Mississippi, which receives complete frames within minutes of being needed on the final assembly line from the nearby Tower plant in Madison.

During the 1990s Tower followed a strategy of globalization through acquisitions, as well as expanded product lines. Sales rose from $167 million in 1994 to $2.2 billion in 2000. Tower took on debt expecting that the acquisitions would produce synergies and growth. However, the company was unable to integrate its many capital-intensive businesses. It was not able to cover its fixed costs, and Tower entered Chapter 11 in 2005. Two years later, the company emerged from bankruptcy by selling most of its assets to the private equity firm Cerberus Capital Management, which acquired Chrysler the same year (Sherefkin 2007a; Walsh 2007).

PAINTING THE BODY: CAPTURING A MOOD

Henry Ford's famous epigram, "People can have the Model T in any color—so long as it's black," captured the distinctive appeal of the Model T during the 1910s. The first Model T's produced between 1909 and 1913 and the last ones produced in 1926 and 1927 were painted bright colors, but the 15 million produced in between came only in black.

Painting had been the most time-consuming step in early car making. Typically, five coats were painted by hand with a brush. Before each coat was applied, the body had to be sanded and varnished, and after each coat, the body took several days to dry. Altogether painting took 18 days, during which time the body had to be stored in a dust-free location (Yanik 1993).

The painting process is still relatively elaborate and expensive. First, a primer layer is applied to steel and plastic components to smooth out irregularities and imperfections and to improve resistance against chipping. Primers may be tinted to reduce the amount of paint needed. A basecoat layer provides most of the coloring, and the final clearcoat layer provides most of the protection. A tricoat layer of micas, aluminum flakes, or other pigments may be added between the basecoat and clearcoat to obtain a more complex metallic, speckled, flat, or three-dimensional appearance.

Many body parts are now painted by electrocoating, which is "an organic coating method that uses electrical current to deposit paint onto a part or assembled product" (Electrocoat Association 2007). The body parts are electrically charged, then immersed in a bath consisting of 80–90 percent oppositely charged deionized water and 10–20 percent resin and pigments. Plastic bumpers and other exterior body parts are coated with adhesion promoters, such as conductive resins and chlorinated polyolefin (CPO), to chemically bond the paint film to plastic parts in injection molding machines. The paint particles are attracted to the metal or plastic surface, neutralized, and baked into a film. The charged particles adhere to the electrically grounded surfaces until they are heated and fused into a smooth coating in a curing oven.

Use of powder coating is increasing in part because of environmental regulations (Powder Coating Institute 2007). Conventional paint solvents discharge into the air during the drying process, but powder coatings contain no solvents. Much of the half-billion-dollar cost of a paint shop goes into ensuring that the waste paint and fluids are disposed of safely (Miel 2002).

Leading Paint Suppliers

Two companies—DuPont and PPG—have been leading paint suppliers through the history of the U.S. motor vehicle industry. A predecessor of PPG was closely associated with Ford's early success, and DuPont was closely associated with GM's early success.

PPG

The source of Ford's black enamel paint was the early twentieth century's leading automotive paint supplier, a predecessor of PPG known as Ditzler Brothers. Peter Ditzler, who had been providing paint for carriages since 1880, joined with his brother Fred to open an automotive paint shop in 1902. Their first automotive customer was the newly formed Cadillac Auto Company in 1902, and Ford followed a year later.

The Ditzlers sold the business to T.W. Conner and Associates in 1913, just as the company was expanding production to meet Ford's increasing demand for black enamel. When Ford belatedly introduced colors for the Model T in 1926, Ditzler was the paint supplier. PPG purchased the Ditzler Color Company in 1928.

PPG transferred Ditzler's operations in 1964 from Detroit to the Forbes Varnish Co. facility in Cleveland. Forbes, founded in 1907, originally produced automotive varnishes, but it switched to industrial coatings during the 1920s. PPG acquired Forbes in 1947 and made the Cleveland facility its principal automotive coatings center.

DuPont

General Motors passed Ford as the leading car seller during the 1920s in part by offering brightly painted cars. General Motors Research Laboratories, under the leadership of Charles F. Kettering, established a Paint and Enamel committee in 1921 to develop colorful fast-drying paint. The committee collaborated with DuPont, which then held a controlling financial interest in GM.

DuPont had been founded as an explosives manufacturer in 1802 by Eleuthère Irénée du Pont (1771–1834), a French citizen and employee of France's central gunpowder agency, who immigrated to the United States in 1799 after being briefly imprisoned during the French Revolution. Black gunpowder was the only product produced by DuPont until 1880. Pierre S. du Pont (1870–1954), the fourth generation of the family to control the company, transformed it from an explosives specialist into a manufacturer of paints, plastics, synthetic fibers, and chemicals.

DuPont's link with GM began when Pierre du Pont bought GM stock in 1914 and was elected a GM director and chairman of the board a year later. When Billy Durant was forced to leave GM in 1920, Pierre du Pont became GM president and his brother Irénée succeeded him as president of DuPont Corporation. The DuPont Corporation, with ownership of one-third of GM stock, rescued the carmaker from near bankruptcy by imposing its then-innovative financial management. The close relationship between the two companies eventually attracted the attention of federal antitrust prosecutors, who filed suit in 1949. Eight years later the U.S. Supreme Court ruled against DuPont, and the company finalized the disposal of its GM shares in 1961.

DuPont developed colorful fast-drying paint during the early 1920s through application of nitrocellulose, which it had been using to make smokeless gunpowder. DuPont chemists, working with cellulose motion picture film in 1920, produced a thick lacquer that was durable and quick drying and could be colored. Trying to prevent film from blowing up or turning to goo, the chemists found that a batch of cellulose, accidentally left in a drum for three days, turned to light-brown syrup. This "syrup" became Viscolac and was sold beginning in 1921 as a fast-drying lacquer for toys and other small objects.

GM engineers found that Viscolac dried too fast for use on cars, but after two years of experiments in collaboration with DuPont, a suitable lacquer called Duco was produced. Duco reduced the amount of time needed for drying from several weeks to two hours. The first car painted with Duco was GM's 1924 Oakland, available in a light-blue color called True Blue.

Paint Colors: Changing Fashion

Color has no impact on a vehicle's performance, and consumers claim in surveys that color is not an important consideration in their purchase decisions. Yet the paint shop is the most expensive portion of an assembly plant—one-half billion dollars per assembly plant—and a color is the most commonly selected adjective when people are asked to describe their vehicles.

Early cars were painted bright primary colors using India enamel paint that lacked durability and faded when exposed to the sun. Henry Ford's black-only policy captured the public imagination as one of his many strategies to keep the price of the Model T low. So-called Japan black enamel (ground pigment in linseed oil) was the only type of paint that dried quickly enough to keep up with the moving assembly line that Ford installed in 1914. Black dried faster than other colors because of the chemical composition of the pigment and resins. To paint other colors on 1,000 cars a day, Ford would have had to set aside 20 acres of covered dust-free space to dry the bodies between coats (Yanik 1993). Lost in Model T mythology is the reality that all but a handful of luxury cars were also being painted black for the same reason.

Forecasting colors that will appeal to consumers is a high-stakes science, not an art. The Color Marketing Group is an organization of 1,100 color designers, and about 50 of them work in the auto industry. Members meet twice a year to forecast the colors that will be featured in manufacturing and services during the next few years.

The motor vehicle industry is often one fashion trend late, according to G. Clotaire Rapaille, founder of Archetype Discoveries Worldwide, a consumer research firm that advises carmakers on what colors to paint vehicles. In the clothing industry, colors are decided a few months in advance, but in the motor vehicle industry, with its relatively long lead time, colors must be decided several years in advance. Popular clothing colors often appear on motor vehicles several years later, by which time clothing designers have moved on to other colors. "Colors represent the mood of the time," according to Rapaille. But motor vehicle designers run the risk that colors may not match the national mood by the time they are introduced (Hakim 2004).

Drab colors of the economically austere 1930s and 1940s gave way to two-toned pastels of turquoise, aqua, pink, and coral during the 1950s. The social turbulence of the 1960s was accompanied by vehicles that were painted lively orange, lemon yellow, candy apple red, and yellow-green. Muted grey and black tones marked the calmer 1970s, and bright reds and blues accompanied the go-go 1980s. The prosperous 1990s brought elegant gold and copper, as well as environmentally aware dark greens (Hakim 2004; Krebs 1997; Sawyers 1993). The somber mood after the attacks on September 11, 2001, increased demand for black, white, gray, silver, and beige.

DuPont and PPG have long tracked color preferences. They agree that silver has been the most popular color in the United States during the first decade of the twenty-first century, having displaced green in 2000. Silver has also been the most popular color throughout the world during the period. The two paint suppliers also agree that white, black, red, and blue follow silver in popularity. However, they don't agree on the market share: silver had 24 percent market share in 2006 according to PPG and only 19 percent according to DuPont.

FROM BUMPERS TO FASCIA

The bumper arguably delivers the biggest bang for the buck of any component. A several-hundred-dollar component can save the motorist thousands of dollars in repair costs. The bumper also provides suppliers with one of the principal entries into the body sector of the industry. According to Harbour Consulting, the percentage of bumpers outsourced by the Detroit 3 increased from 27 percent in 2000 to 56 percent in 2007 (Wortham 2007a).

Today's bumper typically includes a reinforcement bar made of steel, aluminum, or fiberglass sheathed in a TPO (thermoplastic olefin elastomer) cover. Polypropylene foam or plastic "eggcrate" honeycomb is packed between the bar and cover to cushion the impact. Bumpers account for one-fourth to one-third of the motor vehicle industry's purchases of plastics.

During the 1920s thin metal bumper strips attached to the front and rear of the body became standard equipment on cars. As the name implied, the original purpose of the bumper was to reduce damage to the vehicle from inevitable encounters with parked cars, pedestrians, and other hazards on increasingly congested streets. After a bump, replacing a crumpled metal strip was easier and cheaper than repairing a dented body. Elaborately shaped three-dimensional chrome bumpers were added as decoration to complement the aggressive tail fins of the 1950s. Turn signals, parking lights, and back-up lights were sometimes placed inside bumpers that wrapped around headlamps and taillights in the designs from the 1960s.

An Important Safety Feature

The bumper evolved from decoration to a safety feature during the 1970s. The impetus was the correction of a fatal flaw in the Ford Pinto: at least 59 people died from explosions of Pinto fuel tanks crushed in accidents between the rear bumper and axle.

The 1972 Motor Vehicle Information and Cost Saving Act required the National Highway Traffic Safety Administration (NHTSA) to set bumper standards that yielded "the maximum feasible reduction of costs to the public, taking into account the cost and benefits of implementation, the standard's effect on insurance costs and legal fees, savings in consumer time and inconvenience, and health and safety considerations." Beginning in 1972, the NHTSA required bumpers to protect the fuel tank, headlamps, and other body and safety features during front-end impacts of 5 mph and rear-end impacts of 2.5 mph. The rear-end standard was raised to 5 mph in 1979. Bumper standards reached historically high levels between 1980 and 1982, when the bumpers themselves also had to withstand damage in 5 mph impacts.

Regulations have been less stringent since 1983. Bumpers must protect cars from front and rear impacts of 2.5 mph, but the bumpers themselves may now be damaged. The NHTSA defended the relaxation as consistent with the intent of the 1972 law. The new standard contributed to fuel economy because it allowed carmakers to reduce average bumper weight from 85 pounds in 1982 to 72 pounds in 1983. However, the Insurance Institute for Highway Safety, which tests damage to bumpers at 5 mph, claimed that the lower standard added $1,000 to the average vehicle repair cost.

As truck sales soared in the 1990s, the lack of compatibility between car and truck bumpers was heavily criticized by the insurance industry and consumer groups. The bumper on a truck is designed with high clearance—allegedly for off-road capability. It is higher off the ground than the bumper of a car. As a result, in a collision a truck bumper would override a lower car bumper, telescoping the front end of the car back into the passenger compartment. Voluntary standards adopted by nearly all motor vehicle producers, effective in 2009, reduced incompatibility in one of two ways: either by lowering the truck's bumpers and frame rails to the level of cars or by attaching a steel bar called a blocker beam to the truck frame at the same level as car bumpers.

The bumper is playing an increasingly important role in vehicle appearance. Carmakers are designing the front bumper to be integrated with the grille and headlamps into a front-end module and the rear bumper to be integrated with the trunk and taillights into a rear-end module. These integrated front and rear modules are sometimes called fascia in the United States, although the British use the term fascia to describe the interior cockpit combining the instrument panel and dashboard.

Volkswagen's turn-of-the-century New Beetle was regarded as a prototype—it had front- and rear-end modules integrating bumper, fascia, and lights supplied by Plastic Omnium. Bumpers may also integrate electronic systems that assist with parking and maintaining a safe distance in traffic. "'We feel very much that front-end modules are the future,' says Plastic Omnium President Marc Szulewicz. Although some carmakers will initially produce the modules in-house, 'long term they will certainly begin to outsource them'" (Chew 2003).

Carmakers have outsourced bumper production to a number of component-specific specialists who are not major players in provision of other components. The bumper accounts for a major expense, accounting for several billion dollars in annual OEM sales. Consequently, the market for bumpers is highly competitive. Three companies each had about $1 billion of the market.

Flex-N-Gate Corp.

Flex-N-Gate Corp. was founded in 1956 in Urbana, Illinois, to make racks for pickup trucks that featured a flexible roll-up rear gate, hence the company name. The product line was expanded in the 1960s to include truck bumpers. The company remained a small family-owned operation until it was sold in 1980 to Shahid Khan, a native of Pakistan, who started working there in 1970 as an engineering student at the University of Illinois. Khan left Flex-N-Gate in 1978 to start his own bumper company, but he returned two years later as CEO and sole owner. Under Khan, revenues increased from $17 million during the 1990s to $1 billion in 2006. Its 19 U.S. factories as of 2007 were heavily clustered in the Midwest, including six in Michigan, four in Illinois, and three in Indiana.

Meridian Automotive Systems

Meridian Automotive Systems originated as the American Bumper and Manufacturing Co. in Ionia, Michigan. Its largest bumper customer has been Ford trucks and sport utility vehicles. Meridian grew rapidly during the late 1990s through acquisitions, but it entered Chapter 11 in 2005, citing the high price of plastic resin. The company emerged from Chapter 11 a year later, with financial restructuring provided by a consortium of private equity firms. Like Flex-N-Gate, it had 19 U.S. manufacturing facilities in 2007, including seven in Michigan and six in Indiana.

Plastech Engineered Products

Plastech Engineered Products was one of the largest minority-owned Tier 1 suppliers and the second-largest minority-owned plastics firm in the United States, behind Sigma Plastics Group. The company was founded in 1988 when Julie N. Brown acquired a small plastic molding plant in Caro, Michigan. Like Meridian, Plastech grew rapidly during the 1990s through acquisitions, the largest of which was the United Screw and Bolt Co. in 1997. Although a major OEM bumper supplier, Plastech's most rapid expansion came as a Tier 2 supplier of interior trim to Johnson Controls (see Chapter 7). Its three dozen facilities in the United States were also heavily clustered in the Midwest, including 18 in Michigan and nine in Ohio.

In 2008, Plastech filed for Chapter 11 bankruptcy protection. "[L]ike virtually all parts suppliers in Detroit's automotive ecosystem, Plastech has been caught between rising production costs and falling demand for the products in which its parts are used" (McCracken 2008).

OUTSOURCING COMPLETE EXTERIOR MODULES

The pioneering effort to outsource integrated exterior modules was the Chrysler assembly plant in Toledo, Ohio. Chrysler opened the Toledo Supplier Park in 2006 to supply exterior modules, as well as chassis modules, ready for installation at the adjacent Jeep final assembly plant. The bodies moved by conveyors from the Supplier Park to the final assembly line minutes before they were needed, and "Chrysler will have inspectors in the suppliers' plants and has the right to reject assemblies that don't meet quality standards" (Jewett 2004).

Hyundai Mobis subsidiary Ohio Module Manufacturing Co. was given responsibility for assembling "rolling" chassis. The term rolling refers to the fact that the chassis, which includes wheels, axles, and powertrain, could literally be rolled on tires from the supplier shop to where it was needed on the final assembly line.

South Korea's largest supplier, Mobis, was already delivering rolling chassis to Kia's plant in Hwasung, Korea. Mobis was part of the Hyundai chaebol through interlocking ownership. Hyundai owned 60 percent of Kia, which in turn owned 16.2 percent of Mobis, which in turn owned 13.2 percent of Hyundai. Mobis had no North American manufacturing operations when it won the Jeep contract. But Mobis expected to rank among the world's top 10 suppliers by 2010 as an ultra-low-cost supplier.

In awarding the contract to Mobis, DCX passed over Toledo's hometown supplier of rolling chassis, Dana. In the throes of Chapter 11 proceedings, Dana was caught asleep at the switch in its own backyard (see Chapter 11 in this volume; Chang and Chappell 2004).

German-based Kuka Roboter GmbH was given responsibility for welding bodies in a 250,000-square-foot body shop, with an annual capacity of 150,000. Europe's leading manufacturer of industrial robots, Kuka had no experience as an auto parts manufacturer. Its previous auto industry work was building equipment for body shops and assembly lines and helping Chrysler design minivan seats that folded into the floor.

Outsourcing Toledo's paint shop proved more difficult for Chrysler. The contract was first awarded to Durr Industries, which, like Kuka, was a German company with experience in providing equipment rather than parts. Durr planned and built paint shops, as well as cleaning and filtration systems. After two months, Chrysler dropped Durr as paint supplier, citing an unspecified contract impasse (Connelly 2004).

Haden International was next to be given responsibility for the Toledo paint shop. Haden, too, had no experience as a parts supplier. It had developed air pollution abatement and wastewater removal programs for GM's Arlington and Spring Hill assembly plants and water recycling programs at Toyota's Georgetown and Chrysler's Detroit assembly plants. The British-based company was founded in 1816 by brothers George and James Haden. It was best known in the United States for acquiring Carrier (the air conditioning firm) in 1970. Palladium Equity Partners LLC gained controlling interest in Haden in 2001.

Four months before production began, in 2006, Haden "vanished," and its managers "disappeared" from the site. Haden also walked away from contracts to remove paint sludge at Toyota's plant in George-town and Ford's plant in Wayne; to complete a renovation of the New United Motors Manufacturing Inc., California, paint shop; and to treat wastewater at Georgetown. Financial problems were blamed (Chappell 2006a,b; Nussel 2006).

Chrysler assumed responsibility for liens against Haden held by subcontractors at Toledo and placed its own employees in the paint shop. Former Haden employees at Toledo formed a new company to continue to do business with Chrysler.

Replacing Haden as paint shop manager in 2006 was Magna Steyr, a subsidiary of Magna International. Despite Chrysler's original inten-tions, Magna Steyr does not have an equity interest in the Toledo Sup-plier Park.

OUTLOOK AND UNCERTAINTIES

Most exterior suppliers appear likely to remain in the Midwest. As was the case with powertrain, the exterior sector of the parts industry has been heavily clustered in the Midwest because of a similar combi-nation of proximity to inputs and to customers.

Even more so than the powertrain, the exterior is difficult to ship long distance. Body panels and fascia are bulky and fragile and, com-pared to the powertrain, are lower in value. Furthermore, carmakers have retained much of the body stamping work as a core competency. At the same time, some exterior production will drift out of the Mid-west, again for the same reason as powertrain, namely for proximity to foreign-owned assembly plants further south within Auto Alley.

The supplier that may make a particularly strong contribution to the future geography of exterior parts production is Magna International's Magna Steyr division. Magna Steyr did not even have a U.S. production facility until 2005, when it opened a paint shop adjacent to Chrysler's Toledo assembly plant. Magna Steyr at the time was a major supplier in Europe and was set to become one in the United States as well.

Magna International acquired Magna Steyr, then known as Steyr-Daimler-Puch, in 1998. Steyr-Daimler-Puch was created in 1934 through the merger of Steyr-Werke AG and Austro Daimler Puchwerke

AG. Steyr Werke's predecessor was established in 1864 near Steyr, Austria, to make armaments. Puchwerke's predecessor was established in 1899 near Vienna to make bicycles and merged in 1928 with a Daimler body supplier.

From its core competency of making bodies, Magna Steyr expanded into so-called contract assembly, that is, producing entire vehicles for carmakers such as Chrysler and Daimler. Magna Steyr assembled niche vehicles that were sold in volumes too low to be economic for carmakers to assemble themselves, such as convertibles or an American-style Chrysler minivan for the European market. Magna Steyr was also contracted to assemble vehicles whose sales exceeded capacity of the carmakers' own assembly plants. In 2007, Magna Steyr assembled a quarter of a million vehicles at its Austrian plant, including 10 different models for four carmakers.

Magna Steyr made no secret that it wanted to build a similar plant in the United States. "Do we see potential for a North American assembly plant for (subsidiary) Magna Steyr? Absolutely," stated Magna president Mark Hogan (Sherefkin 2007b). "Steyr came within a hair of using that design for such a plant in the U.S.," said [Manufacturing Vice President Wolf-Dietrich] Shulz. He said that "earthmoving equipment was on the ground" at a site somewhere in the South, ready to break ground for a U.S. vehicle project. The project was canceled at the last minute (Chappell 2006c).

When Chrysler was sold to Cerberus in 2007, one of the unsuccessful suitors was Magna. Magna Steyr's experience with assembling entire vehicles and producing modules in Toledo, as well as its position as Chrysler's leading supplier, made it a credible candidate, but analysts have been skeptical of Magna Steyr's ability to bring the European model to the United States. "Magna Steyr has hit a wall . . . [It] has concluded that it has a problem: To grow, big changes are necessary" (Sherefkin 2007b). The first challenge was efficiency: to build 10 different models for four carmakers, Magna Steyr had to provide five assembly lines, six body shops, and two paint shops.

The second challenge was excess capacity in carmakers' own assembly plants. "European contract manufacturing is under pressure. That's because excess capacity at many automakers is making them take back production previously outsourced" (Meiners 2007). Finally, according to Harbour and Associates President Ron Harbour, as carmakers have become more efficient, they "don't have to outsource those low-volume cars anymore" (Sherefkin 2007b).

Notes

1. The City of Detroit purchased the closed stamping plant in 1982 but had to undertake an expensive hazardous materials clean-up operation at the site during the 1990s. Chrysler used the site to construct a new engine plant, which opened in 1998 to supply engines for the Jeep Grand Cherokee, assembled one-half mile south at the company's new Jefferson Avenue assembly plant.
2. Walter Nelson, manager of Ford's Iron Mountain, Michigan, lumber operations, quoted in Sorensen (2003).

5
Supplying the Suppliers

They were a very minor supplier to us, so we don't have an issue. We have replaced them.[1]

The supply base of today's carmakers is structured like a pyramid. On top of the pyramid is the carmaker. Below the carmakers are a small number of Tier 1 suppliers that sell parts directly to carmakers. Tier 1 suppliers in turn purchase materials from Tier 2 suppliers, who purchase from Tier 3 suppliers, and so on down the supply chain.

Tier 1 suppliers and carmakers have different perspectives on the motor vehicle industry than do lower-tier suppliers. For example, is a motor vehicle essentially an aggregation of several thousand parts, or is the whole greater than the sum of the parts? Carmakers favor the holistic view. A motor vehicle is greater than the sum of the individual parts because it is ultimately defined and distinguished primarily through such features as performance, handling, and styling. Large Tier 1 suppliers, responsible for integrating modules and systems, reinforce this holistic perspective.

The perspective of lower-tier suppliers is fundamentally opposite. They are in the business of building a motor vehicle one part at a time. A smoothly performing engine depends on tight-fitting pistons and valves and on well-built brackets and hinges. An attractively styled interior depends on tight-fitting doors and mirrors and on well-built latches and knobs.

Enthusiast magazines such as *Car & Driver* and *Motor Trend* reinforce holistic perspectives in their reviews and commentaries. The quality of an engine is characterized by overall performance in speed and acceleration, and the quality of the interior is characterized by harmonious integration of materials and controls. On the other hand, consumer surveys such as those by J.D. Power and Associates and Consumers Union reinforce a particularistic perspective. Quality is measured by aggregating the frequency with which dozens of specific items cause trouble in particular vehicles.

Ultimately, of course, a motor vehicle is both an aggregation of thousands of individual parts and something greater than the sum. The fundamental challenge—and opportunity—for lower-tier suppliers derives from differences with carmakers and Tier 1 suppliers concerning the relative importance of the two perspectives.

TYPICAL LOWER-TIER SUPPLIERS

Getting a handle on lower-tier suppliers is difficult for the following reasons:

- Lower-tier suppliers are much more numerous than Tier 1 suppliers; major Tier 1 suppliers number in the dozens, whereas lower-tier suppliers number in the thousands.

- Leading databases do not distinguish between Tier 1 and lower-tier suppliers.

- Lower-tier suppliers may make objects with multiple uses, not just for use in motor vehicles.

- Some lower-tier suppliers provide commodities and raw materials from which other suppliers actually fashion the parts.

- Suppliers rarely fall 100 percent into only one tier, so classification is a case-by-case determination based on the tier occupied by most of a supplier's customers. It is even possible for a supplier to operate some of its plants as Tier 1 plants and others as lower-tier plants.

Leading data sources do not permit straightforward identification of a supplier's tier. In the case of a publicly traded company, the annual report and Form 10-K may name the major customers and share of business if it is more than 10 percent. But most lower-tier suppliers are privately owned and therefore do not reveal this information.

The U.S. Census of Manufactures classifies about one-sixth of all suppliers as "other" or "NEC" (not elsewhere classified). Similarly, the database developed for this book, derived from ELM International, classifies one-sixth of all suppliers as providing so-called generic parts, such as brackets, clamps, and fasteners. Another one-sixth of all suppliers are allocated to "miscellaneous" categories within particular systems, such as "miscellaneous engine components." Based on all available information about individual plants, it is likely that most of the companies making "generic" parts are lower-tier suppliers, but this is not a certainty.

Characteristics of Lower-Tier Suppliers

A walk through a typical lower-tier supplier plant reveals little that looks like a contribution to putting together a motor vehicle. Oddly shaped parts are cut or pressed and perhaps several of the pieces are screwed or welded together to form another unfamiliar shape.

The motor vehicle industry includes several thousand lower-tier suppliers, most of which are unfamiliar even to carmakers, let alone to the wider public. Given this arithmetic, summarizing the characteristics of the many thousands of lower-tier suppliers is a formidable challenge. Nevertheless, this chapter attempts to do so. We find that a typical lower-tier supplier is:

- owned by a single individual or family, rather than by a publicly traded corporation. The current owner is often not the first generation of the family involved in the business. Like other small businesses, a lower-tier supplier reflects the values and priorities of the owner.

- a small business, with an average workforce of less than 200 housed in a single facility. In comparison, the 150 largest suppliers in 2007 averaged 11 U.S. plants with 300 employees per plant. Annual sales for lower-tier suppliers are likely to be in the millions of dollars, whereas they are in the billions of dollars for the larger Tier 1 suppliers.

- a specialist in a small number of manufacturing processes, such as stamping or cutting. Compared with large Tier 1 suppliers and carmakers, these firms possess a limited number of capital-intensive presses of a particular size or dies of a particular shape. The distinctive features, assets, and quirks of these specific pieces of equipment, though, are understood in detail. Equipment constrains the variety of products.

- too small to have a professional sales force. Instead, it hires sales representatives, or the owner may do the job.

- sited in a specific community because "the founder lived here." Other communities might now prove more profitable, but even leaving aside the high capital cost of relocation, lower-tier suppliers are rarely footloose firms chasing tax breaks. Instead, it is more likely to be rooted in the owner's hometown through sports, religion, and other community programs.

- feeling pressure from its Tier 1 customers to invest in Mexico, China, and other low-wage countries. Despite strong community roots, lower-tier suppliers are being urged to produce overseas in order to help Tier 1 firms reduce costs. Some lower-tier suppliers have gone along, but most have preferred to stay put.

- located in the Midwest (Figure 5.1). More than three-fourths of plants making brackets, clamps, hinges, fasteners, screws, nuts, bolts, and washers were in the Midwest (Table 5.1). Bearings, seals, and gaskets were less likely to be made there. Overall, more than two-thirds of plants classified as "generic" in our database were in the Midwest.

Although it is difficult to say that any single lower-tier supplier can be considered typical of the thousands, we can offer some good examples of lower-tier suppliers.

Table 5.1 Plants Producing Generic Parts in the Midwest

Generic parts	Number of plants	% in Midwest
Fasteners	118	81.4
Screws, nuts, bolts, and washers	124	79.8
Brackets, clamps, and hinges	186	78.0
Bushings, gears, housing, plugs, and springs	258	65.5
Seals and gaskets	204	52.9
Bearings	60	36.7
Other generic parts	394	64.5
Total generic	1,344	66.4

SOURCE: Adapted by the authors from the ELM International database and other sources.

Figure 5.1 Location of Plants That Supply Generic Parts

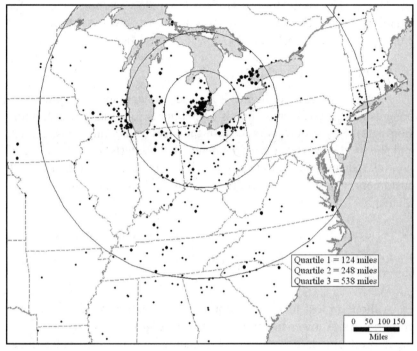

Quartile 1 = 124 miles
Quartile 2 = 248 miles
Quartile 3 = 538 miles

0   50 100 150
Miles

SOURCE: Adapted by the authors from the ELM International database and other sources.

Oakwood Group

The Oakwood Group produces metal speaker grilles and plastic impact absorbers for vehicle interiors. Large Tier 1 interior suppliers such as Johnson Controls and Lear were its major customers. Francois Audi founded the company in 1945, and his son succeeded him as president. The company employed 221 at manufacturing facilities in Taylor, Michigan.

Mid-American Inc.

Mid-American supplies molded thermoplastic parts used in the engine, chassis, and body. Other products include valve shafts, valve lift guides and assemblies, chain tensioners and guides, air shock and fitting assemblies, structural braces, compression caps, and coolant fittings. Major Tier 1 customers for these products have included JCI and Bosch. The company has also made window latch assemblies for Guardian Industries. Mid-American is a minority-owned firm with 180 employees and established in 1972 in Jackson, Michigan.

Shane Steel Processing Inc.

Shane prepares steel before it is used to manufacture engine components (e.g., valves) and chassis components (e.g., stabilizer and torsion bars). Shane detects defects in the steel, and straightens, grinds, and shears steel bars to standards demanded by parts makers. Founded in 1949, Shane employs 80 at its facility in Fraser, Michigan. Tier 1 customers have included Collins & Aikman, Dana, Delphi, Lear, and Siemens.

LARGE LOWER-TIER SUPPLIERS

Although most lower-tier suppliers are small, a handful are large corporations. A lower-tier supplier may have grown large by specializing in producing large volumes of standardized parts, such as bearings, brackets, and latches. Other large lower-tier firms are suppliers of commodities and materials, such as steel and plastic. The distinctive skill demonstrated by these large suppliers is the ability to be the low-cost manufacturer of particular "generic" parts.

Some of the large "generic" parts suppliers were Tier 1 suppliers until "demoted" to lower-tier status by carmakers focusing on module and systems integrators. Others dropped to Tier 2 when Delphi and Visteon were separated from GM and Ford, respectively, in the late 1990s. Finally, from a business strategy perspective, it might be desirable for a company to move to a lower tier. Some large suppliers have deliberately positioned themselves at a lower tier, thereby escaping the not-always-desirable spotlight focused by carmakers on their Tier 1 suppliers.

Large Bearings Suppliers

Bearings are "the invisible heroes inside many mechanical devices" (Nice 2007). Bearings reduce the friction that would otherwise result when one surface slides against another surface. In motor vehicles, bearings play an especially important role in the transmission and wheels.

Ball bearings, the most common and oldest type of bearing, consist of metal balls sandwiched between two ring-shaped liners called races. The smooth steel balls, loosely restrained and separated in a cage, are able to roll with minimal friction in a tight space carved out of the smooth metal surfaces of the two races. Ball bearings were found to be of limited use in motor vehicles, however, because they could not support a heavy load.

Carmakers turned instead to roller bearings, in which cylinders rather than balls are sandwiched between two races. A cylinder can withstand a heavier load than a ball because weight is spread out over a line rather than a single point. Transmissions most commonly have a variation of a roller bearing that is called a roller thrust bearing and is placed between the gears and the rotating shafts. Wheels most commonly have another variation, the tapered roller bearing, which is conically rather than cylindrically shaped.

Timken Co.

Four of the 75 largest suppliers in the United States in 2007 specialized in bearings. The leading U.S. supplier of roller bearings through the century-plus history of motor vehicle production has been Timken Co. Henry Timken, a St. Louis carriage builder, patented the tapered roller bearing in 1898 and one year later, at the age of 68, founded Timken Roller Bearing Axle Co. to make axles equipped with tapered roller bearings. Timken moved the company from St. Louis to Canton, Ohio, in 1901, to be near both its primary customers (the rapidly growing motor vehicle industry) and its principal input (steel).

Axle and bearings businesses were separated in 1909, with Timken Roller Bearing Co. remaining in Canton and Timken-Detroit Axle Co. relocating to Detroit. To control the supply and quality of steel for the bearings, Timken added a steel production facility to its Canton complex in 1916.

Timken has long been the largest employer in Canton, where it is universally known as "Timken's," reflecting the close association of the company with five generations of the Timken family, much as the Ford Motor Co. is often called "Ford's" in Detroit. At its peak in the 1920s, Timken supplied 80 percent of the roller bearings in the U.S. motor vehicle industry. Timken remains the largest bearing supplier in the United States, with one-sixth of the market, but it has fallen to sixth place in worldwide sales. The company's Web site claims that its market share has declined because carmakers, especially Ford, have insisted on having multiple sources of bearings.

Other bearings suppliers

Swedish-based SKF has become the world's largest bearings supplier, and the German-based FAG Group has been the second-largest Europe-based bearing supplier. These two firms have held small shares of the U.S. market. Timken's three chief bearings competitors in the U.S. market are Japanese-based.

NSK. Short for Nippon Seiko Kabushiki Kaisha, NSK is credited with producing the first ball bearings in Japan in 1916. NSK became a major bearings supplier in the United States when it acquired Hoover Ball and Bearing in 1975. The breakup of Hoover also gave Johnson Controls its start in the seat business during the 1980s (see Chapter 7).

NTN Bearings. NTN Bearings, according the company's Web site, entered the bearings business through happenstance: "In 1922 a Swedish vessel carrying a cargo of bearings sank in Kobe harbor. The bearings were auctioned off by the insurance company and the successful bidder was Mr. [Noboru] Niwa. This turned out to be a bonanza, and with the profits Mr. Niwa purchased three foreign-made grinding machines. He installed them in the Nishizono Ironworks, asking Mr. [Jiro] Nishizono, a wizard at technology, to study bearing manufacturing technology" (NTN Bearing Corporation 2007).

Niwa and Nishizono accounted for the two "N's" in the NTN acronym. The "T" came from Niwa's trading company, Tomoe Trading Co., which sold the Swedish cargo, presumably originally produced by NSK. NTN acquired Federal-Mogul's ball bearing division in 1996.

Koyo Corp. Koyo Corp. was founded in Osaka to make bearings in 1921. The company began producing bearings in the United States in South Carolina in 1973. The company, one-fourth owned by Toyota, was merged with Toyoda Machine Works in 2005.

Large Metal-Forming Suppliers

Large Tier 2 suppliers of metal parts, such as brackets and shafts, remain heavily clustered in the Midwest. Proximity to iron and steel inputs as well as carmakers and Tier 1 powertrain suppliers makes a Midwest location important for these suppliers. Two leading examples are Illinois Tool Works and Metaldyne.

Illinois Tool Works

Founded in 1912 by Chicago financier Byron L. Smith to manufacture gears and metal-cutting tools, Illinois Tool Works (ITW) became a manufacturer of thousands of different types of fasteners, latches, and other generic automotive parts. A few of the company's products, such as door handles and seat latch releases, may be recognizable parts of motor vehicles, but the overwhelming majority of its nuts, screws, and clips are not.

ITW has gained a reputation on Wall Street for its unconventional corporate structure: it is decentralized into several hundred highly autonomous operating units, including a couple of dozen that focus on motor vehicle parts. Conventional Wall Street wisdom is that extreme decentralization increases overall corporate overhead because each unit replicates some of the same functions. In rebuttal, ITW claims that high profit margins have been generated by its distinctive "80/20" management system.

ITW operating units are required to rank products, customers, and suppliers from largest to smallest. Invariably, 80 percent of revenues are generated by 20 percent of customers and 20 percent of products, and 80 percent of materials are obtained from 20 percent of suppliers. Unit managers are told to pay attention primarily to the top 20 percent of customers, products, and suppliers, and minimize reliance on or discard altogether the remaining 80 percent. An operating unit may not increase gross revenues and profits until it has increased the rate of return at current level of sales through "80/20."

The Detroit 3 have encouraged ITW to step up as a larger, more prominent Tier 1 supplier, but ITW has declined. Tier 1 suppliers are under a great deal of pressure (e.g., letting in unions) that lower-tier suppliers can escape. By adding engineered parts that require skilled labor, a lower-tier supplier can have more leverage up the supply chain.

As the company name implies, ITW has most of its automotive plants in Illinois, especially in Chicago's outer suburbs. Most of the remainder are in Wisconsin.

Metaldyne

Metaldyne is a leading supplier of sintered powder metal components for powertrains and chassis, including wheel spindles, steering knuckles, hub assemblies, engine dampers and covers, and differential and transfer cases. In 2006 the company merged with Japanese competitor Asahi Tec.

Metaldyne illustrates the blurred distinction between Tier 1 and Tier 2 suppliers. The company sold 38 percent of its output to Tier 1 suppliers, such as Dana, Delphi, International, Magna, TRW, and Visteon. As a Tier 3 supplier, Metaldyne has sold wheel hubs to Tier 2 supplier Timken, which has incorporated them with bearing units before sending them to a Tier 1 supplier.

Carmakers accounted for 62 percent of Metaldyne sales in 2006, and the company expected to gain more Tier 1 business as carmakers outsourced the manufacture of more powertrain parts. In 2003, for example, Metaldyne acquired a metal forging facility in New Castle, Indiana, from its largest customer, Chrysler. Metaldyne's annual report (2006, p. 6) stated, "Currently, OEMs satisfy a significant portion of their metal forming and assembly requirements with in-house production and assembly of purchased components. We [at Metaldyne] believe that, as OEMs seek to outsource the design and manufacture of parts, they will choose suppliers with expertise in multiple metal processing technologies and the ability to design, engineer and assemble components rather than supply independent parts."

Metaldyne has maintained most of its facilities in the Midwest, notably "saving" the former Chrysler New Castle plant from closure by acquiring it and negotiating a more competitive contract with the union. At the same time, Metaldyne has been especially proactive at initiating production activities in China.

Other metal-forming suppliers

Other large metal-forming suppliers produce a wide variety of generic parts that are sold primarily to Tier 1 customers.

Gecom. Gecom is the acronym for Greensburg Equipment and Components Manufacturing, which was opened in 1987 in Greensburg, Indiana, by the Japan-based Mitsui Kinzoku Company. Gecom specializes in closure components such as latches, brackets, and other metal hardware. Gecom has been the principal supplier of closure components to Japanese-owned assembly plants in the United States. A major boon to the company's fortunes came when Honda selected the same community for a new assembly plant in 2007.

Gecom's growth has illustrated a challenge for some suppliers of "generic" parts. For Gecom, the lowly latch has become an electronic component. Embedded in latches are electronics that automatically lock and unlock doors, open gates remotely, protect the vehicle from theft, and warn that doors are ajar.

Grede Foundries, Inc. Grede Foundries, Inc. was founded in 1920 when William J. Grede purchased Liberty Foundry in Wauwatosa, Wisconsin. Grede's grandson was running the company in the twenty-first century. The company produced parts such as cases and hubs from ductile iron castings and bearing caps and pump bodies from gray iron castings. All of the facilities were heavily clustered in the Midwest.

Intermet. Founded in the nineteenth century to produce ductile iron castings, Intermet supplies arms, brackets, covers, cases, housings, and shafts for steering, suspension, and powertrain. Its largest Tier 1 and Tier 2 customers have included Delphi, Metaldyne, Siemens, TRW, and Visteon. The company's dozen plants were generally outside the Midwest, including five in the South and three in Missouri. Intermet filed for Chapter 11 protection in 2004, blaming the rising cost of scrap steel, and it emerged two years later as a private company.

Large Nonmetal Suppliers

Large lower-tier suppliers that make parts from materials other than metal are much less likely to be located in the Midwest. Three examples are ABC Group, Foamex International Inc., and Tomkins.

ABC Group

ABC Group has been the third-largest Canadian-owned parts maker behind Magna and Linamar. ABC, founded in 1974, has claimed to be the number one plastic blow molder. Principal products have included interior parts for instrument panels, seats, and trim, as well as exterior parts for bumpers, running boards, spoilers, and trim. The company supplied the North American market primarily from plants in Canada.

Foamex International Inc.

The leading supplier of polyurethane foam for cushions, headliners, backrests, armrests, and headrests, Foamex was established in 1983 through the acquisition of Scott Paper's foam division. It became a major Tier 1 supplier in 1986 by acquiring Firestone Tire & Rubber's foam division, which had been using the Foamex name. With the emergence of interior integrators, JCI became Foamex's largest customer, accounting for one-half of automotive sales and one-sixth of total corporate sales. Most of Foamex's remaining automotive sales were to Collins & Aikman, Faurecia, Lear, and Magna.

Tomkins

The third-largest British-owned supplier in North America, Tomkins specialized in rubber and polyurethane belts for powertrains. It was the largest supplier of transmission belts. Started in 1925 as a buckle and fastener manufacturer, Tomkins became a major U.S. parts supplier and the leading rubber parts supplier when it acquired U.S.-based Gates Rubber Co. in 1996. Gates traced its origins to 1911 when Charles Gates acquired Colorado Tire and Leather Co., which made steel-studded leather bands that were fastened to car tires to extend their mileage. Gates became a specialist in synchronous timing belts and V-belts.

LEADING SUPPLIERS OF COMMODITIES

Iron and steel are the most important commodities used in motor vehicles, accounting for nearly two-thirds of a car's weight in the early twenty-first century.[2] Plastics and aluminum are a distant second and third, respectively, in materials used by carmakers and suppliers (less than 10 percent each), but both are gaining on steel in terms of overall motor vehicle content.

Iron and Steel

The motor vehicle industry buys much more iron and steel than any other material and is the largest customer of the iron and steel industry. "[B]y far the most influential material during the auto industry's first 100 years was steel" (Winter 1996). Approximately 24 percent of steel produced in the United States was destined for motor vehicles in 2005 (Schnatterly n.d.).

Iron was used to make early engines, but steel was not used in large quantities until the 1920s, when open wooden carriages were replaced with enclosed bodies. Iron and steel content per vehicle rose from 1,500 pounds in 1918 to 3,500 pounds during the 1950s. The weight dropped to 2,600 pounds in the early twenty-first century (Sherefkin 2006a).

Steel is rolled into a thin product through either hot rolling or cold rolling. Motor vehicle producers rely primarily on hot rolled steel for chassis components, such as brake drums, wheels, and suspensions; body components, such as cross and side members, roof frames, pillars, and doors; and drivetrain components, such as transmissions, differentials, gearboxes, and clutches. Because of its appealing surface finish, cold rolled steel is commonly used to stamp the hood, roof, fender, and door panels.

Although the motor vehicle and steel industries have been closely associated for a century, the relationship between them has often been uneasy. Carmakers have reduced steel content in favor of substitute materials, notably plastic and aluminum. For their part, the steel industry, unlike other suppliers, has been independent and powerful enough to stand up to carmakers.

The fundamental divergence of interests between the two industries has been the price of steel. Essentially, low steel prices are good for carmakers and parts suppliers and bad for steelmakers, whereas high steel prices have the reverse effect. Policies such as tariffs and quotas on foreign imports designed to protect U.S.-based steel producers may limit the supply of steel and drive up prices, thereby harming U.S.-based carmakers and parts suppliers. Conversely, open market policies may lower the cost of steel for the U.S. motor vehicle industry, but they expose the U.S. steel industry to foreign competition.

Of the world's six largest steel companies, only Arcelor Mittal owned mills in the United States in the twenty-first century. The other five—Nippon, Posco, JFE, Tata, and Shanghai Baosteel—were all based in Asia and have concentrated on the rapidly growing markets in China, India, and other Asian countries.

In the early twenty-first century, four steelmakers accounted for one-half of sales to the U.S. motor vehicle industry: Arcelor Mittal, AK Steel, U.S. Steel, and Severstal. One-fourth was supplied through smaller steelmakers and minimills. The remaining one-fourth was imported.

Arcelor Mittal

The world's leading producer by a wide margin, Arcelor Mittal was probably the most compelling story in the steel industry in the late twentieth and early twenty-first centuries. Mittal was the brainchild of one man, and it remained a family-run business while becoming the world's largest steelmaker. In 2006 Mittal consolidated its number one position by acquiring Luxembourg-based Arcelor, Europe's leading steelmaker and the second-leading steelmaker worldwide.

Founder, first CEO, and first chairman of the board, Lakshmi N. Mittal was a native of India and son of the owner of a small steel mill in Calcutta. Mittal's wife ran an Indonesian subsidiary, his son was on the board of directors, and other family members held leadership positions.

Mittal Steel and its predecessor LNM Group, founded in 1976, specialized in turning around steel mills viewed as underperforming under previous management. Government privatization programs were the source of several mills.

Mittal entered the U.S. market when its subsidiary Ispat International acquired Inland Steel Company in 1998. Inland, founded in 1893, became a major supplier of automotive steel from its Indiana Harbor Works integrated steel mill located in East Chicago, Indiana. The Indiana Harbor plant supplied about 10 percent of the steel used in motor vehicle production and 5 percent of the total U.S. steel market.

Mittal became the leading steel supplier to the U.S. motor vehicle industry when it acquired International Steel Group (ISG) in 2004. ISG had been formed only two years earlier and had grown rapidly by rescuing several prominent U.S. steel companies from bankruptcy. The financial backing came from the equity investment firm W.L. Ross & Co., and leadership from president and CEO Rodney Mott, previously vice president and general manager of Nucor Steel, one of the most successful minimills.

ISG started in 2002 by acquiring LTV Steel, which had declared bankruptcy two years earlier. LTV began as an electrical construction and engineering firm, Ling Electric Company, in Dallas in 1947. Following several mergers during the 1950s, the company was renamed Ling-Temco-Vought in 1961, which was shortened to LTV during the 1970s. LTV Steel was the country's second-largest steelmaker after a 1984 merger with venerable Cleveland-based firms Jones & Laughlin Steel Corp. (J&L) and Republic Steel Corp.

J&L was established by Benjamin Franklin Jones and James Laughlin in 1853 in Pittsburgh to produce iron. J&L secured a prominent presence along the banks of the Cuyahoga River in 1942 by acquiring Otis Steel Co., which was founded by Charles A. Otis in 1852, also originally an iron forger and the first U.S. firm to make steel in an open-hearth furnace in 1873. Republic Steel, founded in 1899 in Youngstown, expanded rapidly during the 1920s and 1930s to become the third-leading steelmaker in the United States. In 2003, ISG took over Bethlehem Steel Co., which was the nation's second-leading steelmaker behind U.S. Steel when it declared bankruptcy in 2001. Bethlehem, founded in 1857 as Saucona Iron Works in South Bethlehem, Pennsylvania, had the newest large-scale integrated steel mill in the United States, built at Burns Harbor, Indiana, during the 1960s. Acquisition of Acme Steel in Riverdale, Illinois (2002), Weirton Steel in Weirton, West Virginia (2004), and Georgetown Steel in Georgetown, South Carolina (2004), gave ISG three more integrated mills.

AK Steel

AK was smaller than its competitors in overall production, but it held a leading position in supplying the motor vehicle industry. The company sold a higher percentage of its output to carmakers than have the other major steelmakers, although the percentage was declining rapidly in the early twenty-first century.

AK was established in 1989 as a joint venture between U.S. steelmaker Armco Steel (the "A" in the company name) and Japanese steelmaker Kawasaki Steel Corp. (the "K"). Armco began as the American Rolling Mill Co. in Middletown, Ohio, in 1899. Kawasaki, Japan's third-largest steelmaker and world's tenth-largest, was incorporated as a company independent of Kawasaki Heavy Industries, Ltd. in 1950. Kawasaki Heavy Industries began in 1878 as a shipyard company and expanded during the twentieth century to encompass other transportation equipment and machinery as well as steel. AK acquired its one-time parent Armco in 1999.

AK's largest customers were GM and Ford, but its principal competitive advantage was with Japanese-owned carmakers. Toyota bought nearly all of its steel from AK, and other Japanese carmakers were comfortable dealing with another Japanese-managed company in the United States. AK's largest integrated mill, Armco's former home base in Middletown, Ohio, was located further south and closer to Japanese-owned assembly plants than competitors' mills. AK's other integrated mill at Ashland, Ohio, was near Honda's central Ohio complex.

U.S. Steel

U.S. Steel was created in 1901 when the nation's second-largest steel producer, J.P. Morgan's Federal Steel Co., acquired the largest steel producer, Andrew Carnegie's Carnegie Steel Co. Faced with fierce competition from Morgan and a desire to devote full attention to philanthropy, Carnegie agreed to sell his steel company for $480 million, the largest transaction in American industrial history at the time. U.S. Steel immediately became the dominant U.S. steel producer, accounting for two-thirds of production in 1900.

U.S. Steel's principal operations have been in Gary, Indiana, a city built by the steel company to accommodate workers and named for the company's first president, Elbert Gary. Its other integrated steel mills are located in Braddock, Pennsylvania; Fairfield, Alabama; Gary; Detroit; and Granite City, Illinois. The latter two plants were taken over in the Republic acquisition.

Although no longer the monopoly of a century ago, U.S. Steel has remained the largest steelmaker in the United States. The company has been less heavily invested than competitors in the automotive industry, which accounted for only about 14 percent of its sales.

Severstal

Russia's largest steelmaker, Severstal, has not been widely recognized as a major producer of steel in the United States. With $1.8 billion in sales in 2006, Severstal was the fourth-largest supplier of steel to the U.S. auto industry, holding 8 percent of the market (Severstal 2006, p. 45). The company was incorporated in 1993 through the restructuring of Cherepovets Steel Mill, which had been created by the Soviet Union in 1940.

Severstal's U.S. facility was probably the motor vehicle industry's best-known integrated steel mill—the one originally built by Henry Ford as part of the River Rouge complex in Dearborn. In 2004, Severstal acquired the bankrupt Rouge Industries Inc., which Ford had set up as an independent company in 1989.

Other sources of steel

More than one-fourth (28 percent) of steel used by U.S. carmakers in 2006 was imported (AK Steel 2006). Carmakers and other large purchasers of steel typically have not negotiated direct purchases from overseas. The principal channel by which foreign steel enters the United States is through service centers. Service centers purchase bulk quantities of steel from both domestic and foreign sources and perform finishing operations, such as cutting, shearing, and grinding, that otherwise would have to be done by the parts makers. The construction, electronics, shipbuilding, and aerospace industries have also been major customers of steel service centers.

Some automotive steel comes from intermediate processors, such as Shiloh Industries. Founded as a tool and die company in 1950, Shiloh sold $600 million worth of steel products to the auto industry in 2005. Shiloh manufactured blanks, which are two-dimensional shapes cut from flat-rolled steel. Shiloh cleaned, coated, trimmed, and cut steel into shapes that carmakers could stamp into body panels, such as doors and fenders. Blanks were also sent to suppliers to stamp seat frames, bumpers, frames, rails, and other interior, exterior, and chassis components.

Minimills have captured one-fourth of the overall U.S. steel market. Less expensive than integrated mills to build and operate, minimills can locate near their markets where their main input—scrap metal—is widely available. Because the motor vehicle industry utilizes primarily flat steel products, it is not a major direct purchaser of steel from minimills, although some steel produced at minimills is purchased indirectly through service centers. The largest minimill company, Nucor, has not made steel for motor vehicles and asserts that it cannot be done by a minimill. The primary use of minimill steel in the auto industry has been for wiring.

ThyssenKrupp, Germany's leading steel producer, entered the U.S. market by constructing a mill in Mobile, Alabama, scheduled to open in 2010. "Proximity to automakers and their suppliers was a key factor in ThyssenKrupp's decision to build in the South" (Wortham 2007b).

Despite these alternatives, the number of sources of steel in the United States has become too small for carmakers' comfort. "GM once negotiated with nine steel makers. Now just four major integrated steel mills are at the table today" (Sherefkin 2006a). Carmakers have traditionally negotiated simultaneously with three steel producers during the engineering phase before awarding contracts for actual manufacturing. A savvy steelmaker would submit designs that, if adopted, placed it in a strategic advantage when manufacturing contracts were issued. However, as the number of steelmakers willing to play the game declined, carmakers could no longer count on getting three independent designs and bids.

Plastics

The average plastic content per passenger vehicle increased from 150 pounds (6 percent of total vehicle weight) in 1988 to 250 pounds (9 percent) in 1997 and to 300 pounds (11 percent) in 2007. Plastic components accounted for $11 billion, or 5 percent of the overall supplier industry, in 2000 (Flanagan 2001; Miller 2005).

Leading suppliers of plastic products to carmakers and suppliers have been BASF Corp. and Dow Automotive, each with about $600 million in annual North American motor vehicle sales in 2005. The motor vehicle industry has accounted for only about 10 percent of overall sales at both companies. BASF has been the world's largest supplier of plastics to the motor vehicle industry and Dow the largest in North America.

BASF

BASF has supplied the motor vehicle industry primarily with styrenes and polyurethanes used for molding plastic parts. Because of its ability to withstand high thermal and mechanical stresses, BASF plastic has been used in the engine, including camshaft timing gears, engine covers, air intake modules, oil filter housings, and cylinder head covers. Several fuel line components have been molded from plastic, and electrical components have also been encased in plastic. In other systems, BASF plastic has been used to make gearshifts for the drivetrain, steering columns for the chassis, and headlamp reflectors for the body. BASF has also supplied chemicals to the motor vehicle industry, including antifreezes, brake fluids, and coatings.

Badische Anilin- & Soda-Fabrik AG (BASF) was founded by Friedrich Engelhorn in 1865 to produce dyes from coal tar. The company became heavily involved in developing fuels, synthetic rubber, and coatings for motor vehicles during the 1920s. BASF merged with Hoechst, Bayer, and others into I.G. Farbenindustrie AG in 1925, but the companies were separated again in 1952. The company had about 40 plants in the United States, specializing in particular segments, such as coatings, polyurethanes, styrenes, or chemicals, but none was exclusively devoted to motor vehicle production.

Dow

Dow Automotive has been a small piece of Dow Corporation. It employed only 1,500 of the company's 46,000 employees. Dow Automotive has supplied plastics, plastic parts, adhesives, and sealants to carmakers and suppliers. Products have included polypropylene, nylon, ABS, polycarbonate, SAN, crystalline polymers, thermoplastic urethanes, adhesive films, engineering plastic blends (like PC/ABS), polyurethane, and vinyl ester resins.

Dow Chemical Co. was incorporated in 1897 by Herbert H. Dow to manufacture bleach. Dow Automotive was formed in 1988 as a business group and became a separate industry-focused business unit in 1999. As with BASF, Dow has been organized into several operating segments, such as chemicals, hydrocarbons and energy (called oil & gas at BASF), agriculture, plastics, and so-called performance plastics (which includes motor vehicle parts).

Compared with BASF, Dow has focused more on interior trim, such as instrument panels, knee bolsters, glove boxes, and airbag covers. It has also supplied body trim, panels, and lighting surrounds, as well as electrical, cooling, and fuel systems for the engine.

Only two Dow plants have been devoted primarily to automotive parts, and both are located in the Midwest—in Hillsdale, Michigan, and Kankakee, Illinois. Dow Chemical has maintained 34 other manufacturing facilities in North America.

Aluminum

Aluminum was the third most used material in vehicles in 2000, and its use was growing the fastest. The amount of aluminum in an average car increased from 90 pounds in 1977 to 236 pounds in 2005 and to an anticipated 345 pounds in 2009 (American Iron and Steel Institute 2005).

Aluminum has been relatively expensive to cast, about $2.50 per pound compared with 40.5¢ per pound for iron in the early twenty-first century. Nonetheless, aluminum was being used more because it has been the most effective way to cut vehicle weight and therefore improve fuel economy. Fascia, fenders, hoods, doors, and trunks of higher priced vehicles have been molded from aluminum rather than plastic.[3]

The major supplier of primary aluminum and fabricated aluminum products to carmakers and suppliers has been Alcoa Inc. Alcoa's predecessor, Pittsburgh Reduction Co., was established in 1888 to produce pure aluminum. The company's name was changed to Aluminum Company of America in 1907.

Alcoa has several dozen business segments, including four that have supplied the motor vehicle industry. Alcoa-Fujikura Ltd. Automotive, a joint venture with Japanese wire- and cable-maker Fujikura, made copper and fiber optic wiring harnesses. The Alcoa Automotive Castings segment made chassis components, such as subframes, cradles, knuckles, brackets, control arms, and other suspension parts. The Alcoa Cast Auto Wheels segment, as the name implies, was a major supplier of aluminum wheels. The Alcoa Automotive segment supplied aluminum bodies for niche vehicles, as well as body parts such as hoods, tailgates, van doors, radiator enclosures, and engine cradles.

REDUCING PRICE WHILE RAISING VALUE

Tier 1 suppliers, who are the principal focus of this book, have regarded lower-tier suppliers as necessary, but very junior, partners in the motor vehicle production process. Carmakers have viewed lower-tier suppliers as even more marginal to their core operations. Lower-tier suppliers, providers of generic bin parts, manufactured to specifications, have been seen as answerable only to price. Low price has not been merely the most important consideration in negotiations with lower-tier suppliers—it has usually been the only consideration.

Lower-tier suppliers have few direct contacts with carmakers because they work primarily with Tier 1 suppliers. The exception is companies that are both Tier 1 and Tier 2 suppliers. By necessity, they work both directly with carmakers as Tier 1 suppliers and indirectly with carmakers through their Tier 1 customers. Despite—or perhaps because of—their relatively limited direct contact with carmakers, lower-tier suppliers hold especially outspoken opinions on the behavior of the Detroit 3. Systematic differences are seen between doing business with the Detroit 3 and with international carmakers. In short, the Detroit 3 are characterized as specifications oriented, whereas international carmakers are results oriented.

By specifications oriented, lower-tier suppliers are referring to two particular characteristics of Detroit 3 purchasing. First, the perception is widespread among lower-tier suppliers that the Detroit 3 care only about price. Before lower-tier suppliers are called, a Tier 1 supplier has already made a pricing commitment to a carmaker. A lower-tier supplier must provide a price quotation quickly to the Tier 1 supplier, then engineer and produce the part within the set price.

Lower-tier suppliers are being asked to participate more in the design and engineering of integrated modules and systems. But because they are manufacturing only a small piece of the system or module, they feel that they are the last in the industry to know about new product development—barely in advance of the general public. As a result, they claim to receive information too late in the process to be able to identify cost savings before a design is frozen.

For their part, carmakers and Tier 1 suppliers feel they need to intrude into the performance of lower-tier suppliers because of quality control issues. Lower-tier suppliers are held accountable for quality through "traceability." Every part is bar-coded at each stage in the production process. A steel part, for example, can be traced back to the heat treatment at the steel mill.

Lower-tier suppliers see themselves as performing a very different role in the production process. They believe that carmakers and Tier 1 suppliers have become primarily assemblers and marketers, while shedding engineering capabilities they once possessed. Carmakers and Tier 1 suppliers once had more knowledge of mechanical engineering than lower-tier suppliers, but they now allegedly have less.

Lower-tier suppliers believe that they are being asked to design and engineer individual parts that carmakers and Tier 1 suppliers no longer actually know how to make. This loss of knowledge, lower-tier suppliers allege, stems from decisions by carmakers and suppliers to employ fewer mechanical engineers than in the past while outsourcing more responsibilities to lower-tiers.

For example, when GM made most of its own parts, it also did most of its own stampings. Even when still part of GM during the 1980s, Delphi started outsourcing stamping. Stamping equipment was moved out of Delphi facilities into Tier 2 suppliers. As an independent company, Delphi owned the stamping dies, but the dies were actually made and used by Tier 2 suppliers. Theoretically, Delphi could pull the dies from the suppliers, although it never did.

Delphi no longer has the knowledge to use the dies because it no longer employs knowledgeable mechanical engineers. Lower-tier suppliers view Delphi's gap in knowledge of dies as a money-making opportunity—the longer a die lasts and the fewer times it must be refurbished, the more profitable it is.

OUTLOOK AND UNCERTAINTIES

Lower-tier suppliers believe that they are now the guardians of two critical types of knowledge about manufacturing. Lower-tier suppliers assert that they are being asked to make the parts that are too complex for carmakers and Tier 1 suppliers given their diminished engineering expertise. Lower-tier suppliers claim that they know how to design indi-

vidual parts to perform assigned duties. They understand how parts behave in real-world conditions, depending on choice of material, shape,
and size. The hard-to-make parts are allegedly being passed down the
supply chain: the lower the tier, the harder the part is to make.

Second, lower-tier suppliers believe that only they understand the
manufacturability of an individual part, in other words the relationship
between the process and the product. Because a particular product is
made on a particular machine, sensitive product design is based on
understanding the mechanics and tolerance of the machine on which
the product will be made. Lower-tier suppliers claim that, because of
their knowledge of manufacturability, they are called in—belatedly—
to solve costly production problems that are too detailed for carmakers and Tier 1 suppliers to address. For example, Tier 1 suppliers may
not be considering how new stronger lightweight metals behave when
pressed into shapes, or how dies and presses operate when lubricated
with different liquids.

Lower-tier suppliers report that they are often brought into the production process to solve a problem caused by an inferior part that another company supplied at a lower price. The challenge for lower-tier
suppliers is to convince carmakers and Tier 1 suppliers that their manufacturing expertise can add value in the production process and that
they should not be regarded merely as sources of generic parts.

Notes

1. Bo Andersson, GM worldwide purchasing chief, referring to the plant closure of
   Tier 3 supplier Chatham-Borgstena Automotive Textiles in Sherefkin (2005).
2. The average vehicle weighed 3,927 pounds and contained 2,419 pounds of steel,
   or 61.6 percent, in 2005 (American Iron and Steel Institute 2007) .
3. Aluminum's penetration has increased from 39 kg (3 percent) in 1976 to about
   89 kg (7 percent) in the mid 1990s (Becker 1999 cited in Kelkar, Roth, and Clark
   2001).

Part 2

Carmaker–Supplier Networks: How Close Is Close Enough?

Parts plants are like planets revolving around a star, the final assembly plant. Some parts plants are arrayed in very tight orbits within a few miles of an assembly plant, whereas others are in wide orbits thousands of miles away; most lie between these two extremes. This section of the book explores three key elements of the auto industry's producer–supplier networks: the tightness of the collection of orbits around the various assembly plants, the distinctive character of suppliers orbiting most closely around assembly plants, and the physical ties facilitating movement of parts within networks.

Parts production and final assembly operations are among the most co-located industry pairs in the United States (Ellison and Glaeser 1997). Colocation has long been of interest to both economists and geographers. Alfred Marshall argued in 1920 that businesses localize in response to a number of factors, including capturing technological spillovers, achieving a greater variety and lower costs of intermediate inputs, and pooling labor markets to promote a larger and deeper supply of workers.

Colocation is a distinctive feature of many "bulk-gaining" products. A bulk-gaining product weighs more or takes up a greater volume than its inputs, whereas a bulk-reducing product weighs less or takes up less volume than its inputs. Bulk-gaining products are more likely to be made near their customers because shipping costs tend to be less for the relatively compact inbound parts than for the relatively bulky outbound finished goods. Conversely, bulk-reducing products are more sensitive to the location of inputs.

Motor vehicle assembly is a classic example of a bulk-gaining industry because finished vehicles are much bulkier than the sum of their parts. Consequently, final assembly plants are located primarily to minimize transportation costs to customers. Parts that are bulky, awkward, and fragile, and therefore more expensive to ship (e.g., seats and bumpers), are more likely to be made near the customer (the final assembly plant) to minimize shipping costs.

Some carmakers have constructed relatively tight networks of suppliers around their assembly plants, with a high percentage of parts plants less than a one-day drive away, whereas others have preferred looser networks. Underlying the development of closely linked networks of suppliers and carmakers has been the widespread adoption of just-in-time (JIT) delivery in the auto industry. Carmakers now require that parts arrive at their final assembly plant shortly before needed rather than far in advance.

As a result, suppliers have been forced to locate facilities in places where JIT delivery to a final assembly plant is feasible. However, JIT delivery does not mean that suppliers must be immediately next door to final assembly plants. The distance from parts plants to the assembly plant "node" actually can be divided into three groups: those within a one-hour driving radius, those within a one-day radius, and those further than one day away.

The tightness of the network of suppliers around an assembly plant determines its regional economic footprint. That is important because states and localities often provide large sums to attract final assembly plants. These subsidies have been justified because they are said to attract not only a final assembly plant but a large number of parts plants as well. Some of these forecasts may have been overstated because they got the geography wrong.

6
The Closely Linked Supply Chain

Kia has told Georgia officials that it envisions only five or six new supplier plants being necessary to support the Georgia auto plant.(Chappell 2006d)

U.S. assembly plants together receive 2 billion pounds worth of parts per day in 20,000 shipments, some from nearby and some from the other side of the planet (Cottrill 2000; Penske Logistics 2007). In an industry characterized by colocation, physical proximity is mutually reinforcing. Assemblers prefer to have multiple suppliers located nearby to ensure reliable delivery of parts. Suppliers in turn prefer to have several assembly plants within a day's drive of their operations.

Lean production has sought to root out and eliminate waste wherever it exists in the production process. One of the most striking examples of a wasteful practice in mass production has been the stockpiling of parts in the final assembly plants. Parts would be piled high and crammed into every corner of the shop floor.

The parts that piled up in the final assembly plants may not have been needed in actual production for some time—if at all. At the end of the model year, leftover parts would be thrown away. Ford's Chester, Pennsylvania, assembly plant was said by David Halberstam (1986) to have "dumped thousands and thousands of useless parts into the nearby Delaware River . . . The people in Chester joked that you didn't have to swim the Delaware, you could walk across on the rusted parts of 1950 and 1951 Fords."

Lean production has changed these wasteful practices. Not every carmaker may have absorbed all the lessons of Japanese-inspired lean production, but they have all recognized the economic benefits of eliminating inventory. The diffusion of JIT has caused a significant decline in inventory of parts and finished goods at assembly plants as it is now standard practice for most parts to arrive at final assembly plants only shortly before they are needed on the assembly line. The burden of making JIT work has fallen primarily on the suppliers. Helper and Sako

(1995) found that the practice of making more frequent deliveries of smaller batches has resulted in some increase in stockpiling at supplier companies.

Does the application of JIT influence where supplier plants locate relative to their assembly plant customers? One would expect tighter operational linkages with suppliers to lead to tighter physical linkages between assembly and supplier plants. Yet only some parts must be produced within an hour of the final assembly plant to meet JIT delivery requirements. Suppliers of such parts needed to relocate their production facilities. Chapter 7 highlights the seat, the most prominent example of a part that is invariably produced within an hour of a final assembly plant. JIT production, however, does not require all parts makers to locate that close to a final assembly plant. For most parts, being within one day's driving distance from an assembly plant is sufficient. Other parts can be made even further away and still reach the assembly plant when needed because the availability of a well-developed transportation infrastructure in combination with state-of-the-art logistics services allows production facilities to be closely linked operationally even though physically they can be quite far apart from one another.

JUST-IN-TIME PRODUCTION

The production of seats illustrates how tight today's linkages between assembly and supplier plants can be. At the seat-making plant, action is triggered when the final assembly plant sends a fax or e-mail outlining the schedule of seats needed for the next 10 days. A second communication pinpointing the precise moment when each seat is needed arrives only eight hours in advance of actual delivery.

The detailed communication from the final assembly plant documents not merely the specific vehicles that will be assembled during the day but, even more importantly, the order in which they will be built. The seat plant subsequently has to put together various styles of seats from leather, foam, frame, and wiring in accordance with the assembler's specific needs. After a hundred or so seats have been produced—sufficient to keep the final assembly line rolling for a couple of hours—they are loaded onto a truck in "backward" order; that is, the first one needed at the final assembly plant is the last one loaded onto the truck.

Elements of JIT

The concept of JIT, which was pioneered in postwar Japan as a survival strategy, has been one of the foundations of lean production (Womack, Jones, and Roos 1990). "Supply chain managers have two primary goals: reduce inventory and avoid delays. For years, just-in-time delivery has been the preferred method for meeting those goals" (Haight 2004). "[A] 1991 survey conducted by Advanced Manufacturing resulted in a PriceWaterhouseCoopers white paper that found that 92 percent of manufacturers believe that just-in-time delivery by key suppliers is now a critical success factor" (Pescon [2001] cited in Polito and Watson [2006]).

Under lean production, parts do not arrive where needed along the final assembly line until shortly before installation in the vehicle. Related to the implementation of JIT has been a considerable change in the relationship between assemblers and suppliers. In the past carmakers relied on hierarchical coordination of information and control over technology within their own company to solve the complex task of manufacturing cars. Now, in order to allow for JIT to achieve its full potential, tight organizational and informational linkages are extended outside a plant's boundaries to include its suppliers and their operations, and possibly their suppliers in turn (Klier 1995).

Aided by widespread use of information technology to track parts and orders, JIT has become the standard for carmakers, as well as for other manufacturers and retailers. According to this approach, the various operations within the assembly plant are linked with one another so as to expedite the process of filling orders. The underlying principle of JIT production is to reduce the time from when an order for a product is placed until the finished product is shipped to the customer. Such linkages now extend to an assembly plant's supply base, ideally connecting the entire supply chain.

For parts makers, JIT starts with an order from a carmaker. Instead of producing according to a preset schedule, suppliers operate according to a so-called pull system, in which the flow of materials through the various stages of production is triggered by what is needed in the next stage, and ultimately by the customer. For carmakers, maintaining a continuous and tightly controlled flow of parts allows for flexible modification of production changes in the demand for the final product.[1]

To capture the financial advantages of JIT, suppliers have developed production techniques that reduce inventory. As a result of lower inventory inside a plant, problems affecting production quality such as a faulty machine tool will become apparent more quickly. In addition, the production process itself can be continuously improved. Implementing JIT therefore can improve a plant's production quality.

Prior to JIT, the traditional supply chain of the Detroit 3 automakers was characterized by the carmaker procuring most parts and components from their own parts divisions. For parts sourced from outside companies, the Detroit 3 typically dealt directly with several thousand independent supplier companies. Contracts with suppliers were bid on spec and typically ran no longer than a year. After one year they were put up for bid again and typically awarded to the lowest bidder for the next year.

Under JIT, contracts between assemblers and Tier 1 suppliers tend to be longer term, covering the life of a particular model. Carmakers directly interact only with a handful of Tier 1 suppliers responsible for entire subsystems or modules, who in turn procure parts and services from their own suppliers to deliver a highly integrated part to the assembly line. Many of these suppliers have also taken on research and development functions. A number of carmakers have set up so-called supplier support organizations to help improve the efficiency of operations at their suppliers.

To help their suppliers master the challenges of JIT, Japanese carmakers have created a disciplined system of delivery time periods. They also deliberately smooth their production schedules to avoid big spikes in demand. Suppliers in turn are encouraged to ship only what is needed at the time.

Challenges in JIT Delivery

JIT has proven an effective tool for improving a manufacturer's bottom line, but it is not without its challenges. Pescon ([2001] cited in Polito and Watson [2006]) identified five major constraints in JIT: 1) customer-driven and economic conditions, such as raw material price fluctuations; 2) logistics and interruption in the supply chain as a result of, for example, labor disputes and natural disasters; 3) organizational culture conflicts with JIT, such as piecework rather than hourly wages; 4) intractable accounting and finance practices; and 5) slow adoption of JIT because of resource constraints on small suppliers.

In the auto industry, the second constraint has been especially important. Chapter 8 specifically addresses the logistics aspect of the supply chain. Even the most carefully made plans are subject to myriad uncontrollable factors—labor issues, equipment failure, political unrest, and severe weather (Haight 2004).

A tightly linked supply chain has proven vulnerable to labor disputes. In 1998, for example, the UAW struck GM parts plants in Michigan that were the sole suppliers of such parts as spark plugs, filters, fuel pumps, and instrument clusters. Loss of output quickly fed through the company's entire supply chain and essentially shut down the vast majority of its North American production facilities in less than two weeks. Absent JIT, larger buffer stocks of these parts would have been able to better insure against the strike-related loss of output.

The most significant political factor constraining logistics has been the need to move parts across international borders. Large amounts of material and components are crossing into the United States from Canada and Mexico (for a detailed discussion, see Chapter 13). If trucks experience delays crossing the Canadian and Mexican borders, it can be difficult to meet JIT requirements.

Canada's Ontario auto-producing center is within one day's driving distance of most U.S. assembly plants, and parts plants in Windsor are within one hour of Detroit assembly plants. Conversely, Ontario assembly plants are within one day's drive of most U.S. parts plants. After the September 11, 2001, attacks, the issue of the security of the Canada–U.S. border became suddenly much more visible. Commerce between Michigan and Canada halted when the United States closed all of its borders for five days.

Under normal conditions, assembly plants in Detroit set the same delivery schedules for suppliers regardless of whether they are located in Michigan or Ontario, essentially treating the border as invisible. Though traffic delays at the two Detroit River border crossings are common occurrences, the complete shutdown of trade after 9/11 was unprecedented. Thousands of parts shipments required at U.S. assembly plants were then stuck at the border. Assembly plants on the Detroit side of the border scrambled to maintain production without parts that routinely arrived from the supplier base in southwestern Ontario. To maintain deliveries from Canadian suppliers after the border was closed, U.S. companies ferried Canadian-built components on barges across the Detroit River, with the tacit approval of immigration officials.

Beyond the immediate impact of 9/11, the border has remained a serious logistics issue for Canadian suppliers. "Some Canadian companies have responded by lengthening delivery schedules or setting up warehouses across the border to stockpile parts" (*The Economist* 2008, p. 40).

Particularly acute has been congestion on the Ambassador Bridge from Windsor into Detroit. Goods carried on the Ambassador Bridge—primarily auto parts—account for one-fourth of the value of all trade entering the United States from Canada. The only other border crossing in the Detroit area, the Detroit–Windsor Tunnel, is too narrow to accommodate large trucks. Otherwise, the nearest border crossing is the Blue Water Bridge between Sarnia, Ontario, and Port Huron, Michigan, about 60 miles north of Detroit.

Two engineering problems have hampered traffic entering the United States on the Ambassador Bridge. First, the Canadian side of the bridge has not been directly linked to the country's high-speed road network. Route 401, the principal expressway through Ontario's automotive production corridor, terminates 5 miles from the bridge. During peak delivery times, trucks face considerable delays in stop-and-go traffic through the streets of Windsor.

Second, once on the Ambassador Bridge, truckers often face further delay because of backups at the U.S. customs and immigration station on the Detroit side. Large corporations making frequent deliveries have expedited clearance through special bays, but the bridge itself has only one lane entering the United States, so during peak periods, trucks designated for expedited clearance may be caught in a backup on the bridge itself, intermingled with vehicles subject to more intense scrutiny and therefore unable to maneuver to their special clearance lane on the U.S. side.

Compounding the challenge of adding capacity from Canada to Michigan is the fact that the Ambassador Bridge is privately owned by Manuel J. (Marty) Moroun, through the U.S.-based Detroit International Bridge Company and its Canadian subsidiary Canadian Transit Co. Both the State of Michigan and Moroun have proposed building a new bridge across the Detroit River (Davey 2007).

Similarly, on the border between the United States and Mexico, material moves more easily out of the United States than into it. Movement of material south from the United States to Mexico has been relatively straightforward.

Northbound has been another matter. "Notwithstanding the freedoms of NAFTA, Mexican law requires that all domestic over-the-road shipments be handled by Mexican carriers" (Bowman 2000). The northbound Laredo crossing has proved especially notorious. "Veterans of U.S.–Mexico trade have long complained of the punishing delays that trucks experience in crossing the border, especially at Laredo. Competing with armies of passenger cars, and depending on the attitude of customs officials toward a particular shipment, they may take hours or even several days to reach the broker on the other side. A busy day finds trucks backed up for several miles" (Bowman 2000).

NETWORKS OF SUPPLIERS AND ASSEMBLERS

Data for each of the 4,268 supplier plants in the United States, Canada, and Mexico identified in this study included the names of the carmakers that served as customers for the products. Some suppliers shipped exclusively to one carmaker, but most had multiple customers per plant. Networks of suppliers could be constructed around the final assembly plants of each of the carmakers. These networks can be depicted through maps of suppliers surrounding the assembly plants of individual carmakers.

Distances between suppliers and assembly plants were calculated as straight-line distances between the respective coordinates of the plants' Zip codes. Due to the presence of an excellent road network, straight-line distances rather accurately approximate travel times (Klier 1995, 2000). The principal limitation in constructing the networks is that the database shows customers by name of the carmaker rather than address of the assembly plant. For example, a parts maker located in Ypsilanti, Michigan, might report its customers as Ford and Mitsubishi. If the customer operates only one assembly plant in the United States (like Mitsubishi), then the address of the parts plant's customer is identifiable and the distance between the parts plant and the assembly plant can be computed. When this database was constructed, five companies were assembling vehicles at only one plant: 1) AutoAlliance in Flat Rock, Michigan; 2) BMW in Greer, South Carolina; 3) Mercedes-Benz in Vance, Alabama; 4) Mitsubishi in Normal, Illinois; and 5) Subaru in Lafayette, Indiana.

The three largest Japanese-owned carmakers—Honda, Nissan, and Toyota—all had more than one U.S. assembly plant at the time this database was created. Nonetheless, networks of suppliers around their assembly plants could be constructed in all three cases.

Honda started operating its Marysville, Ohio, assembly plant in 1982 and built a second one in 1989 three miles away in East Liberty; because the two were so close to each other, it did not matter for this analysis which one was the customer for a particular supplier. Honda's assembly plants in Lincoln, Alabama, which opened in 2003, and in Greensburg, Indiana, which opened in 2008, were too new to affect the database.

Nissan built its first U.S. assembly plant in Smyrna, Tennessee, in 1983 and added a second assembly plant in 2001 in Canton, Mississippi, which was also too new to affect this study. Similarly, at the time of this study, Toyota had one assembly complex, with two lines, in Georgetown, Kentucky. Toyota added plants in Princeton, Indiana (2001); San Antonio, Texas (2006); and Tupelo, Mississippi (2008). Again, however, these were too new for the database. Toyota's joint venture assembly plant with GM in Fremont, California, was identified separately in the database as NUMMI (New United Motors Manufacturing Inc.). Honda and Toyota also built assembly plants in Ontario during the 1980s, Honda in Alliston and Toyota in Cambridge. Toyota added another Ontario plant in Woodstock in 2008.

The Detroit 3 together operated about 30 U.S. assembly plants at the time of this study, so the data did not permit construction of individual supplier networks for each of the assembly plants. The exception was GM's Saturn division, which was identified by parts makers as a customer distinct from the rest of GM, and at the time of this study, the vast majority of Saturns were produced at the assembly plant in Spring Hill, Tennessee.

The Key Networks

Each of the network maps presented in this section of the book has included three concentric circles drawn around an assembly plant. These circles represented quartiles of the distance from the suppliers to the assembly plant. The closest one-fourth of all suppliers to that carmaker were located within the inner circle, the next closest fourth were between the inner and middle circle, the third closest quartile were between the middle and the outer circle, and the final quartile were beyond the outer circle. In other words, one-half of suppliers were within the middle circle and three-fourths within the outer circle. Thus, the radius of the middle circle represents the median distance for shipment of parts to the particular assembly plant.

Mitsubishi, for example, had one-fourth of its parts suppliers located within 245 miles of its assembly plant in Normal, Illinois. Most of these suppliers were in Illinois, Indiana, western Michigan, and western Ohio. Another one-fourth of the suppliers were between 245 and 337 miles from Normal, primarily in southeastern Michigan, central Ohio, and Kentucky. Three-fourths of suppliers were within 557 miles of Normal, with the additional suppliers coming primarily from eastern Ohio and Ontario (Figure 6.1). The median distance from the Mitsubishi plant for all suppliers was thus 337 miles.

For carmakers with more than one assembly plant in the United States, decisions had to be made concerning the location of the centroid of the concentric circles. For Honda and Toyota, the selected centroid for the circles was their first and still largest assembly operation at Marysville and Georgetown, respectively. The Big 3 centroids were all placed in southeastern Michigan because the area was home to about one half of their U.S. assembly plants in 2007.

Honda's supplier network

Honda, the first Japanese carmaker to assemble vehicles in the United States, put together a supplier base clustered tightly in western Ohio, near its Marysville and East Liberty assembly plants, which were constructed 3 miles from each other on opposite sides of a disused test vehicle track acquired from the State of Ohio. Most of the engines destined for Marysville and East Liberty were made in Anna, Ohio, 35 miles west of the assembly complex. Transmissions came from a plant

Figure 6.1 Location of Mitsubishi's Suppliers Relative to Its Final Assembly Plant in Normal, Illinois·

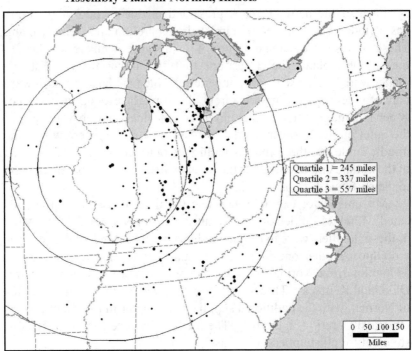

SOURCE: Adapted by the authors from ELM International database and other sources.

in Russells Point, Ohio, 25 miles west. Seats were made 30 miles east of the complex by Honda affiliate TS Tech in Reynoldsburg, Ohio.

In 2006 the company announced the construction of an engine plant near its Alliston, Ontario, assembly facility. That move made available much needed production capacity at its Anna, Ohio, engine plant, supporting the construction of a new assembly plant in eastern Indiana to open in 2008.

One-fourth of Honda's North American suppliers were within 149 miles, one-half within 288 miles, and three-fourths within 449 miles (Figure 6.2). Thus, around three-fourths of Honda suppliers were within one day's drive of Marysville and East Liberty. "[A]s trucking costs rise, the idea of moving some suppliers closer to Honda's property 'is beginning to make more financial sense.'"[2] Yet, even though Honda had one of the tightest supplier networks, only 2 percent of its inde-

pendently owned suppliers were located within 60 miles of the western
Ohio assembly plant complex. JIT has not meant "right next door" for
Honda.

Two decades after arriving in Ohio, Honda decided to build its third
U.S. assembly plant in Lincoln, Alabama, 40 miles east of Birmingham.
The Ohio supplier plants lay 700 miles to the north, well beyond the
one-day delivery range. Consequently, Honda constructed a second set
of facilities in the Deep South. An engine plant was placed in the same
Lincoln campus with the assembly plant. Transmissions came from Tallapoosa, Georgia, 60 miles to the east, just across the Alabama state
line. TS provided seats from Boaz, Alabama, 50 miles to the north.

Honda's Deep South facilities were not expected to induce a large
number of suppliers to locate new facilities in their immediate vicinity.

**Figure 6.2 Location of Honda's Suppliers Relative to Its Final Assembly
Plants in Marysville and East Liberty, Ohio**

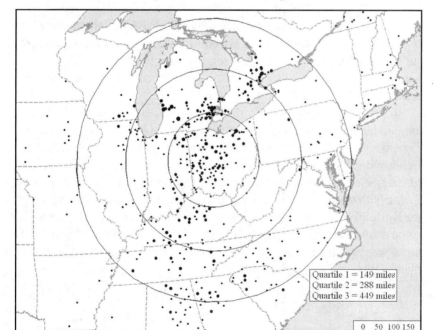

SOURCE: Adapted by the authors from ELM International database and other sources.

"Most of Honda's suppliers operate factories nearer to Honda's older assembly plants in central Ohio and Ontario. Although Honda used 620 North American Tier 1 suppliers, only about 20 operated near its Alabama plant" (Chappell 2004c).

Honda's limited commitment to the Deep South was revealed in a response to a reporter's question, "Will we see another wave of [Honda] supplier plants coming into Georgia?" Honda's answer was, "No, not really. We will continue to make transmissions in Ohio. Transmission manufacturing is such a capital-intensive operation that it probably wouldn't make sense for our suppliers to invest in two locations to support us."[3]

Toyota's supplier network

Toyota's network of suppliers was not as spatially clustered as Honda's. The heart of Toyota's U.S. network was tied to a 300-mile east–west stretch of I-64 between its assembly plant in Princeton, Indiana, and its powertrain plant in Buffalo, West Virginia. A second 300-mile north–south corridor extended south from I-64 to an engine plant in Huntsville, Alabama, and an assembly plant in Tupelo, Mississippi (to open in 2009). Near the intersection of the two corridors, in central Kentucky, was positioned Toyota's largest North American manufacturing complex, at Georgetown (Figure 6.3).

Toyota had seven final North American assembly plants opened or announced as of 2007. They were located in Georgetown; Princeton; Tupelo; San Antonio, Texas; and Cambridge and Woodstock, Ontario. In addition, there was the NUMMI joint venture in Fremont, California. Adjacent to the Georgetown and Cambridge assembly plants were facilities that supplied most of their engines. Gaps were filled in part by the Buffalo, West Virginia, engine plant. The Buffalo plant also supplied some of the engines installed at Fremont. The Princeton and San Antonio assembly plants received some of their engines from the Huntsville plant. Thus, in 2007 approximately

- 40 percent of Toyota's engines were made adjacent to final assembly plants;
- 15 percent were shipped about 300 miles north (from Alabama to Indiana);

Figure 6.3 Location of Toyota's Suppliers Relative to Its Final Assembly Complex in Georgetown, Kentucky

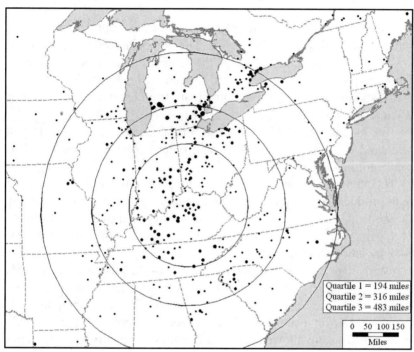

Quartile 1 = 194 miles
Quartile 2 = 316 miles
Quartile 3 = 483 miles

0 50 100 150
Miles

SOURCE: Adapted by the authors from ELM International database and other sources.

- 15 percent were shipped about 300 miles north (from West Virginia to Ontario);
- 15 percent were shipped west about 2,500 miles (from West Virginia to California); and
- 15 percent were shipped across the Pacific from Toyota facilities in Japan.

In other words, Toyota eschewed Honda's strong preference for close spatial linkage between assembly and powertrain sources. Whereas nearly all of Honda's powertrain needs were produced within an hour or so of final assembly operations, Toyota triaged its captive powertrain supply base into roughly equal portions by distance. A bit more than one-third of Toyota engines were delivered to final assembly plants within one hour, one-third within one day, and one-third in more than one day.

Like Honda, Toyota had only 2 percent of its suppliers positioned within one hour of assembly plants. The notable exception, as always, was the seat assembler. Most of the seats were shipped to Toyota's Georgetown assembly plant from Nicholasville, Kentucky, 25 miles away, and to the Princeton assembly plant from Lawrenceville, Illinois, 35 miles away.

By assembling vehicles in California, Texas, and Baja, Toyota stretched its supply chain wider than other carmakers. The NUMMI joint venture in California, opened in the early 1980s, could be regarded as Toyota's preliminary investigation for testing the ability to conduct lean production in North American factories. Separated by the Pacific Ocean from Japanese suppliers and by several thousand miles from the U.S. parts production center, NUMMI has depended on especially complex logistics arrangements.

With 80 percent of its parts sourced east of the Mississippi, NUMMI relied on a number of parts consolidation centers. Parts suppliers shipped their output to one of these centers, located in El Paso, Memphis, Chicago, and Detroit. From there the parts were transported to the assembly plant. This system allowed the assembly plant inventory to be no larger than four hours (*Ward's Automotive Reports* 1997). The Baja plant did not add much additional weight to the Southwest in Toyota's footprint because it produced only a small number of pickup trucks from little more than knocked-down kits.

The decision to build an assembly plant in Texas, though, could not be dismissed as an anomaly. Toyota officials justified the location for marketing reasons. What better way to establish credentials as a seller of large trucks—Toyota's weakest product segment—than to build them in Texas, the world's largest V-8 truck market. But even if Toyota increased net revenue by prying away many of Texas's loyal Ford and GM truck owners, the operative word was "net." Someone had to cover the "tyranny" of geography—the additional costs of shipping parts into Texas and shipping out assembled vehicles, which was at least several hundred dollars per vehicle. If Toyota did not absorb the penalty, then it would fall to its suppliers, haulers, or customers or all of the above.

Detroit 3 supplier networks

Differences are immediately visible in the distribution of the supplier networks of the Detroit 3 and of Japanese-owned carmakers. The Detroit 3 networks contained more suppliers, were more tightly clustered around assembly plants, and were located further north.

The supplier networks of Chrysler, Ford, and GM were nearly identical (Figures 6.4, 6.5, and 6.6, respectively). One-fourth of the suppliers to each of the Detroit 3 were located within approximately 135 miles of Detroit, essentially southern Michigan with the addition of small portions of western Ontario and northern Ohio. One-half of all suppliers were within 275 miles of Detroit, encompassing the Great Lakes region between Milwaukee and Buffalo, as well as the auto-producing portion of Ontario. Another one-fourth of suppliers were located between 275 and 613 miles away, extending primarily into the South. The most distant one-fourth of Detroit 3 suppliers were widely scattered, with the largest number in Mexico.

Suppliers to GM's Saturn brand were identified separately in the database for this project. Saturn's supplier network was scattered over a much larger area than was the case for other Detroit 3 assembly plants. Relatively few suppliers chose to locate close to Saturn's Tennessee assembly plant. The circle encompassing one-fourth of Saturn suppliers had an extremely large radius of 321 miles (Figure 6.7). One-half of Saturn suppliers were within 482 miles, and three-fourths within 559 miles. Saturn used many suppliers based in the Great Lakes that did not choose to add facilities in Tennessee to be near Saturn. With most of its suppliers located more than one day away, Saturn had to depend on logistics operations to meet JIT requirements.

Comparing Networks by Location

Networks of suppliers around assembly plants located in the Deep South could be compared to those located in the Upper South and Midwest. Differences—and similarities—among the networks illustrate fundamental features underlying the geography of carmaker–supplier linkages.

The four Deep South assembly plants for this comparison were BMW in South Carolina, Mercedes-Benz in Alabama, and Nissan and Saturn in Tennessee. Five assembly plants in the Upper South and Mid-

**Figure 6.4 Location of Chrysler's Suppliers Relative to Its Final
Assembly Plants in Southeastern Michigan**

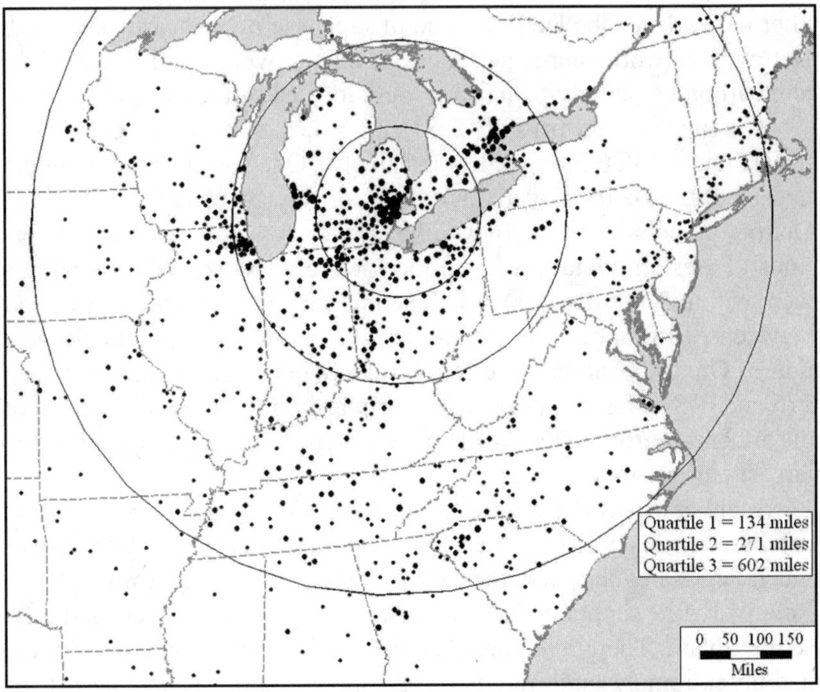

Quartile 1 = 134 miles
Quartile 2 = 271 miles
Quartile 3 = 602 miles

0   50 100 150
Miles

SOURCE: Adapted by the authors from ELM International database and other sources.

west were Honda in Ohio, AutoAlliance (Mazda) in Michigan, Mitsubishi in Illinois, Subaru in Indiana, and Toyota in Kentucky.

The five Upper South and Midwest assembly plants were relatively
old, having all been opened during the 1980s (Table 6.1). Three of the
four Deep South plants were opened more recently, in the 1990s. This
reflected the southern drift of the U.S. motor vehicle industry, which is
discussed in more detail in Chapter 11.

The nine final assembly plants had a mean of 425 suppliers and a
median of 340. The five Upper South and Midwest plants had a mean
of 457 suppliers, 19 percent more than the average of 385 for the four
southern plants. The three best-selling brands—Toyota, Honda, and
Nissan—had a much higher mean of 692 suppliers. Assembly plants
that produced fewer vehicles had correspondingly fewer suppliers.

Figure 6.5   Location of Ford's Suppliers Relative to Its Final Assembly Plants in Southeastern Michigan

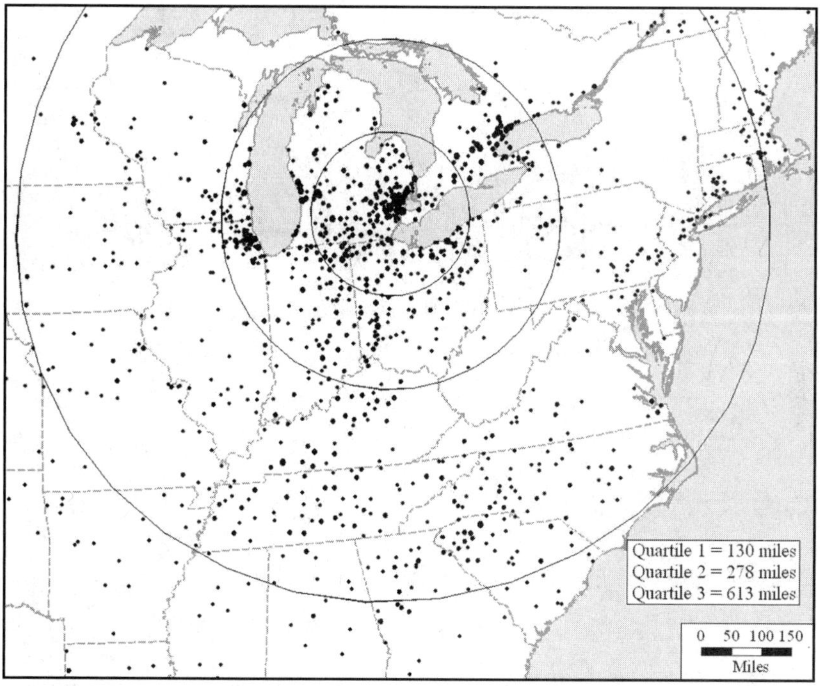

Quartile 1 = 130 miles
Quartile 2 = 278 miles
Quartile 3 = 613 miles

0   50 100 150
Miles

SOURCE: Adapted by the authors from ELM International database and other sources.

Five more assembly plants were added to the analysis of suppliers located within a one-day drive, including three in the Upper South and Midwest (Honda and Toyota in Ontario and Toyota in Indiana) and two in the Deep South (Honda in Alabama and Nissan in Mississippi). The average median distance from the 14 final assembly plants listed in Table 6.2 to each of their several hundred suppliers was 440 miles. In other words, half of the suppliers were located beyond 440 miles, which is just within the 450-mile industry standard for the distance a truck can cover in one day. The average median distance to suppliers was considerably less from the eight Upper South and Midwest plants than from the six Deep South ones, 317 miles from the eight northern plants compared with 602 miles from the six southern ones. Median distance from the eight Upper South and Midwest assembly plants to

**Figure 6.6 Location of GM's Suppliers Relative to Its Final Assembly
Plants in Southeastern Michigan**

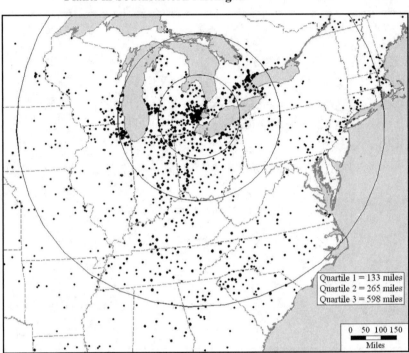

SOURCE: Adapted by the authors from ELM International database and other
sources.

their suppliers ranged from 238 miles for AutoAlliance to 372 miles for
Toyota/Indiana. For the six Deep South plants, the median ranged from
497 for Saturn to 776 for Nissan Mississippi.

The supply base of the Upper South and Midwest assembly plants
was much more likely than the Deep South ones to be located within
the one-day driving range of 450 miles. All eight of northern plants had
between 60 percent and 75 percent of their supplier base located within
450 miles. Together they averaged 68 percent. Incidentally, all eight of
the assembly plants were also located within 450 miles of Detroit. The
six Deep South assembly plants had an average of just under one-third
of their suppliers within 450 miles, with figures ranging from 14 to 41
percent.

Figure 6.7 Location of Saturn's Suppliers Relative to Its Final Assembly Plant in Spring Hill, Tennessee

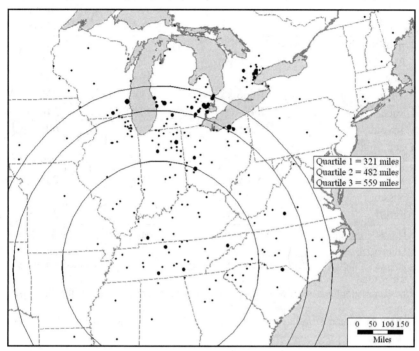

Quartile 1 = 321 miles
Quartile 2 = 482 miles
Quartile 3 = 559 miles

0 50 100 150
Miles

SOURCE: Adapted by the authors from ELM International database and other sources.

Results were different for the percentage of suppliers within 60 miles, or roughly within a one-hour driving distance, of the various assembly plants (Table 6.3). The 60-mile distance was chosen to capture plants that locate close enough to allow multiple daily deliveries using the same truck. On average, only 5 percent of suppliers were located within 60 miles of their customers. Thus, locating within one hour of a final assembly plant was not a critical factor for the vast majority of suppliers.

The percentage of suppliers within 60 miles did not vary significantly between the two groups of assembly plants. The six Deep South plants together had 6 percent of their suppliers within one hour, whereas the eight Upper South and Midwestern ones had 4 percent. The actual count was also virtually identical: an average of 21 parts plants were

Table 6.1 Location, Year Opened, and Number of Suppliers for Selected Assembly Plants

Carmaker	State	Year opened	Number of suppliers
Upper South and Midwest			
AutoAlliance	Michigan	1987	336
Honda	Ohio	1982	667[a]
Mitsubishi	Illinois	1987	335
Subaru	Indiana	1989	340
Toyota	Kentucky	1987	606[b]
Deep South			
BMW	South Carolina	1994	158
Mercedes-Benz	Alabama	1997	234
Nissan	Tennessee	1983	803[c]
Saturn	Tennessee	1990	346

[a] Honda's suppliers to its Alabama and Ontario assembly plants are included in the Ohio total.

[b] Toyota's suppliers to its Indiana and Ontario assembly plants are included in the Kentucky total.

[c] Nissan's suppliers to its Mississippi assembly plant are included in the Tennessee total.

SOURCE: Adapted by the authors from the ELM International database and other sources.

within 60 miles of the 8 Upper South and Midwest assembly plants and 19 were within 60 miles of the 6 Deep South ones.

The variation in percentage and number of suppliers within 60 miles fluctuated much more within groups than between them. Nine assembly plants had less than 5 percent of suppliers and two had about 15 percent. The number of suppliers within 60 miles ranged from 48 for AutoAlliance to 3 for Mitsubishi and Toyota/Indiana. That AutoAlliance had the highest number of suppliers located within a 60-mile radius was not surprising, because the plant is located in southeastern Michigan, just south of Detroit, surrounded by the highest concentration of supplier plants anywhere in the country.

The location of suppliers by country was similar across networks (Table 6.4). Honda and Toyota both had assembly operations in Canada, hence their elevated share of suppliers based in Ontario. By the same token, Nissan had a large share of Mexican suppliers due to its greater

Table 6.2 Suppliers within One Day's Driving Distance of Selected Assembly Plants

Carmaker	State or province	Median distance to suppliers (miles)	Suppliers within 450 miles (%)
Upper South and Midwest		317	68
AutoAlliance	Michigan	238	71
Honda	Ohio	268	75
Mitsubishi	Illinois	342	65
Subaru	Indiana	282	69
Toyota	Kentucky	321	73
Honda	Ontario	369	62
Toyota	Indiana	372	66
Toyota	Ontario	345	64
Deep South		602	29
BMW	South Carolina	523	41
Mercedes-Benz	Alabama	688	23
Nissan	Tennessee	505	35
Saturn	Tennessee	497	39
Honda	Alabama	621	22
Nissan	Mississippi	776	14
Mean		440	51

SOURCE: Adapted by the authors from the ELM International database and other sources.

footprint there. Nissan's North American supplier network was large because it included a sizeable number of suppliers based in Mexico. With the exception of Volkswagen, Nissan was the only "foreign" automaker that has a notable presence in Mexico, where it operates two assembly plants.

Data for suppliers around the NUMMI plant were also examined. As the only remaining assembly plant in California, far from the heart of the U.S. auto industry, median distance to suppliers was 2,007 miles, much higher than for any other assembly plant. Only 6 percent of NUMMI's suppliers were within 450 miles, and only five suppliers, or 2.5 percent of its total, were within 60 miles.

Table 6.3 Suppliers within One Hour's Driving Distance of Selected Assembly Plants

Carmaker	State	Number of suppliers within 60 miles	Suppliers within 60 miles (%)
Upper South and Midwest		21	4
AutoAlliance	Michigan	48	14
Honda	Ohio	29	4
Mitsubishi	Illinois	3	1
Subaru	Indiana	7	2
Toyota	Kentucky	11	2
Honda	Ontario	34	5
Toyota	Indiana	3	1
Toyota	Ontario	35	6
Deep South		19	6
BMW	South Carolina	26	17
Mercedes-Benz	Alabama	22	9
Nissan	Tennessee	13	2
Saturn	Tennessee	8	2
Honda	Alabama	20	3
Nissan	Mississippi	23	3
Mean		20	5

SOURCE: Adapted by the authors from the ELM International database and other sources.

OUTLOOK AND UNCERTAINTIES

Close linkage between an assembly plant and its network of suppliers is crucial for efficient operation in the contemporary environment of lean inventory with JIT delivery. For most suppliers, close linkage means a physical location within a one-day delivery range of the assembly plant. Regardless of whether an assembly plant is located in the Great Lakes or the southern portion of Auto Alley, roughly three-fourths of its suppliers will be situated within one day.

At the same time, close linkage does not mean suppliers must locate next door to the assembly plant. In fact, few suppliers are within a one-

Table 6.4 Mexican and Canadian Suppliers to Selected Assembly Plants

Carmaker	State	Suppliers in Canada (%)	Suppliers in Mexico (%)
Upper South and Midwest			
AutoAlliance	Michigan	9.8	6.0
Honda[a]	Ohio	10.6	6.8
Mitsubishi	Illinois	9.3	3.6
Subaru	Indiana	7.1	5.0
Toyota[b]	Kentucky	10.1	6.4
Deep South			
BMW	South Carolina	1.9	13.9
Mercedes-Benz[c]	Alabama	8.1	31.2
Nissan[d]	Tennessee	4.0	32.0
Saturn	Tennessee	9.8	2.6

[a] Honda's suppliers to its Alabama and Ontario assembly plants are included in the Ohio total.

[b] Toyota's suppliers to its Indiana and Ontario assembly plants are included in the Kentucky total.

[c] The Mercedes network includes a number of Chrysler suppliers, some of which are located in Mexico.

[d] Nissan's suppliers to its Mississippi assembly plant are included in the Tennessee total.

SOURCE: Adapted by authors from ELM International database and other sources.

hour drive of an assembly plant. Invariably, the seat supplier will be within the one-hour radius, as are some stamping and trim shops.

That most suppliers are within one day but not within one hour is critical to local government attempts to entice new plants. Government subsidies exceeding $100,000 per job for final assembly plants have been justified because of the multiplier effect: each new assembly job generates several new supplier jobs. However, most of the new supplier jobs are destined for political jurisdictions other than the one enticing the final assembly plant.

Especially challenging for the future of tightly linked networks of carmakers and suppliers is the globalization of supply chains. With final assembly plants in the United States receiving more than one-fourth of their components from other countries—as discussed in Chapter 13— JIT has become harder to sustain when it is stretched around the world.

"How do suppliers maintain JIT delivery when weeks are added to a delivery cycle that previously was measured in hours or days? 'Current automotive supply chains were built around just-in-time production and very short lead times,' notes Mark Bünger, senior analyst at Forrester Research, Cambridge, Massachusetts. 'When these companies start sourcing from overseas, this dramatically increases the complexity'" (Murphy 2004).

Notes

1. For an extensive description of lean manufacturing, see Schoenberger (1987).
2. Larry Jutte, Honda of America Manufacturing senior vice president and general manager of parts and procurement, quoted in Chappell (2005d).
3. Larry Jutte, Honda of America Manufacturing senior vice president and general manager of parts and procurement, quoted in Chappell (2004d).

7
Seat Supplier Right Next Door

Automakers encouraged Tier 1s to get big enough to handle the outsourcing of big chunks of the vehicle, but then reversed course and reassumed some of those responsibilities. (Sherefkin 2006b)

The previous chapter showed that three-fourths of parts plants are located within a one-day drive of the final assembly plants, but only a few were within a one-hour drive. Invariably, one of the handful of parts plants within the one-hour radius of the assembly plant is a seat supplier.

Finding seat suppliers very near final assembly plants derives in part from the economic geography of seat production. A vehicle seat comprises three principal components. The frame, which is mainly metal, provides the basic skeleton for the seat and transfers the load to the body of the vehicle. The padding is primarily polyurethane foam molded to shape. The external skin is cut from fabric, leather, or vinyl and sewn to shape.

A finished seat occupies a much greater volume than the sum of these individual inputs. Thus, like other bulk-gaining products, seats will normally be produced most efficiently near the customer. A seat is fragile as well as bulky, and it comes in a rather large number of varieties for a given model. So long-distance shipping of a finished seat is much more difficult and expensive than long-distance shipping of the constituent parts of a seat.

The distinctive organization of this sector of the auto industry has also favored especially tight colocation with final assembly. A low value-added component that was considered peripheral to the vehicle's performance or profit, the seat was one of the first parts that the Detroit 3 carmakers outsourced to independent suppliers and placed on JIT delivery to final assembly plants. Clearing out the massive inventory of cushions, frames, and covers from Detroit 3 final assembly plants was the most visible harbinger of JIT delivery during the 1980s. Japanese-owned carmakers in the United States outsourced seats from the start.

Also contributing to the distinctive geography of seat production has been the consolidation of the sector into a handful of major suppliers. An assembly plant obtains most if not all its seats from a single source, and the supplier in turn typically dedicates a single facility to producing seats for that assembly plant.

The fate of an assembly plant determines the fate of a seat plant. For example, assembly plant closures by GM in Atlanta and by Chrysler in Newark, Delaware, resulted in the closure of nearby Lear seat-making plants. By the same token, to support Honda's assembly plant in Greensburg, Indiana, which opened in 2008, TS Tech, Honda's primary seat supplier in North America, opened a new plant in 2008, just 45 miles away in New Castle, Indiana. This colocation recalls the pattern used during the era of vertical integration, when the Detroit 3 carmakers typically located a stamping facility near each assembly plant to supply it with bodies (see Chapter 4).

The seat may play a less central role than other systems in vehicle performance, but the powertrain, chassis, and electronics perform their functions largely unseen, and the exterior catches the eye of motorists only fleetingly as they get in and out of the vehicle. It is while sitting in the interior that the driver most experiences the convenience of a modern vehicle, and the passenger experiences its comfort. In addition the interior is one of the most self-contained parts of the vehicle, so it is relatively easy to isolate it for outsourcing.

As a result, the interior has been the portion of the vehicle where producer–supplier relations have been most transformed. "The process of outsourcing entire modules to Tier 1 suppliers and delegating responsibility for the design and subcontracting has probably gone furthest in interiors and seats" (Van Biesebroeck 2006, p. 209). A handful of companies stand ready, willing, and able to supply carmakers with entire interiors ready to snap into place on the final assembly line. Other interior suppliers, including some of the industry's largest, have been relegated to Tier 2 status, shipping much of their output to the three interior suppliers rather than directly to carmakers. Consequently, the interior has been the most rationalized sector of the auto supplier industry. It is also the least globalized—both of the leading interior suppliers in the United States are U.S.-based.

IT ALL STARTED WITH SEATS

Nowhere is the name Johnson or Lear visible inside a motor vehicle; it is Ford or Toyota stamped on the steering wheel, instrument panel, and doorpost. Yet Johnson Controls Inc. (JCI) and Lear Corp. deserve as much credit as the carmakers for the look and feel of the passenger compartment. These two interior specialists have ranked among the largest suppliers in North America.

In contrast with many of the other leading North American suppliers, which are venerable survivors from the early days of the automotive industry, these two large interior suppliers rose to prominence much more recently. Neither Lear nor JCI has a long history in the automotive industry: Lear entered the parts business in 1964 and JCI in 1978. Both grew rapidly during the late twentieth century by being in a position to respond to carmakers' demand for JIT delivery of complete seats ready to install on the final assembly line. Into the twenty-first century, they evolved from mere "suppliers" to "integrators" of interiors.

The lowly seat made an unlikely candidate to spearhead a revolution in producer–supplier relations. The seat was an afterthought through the first century of motor vehicle production. For its first Model A in 1903 Ford spent a mere $16 per vehicle (representing 4 percent of production costs) on seats, which were cushions purchased from body builder C.R. Wilson to cover wooden slats (Table 2.1). In 2006, the seat represented 30 to 40 percent of the total interior cost (Lear Corporation 2006, p. 7).

Replacement of open carriages with enclosed passenger compartments in the 1920s generated demand for more substantial seats. Minimally structured sofas, not unlike those typically found in the living rooms of modest American homes, were chopped down to fit the more limited space and installed in cars. Most new car buyers bought aftermarket covers to protect the seats from wear and tear as well as throw a dash of style and color over the drab gray factory-delivered surface.

GM's empire within an empire, Fisher Body division, produced most of GM's seats, mainly in the same Flint plant where the famous 1937 sit-down strike forced the company to recognize the UAW union. Ford naturally made most of its seats inside its sprawling Rouge complex. Chrysler too made most of its seats in Michigan. To manufacture seats, the Detroit 3 purchased most of the parts from multiple sources through annual contracts awarded by price.

When the Detroit 3 started to demand delivery of complete seats on a JIT basis during the 1980s, the numerous suppliers of frames, cushions, and covers were thrown into disarray. To deliver complete seats, suppliers once content to specialize in one seat-related component had to figure out how to get the other components—by acquiring competitors, setting up new facilities, or subcontracting to specialists. And to assure JIT delivery, a seat supplier had to build a final seat assembly plant adjacent to the customer's final assembly plant. The required investment and risk proved too much for most seat makers.

Left standing from the shakeout were JCI and Lear; each controlled roughly 40 percent of the North American market during the first decade of the twenty-first century. Magna International (discussed in Chapter 4) had about 10 percent of the North American seat market, and several foreign-based companies divided the rest. For both JCI and Lear, supplying seats represented a significant departure from long-standing core competencies in other industrial sectors. Both had esoteric connections to the early motor vehicle industry, but these connections were unrelated to making seats.

The JCI–Lear battle for the seat market turned into the auto industry's version of the nuclear arms race (a rump race?). Never mind alternative fuels, variable transmissions, and electronic suspension, billions were poured in researching the derriere of the American motorist (it's getting larger). What better opportunity was there to envelop the American motorist in more comfort? With the market long since cornered, seat makers have had to search for new ways to add content. Cavernous minivans and sport utility vehicles have offered especially fertile territory for suppliers to configure endless seating permutations.

Sofa-style "bench" seats have long given way to what were originally called "bucket" seats. No longer can a tired motorist (or amorous couple) stretch out across a bench—each passenger is now individually wrapped up inside a self-contained "captain's chair." Seats are being shaped to be more ergonomic, and the addition of headrests and child supports make them safer. Materials are more durable, waterproof, stain resistant, and breathable. Thinner seats leave room to stuff yet more features into the interior.

Ultimately, though, the seat supplier battle between JCI and Lear has been waged largely on trim, colors, and other cosmetic features. An executive at one of the two dominant seat suppliers, unable to restrain his enthusiasm for the company's newest seat, apologized that the specific features had to remain secret, although assurance was given that the new seat would "shock and awe" the authors, not to mention the American public, when it was unveiled.

Lear: From Jets to Seats

The name Lear is probably most widely recognized as a brand of small jet airplanes, and in fact, inventor and entrepreneur William Lear (1902–1978) started the first company bearing his name during the 1930s to fit planes for use by executives. Lear Inc. grew rapidly during World War II as a supplier of electronic aviation guidance to the military. Unable to convince his business partners to invest in the up-and-coming but still economically risky passenger jets, Bill Lear sold his interest in Lear Inc. in 1959. The company merged with Siegler Corp. three years later to form Lear Siegler, Inc., a major defense contractor during the Vietnam War.

Bill Lear went on to create Learjet in 1962. The Wichita, Kansas, company soon became the leading supplier of corporate jets to executives and other wealthy individuals who could afford a private and flexible alternative to scheduled airlines. He sold Learjet in 1967 to Gates Rubber Co., by coincidence also a major automotive parts supplier at the time. After several more transfers, Learjet became a division of Québec-based Bombardier Aerospace.

Bill Lear was restless. He would develop an innovative consumer product with high-tech electronics by the standards of the time, establish a company to manufacture it, sell his interest in the company a few years later, and then repeat the cycle with a fresh idea. Prior to his work in aviation, he was an early contributor to the development of car radios. He patented the first workable car radio in 1922, and formed the Radio Wire and Coil Co. to build them. He assigned the patent two years later to a newly established company called Motorola (short for "Motor Victrola"; see Chapter 14). Four decades later, he invented a more fleeting contribution to automotive audio equipment—the eight-track tape system—first offered on 1966 Ford models.

Lear Siegler expanded rapidly during the 1960s in a variety of sectors, many unrelated to defense work. One of the more obscure of its 47 divisions and subsidiaries was American Metal Products, a producer of metal tubes, founded in 1917 in Detroit by Frederick Matthaei (1892–1973). Aircraft companies bought some of them, but its largest customers during the 1920s were Ford and GM, which shaped the metal tubes into seat frames. American Metal added Chrysler and several automotive parts makers as customers during the 1930s, exceeded $1 million sales for the first time in 1939, and expanded from 18 employees in 1917 to 900 in 1941. When it was acquired by Lear Siegler in 1964, American Metal had become the largest independent supplier of parts for seat frames in the United States. American Metals was renamed General Seating Division in 1975.

A leveraged buyout by investment bankers Forstmann & Little in 1987 resulted in the sale of all Lear Siegler assets except General Seating, which was incorporated as Lear Siegler Seating Corp. About 30 of the seating division's managers acquired the company a year later and took the company public, on the New York Stock Exchange, in 1994.

Lear emerged in the 1990s as one of the two leading suppliers of complete seats primarily through acquisition of seat facilities from Ford in 1993, GM in 1998, and ITT (its Automotive Seat Sub-Systems Unit) in 1997. Lear also established a joint venture in 1987, called General Seating of America, with Japanese supplier NHK Spring Co., to supply seats to Subaru's Lafayette assembly plant, from nearby Frankfort, Indiana.

Johnson Controls: From Thermostats to Seats

JCI similarly originated as a manufacturer of a product unrelated to the auto industry, in this case, the thermostat. Warren S. Johnson, a professor at the State Normal School in Whitewater, Wisconsin (now University of Wisconsin Whitewater), invented the electric room thermostat in 1883. With a group of Milwaukee investors, he incorporated Johnson Electric Service Co. in 1885 to manufacture, install, and service automatic temperature regulation systems for offices and other nonresidential buildings. The company was renamed Johnson Controls in 1974.

Johnson developed other products during the late nineteenth century, including beer carbonators, steam couplers for trains, and push-button toilets. The company also built some cars and trucks during the first decade of the twentieth century. After Johnson's death in 1911, the company concentrated solely on nonresidential temperature controls. It did enter the automotive aftermarket parts business in 1978 by acquiring Globe-Union, Inc., the country's largest producer of private-label lead-acid automotive batteries.

Hoover Universal

JCI became an original equipment interior parts supplier in 1985 when it bought Ferro Manufacturing Corp. and Hoover Universal, Inc. Ferro, a privately held company founded in 1915, made car door latches, window regulators, seat tracks, and recliners.

The key acquisition was Hoover Precision Products Inc., founded in 1913 by Leander J. Hoover in Ann Arbor, Michigan, to make steel balls for the automotive industry. Hoover became a seat supplier through acquisition of Universal Wire Spring Inc., which made seat springs, in 1960, and Stubnitz Greene Corp., which made seat frames and molded urethane foam, in 1964. When acquired by JCI, Hoover had recently become the first supplier able to deliver complete seats on a JIT basis ready for installation on the final assembly line.

As its seat business expanded rapidly—from $200 million in 1985 to $1.2 billion in 1991 and $2.6 billion in 1993—JCI disposed of Hoover's other businesses. Eighteen plants were sold to Citicorp Venture Capital, which formed Hoover Materials Holding Group Inc. Hoover's Ball Products Division was sold in 1990 to Japanese bearing-maker NSK. JCI did retain its original thermostat business.

JCI's Joint Ventures

JCI grew in part through acquiring Chrysler's seat operations in 1994, but it could not keep pace with Lear's torrid buying spree. Instead, JCI fueled much of its expansion through several joint ventures with Japanese suppliers and minority-owned U.S.-based suppliers.

JCI's first joint venture, called Trim Masters, was established in 1987 with Toyota keiretsu Araco Corporation to supply seats to Toyota's U.S. assembly plants. Araco remained in the shadow of JCI until

2004, when it became part of Toyota Boshoku Co. Following in the footsteps of other Toyota keiretsu firms Aisin and Denso, Toyota Boshoku emerged as a major interior integrator and competitor to JCI in the early twenty-first century (see Outlook and Uncertainties at the end of the chapter).

Trim Masters had seat assembly plants in Nicholasville, Kentucky, to serve Toyota's Georgetown assembly plant, and in Lawrenceville, Illinois, to serve Toyota's Princeton assembly plant. The joint venture also had facilities to cut and sew leather, cloth, and vinyl in Harrodsburg and Leitchfield, Kentucky; Muncie, Indiana; and Torreon, Mexico. Trim Masters also did injection molding and vacuum forming for door trim at Bardstown, Kentucky, and Modesto, California, as well as Lawrenceville.

The Lawrenceville plant, which supplied Toyota, became entangled in a complex web of ownership. Trim Masters sold the plant in 2001 to a newly formed company named Automotive Technology Systems. Trim Masters—itself a joint venture between JCI and Araco—retained 49 percent ownership in the new company. Majority control passed to Ernie Green Industries, Inc.

Why Ernie Green? With Ernie Green holding majority control, Automotive Technology Systems could apply for minority-ownership certification from the National Minority Supplier Development Council. Ernie Green was a football star at the University of Louisville between 1958 and 1961 and with the Cleveland Browns in the National Football League between 1962 and 1968.

The one-time football star claimed that his success at selling to Japanese carmakers began with a chance encounter with a Toyota executive in 1988. Green had recently acquired Florida Production Engineering Inc., a small supplier of plastic wheel trim: in Green's words "a horrible company." Although Green was not one of its suppliers, Toyota agreed to send a consultant team to reorganize Florida Production along Toyota Production System principles.

Ernie Green Industries, founded in Dayton, Ohio, started supplying Honda with plastic wheel covers in the early 1990s. Honda asked Green to acquire and run a troublesome plastics supplier and repaid the favor in 1999 with a large contract to supply front and rear suspensions to its Marysville and East Liberty assembly plants. Honda had been making the components at its Anna, Ohio, engine plant, and wanted to devote more plant space to engine production. With no experience producing that component, Ernie Green Industries officials spent a year observing how Honda made suspensions before opening a parts plant in Marion, Ohio (Chappell 2001). Sourcing parts from Ernie Green gave Honda an opportunity to increase purchases from minority-owned suppliers. More than half of Ernie Green's $636 million sales in 2003 comprised original equipment to Honda. GM and Toyota were also important customers.

To supply Nissan's Smyrna, Tennessee, assembly plant, JCI set up a 50–50 joint venture in nearby Murfreesboro with Nissan keiretsu Ikeda Bussan Co. When Nissan, under the leadership of Carlos Ghosn, severed many of its keiretsu links, JCI bought out Ikeda's half of the Murfreesboro joint venture. In 1996 JCI created a third joint venture, called Bridgewater Interiors, with Epsilon, LLC to produce seats and other interior components. Because Epsilon was minority owned, the joint venture was also certified as minority owned. Bridgewater supplied seats to Honda's truck plant in Lincoln, Alabama.

The joint ventures gave JCI a strong tactical advantage in the seat market. The Detroit 3, under pressure to increase sourcing through minority-owned suppliers, could buy seats from Bridgewater. And the leading Japanese transplants, reluctant to deal with a heavily unionized purely "American" company like Lear, could still source seats to JCI indirectly. One-third of JCI's North American sales were being generated by transplant business into the twenty-first century. "The thing that jumps out about Johnson Controls is their broad customer base . . . They do probably the best job of any American company with the new domestics, especially the Japanese transplants."[1] Only one-third of JCI's sales went to the Detroit 3 in 2006, compared to 61 percent for rival Lear (Merrill Lynch 2007, pp. 71, 74).

Other Seat Suppliers

To increase competition, the Detroit 3 encouraged new entrants into the seating business. "The car companies are uncomfortable having just two choices in global seating suppliers."[2] Especially uncomfortable has been GM, still hoping for a return to the good old days of multiple sourcing and annual competitive bidding. Magna International, Faurecia, and TS Tech hold most of the market not held by JCI and Lear.

Magna International

Magna International was the third leading seat supplier in the United States, with 10 percent of the market (see Chapter 4). Magna became a major seat supplier in 1996 when it acquired Douglas & Lomason, the fifth-largest seat maker at the time.

Faurecia

Faurecia was Europe's leading seat maker and third worldwide behind Lear and JCI. Faurecia was created when French seating specialist Bertrand Faure acquired Ecia, a former PSA Peugeot Citroën captive that had been spun off. Bertrand Faure had already entered the U.S. market through a joint venture with Japanese supplier Fuji Kiko Co. called Dynamec, Inc., which made seat reclining devices and seat adjusters at a plant in Walton, Kentucky. GM encouraged French seat maker Faurecia to enter the North American market by awarding it a contract in 1999 to deliver fully assembled seats for its high-volume Chevrolet Malibu beginning in 2004.

Faurecia may have expanded too quickly in North America. Its North American operations lost $108 million in 2006, fueled by poor initial contracts that failed to adjust for the rising cost of steel and resins. After opening 14 new facilities in North America in three years, Faurecia had to put further growth on hold. "You can't build a castle on quicksand. We've got to throw some cement into the quicksand pool before we continue," was the picturesque way its North American president James Orchard put it in 2007 (Wortham 2007c).

TS Tech

Honda's principal seat supplier, TS Tech, was founded in 1954 as the seat division of Teito Fuhaku Kogyo Corp. The division was made an independent company in 1960 and was known as the Tokyo Seat Co. until 1997 when it changed its name to TS Tech Ltd. TS initially made seats for motorcycles, Honda's first product line. In addition to seat assembly plants near Honda's Alabama, Indiana, and Ohio final assembly plants, TS Tech has set up Tri-Con Industries to stamp seat frames and TS Trim Industries to make foam, seat covers, and other seat components. TS Tech and Bridgewater split the seat contract at Honda's Lincoln, Alabama, truck plant. TS Tech also built a dedicated seat plant near the Honda assembly plant in Greensburg, Indiana, opened in 2008.

Seat Plant Locations

Overall, seats are less likely than most components to be made in the Midwest. Half of seat parts are made in the Midwest (Table 7.1). The distribution of seat plants closely resembles that of final assembly plants, as expected given the especially high degree of colocation between the two.

The overall share of seat plants in the Midwest has also been lowered by the fact that plants of nonmetal parts do not depend on Midwest sources of steel. Covers and padding in particular have been sourced to plants in the South along with the majority of the U.S. textile and furniture industries (see the next section).

Lear Plant Locations

Lear operated 29 seat-making facilities in 2006, including 12 in Michigan; 4 in Missouri; 3 in Indiana; 2 each in Alabama and Ohio; and 1 each in Delaware, Kentucky, South Carolina, Tennessee, Texas, and Wisconsin (Lear Corporation 2006, p. 18). A number of the Michigan plants specialized in seat parts, such as frames and foam. Most of the plants outside Michigan were sited to provide finished seats to nearby assembly plants.

For example, Ford assembly plants in Hazelwood, Missouri, and Louisville, Kentucky, and GM assembly plants in Wentzville, Missouri,

Table 7.1 Interior Parts Plants in the Midwest

Type of plant	Number of plants	% in Midwest
Seats and seat components	269	49.4
Headliners, carpeting, sound deadeners	234	56.0
Interior door panels	136	63.2
Handles, mirrors, labels, pedals	95	78.9
Dashboard	86	60.5
Miscellaneous and not specified	350	64.6
Total interior	1,170	60.1

SOURCE: Adapted by the authors from ELM International database.

and Arlington, Texas, received seats from Lear in the same communities. Ford's Chicago assembly plant and GM's Lordstown, Ohio, assembly plant received seats from Lear facilities in nearby Hammond, Indiana, and Warren, Ohio, respectively.

JCI Plant Locations

JCI had 34 seat-related plants in 2006, including seven in Michigan; four each in Kentucky and Ohio; three in Tennessee; two each in Georgia, Missouri, and Texas; and one each in Alabama, California, Illinois, Indiana, Louisiana, Mississippi, New Jersey, Oklahoma, Virginia, and Wisconsin. As with Lear, the JCI seat plant distribution closely followed final assembly plant distribution, with the addition of plants primarily in the Midwest to produce seat parts.

THE REST OF THE INTERIOR

Suppliers have used the term "trim" to refer to the portions of the interior other than seats. The interior trim sector struggled much more than the seat sector in the early twenty-first century. While seat suppliers were able to add value to their product, interior trim suppliers faced the opposite trend. Trim became an increasingly low-cost product driven by commodity prices. Interior trim suppliers tried to survive through involvement of equity investment firms motivated entirely by squeezing costs from the production process, but not all succeeded.

Interior Trim Modules

Interior trim consists of four principal modules: dashboard, door panels, floor cover, and headliner. Interior trim also includes smaller hardware such as handles, labels, and pedals.

The dashboard houses the gauges that are supplied by electronics specialists, who are responsible for adding most of the value to this component (see Chapter 14). The dashboard was originally a metal plate that separated the passengers from the engine. By the 1930s, the plate was being stamped into a decorative shape. Since the late twentieth century, the dashboard has been made of softer plastic to protect occupants in a crash.

Early doors were little more than slats of wood hinged to one pillar and latched to another. Today's doors are quite different. They are more like sandwiches with different "bread" on each side of the filling. The outer side of the sandwich is usually stamped from metal. The inner side was also once stamped from metal with bits of fabric glued to it. Now, the inner side of the door is typically molded from plastic, such as thermoplastic olefin (TPO). Between the inner and outer door panels are acoustical and restraint systems, as well as locks, regulators, speakers, adjusters, wiring, and other electronic components mounted on steel or plastic carriers.

As with other interior components, door panels were once constructed at final assembly plants but are increasingly shipped as complete modules. A full door module (a level 3, in industry vernacular) includes inner door trim panel, hardware, glass, and outer body panel. Painted door structures arrive at a module manufacturer's plant, where latches, regulators, glass, electronics, soft trim, and other parts are attached. In North America, about 8 percent of front doors, 11 percent of rear doors, and 33 percent of rear liftgates were delivered as modules by outside suppliers in 2001. The leading supplier of door modules, with 40 percent of the world market, was Brose Fahrzeugteile GmbH (Broge 2002).

When passenger compartments were enclosed in the 1920s, textiles were placed on the roof and floor for decoration, as well as for insulation from noise and cold. Carpet was laid on the floor, and fabric glued to a shell known as a headliner was fitted into the roof (Fung and Hardcastle 2001).

Headliners and flooring have played leading roles in making the passenger compartment quieter. Allowing some outside noise to reach the interior was traditionally regarded as a necessary safety feature, permitting drivers to listen for horns, emergency sirens, squealing brakes, skidding tires, and other evidence of traffic and road hazards. Keeping out exterior noise became increasingly important as American motorists chose instead to listen to music and chat on cell phones. "When a consumer test drives a car, they notice how quiet it is in the compartment."[3] "The traditional way to make a car quiet was to determine where noise was coming in and then stick enough engineered weight between the listener and the noise to stop the sound. The problem is that that ties your noise performance directly with the weight. In a world where we're looking at composites and aluminum bodies, I'd have to put back in all that weight they just took out of the body."[4]

Headliners and carpets were made of woven fabric for most of the twentieth century. Carpet could be laid directly on the floor, whereas headliner fabric was glued to a foam backing that was in turn glued to the roof. Woven fabrics suitable for the home did not hold up well under the rougher conditions of the motor vehicle. Headliners sagged when intense summer sun heat melted the glue. Mats were placed on top of the carpets to protect them from dirt and punctures.

Nonwoven fabric became popular in Europe and Japan during the 1990s and in North America a decade later. Nonwoven headliners were made of polyester fibers locked together through a process known as needle-punch technology. They were also made of a composite of porous materials like foam, fibers, synthetics, and cotton (Armstrong 2004b). The foam base was no longer needed, thereby making nonwoven fabric cheaper, lighter, and more durable than woven fabric (Kisiel 1996).

Faced with demand for a quieter passenger compartment, leading headliner and carpeting suppliers became acoustical systems suppliers. An acoustical expert could ensure that each component contributed to the desired overall sound and noise conditions. Acoustics once sourced piecemeal have been purchased from single suppliers with expertise in balancing materials in the various components to achieve the desired overall effect (Wilson 2002a).

Interior parts other than seats are more likely than average to be produced in Michigan and other Midwest states (Figure 7.1). About one-third of these interior plants have been located in Michigan and another one-third elsewhere in the Midwest (Table 7.1).

Struggling Interior Trim Suppliers

Suppliers of these various interior parts have struggled. Of the two largest U.S.-owned suppliers of interior parts other than seats in 2006, one (Dura) entered Chapter 11, and the other (Collins and Aikman) went out of business.

Figure 7.1 Interior Parts Plants

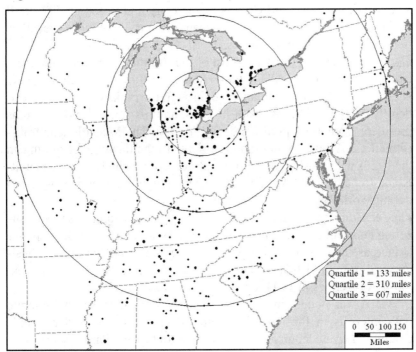

Quartile 1 = 133 miles
Quartile 2 = 310 miles
Quartile 3 = 607 miles

0   50 100 150
Miles

SOURCE: Adapted by the authors from ELM International database and other sources.

Collins & Aikman

The leading supplier of interior components other than seats at the beginning of the twenty-first century was Collins & Aikman Corporation (C&A). It accounted for one-half of the seat fabric and flooring and one-fourth of the headliners in 2004. It was also the largest supplier of dashboards, with one-third of the market, and the second-largest supplier of door panels, with one-sixth of the market. The company claimed to be supplying parts for 90 percent of the vehicles assembled in the United States. Yet, in 2005, it was bankrupt.

C&A's predecessor, G.L. Kelty & Co., was founded in 1843 by Gibbons L. Kelty as a window shade shop in New York City. Kelty's nephew Charles M. Aikman joined the firm as a partner in 1870 and bought half ownership after Kelty's death in 1889. The other half was owned by William G. Collins. The two formed Collins & Aikman in 1891, with Aikman as president and Collins as secretary and treasurer. The retail business was closed in the late nineteenth century in order to specialize in heavy upholstery-type fabrics.

Management of C&A for most of the twentieth century came from two generations of the McCullough family. Willis G. McCullough, who started at C&A as a salesman, rose through the ranks to serve as president from 1929 until his death in 1948, and his son Donald served as president from 1961 until his death in 2000. The McCulloughs transformed C&A into an automotive-oriented manufacturer beginning in the 1920s with seat and headlining fabric. Motor vehicle fabric accounted for 75 percent of C&A business when civilian production was halted during World War II.

C&A diluted its motor vehicle focus when it acquired several carpeting and wall covering firms during the 1960s and 1970s. In response to increased outsourcing, C&A sold off most of its nonautomotive businesses during the 1990s. Motor vehicle parts increased from 59 percent of C&A revenues in 1994 to 96 percent in 1999.

C&A was bought in 1986 by Wickes Companies, a conglomerate with interests in furniture, home improvement stores, and women's clothing. Private equity firm Heartland Industrial Partners acquired C&A in 2001. One of Heartland's founders, David A. Stockman, became chairman of the board of C&A in 2001 and CEO in 2003.

Stockman had been elected to Congress in 1976 at age 29. His articulate advocacy of supply-side economics gained him appointment as director of the Office of Management and Budget (OMB) from 1981 to 1985. After resigning from OMB, he became a managing director at Salomon Brothers, Inc., and an original partner and a senior managing director of the Blackstone Group, before setting up Heartland in 1999, in part because of Blackstone's reluctance to invest in C&A.

Heartland struggled to achieve the cost savings promised in its many acquisitions, especially at C&A, which lost $35.6 million in 2001. Stockman took over as CEO in 2003, and immediately cut 14 percent of the workforce in a bid to reduce losses. However, the company had a very high exposure to the Detroit 3, and it was highly leveraged. When the company ran into trouble refinancing its debt, it was forced to file for Chapter 11 bankruptcy protection in 2005. Stockman was forced to resign as CEO and was charged with falsifying information about the company's perilous financial condition. After auctioning off or closing down its operations, C&A went out of existence in 2007.

Dura Automotive Systems

Dura was the leading supplier of interior control components, such as seat adjusters, gear shifters, parking brakes, pedals, cables, and steering columns. The company also produced glass components, door modules, and exterior trim.

Dura was formed in 1990, when the Minneapolis-based holding company Hidden Creek Industries acquired Wickes Dura Automotive Hardware and Mechanical Components division from New York financial investment firm Wasserstein Perella. The founder and first chairman of Hidden Creek was S.A. (Tony) Johnson, an 18-year veteran of Cummins Engine Co. He was also president and chief executive officer of Onan Corp. from 1981 to 1985 and chief operating officer of Pentair, Inc. from 1985 to 1989.

In addition to Dura, Hidden Creek operated three other parts makers: Automotive Industries, J.L. French Automotive Castings, and Tower Automotive. Johnson "kept costs low at his operating companies through a centralized management team of just 10 people" (Sherefkin 2006b). However, French and Tower joined Dura in seeking bankruptcy protection, and Automotive Industries was sold to Lear, where it formed the basis of a struggling interior trim segment of Lear's interior integration strategy. "All four [Hidden Creek parts-making] companies illustrated the grow-at-all-costs roll-up strategy used by financiers in the 1990s to win more Detroit 3 outsourcing business. Typically the strategy involved investors who made serial acquisitions of parts suppliers to offer one-stop shopping for automaker customers" (Sherefkin 2006b).

Dura Automotive filed for bankruptcy protection in 2006 following a sharp drop in revenue. "A significant part of that revenue loss came from Lear Corp.'s decision to take in-house the seat adjusters Dura manufactured . . . Most of Dura's business was with the Detroit 3 carmakers, but one-fourth was with other tier one suppliers, especially Lear, its third leading customer behind GM and Ford. However, Dura found itself in competition with Lear. Instead of buying seat tracks from Dura for GM vehicles, Lear started making them itself" (Sherefkin 2006b).

INTERIOR SYSTEMS INTEGRATORS

At the beginning of the twenty-first century sourcing an integrated interior from a single supplier appeared very attractive to carmakers. A single supplier could ensure that the main interior modules were designed as a harmonious whole and fit together well. Fibers for seat covers, headliners, and carpets could be obtained from the same batch and colored together, as could plastic and wood trim on the door panels and cockpit.

The importance of the interior for comfort and convenience, rather than for performance, seemed to make it especially appropriate for outsourcing as a single integrated module to a single supplier. An attractive interior must blend materials harmoniously, match colors closely, fit pieces snugly, arrange controls conveniently, and provide ergonomics suitably. Expertise in creating and building interiors has less to do with advanced engineering than with coordination of hundreds of parts. This seemed a suitable job for an integration specialist.

JCI and Lear were the two principal suppliers to emerge as interior integrators into the twenty-first century. Their strategy was implemented by way of numerous acquisitions during the 1990s.

Interior Integration at JCI

JCI's major acquisition was Prince Corp., the sixty-first-largest parts supplier at the time, with $425 million in North American OEM sales at the time of the acquisition in 1996. Prince was founded in 1965 by Edgar Prince in Holland, Michigan, to make machine tools and auto parts. Under Edgar Prince's long-time leadership, the company remained extremely insular. All seven of its U.S. manufacturing facilities as well as research and corporate offices were in Holland, Michigan. The company had a minimal presence overseas other than one plant in Mexico, and it did not even maintain a sales office in the Detroit area.

Prince made headliners, door panels, and other individual interior components, such as consoles, grab handles, visors, armrests, and storage compartments. The Prince acquisition gave JCI the ability to supply all five major interior systems except instrument panels. Adding Prince increased JCI's share of the U.S. headliner market, for example, from 9 percent to 21 percent.

Edgar Prince gave only one authorized media interview, around 1980, and vowed never to speak on the record again because he felt he had been misquoted (Gardner 1996). After he died in 1995, his widow Elsa briefly ran the company and then sold it within a year to JCI. The machine tool business, Prince Machine, was sold in 2000 to Italy-based Idra Presse, and the combined company known as IdraPrince became the world's largest supplier of die casting equipment.

Despite its insularity, Prince had a reputation for innovation, such as buttons on the sun visor that open garage doors and enable security systems. Prince claimed to hold more patents than any other parts supplier except one—JCI—which was thus its most logical merger partner. JCI gave Prince considerable autonomy and maintained the corporate offices and technology center as well as the manufacturing facilities in Holland.

To make instrument panels, JCI established a joint venture with Japanese manufacturer Inoac Corp. in 1996. The joint venture produced instrument panels and other interior components under the name Intertec Systems, LLC, at a plant in Bardstown, Kentucky.

Interior Integration at Lear

Lear made 14 major acquisitions between 1995 and 1999. The three most significant acquisitions in Lear's transformation from seat supplier to interior integrator were Automotive Industries Holding Inc. (AIHI) in 1995, Masland Corp. in 1996, and United Technologies Automotive (UTA) in 1999. The AIHI, Masland, and UTA acquisitions gave Lear the ability to produce all major interior components.

AIHI was an interior door panel specialist with 8,000 employees at 14 U.S. and 8 foreign manufacturing facilities. The acquisition also brought Lear capabilities in armrests, center consoles, sun visors, package shelves, and other interior molded trim.

Masland Corp., acquired in 1996, was a leading manufacturer of carpeting, acoustical products, and luggage compartment trim. It was the fifty-fifth-largest supplier in 1996, with $500 million in sales and 3,000 employees. Founded in 1866 by Charles H. Masland to make textiles, the company produced automotive carpet beginning in 1922 with the Ford Model T. UTA had been the automotive division of United Technologies Corp. (UTC).

UTC's predecessor, United Aircraft and Transport Corp., was created in 1929 through the merger of several pioneering aviation firms, including Pratt and Whitney, which made aircraft engines; Sikorsky, which made helicopters; and Boeing Airline & Transport, which made airplanes and offered scheduled service. Federal government opposition to consolidation of airlines with manufacturers resulted in division of United into three companies in 1934: United Air Lines Transport (predecessor of United Airlines), Boeing Airplane Co. (manufacturer of airplanes), and United Aircraft Co. (manufacturer of engines and helicopters).

United Aircraft changed its name to United Technologies Corp. in 1975 when it began to diversify away from aircraft production through such acquisitions as Otis Elevator in 1976 and Carrier heating and air conditioning in 1979. UTC was one of the largest motor vehicle suppliers during the 1990s, but the sector accounted for only 10 percent of the company's total sales and an even lower share of profits when it was sold to Lear.

System Integration in Reverse?

JCI and Lear may be ready, willing, and able to supply entire interiors, and a few such orders were received from the Detroit 3. But early in the twenty-first century carmakers pulled back and hesitated to continue single sourcing of entire interiors.

Despite clear benefits of efficiency and quality in having a single supplier, carmakers were reluctant to turn over so much authority to a single supplier, fearing loss of control in the development and manufacturing processes. "[T]hey [GM officials] are re-examining their total interiors strategy . . . They have said they want to increase their involvement in the Tier 2 and Tier 3 sourcing decisions and relationships."[5] Consequently, carmakers have taken back control over interior design and selection of Tier 2 suppliers of interior components. "GM believes it can more effectively control costs and quality by bringing more work in-house" (Van Biesebroeck 2006, p. 209).

Forced to sell components and modules one at a time, the large interior integrators have struggled to make each portion of their firms profitable. In particular, the interior trim segment has proved less profitable than the seat assembly segment, calling into question the business model of interior integration. This has dragged down profits for the entire companies and forced them into cutbacks (Bowens and Sedgwick 2005).

Lear felt a "severely negative impact" on its financial position (Merrill Lynch 2007). As a result, the company shed its low value-added interior trim portion of the business. Collins & Aikman decided to auction itself off when it could not come up with a profitable business plan that would have allowed it to emerge from Chapter 11.

OUTLOOK AND UNCERTAINTIES

Regardless of the structure of the interior sector, seat plants in a JIT production environment continue to be located within 60 miles of an assembly plant. This relationship holds for every assembly plant in North America. It is driven by the bulkiness of seats and the large number of variations in seats for a given car model.

What is in play, however, is the future role of interior suppliers. As the Detroit 3 have backed away from commitments to interior integrators, market leader Toyota has moved in the opposite direction. In 2004 Toyota Boshoku, through the merger of several Toyota keiretsu companies, became Toyota's interior integrator. In its 2006 annual report, the company described itself as "an automotive systems supplier that considers the automobile's interior space in its totality, including seats, door trim, headliners and carpets (but excluding instrument panels). It integrates everything from conceptualization through product development, design, procurement and production" (Toyota Boshoku 2005, p. 3). Given its high dependency on a single customer, the fate of Toyota Boshoku as a systems integrator was tied to the future of Toyota. As Toyota was growing rapidly, Toyota Boshoku was likely to do so as well.

The wildcard in the restructuring of the interior sector has been private equity investors, which were especially active in investing in the motor vehicle parts sector during the first decade of the twenty-first century. Starting in 2005, Wilbur Ross, a self-made billionaire turned private equity investor, created International Automotive Components (IAC), designed to be "an interiors powerhouse in North America and abroad through the select purchase of financially troubled assets" (Barkholz 2007a). IAC's rationale was one of scale, not of systems integration. Prominent among its assets were interior trim plants formerly operated by Collins & Aikman and Lear (Snavely 2007a). The company quickly became one of the world's 40 largest suppliers. Instrument panels and door panels were responsible for more than half of IAC's sales (International Automotive Components 2007).

Notes

1. Donald Montroy, CSM Worldwide analyst, quoted in Wernle (2005c).
2. Eric Goldstein, Bear Stearns analyst, quoted in Sherefkin (1999b).
3. Betsy Meter, KPMG partner, quoted in Armstrong (2004b).
4. Jeff VanBuskirk, vice president of systems engineering and development for Rieter Automotive North America Inc., quoted in Armstrong (2004b).
5. Doug DelGrosso, Lear COO, quoted in Bowens and Sedgwick (2005).

8
Delivering the Goods

*We see a transmission not as a whole part, but as hundreds
of boxes of parts of all different shapes and sizes, each with
its own part number and its own location in warehouses we
have to manage.*[1]

The task of connecting the complex chain that links parts makers
with final assembly plants has been outsourced to logistics specialists.
Transport management is not a core competence of either carmakers or
parts suppliers. With widespread diffusion of just-in-time delivery, demand for pinpoint timing of several hundred daily deliveries per assembly plant has exceeded the capabilities of carmakers and suppliers, many
of whom traditionally relied on hand-drawn production flow charts. So
logistics specialists now sort out scheduling and hauling of parts from
lower tier to higher tier suppliers and from suppliers to assemblers.

"Logistics is a key foundation of our production system," according to Glenn Uminger, who was general manager of logistics at Toyota
Motor Manufacturing North America Inc. in 2004, "because if we don't
move material efficiently and in small lots we might lose many of the
benefits our production system principles stand for" (Terreri 2004).
"Logistics" is most simply "having the right thing, at the right place, at
the right time," according to *Logistics World* magazine (2008). For all
of its vaunted production system, Toyota was still sorting out delivery
routes with "plastic and crayons" in 2001, according to Uminger (Shea
2001).

> "[M]anufacturing gurus" effectively assume that the economic
> universe revolves around manufacturing . . . Those evaluating the
> economy and the future without the manufacturing bias typically
> see quite a different economic universe. The "supply chain" uni-
> verse would seem to provide an alternative concept to the "manu-
> facturing" universe—a universe where manufacturing is simply
> viewed as a link in the worldwide supply chain that includes all of
> the activities required to supply worldwide need. (McKee 2004a)

3PLS: MOVING THE FREIGHT AND MANAGING THE CHAIN

Logistics are provided by specialists known as third-party logistics (3PL) providers. A 3PL is an outsourced provider that manages all or a significant part of an organization's logistics requirements and performs transportation, location, and sometimes product consolidation activities (Logistics List 2006).

Logistics costs have risen in the United States from $521 billion in 1985 to $773 billion in 1995 and $1,305 billion in 2006. As a percentage of GDP, though, logistics costs declined from 12.3 percent in 1985 to 10.4 percent in 1995 and 9.9 percent in 2006. A sharp decline in inventory, as noted in Chapter 6, has accounted for most of the decline (Andel 2007; Wilson 2007).

The distinctive contribution of 3PLs in the production process has been to arrange two types of services for their customers: freight management and supply chain management. Freight management is arrangement of shipment of goods either through direct ownership of transport companies or through negotiations with other carriers. Supply chain management is coordination of pickup, storage, and delivery, often on a just-in-time basis.

In the logistics industry freight management is known as asset-based service because it involves the physical transfer of the goods. Supply chain management is known as non-asset-based service because it involves the flow of information about the goods. According to O'Reilly (2006), 46 percent of 3PLs were asset based in 2006, 19 percent were non-asset based, and 37 percent were both (O'Reilly's numbers totaled more than 100 percent). "Asset-based providers tout their investment in equipment, and the control they can leverage in coordinating transportation processes; non-asset 3PLs claim to bring a more objective and flexible approach to negotiating and securing capacity" (O'Reilly 2006).

Freight Movement

The physical transfer of goods requires two types of tangible assets. One is transportation equipment, including trucks, trains, ships, and airplanes, for hauling the goods from one place to another. The second type of tangible assets is buildings for storage and transfer of the goods.

Shipping

"On the transportation side, 3PLs are all the rage, as businesses find it increasingly irksome to manage rising fuel expenses, capacity and truck driver shortages, and equipment costs . . . reducing transportation costs is the top concern among their customers" (O'Reilly 2006). Transportation accounted for $801 billion of the $1,305 billion total logistics cost in the United States in 2006. Trucking accounted for $635 billion, other transportation for $166 billion, and carrying costs and administration for the remainder (Wilson 2007).

Passage of the Motor Carrier Act in 1980 substantially deregulated the trucking industry, enabling subsequent changes in the structure of the industry. The Motor Carrier Act of 1935 had given authority to regulate the trucking industry to the Interstate Commerce Commission, which had been regulating railroads since 1887. "ICC regulation reduced competition and made trucking inefficient . . . Truckers with authority to carry a product, such as tiles, from one city to another often lacked authority to haul anything on the return trip" (Moore 2002).

The regulatory environment made it virtually impossible for a trucking firm to add a new route except in the rare circumstance that no competitor opposed it. "The result was often bizarre. For example, a motor carrier with authority to travel from Cleveland to Buffalo that purchased another carrier or the carrier's rights to go from Buffalo to Pittsburgh was required to carry goods destined for Pittsburgh through Buffalo, even though the direct route was considerably shorter. In some cases carriers had to go hundreds of miles out of their way, adding many hours or even days to the transport" (Moore 2002). The 1980 Motor Carrier Act eliminated most restrictions on destinations that a carrier could serve, commodities that could be carried, and routes that could be used.

In the deregulated environment, trucking companies are offering three basic types of runs: dedicated contract carriage, less-than-truckload shipments, and milk runs. Dedicated contract carriage and less-than-truckload shipments were updated versions of long-standing forms of shipping. A moving van completely filled with the contents of an old house and completely unloaded at a new house is an example of a dedicated contract carriage. A mattress delivered from a furniture store that shares space with other furniture destined for other homes is an example of a less-than-truckload shipment.

In the motor vehicle industry, some trucks have offered dedicated contract carriage: they were completely filled with a single supplier's components and completely unloaded at a final assembly plant. Johnson Controls, for example, has delivered seats to final assembly plants in trucks that it has owned and operated. Less-than-truckload, though, has become less common in the motor vehicle industry than in the past because it has been superseded by the milk run.

A milk run or common carrier route is a routine trip involving stops at many places. A milk run visits a large number of suppliers on a recurring predictable schedule, such as the same time every day or week. It is more efficient than less-than-truckload for small batch delivery. Once limited to picking up routine parts from smaller suppliers, the milk run has become an important tool in just-in-time delivery because smaller batches can be sent more often than with dedicated truckloads. "We know we have to sacrifice some mileage, but the benefits are steady and level flows of material and higher order frequencies," stated Toyota's Glenn Uminger (Terreri 2004).

Distribution

The Detroit 3 traditionally took direct responsibility for most of their warehousing operations. Parts made in Michigan were stored until a sufficiently long train of fully loaded boxcars was ready to be put together for shipment to a branch plant. In the trucking era, distribution centers still play an important role, although parts come and go more quickly. GM ranked fifth in the United States in 2004 in square footage of privately or exclusively owned warehouse space, with 24 million square feet, behind UPS, Wal-Mart, Target, and Sysco.

Among logistics firms, DHL has been by far the largest owner of public or shared warehouse space, with 73 million square feet in 2005. Second-place UPS Supply Chain Services had 28 million square feet, which was counted separately from UPS delivery service's 78 million square feet (McKee 2004b). Warehousing accounts for about 10 percent of all logistics expenditures, small compared with the actual hauling of the goods, but production costs increase as inventory sits on the shelf of a warehouse. Therefore traditional warehousing is being replaced with cross-docking operations.

Cross-docking represents the physical receipt of goods and their immediate transfer to the next onward phase without the goods ever being brought into inventory. The 3PL operating the cross-docking facility unloads deliveries from multiple sources, sequences the parts, and delivers them to the appropriate locations along the final assembly line as needed. For example, deliveries into Toyota's assembly plant do not come directly from each of the company's 500 parts suppliers. Instead, parts are first shipped from suppliers to one of eight crossdocks. Upon arrival, products delivered from suppliers are unloaded and quickly repacked for delivery to an assembly line.

According to Glenn Uminger, "Crossdocks accumulate shipments from a region. Those shipments then get split according to plant requirements and are shipped directly from the crossdock to the plant . . . The crossdocks are located where we need them, based on volume" (Terreri 2004). Most parts sit at a Toyota crossdock for less than six hours, none for more than 12 hours. Parts are packaged in small standardized boxes that fit together like Legos to facilitate transfer from the crossdocks to the assembly plant.

Toyota no longer includes the term "inventory" in its corporate vocabulary—material flows continuously into its assembly plants, just as it does into competitors' plants operated on a just-in-time basis. Instead, Toyota refers to heijunka, or level flow, as the key concept in its production system concerning the movement of parts from its suppliers to its assembly plants. Reflecting Toyota's evolving view of materials handling, Mr. Uminger's job title changed from assistant general manager for production control in 2001 to general manager of logistics in 2004 (Shea 2001).

Supply Chain Management

The process of planning for the movement of all materials, funds, and related information, from pickup of raw materials to delivery of finished products, is called "supply chain management" (*Logistics World* 2007). "The supply chain is an integral part of the entire manufacturing process."[2]

To explain the purpose of supply chain management, 3PLs like to use diagrams. Typically, a "before" diagram shows a customer, such as a final assembly plant, at the center, connected to many freight haulers. The "after" diagram instead places the 3PL firm at the center, connected to many freight haulers at one end and the customer at the other end.

Penske Logistics, hired by Ford in 1999 as its lead logistics provider, described the inefficient logistics arrangements that it inherited from Ford:

> Penske Logistics began its relationship with Ford in 1996 as lead logistics provider (LLP) for Ford's assembly plant in Norfolk, Virginia. At the time, each of Ford's 20 North American assembly plants managed its own logistics operations. A decentralized approach provided total control of logistics at the plant level, but presented costly redundancies in materials handling and transportation.
>
> Under the plant-centric approach, suppliers would make multiple deliveries of the same parts to different plants. A supplier would pick up a small load, deliver it to one plant, pick up another small load of the same parts and deliver it to another plant. Carriers with half-empty trucks would often cross routes with each other en route to the same plant. (Penske Logistics 2007)

At a Ford assembly plant, "it was not uncommon on any day to have 22 different trucks arriving at the same part source to make pick-ups for 22 different locations" (Shister 2005). Aside from being highly inefficient, this design allowed for excessive inventory and storage costs at the plant level.

To better facilitate supply chain management, a 3PL plans the distribution network for a carmaker, optimizing routes across its plants to minimize fleet size and mileage. The 3PL rarely does all of its own hauling and some do none, so individual carriers are hired, presumably at favorable rates given the large scale of freight hauling being purchased by the 3PL. Information technology plays a key role in managing logistics and supply chain functions, including processing orders, inventory management, forecasting and planning, warehouse management, transport management, and tracking. Systems keep track of parts and provide visibility for each one from production to delivery.

Tight inventory control is crucial within a lean production process. Management of in-line sequencing typically begins with broadcasts from the assembly plant listing which cars are soon to move onto the assembly line and what components or subassemblies are required and in what order. "'What we have noticed is that the time requirements of the broadcasts keep getting shorter and shorter,' according to Penske Logistics senior vice president-automotive Ed Cumbo. 'We used to sometimes have four hours, but today it is mostly 90 minutes'" (Murphy 2004).

In accordance with principles of heijunka, Toyota identifies 12 delivery times during an eight-hour work shift, 40 minutes apart from each other. The company specifies the quantity of each part needed during each of the 12 deliveries. A typical two-shift daily operation therefore has 24 available delivery slots. "How we use those 24 order slots depends on the supplier, the volume, the distance and the efficiencies," according to Mr. Uminger (Terreri 2004).

Ideally, equal quantities of the part could be delivered each time, but that is not always possible. In some cases, the line may be running at a faster or slower speed during the various 40-minute periods, or the mix of specific models coming down the line may vary. In other cases, the nature of the part itself may not be amenable to 40-minute delivery intervals. In response to changing volume demand, Toyota can shift the number of daily deliveries of a particular part to any number that will divide into 24.

The Detroit 3 have tried to emulate the Toyota system, but they have some catching up to do. "In regard to supply-chain management, the Big Three U.S. automakers have publicly adopted some version of lean manufacturing and JIT logistics. Our [Liker and Wu] data showed, however, that there was still room for improvement. The same suppliers had much leaner operations within their plants and in their logistics when serving Japanese customers" (Liker and Wu 2000, p. 92).

Leading Motor Vehicle 3PLs

As 3PL services have expanded rapidly, firms have been consolidating into fewer larger firms. Worldwide, the largest 3PL—DHL—had $31 billion in revenue in 2006, and the next four combined had $44 billion.

Four of the world's five largest 3PLs in 2007 were European owned: DHL, Kuehne + Nagel International, Schenker, and Panalpina. UPS, based in the United States, was the only non-European firm to crack the top five.

> History, empire and exports helped create the large European 3PLs . . . [The top European 3PLs] have been leading forwarders and transportation management 3PLs in Europe for decades . . . European countries, which have always had significantly more cross-border traffic, have relied more on outsourcing than Americans, especially since World War II . . .
>
> Over the last few years nearly every company in Europe has been able to take some advantage of the free movement of goods across borders. This shift has been good for the large European 3PLs, but cultural differences still prevent centralization of operations at U.S. levels. Most 3PL operations in Europe still have to be designed on a country-by-country basis to be effective. (Foster and Armstrong 2004)

The five largest 3PLs serving the U.S. auto industry in 2007 were Ryder, Penske Logistics, UPS, CEVA Logistics, and DHL. Only two of the five—DHL and UPS—are also ranked among the five largest 3PLs worldwide in 2007. CEVA, Penske, and Ryder were the world's eighth, fourteenth, and fifteenth largest, respectively (Armstrong and Foster 2007).

Ryder

The largest 3PL serving the U.S. auto industry has been Ryder Logistics. The company was started in 1933 by James A. Ryder in Miami, Florida, with one truck. Ryder was the largest hauler of finished vehicles in the United States when it decided to get out of the business of directly running its own trucks. The company sold Ryder Freight System in 1989, the One Way Consumer Truck Rental division in 1996, and the Automotive Carrier division in 1997.

Instead, Ryder has concentrated on arranging hauling for its customers, as well as leasing and renting vehicles. The acquisition of a logistics management company, LogiCorp, in 1994 made Ryder the leading provider of inbound logistics in the U.S. automotive industry. "Ryder doesn't drive trucks or move packages, they manage information: procurement support, carrier relationships and performance, freight billing, auditing, and payment, and negotiate rates for transportation" (Konicki 2001).

Ryder's relationship with Chrysler has been particularly strong:

> [Chrysler] outlines for Ryder the network surrounding a particular
> physical location, including what will be built at that location, the
> preferred supplier sources, rate structures, available equipment,
> and densities. Ryder then designs a proposed logistics network de-
> tailing when certain trucks will be loaded at a particular supplier,
> the departure time of these trailers from the supplier, when parts
> will be delivered at a particular plant, and when that truck will be
> unloaded. (Terreri 2004)

For GM, Ryder has optimized the logistics network and manages
inbound freight at Saturn's Spring Hill final assembly plant. Penske
manages the work inside Saturn's logistics optimization center, while
Ryder manages the milk runs from suppliers to the center as well as
shuttles from the center to the final assembly plant one mile away.

Penske

The other leading U.S.-owned auto industry 3PL has been Penske
Logistics, a subsidiary of Penske Truck Leasing, the largest truck rental
and leasing company in the United States. Founder Roger S. Penske
was well known as a successful race-car driver during the 1950s and
1960s, then as sponsor of a successful NASCAR racing team after retiring as a driver in 1965. Penske also acquired new-car dealerships and
parts suppliers.

The major work of Penske Logistics has been with Ford. As described earlier in the chapter, Penske created, implemented, and operated a centralized logistics network for handling all inbound materials
handling at Ford's assembly and stamping plants.

Penske trained more than 1,500 suppliers on a uniform set of pro-
cedures and logistics technologies. Carriers were required to follow
routes set by Penske and to pick up and deliver within 15 minutes of
schedule. Loads were tracked through satellite communications and engine monitoring systems on all trucks. Shipments were consolidated
at 10 Order Dispatch Centers (ODCs). *World Trade Magazine* named
Ford Manufacturer of the Year for Global Supply Chain Excellence in
2005. The award cited a 15 percent reduction in plant inventory and a
clearer understanding of the variation in freight costs among individual
plants and carriers (Shister 2005).

UPS

Third among U.S.-owned firms in the auto industry was UPS Supply Chain Solutions. The company was the largest U.S.-based 3PL overall, and it was ranked fourth internationally in 2007. UPS created a Logistics Group in 1993 to provide supply chain management and an Automotive Services unit within its Logistics Group in 2000. Logistics accounted for only $8 billion of the company's $48 billion revenues in 2006, with the bulk generated by package delivery. UPS has been a highly recognizable brand in the United States for its fleet of brown package delivery trucks.

The company, originally known as American Messenger Co., was founded in Seattle, Washington, in 1907, by 19-year-old James E. Casey. Messages telephoned to the company's office were delivered by Casey's brother George and several other teenagers on foot or bicycle. As the messenger business declined, the company refocused on package delivery, especially for retailers. Large department stores in Seattle were the company's major clients. The company also delivered special delivery mail in the Seattle area for the Post Office.

UPS expanded beyond Seattle during the 1920s, but growth was hindered by federal and state regulations prohibiting common carrier competition with the Post Office. Interstate Commerce Commission authority was needed for each state border that was crossed, and each state had to authorize the movement of packages within its borders. Packages often had to be transferred between several carriers before they reached their final destinations. UPS battled federal and state regulators for two decades beginning in the 1950s for the right to carry packages across state lines. Not until 1975 did UPS become the first package delivery company permitted to delivery anywhere in all 48 contiguous states.

CEVA

CEVA, the leading automotive 3PL worldwide, was created in 2006 when the British-based Apollo Management equity firm acquired and renamed the logistics operations of TNT. Apollo shed underperforming contracts, standardized processes worldwide, and integrated divisions, and concentrated on six high-performing sectors, including automotive, which accounted for 40 percent of CEVA's revenue in 2006 (Armstrong and Foster 2007).

The predecessor of TNT was Thomas Nationwide Transport, founded in 1946 by Ken Thomas to provide express delivery service in Australia. A logistics division set up in the United Kingdom in 1985 became the motor vehicle industry's largest 3PL during the 1990s.

TNT started logistics services in North America during the 1980s and became a major player when it acquired logistics provider CTI LOGISTX in 2000 from rail and shipping company CSX Corporation. CTI, originally Customized Transportation Inc., was established in 1981 and became a subsidiary of CSX in 1993.

TNT was acquired in 1996 by the Netherlands postal service Koninklijke PTT Nederland (KPN), which had been privatized by the Dutch government seven years earlier. Until the holding company for TNT Logistics and Royal TPG Post was sold to Apollo, it was the largest private employer in the Netherlands.

DHL

DHL was the world's largest 3PL in 2006, with revenues twice as high as the second largest 3PL. When it was created in 1969, DHL initially specialized in international air express. It was named for the initials of the three founders, Adrian Dalsey, Larry Hillblom, and Robert Lynn. DHL was sold to the German post office Deutsche Post World in 2002, and it became the largest 3PL when it acquired the British-based logistics firm Exel in 2005.

Exel in turn had become the leading 3PL through a 2000 merger of two venerable British firms, National Freight Company Ltd. and Ocean Steam Ship Company. National had moved into contract logistics using Exel as a brand name in 1989. Ocean, founded in 1865, was a freight forwarding firm, originally (as the name suggested) by sea. Exel "was made from two British companies meant to be merged together. [National's] contract logistics and [Ocean's] freight forwarding have complemented each other well" (Foster and Armstrong 2004). Exel's distinctive contribution to auto industry logistics had been leadership in developing supplier parks in Europe (see below).

COORDINATING AND MANAGING LOGISTICS

"The utter lack of coordination among 3PLs, carriers, parts suppliers and OEMs is a modern equivalent of the Tower of Babel story."[3] Difficulties include the following: inadequately developed company networks, insufficiently defined tasks and responsibilities within company networks, slow implementation of optimization activities because of poor information and coordination management, and difficulties in calculating and allocating cost and savings between partners (European 4PL Research Club n.d.). "Each car manufacturer has its own system and each logistics provider has its own system. If you're a supplier that does 70 percent of your business with one OEM then that's great. If you are ArvinMeritor or Robert Bosch and you are doing business with everybody, then all of a sudden you are working with seven, eight different systems to do the same thing."[4]

Two basic strategies have emerged to organize the complexities of logistics. One has been to add another layer of logistics management: in other words, to manage the managers. The other has been to add another layer of physical facilities: in other words, the staging areas.

4PL Logistics: Adding Value or Adding Cost?

The term 4PL (Fourth Party Logistics) has sometimes been applied to the coordination by a single logistics firm of all companies involved along the supply chain. "The definition of a 4PL is to manage 3PLs."[5]

A 4PL addresses the challenges of coordinating multiple 3PLs "through the integrative approach of designing, coordinating, and controlling agile supply networks. The decisive task of the 4PL provider is to embrace the process integration of single, independent companies in an overall concept with the objective of enhancing the quality and efficiency of the value chain and thereby unlocking competitive advantage" (European 4PL Research Club n.d.).

A 4PL is different from a 3PL because it plans, steers, and controls the flow of information and capital, not just material, in accordance with a client's long-term strategic objectives (Figure 8.1). The essence of a 4PL is integrating information management with coordination of multiple 3PLs. A 4PL does not actually supply the underlying logistical

Figure 8.1 Hierarchy of Supply Chain Management

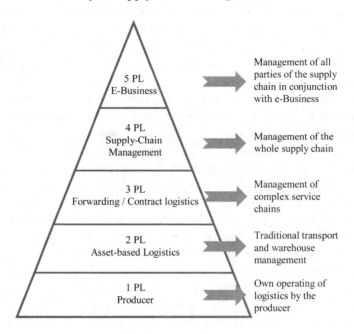

SOURCE: Adapted by the authors from the Hoyer Web site (http://www.hoyer-group
.com/logistikE/html/3pl4pl.html).

services, a job still reserved for 3PLs. "The rise of 4PLs stems in part from the fact that outsourcing is now a global endeavor. The management and integration of dispersed logistics players—each bound by local variations in language, currency, trade law, and so on—is an enormous undertaking. In hiring a 4PL, an enterprise must find a partner that understands its special logistics needs, one that can share in the risks and rewards of reinventing a significant portion of its business" (Schwartz 2003).

A 4PL needs IT capabilities, including Web-based capabilities, so that it can manage each logistics participant throughout the supply chain, as well as control inventory and shipments. Armed with this capability and information from each link in the supply chain, the 4PL can optimize inventory, transportation, and warehousing.

The leading IT provider of 4PL services was Accenture, formerly Andersen Consulting, which actually trademarked the term "4PL" in 1996. Accenture defined 4PL as "an integrator that assembles the resources, capabilities and technology of its own organization or other organizations to design, build, and run comprehensive supply-chain solutions" (Bumstead and Cannons 2002). According to Accenture associate partner James W. Moore, "The key thing that is happening in the supply chain is that time now is often more important than geography," and management of time is an IT skill. "The core value offered by 4PLs is in managing and integrating the flow of information between hundreds of outsourced supply chain partners and the enterprises that employ them. '4PLs manage other 3PLs and transportation carriers to execute the work and oversee the solution design and performance of those entities that work for them,' states Tom McKenna, senior vice president of logistics engineering at Penske Logistics" (Schwartz 2003).

Leading 3PLs have questioned the need for an additional player. They argued that putting another layer in the supply chain raised costs without adding value. Haulers claimed that consultants created the 4PL concept simply to siphon off an ongoing revenue stream from the 3PLs. The larger 3PLs were ready and able to provide the coordination services, which they preferred to call "logistics integrator" or "lead logistics provider," both terms that have been around for a long time (Hoffman 2000).

The term "4PL" itself has rankled 3PLs, as it was trademarked, and by an IT firm to boot. Ryder CEO Gregory Swienton said, "I hate the term 4PL. I even hate the term 3PL. We say 'lead logistics'" (Armbruster 2002b). Other 3PLs "deftly hijacked the new 4PL term to give them license to move into other higher margin areas of the supply-chain" (Bumstead and Cannons 2002).

Vascor and Vector have been the leading 4PLs associated with the U.S. motor vehicle industry. The two were created by Toyota and GM, respectively, specifically to coordinate their complex logistics. However, because of widespread hostility to the term among the 3PL community, neither Vascor nor Vector has been referred to as a 4PL.

Vascor, Toyota's 4PL

Toyota turned over 4PL responsibility for its Georgetown complex to Vascor, Ltd. in 1987. The company's name was an acronym for "value-added service corporation." Vascor was a joint venture between Fujitrans Corp. and APL Logistics. Fujitrans was a shipping company, founded in Nagoya, Japan, in 1952. The company owned a fleet of ships and specialized primarily in freight handling and warehousing within Japan. APL, originally American President Lines, was created in 1848 to carry passengers on the S.S. California from New York to San Francisco for the gold rush. The company established the first trans-Pacific route between the United States and China in 1867. APL was acquired in 1997 by the much smaller NOL Group, founded in 1968 as Neptune Orient Lines, based in Singapore and one-third owned by the Singapore government.

Vascor has played a dual role for Toyota as operator and coordinator. As operator, Vascor would get a month's worth of milk-run routes to pick up from a network of 500 suppliers. Vascor delivered to one of eight crossdocks that Toyota's 3PLs operated for the company. In that function, Vascor also coordinated the outbound movement of finished vehicles to dealers.

Vascor has managed the various transportation and distribution service providers to get parts into the plants on a just-in-time basis. Routes have been structured precisely to get seats, interior trim, and other parts from suppliers or sequencing centers to plants in accordance with production schedules. Vascor assigned routes to partner carriers, schedules less-than-truckload shipments, and organizes intermodal transfers. Given the need for a precise timetable of truck arrivals at the plant because of sequencing, global positioning systems have been used to track the milk-run fleet. If a driver encountered an "exception"—that is, is running late—Vascor immediately informed a large number of people at Toyota (Terreri 2004).

Vector, GM's 4PL

Vector was established in 2000 to run GM's supply chain in the United States. Controlling interest was originally held by Menlo Worldwide, a leading 3PL that was founded in 1990.

CNF, originally Consolidated Truck Lines, combined several Portland, Oregon, freight companies that were acquired in 1929 by Leland James. A decade later, to provide his freight company with suitable trucks, James established Freightways Manufacturing Co., later known as Freightliner Corp. CNF became a leading international freight forwarder specializing in heavy air cargo, especially after acquiring Emery Air Freight Corp. in 1989. Menlo Logistics was established in 1990 to meet distribution services beyond traditional trucking and air freight.

CNF spun off its original trucking operations into a separate company in 1996. Viewed as uncompetitive, saddled with a high wage unionized workforce, the spun-off freight hauler declared bankruptcy in 2002. CNF was restructured around Emery Worldwide air freight service and Menlo Logistics (Cottrill 2000).

CNF provided Vector with the initial funding, skills, and technology to manage GM's global network of logistics service providers. GM provided strategic planning and worked with Vector to identify projects to move from GM staff over to Vector (Bumstead and Cannons 2002). Vector's first accomplishment was a redesign of GM's Logistics Inbound Material Network to reduce the aggregate travel of all inbound carriers by 44 million miles in 2004. At 6.2 miles per gallon per truck, the reduction saved 7 million gallons of diesel fuel and $59 million.

GM bought out Menlo in 2006 and brought Vector in-house. "GM apparently came to the conclusion that managing inbound supply chain operations had become a core competency that it wanted to manage itself" (Armstrong and Foster 2007, p. 32).

Staging Deliveries

Carmakers have also addressed the complexities associated with the frequency and volume of deliveries to their assembly plants through establishment of satellite facilities, including supplier parks and distribution centers. These facilities are not warehouses storing large inventories of not-yet-needed parts. Rather, they move parts quickly from suppliers to final assembly in a logical sequence that can be handled more smoothly in a building dedicated to the purpose rather than inside the final assembly plant.

Supplier parks

A supplier park is a campus containing a number of suppliers situated in close proximity to a final assembly plant. In Europe, supplier parks have been opened by Ford near assembly plants in Valencia, Spain, and Saarlouis, Germany, and by Nissan near its assembly plant in Sunderland, England. Traffic congestion in Germany and the remoteness of southern Spain and northern England from Europe's supplier base influenced the decision to establish supplier parks there. Supplier parks have also been opened in developing countries like India, where poor roads make just-in-time delivery difficult, and utilities such as water and electricity are hard to get.

In the United States, Ford opened the first full-fledged supplier park in Chicago. Ford has been assembling cars at its Torrence Avenue plant located on the far South Side of Chicago, on the banks of the Calumet River, since 1924. As production of the Taurus car neared the end of its run at the Chicago assembly plant, Ford officials weighed their options. On the plus side, the plant had a productive workforce amenable to flexible work rules, and a local government willing to do what it would take to keep the plant open. On the other hand, the plant was Ford's oldest and faced severe logistics challenges. Ultimately, Ford decided to retool the plant for new models.

Logistics issues would be addressed by opening a supplier park adjacent to the assembly plant. Ford's Chicago supplier park would be designed to reduce shipping costs and inventory, to allow more flexibility to changes in production mix, and to more quickly identify (and solve) quality problems.

Ford began talking with local government officials about the supplier park idea in 1999. A deal was announced a year later. A supplier park was to be located on a contaminated site, formerly occupied by Republic Steel, adjacent to the Torrence Avenue assembly plant. Ford's real estate arm, Ford Land, chose CenterPoint Properties Trust, the largest owner and developer of industrial property in Chicago, to manage the supplier park and to entice Ford suppliers to lease space there.

Naturally, local government incentives were forthcoming. Ultimately, the city of Chicago and state of Illinois split about evenly $100 million in roadway improvements, including the relocation of Torrence Avenue 100 feet to the east to accommodate new loading-dock facilities for the assembly plant. The state provided $4.8 million in Illinois FIRST funds for urban brownfield restoration, plus $6 million for job training. The city also contributed $11 million in tax increment financing (Kachadourian 2000; Mayne 2002).

Initially attracted to the supplier park were nine suppliers, a mix of large and small. Five large tenants included Brose Automotive, Plastech Engineered Products, Tower Automotive, Visteon, and ZF Group.

Ford's Chicago assembly plant received door modules from Brose, plastic body parts from Plastech, floor pans and chassis components from Tower, instrument panels and engine-related components from Visteon, and suspension components from ZF. S-Y Wiring Technologies, a joint venture between two large suppliers, Siemens VDO Automotive Group and Yazaki Corp., supplied wiring to both Ford and the other suppliers in the park.

Two smaller suppliers attracted to the supplier park were Sanderson, which supplied stampings, and Summit Polymers, which supplied plastic parts. The ninth original tenant, Conau-Pico, was not actually a parts supplier; rather it was the largest supplier of automation equipment for assembly plants.

For all of the hype about the supplier park, the most important components still arrived at the Chicago assembly plant through conventional sources. Engines and transmissions came from Ford's powertrain facilities in Ohio. Stampings came from Ford's 1940s-era Chicago Heights facility, 10 miles south of the assembly plant. Lear Corp., as was its custom, built its own seat plant one-half mile from the Ford assembly plant and supplied headliners and other interior parts from a facility in Hammond, Indiana, 5 miles away.

Ford reported that the average distance materials had to be transported to the Chicago assembly plant declined from 457 miles for Taurus production to 121 miles for the new models (Mayne 2002). The figure was probably the average distance traveled by the 600 trucks arriving each day at the assembly plant, and was not weighted by value or weight of the individual components.

Did Ford's Chicago supplier park represent the wave of the future? Two *Automotive News* headlines two months apart equivocated

- "Automakers See Payoffs in Supplier Parks" (August 5, 2002), and
- "Automakers Are Divided on Supplier Parks" (October 7, 2002).

The first article, complete with a sketch of the then-future Chicago supplier park that inevitably bore little resemblance to the completed complex, emphasized Ford's perspective. "Besides improving logistics itself and the cost to ship, it provides the ability to sequence directly to the assembly plant door," according to Roman Krygier, then Ford's group vice president of manufacturing and quality. "Quality gets a significant improvement because you don't have a long pipeline, and response to change is much better. It's hard to mention all the benefits because what you really do is link the supplier" (Wilson 2002b).

Two months later, *Automotive News* reported, "Supplier parks—the concept of housing major suppliers next to assembly plants—aren't quite working out as planned." Toyota and Honda in particular did not seem especially fond of the supplier park concept. "Toyota developed an electronic version of its kanban, or card, reordering system that adjusts to shopping time from more distant suppliers to smooth the flow of parts." And Honda has relied on a crossdock system (Cullen 2002). In other words, if Toyota and Honda already managed their inbound freight efficiently, what value would a supplier park add for them? The fact that Ford did not roll out supplier parks across its North American assembly operations supported the second point of view.

Supplier parks have been implemented, however, by a number of assembly facilities located at the southern end of Auto Alley, such as Toyota's truck plant in San Antonio and Nissan's assembly plant in Mississippi. If an assembly facility is at the fringe of or actually outside Auto Alley, a supplier park is a way to make up for the lack of a well-developed regional supply base.

A different model of bringing a select group of suppliers close to the assembly line has been put into place at Chrysler's Toledo assembly plant. Here a small number of strategic suppliers have been brought into the assembly plant (see Chapter 11).

Distribution centers

Distribution centers are being built as staging areas to facilitate the timely arrival of parts at final assembly plants. Carmakers now require delivery of parts not merely on a just-in-time basis, but more importantly, in the correct sequence. Rather than just-in-time, this trend has been called just-in-sequence. In order to meet these requirements, the line between supplier and logistics provider sometimes gets erased. State-of-the-art distribution centers perform a number of so-called sequencing and kitting operations. The value added consists not in producing parts but in getting them ready to be sent to the assembly line in the right order of the available variations. A sequencing and kitting operation can also include unpacking and prepping parts for assembly. An example is plants that put tires on wheels (not producing either of these two parts). A small company named T&W Assembly in 2005 supplied all the three Mississippi-based assembly plants from three dedicated distribution centers with tires and wheels.

Carmakers tell suppliers what specific vehicles will be built on which days. "The suppliers then determine what assemblies to make—interior dashboards, for instance—produce them, then sequence delivery in the exact order of the manufacturing production run" (Harrington 2007).

A distribution center (DC) may serve a single assembly plant or it may serve multiple assembly plants. "A 3PL may pick up material from nearby suppliers, crossdock it, split out what's going to the local OEM plant, and load the rest on a truck for delivery to another DC or plant," according to Vascor vice president Jim Brutsman (Harrington 2007).

Just-in-time meant frequent deliveries from suppliers to final assembly plants in small batches. Just-in-sequence has meant moving larger batches less frequently from suppliers to distribution centers and then moving small batches more frequently from distribution centers to final assembly plants. "Instead of a 3PL delivering to an assembler from a supplier 16 times a day, it may go to the supplier twice a day, bring the materials to the DC, then move from there 16 times to the OEM plant." This arrangement trades transportation costs for distribution center costs (Harrington 2007).

According to another Vascor vice president, Dan Greenberg,

> The plant still receives the same 16 deliveries, but the external flow makes more economic sense. If, for example, the 3PL moves material from a supplier 100 miles away from the OEM, a roundtrip runs 200 miles. Delivering 16 times a day equals 3,200 miles.
>
> If, on the other hand, the 3PL moves material from the supplier twice a day in larger quantities, and puts the shipments in a distribution center close to the OEM's plant, travel distance is reduced to 400 miles. (Harrington 2007)

OUTLOOK AND UNCERTAINTIES

Efficient logistics is the thread that holds together all of the changes in producer–supplier relations outlined in this book. It has made feasible the business model by which carmakers outsource most of the value of the vehicle to independent suppliers. Large modules can arrive at the final assembly line ready for installation moments before needed, eliminating costly inventory. "Clearly, logistics outsourcers are using 3PL partnerships to strategically shift the way they approach and manage their supply chains. It's no longer simply a matter of cutting costs or accessing capacity. 3PLs and their customers are digging deeper into the supply chain to look at how they can apply technology to business processes—beginning with suppliers and inbound product movement—to reduce inventory, match available capacity to demand, and streamline costs in a more organic way" (O'Reilly 2006).

Thanks to efficient logistics, the network of suppliers around an assembly plant described in Chapter 6 can be rather loose. Suppliers do not have to be bunched up in the immediate vicinity of an assembly plant, competing for the same labor supply and infrastructure investment. The most important unit of delivery time is one day, not one hour, thanks to efficient logistics.

The challenge for carmakers is that they have outsourced logistics to companies that, with some exceptions, do not have historic ties to the auto industry. In other words, 3PLs know computers and spreadsheets, but how well do they know seats and engines? Even more challenging for carmakers will be integrating parts sourced from China into the supply chain. To date, China has been the source of a small but growing percentage of components used in the United States. As carmakers stretch their supply chains around the globe, many are seeking help from large 3PL providers.

> [S]ourcing and manufacturing in China ties up an additional six weeks' worth of capital while goods are in transit. It is vital that companies stay on top of where that inventory is at any point in time and be able to make decisions to keep the supply chain flowing. Lead logistics 3PLs have the state-of-the-art systems, the web-based track-and-trace interfaces, and the event management capability needed to manage these long, risky supply chains. The next tier of 3PLs below the Top 25 does not yet have these systems or these abilities. A big differentiator between the major-league 3PLs and everyone else is the ability to spend the money and build this systems capability. (Foster and Armstrong 2004)

The challenge for suppliers is somewhat different. Because they ship to more than one carmaker, they must work with more than one

3PL. The benefits they have been receiving in streamlined delivery schedules have been at least partially offset by the costs they have incurred in having to learn the distinctive practices of several 3PLs. "The one-stop shop philosophy is no longer as practical as it once was. Businesses have less flexibility with only one 3PL, particularly when planning contingencies or shifting in and out of markets. Having multiple logistics providers also gives companies greater leverage to benchmark performance, which in turn holds 3PLs accountable for meeting expected service requirements" (O'Reilly 2006).

Despite initial claims that the arrival of just-in-time production would considerably tighten the physical linkages between assemblers and their suppliers, we observe a rather loose geographical connection of the supply chain. Key to this development is the availability of a well-developed transportation infrastructure. In combination with the use of logistics services, it allows production facilities to be closely linked operationally without having to be physically close.

Notes

1. Bill Naples, transportation manager, Ford Customer Service Division, Livonia, quoted in Terreri (2004).
2. Tim Connearney, materials director for Saturn, quoted in Terreri (2004).
3. Tom Jones, Ryder Logistics official, quoted in Buss (2004).
4. Vic Giardini, supply chain management director, ArvinMeritor, quoted in *Automotive Logistics* (2004).
5. Jim Allen, CNF spokesman, quoted in Armbruster (2002a).

Part 3

Shifting Fortunes along Auto Alley

When GM, Ford, and Chrysler controlled more than 90 percent of the U.S. auto industry as "the Big Three," southeastern Michigan was the center of auto manufacturing, research, and administration, and "Detroit" was a one-word term that encompassed the totality of the U.S. auto industry. At the peak of their dominance during the 1950s, the Big Three employed more than 400,000 people in Michigan. As described in earlier chapters, parts suppliers even more than carmakers were clustered in Michigan.

As the Big Three—now more accurately referred to as the Detroit 3—lost market share to foreign-owned carmakers, "Detroit" became shorthand for the declining remnants of the industry still in the hands of GM, Ford, and Chrysler. Michigan auto industry employment declined about 6 percent per year during the early twenty-first century.

Despite Michigan's decline, at a national scale the U.S. auto industry remains very highly clustered in a small portion of the country. More than three-fourths of auto industry jobs and facilities are packed into an area that comprises only 2 percent of the land of the United States.

The auto-producing area has a distinctive shape: a narrow corridor roughly 700 miles long and often less than 100 miles wide through the interior of the United States between the Great Lakes and the Gulf of Mexico. The spine of the corridor is formed by two north–south interstate highways, I-65 and I-75, which run within 100 miles of each other for the most part. East–west interstates including I-40, I-64, and I-70 form ladders connecting the two north–south routes. The corridor is commonly referred to as Auto Alley.

Interstate 65 runs 1,000 miles between Gary, Indiana, near Lake Michigan, and Mobile, Alabama, near the Gulf of Mexico. The Auto Alley portion of I-65 passes through Indianapolis, Indiana; Louisville, Kentucky; Nashville, Tennessee; and Birmingham, Alabama. Interstate 75 runs 2,000 miles between Sault Ste. Marie in Michigan's Upper Peninsula and Fort Lauderdale, Florida. Within Auto Alley, I-75 passes through Detroit and Flint, Michigan; Toledo,

Dayton, and Cincinnati, Ohio; Lexington, Kentucky; Knoxville and Chattanooga, Tennessee; and Atlanta, Georgia.

Seven hundred miles south of Michigan, Alabama was one of the poorest states in the country for much of the twentieth century. Per capita income and car ownership rates were 50 percent lower in Alabama than in Michigan in 1950. Investment in all-new and expanded factories totaled $35 million in Alabama in 1952 compared with $218 million in Michigan, and manufacturing wages totaled $700 million in Alabama compared with $6 billion in Michigan.

This section examines reasons for the industry's clustering in Auto Alley between Alabama on the south and Michigan on the north. Michigan remains a major center of automotive production, but most of the industry's growth of late has been further south. As a result, Alabama was tied with Illinois and Indiana for fourth place in number of assembly plants in 2007, behind only Michigan, Ohio, and Missouri.

The first chapter of this section describes the emergence and current structure of Auto Alley. The nature of the parts produced as well as the nationality of the supplier company influence specific locations within Auto Alley. Chapters 10 and 11 describe the pull towards the southern end of Auto Alley for several types of parts, including tires and glass (Chapter 10) and chassis (Chapter 11).

Chapter 12 explains how labor was the principal factor underlying the relative attractiveness of the southern end of Auto Alley as the location of choice for new assembly plants and parts suppliers. Of critical importance has been the difference between the northern and southern ends of Auto Alley in labor relations, especially the role of unions.

9
Emergence of Auto Alley

To be honest, five years ago, I didn't even know where Alabama was, much less think that I would be living there.[1]

Auto Alley became the home of the U.S. auto industry primarily because of transport costs. The most critical transport factor for carmakers is the cost of shipping vehicles from final assembly plants to customers. Because assembled vehicles are bulky and fragile and tie up a lot of capital, it is imperative that they be delivered to customers as quickly as possible.

At first glance, the optimal location for an assembly plant would be the point that minimizes the aggregate travel to all of its customers throughout the United States, as well as Canada and Mexico. Each model would have its own optimal location, depending on the particular distribution of its customer base. For a vehicle with a similar market share in every region of the country, the optimal location would probably be near the center of U.S. population, which is currently in Missouri.

In reality, Missouri is west of the optimal location, because the cost per mile of shipping vehicles is not uniform. For vehicles that leave the assembly plant by truck, delivery that takes more than one day adds considerable cost. If overnight travel is required, the vehicles may as well be loaded on trains, which have a much higher cost per mile than trucks for short distances but a lower cost per mile for long trips. So the optimal location for an assembly plant is actually the point that maximizes the number of customers who can be reached within a one-day drive. For most carmakers, that optimal location is somewhere in Auto Alley (see Figure 9.1).

Figure 9.1 Close-up of Auto Alley

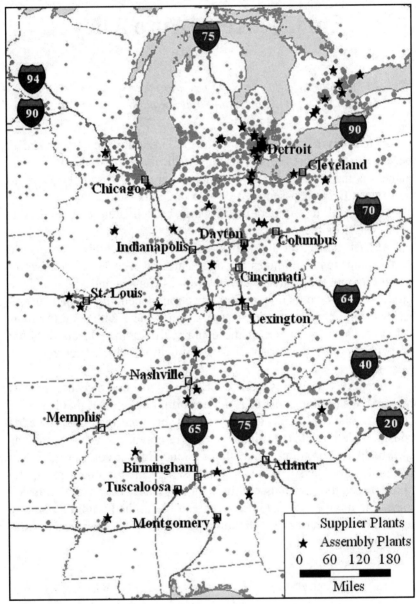

NOTE: Empty boxes denote cities.
SOURCE: Adapted by the authors from ELM International and other sources.

BEFORE AUTO ALLEY

The geographical arrangement of motor vehicle production in the United States has changed three times. The first geographical change took place around 1900 and the second around 1910. The third geographic shift, which resulted in the creation of the modern Auto Alley, began about 1980.

When commercial production began in the 1890s, most motor vehicles were produced in the Northeast, between Boston and Philadelphia. Most customers for early vehicles were also in the Northeast, which was the wealthiest, most populous, and most densely built-up region in the United States at the time.

When the industry was still in its infancy, most motor vehicle production shifted to southeastern Michigan during the first decade of the twentieth century. By 1913, 80 percent of U.S. motor vehicle production was concentrated in the area. As explained earlier in the book, Michigan had already been established as the center of production for key components, notably gasoline engines and carriage bodies. Production also clustered in Michigan because venture capital was more readily available there than it was from the staid banks of Wall Street.

Between the 1910s and 1980s, most parts were produced in Michigan, but carmakers opened branch assembly plants (that is, assembly plants producing the same models as a plant in the Midwest) elsewhere in the United States, near big cities, such as Los Angeles and New York. Carmakers calculated that it was much cheaper and safer to ship parts long distances and put together finished vehicles as close as possible to customers.

Since the late 1970s, nearly all new final assembly plants and most parts suppliers have been located within Auto Alley. Branch assembly plants elsewhere in the country have been closed. Facilities have been located in various places within Auto Alley, depending on the particular needs and priorities of the company.

Branch Assembly Plants

Between the two world wars, the Detroit 3 made most of their parts in Michigan and shipped them to branch assembly plants around the country. Ford pioneered construction of branch assembly plants as part of its strategy of minimizing Model T production costs in order to reduce its selling price and make it affordable for most Americans.

Ford's brilliant first sales manager, Norval Hawkins, proposed "establishment of assembling plants all over the world, and shipping in knockdown condition from the plant in Detroit the pieces and parts that went to make up this car." Hawkins "spent six weeks in loading, unloading and reloading freight cars to find out just how they could pack the stuff in . . ." (Goodenough 1925, p. 183). He eventually determined that the equivalent of 26 vehicles could be shipped in knocked-down form in railroad cars in the same space as seven or eight fully assembled ones (*Dodge et al. v. Commissioner of Internal Revenue* 1927).

Ford's first branch assembly plant was opened in Kansas City in 1912. By 1917, Ford was assembling identical Model T's in 30 locations, including Highland Park, Michigan. Ford embarked on a second wave of construction of branch assembly plants during the 1920s, including several at new locations, as well as larger, more modern replacements for most of the ones built only a decade earlier. Ford's all-time high of 32 branch assembly plants was reached in 1925 (Rubenstein 1992). About half of the plants were permanently closed during the Depression. Ford resumed production after World War II with 15 branch assembly plants, 11 for Ford and 4 for Lincoln and Mercury (Rubenstein 1992).

Ford made nearly all of the parts at its Highland Park complex and shipped them by rail to the branch assembly plants. Parts purchased from suppliers, notably bodies and tires, were shipped directly to the branch assembly plants rather than through Highland Park. Railroad companies charged between second- and sixth-class rates to ship parts, much lower than the rate charged for assembled vehicles, which was 10 percent above first class (*Dodge et al. v. Commissioner of Internal Revenue* 1927).

GM and Chrysler also adopted the strategy of making most of their parts in Michigan and shipping them to final assembly plants around the country. During the 1950s, GM assembled identical Chevrolet models at 10 branch assembly plants and a combination of Buick, Oldsmobile, and Pontiac models at seven branch assembly plants.[2] At a U.S. Senate hearing in 1956, GM officials displayed maps showing the boundaries of the market areas surrounding each branch assembly plant, as well as financial data explaining the attraction of the branch assembly plant model.[3]

Smaller carmakers emulated the branch assembly plant model to a lesser extent. Before and after World War II, Chrysler maintained three branch assembly plants in addition to four "home" plants in the Detroit area. The Los Angeles area, home to an especially large and growing car market, had nine branch assembly plants in the 1950s, including two each owned by Ford and GM and one each by Chrysler, Nash, Kaiser-Frazer, Studebaker, and Willys-Overland. By the 1990s, all nine had been closed (Rubenstein 1992, pp. 95–96).

The branch assembly plant model worked as long as a carmaker was producing a variety of trim and body styles on a single platform for national distribution. When it controlled half of the U.S. market in the 1950s, GM had only three platforms, each differing only slightly in size. Each branch assembly plant was thus producing the same vehicles for regional distribution. Thus, a Chevrolet or Ford sold in southern California would have been assembled in Los Angeles, and one sold in the Southeast would have been assembled in Atlanta.

Parts: East–West Auto Alley

For most of the twentieth century, parts plants that were not in Michigan were arrayed in a 700-mile east–west corridor between upstate New York and southeastern Wisconsin along the southern rim of Lakes Ontario, Erie, and Michigan. This southern Great Lakes region, which also included the northern portions of Illinois, Indiana, and Ohio, had been home to numerous automotive pioneers during the late nineteenth century, before the industry clustered in southeastern Michigan. Two examples discussed in Chapter 10 are the tire industry in Akron and the glass industry in Toledo.

As the Big 3 expanded production after World War II, they sited many of their new parts plants in southern Great Lakes states other than Michigan. They were attracted by a combination of proximity to raw materials—steel mills were also clustered in the region (see Chapter 5)—and to customers in the Detroit area. By locating outside Michigan, the new parts plants were less likely to compete against existing parts plants for skilled labor in a tight market.

Prior to World War II, Ford had only two parts plants outside Michigan. Glass was produced in St. Paul, Minnesota, and steering wheels in Hamilton, Ohio. In comparison, during the 1950s, Ford opened nine new parts plants in Ohio, including three each for engines and drivetrains, and one each for stamping, casting, and electrical accessories. Ford's vice president of operations D.S. Harder, in charge of selecting new plant sites, stated that "taxes were a consideration in Ford's move to Ohio" (Rubenstein 1992, p. 104).

GM had more parts plants than did Ford in Great Lakes states other than Michigan during the interwar years. GM parts centers included several communities in upstate New York, northern New Jersey, northern Indiana, and Ohio. The leading center for GM parts production outside of Michigan was Dayton, Ohio.

Dayton Engineering Laboratories Company (later shortened to Delco) made its first product for the auto industry in 1909, an electric starter that eliminated the difficult and dangerous task of hand-cranking the engine. As part of William C. Durant's wheeling and dealing, Delco was acquired in 1916 by United Motors, which in turn was acquired by GM two years later. Delco CEO Charles F. Kettering was appointed head of the newly established GM Research Laboratories in 1920. Among the parts GM produced in Dayton were shock absorbers, brakes, air conditioners, and steering wheels.

A 1940 economic geography book delineated a "Central Automobile District" that encompassed southeast Michigan, northwest Ohio, and northeast Indiana (Colby and Foster 1940, cited in Ballert 1947). Three-fourths of the nation's motor vehicle employment was clustered in this district, including one-half in the Detroit area and one-fourth in the rest of the area. Michigan had 60 percent of all parts employment (Detroit City Plan Commission 1944, p. 5, cited in Ballert 1947). Most of the remaining one-fourth was found in the rest of the so-called American Manufacturing Belt between the Atlantic Coast and Lake Michigan.

The most detailed study of the mid-twentieth-century southern Great Lakes supplier network was a 1951 University of Michigan thesis by G.R. Henrickson. Henrickson documented the sources of parts at GM's Buick City assembly plant in Flint, Michigan, which was then one of the world's largest and employed 22,000 workers who produced 2,000 cars a day. With information from Buick's purchasing department, Henrickson identified the origin of 50 leading parts, including bodies, carburetors, mufflers, spark plugs, wheels, tires, engine mounts, and fan belts. Suppliers included plants owned by GM and by independent companies. He also compared Buick City's 1951 supplier base with that of the first decade of the twentieth century when Buick was founded.

Buick suppliers during the first decade of the twentieth century were spread out through the Northeast from Massachusetts, Rhode Island, Connecticut, and New Jersey on the east and through Pennsylvania, Ohio, Indiana, Michigan, Illinois, and Wisconsin on the west. After gaining control of Buick in 1904, Billy Durant enticed key suppliers to move to Flint. As a result, Buick City's suppliers during the 1950s were more concentrated in Michigan, Indiana, and Ohio than a half-century earlier.

Henrickson found that 23 percent of Buick's suppliers were located within 60 miles and 81 percent within 450 miles of the Flint assembly plant (Figure 9.2). At first glance his results are remarkably similar to the footprint of twenty-first-century auto supplier networks, as shown in Chapter 6. However, the appearance of similarity is somewhat deceiving. Today, a distance of 450 miles represents a one-day driving radius for a truck, but in 1951, when most deliveries were by rail, it would have taken more than one day because of time lost loading and unloading.

Buick's 1951 suppliers within the 450-mile radius were arrayed in an east–west configuration along the southern Great Lakes. The creation of an east–west supply base along the southern Great Lakes after World War II resulted in a sharp decline in auto industry jobs in Michigan. In just four years, between 1954 and 1958, the percentage of U.S. motor vehicle jobs located in Michigan declined from 53 percent to 43 percent. Michigan's share of U.S. motor vehicle employment thus declined most sharply not in the twenty-first century, but a half-century earlier.

The vehicle systems most likely to relocate outside Michigan were the engine and drivetrain. Independent suppliers of powertrain parts followed their Detroit 3 customers out of Michigan and into adjacent southern Great Lakes states. The legacy of Detroit 3 investment in the Midwest after World War II continues to shape the geography of powertrain parts production in the twenty-first century.

Figure 9.2 Buick City Suppliers, 1951

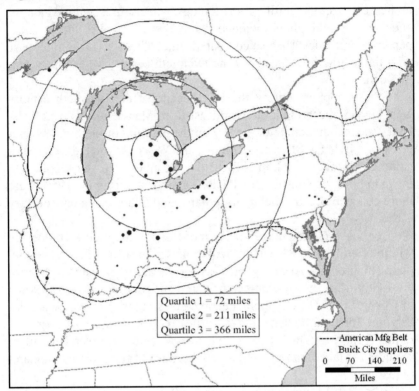

Quartile 1 = 72 miles
Quartile 2 = 211 miles
Quartile 3 = 366 miles

----- American Mfg Belt
· Buick City Suppliers
0   70   140   210
Miles

SOURCE: Henrickson (1951).

During the early twenty-first century, Michigan's auto job losses were tied to vertical disintegration and declining fortunes of the Detroit 3 carmakers. In contrast, after World War II, Michigan's losses were linked to an increase in vertical integration and the strengthening of the Detroit 3. Also varying between the two time periods has been the destination of jobs leaving Michigan. After World War II, parts production moved from Michigan to other Midwest states, but in the early twenty-first century, it moved from Michigan to the South.

THE NORTH–SOUTH AUTO ALLEY

The term *Auto Alley* was first employed to refer to investment decisions made by Japanese carmakers during the 1980s. When they decided to build assembly plants in the United States, at first known as *transplants*, Japanese firms for the most part shunned Michigan and the adjacent Great Lakes area. Auto Alley was also called the *kanban* highway, after the Japanese word for just-in-time.

The southern drift of the U.S. auto industry has occurred in three distinct periods. First, during the 1980s, new plants were located primarily between southern Ohio and central Tennessee. A second wave of new plants built during the 1990s was centered on the southernmost portion of Auto Alley, especially Alabama and Mississippi. A third wave of investment in the first decade of the twenty-first century focused on filling in gaps in Auto Alley that had not been selected during the first two waves.

Auto Alley First Appears

The Ohio River runs 981 miles from the Monongahela and Allegheny rivers at Pittsburgh to the Mississippi River at Cairo, Illinois. During the nineteenth century, the Ohio divided free states from slave states. In the twenty-first century, the Ohio River divides Auto Alley into two portions. North of the river lies the auto industry's traditional Midwest auto-producing region, centered on southeastern Michigan and portions of Illinois, Indiana, Ohio, and Wisconsin along the southern Great Lakes. As recently as 1979, only 5 of 55 U.S. assembly plants were located in Auto Alley south of the Ohio River (Figure 9.3). Since then, a new center of automotive production has emerged south of the Ohio River, centered on Kentucky and Tennessee and thrusting further southward.

Japanese assembly plants

Honda was the first Japanese carmaker to assemble vehicles in the United States, beginning in 1982. Ardently wooed by Ohio governor James Rhodes, at a time when most American politicians shunned Japanese manufacturers, Honda built an assembly plant in Marysville, a

**Figure 9.3 Light Vehicle Assembly Plants in the United States and
Canada, 1979**

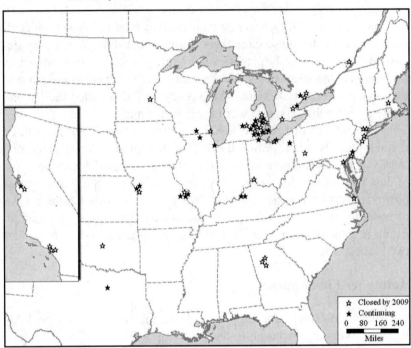

NOTE: Projections made to 2009 are based on manufacturers' announced plant openings and closings as of March 2008.
SOURCE: Adapted by the authors from the *Ward's Automotive Yearbook* database.

few miles west of the Columbus bypass. Although a rural location not
traditionally associated with motor vehicle production, the Marysville
site did not appear to represent a sharp break with the industry's long-
standing Midwest orientation.

It was the second Japanese carmaker that represented the dramatic
break with past location patterns. Nissan was also recruited heavily by
Governor Rhodes and came close to joining Honda in Ohio. But in
1983, Nissan went to Smyrna, Tennessee, a tiny community with no
ties to the auto industry in a region with limited ties to the auto industry (nearby Nashville had a Ford glass plant). As a result of what was
then an extremely remote location, the Nissan plant was farther than the
typical assembly plant from its supplier base (see Chapter 6).

Nissan's location remained a southern outlier as the next three Japanese-run assembly plants opened. NUMMI, a GM–Toyota joint venture, took over a closed GM plant in Fremont, California. AutoAlliance, a Mazda–Ford joint venture, selected Flat Rock, Michigan, site of the state's only Japanese-run assembly plant. Diamond-Star, the original name of a Mitsubishi–Chrysler joint venture, went to Normal, Illinois.

Toyota was responsible for filling in the gap between Nissan and the other transplants and clearly set the pattern of southern drift (Figure 9.4). As the best-selling and most successful of the Japanese carmakers, Toyota moved more slowly than its competitors. When it finally decided to build its own final assembly plant in the United States, Toyota locat-

Figure 9.4 Light Vehicle Assembly Plants in the United States and Canada, 1990

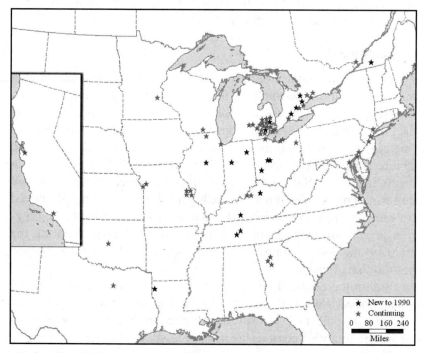

NOTE: Black stars represent new plants that opened between 1979 and 1990; replacement plants are not shown as new. Projections made to 2009 are based on manufacturers' announced plant openings and closings as of March 2008.

SOURCE: Adapted by authors from the *Ward's Automotive Yearbook* database.

ed in the small town of Georgetown, near Lexington, Kentucky, in the middle of the nation's most famous horse farms in bluegrass territory.

The Detroit 3 also contributed to the creation of Auto Alley during the 1980s by opening several new plants in the region while closing many of their coastal plants. GM built new plants in Bowling Green, Kentucky; Fort Wayne, Indiana; Moraine, Ohio; and Spring Hill, Tennessee. GM also replaced several older plants in Auto Alley during the 1980s.

Meanwhile, the Big 3 had ended the branch plant system in the 1960s when they started to produce models of varying sizes that could not be assembled on the same line. Assembly plants that once distributed vehicles to a regional market were converted to production of one or two specialized models for sale throughout the United States and Canada. Coastal assembly plants were closed because the cost of shipping from them to customers throughout the continent was much higher than it was from assembly plants in Auto Alley.

Parts plants

The data that inform our analysis (see Chapter 1) provide us with information on the start-up year for most of the supplier plants we observed operating in 2006. Therefore we can make inferences regarding the geographic pattern of plant openings for these plants. A decade before the arrival of the Japanese carmakers, the South had already started to lure parts plants. During the 1970s GM opened 10 parts plants in the South. These plants primarily produced electrical components and powertrain parts that did not require highly skilled workers. GM hoped (in vain) to pay lower wages and avoid unions (see Chapter 12). Eighteen percent of parts plants we observed in 2006 opened during the 1970s in the South, compared to only 9 percent of those that opened prior to that (Table 9.1).

Within the South, the Carolinas and Georgia attracted the largest number of parts plants through the 1970s. The pattern was set primarily by European parts makers, especially French and German, who came to regard the southeast coast as the most accessible for trade.

The southern gain during the 1970s was only partially at the expense of the Midwest. The Midwest as a whole had 66 percent of parts plants prior to 1970 and 57 percent of those that opened during the

Table 9.1 Percentage Distribution of Parts Plants by Decade of Opening

Location	Before 1970	1970–79	1980–89	1990–99	2000–06	Total	Number
Midwest	65.6	57.4	55.5	51.7	26.5	58.2	1,463
South	9.2	18.0	22.8	29.8	61.4	19.1	481
Other	25.1	24.7	21.7	18.5	12.0	22.6	569
Total number	1,010	373	604	443	83	100	2,513

NOTE: This table presents information on the start-up year of supplier plants that were observed in 2006. The Midwest is defined as Indiana, Illinois, Michigan, Ohio, and Wisconsin; the South is defined as Alabama, Georgia, Kentucky, Mississippi, and Tennessee; and other is everywhere else. Columns may not sum to 100 due to rounding.
SOURCE: Adapted by the authors from ELM International and other sources.

1970s; the rest of the country, excluding the South, stayed at 25 percent through the 1970s (Table 9.1).

The percentage of parts plants locating in the South increased from 18 percent during the 1970s to 23 percent during the 1980s. More significant was the shift in the location of plants within the South, from the Atlantic coast to Auto Alley. Two-thirds of parts plants located in the South during the 1980s went to Kentucky or Tennessee, the two principal states at the southern end of Auto Alley, compared to only 45 percent during earlier decades.

Changes were also occurring within the Midwest prior to the emergence of Auto Alley. Michigan's share of the nation's parts plants increased during the 1970s, whereas the other four states of the region declined. The Detroit 3's Michigan stronghold was not yet under attack. However, during the 1980s, the pattern reversed. Michigan's share of new parts plants declined from 32 percent to 20 percent, whereas the other four Midwest states increased from 25 percent to 35 percent.

The increasing share of parts plants in the upper South (Kentucky and Tennessee) and lower Midwest (Indiana, Illinois, and Ohio) during the 1980s matched the distribution of new assembly plants. As Japanese carmakers started production in these regions, suppliers followed.

Auto Alley Pushes into the Deep South

Auto Alley pushed farther southward during the 1990s. After the initial period of Japanese investment during the 1980s, a several-year gap occurred before the arrival of a second wave of foreign-owned assembly plants. During the 1990s, the southern end of Auto Alley was extended from central Tennessee nearly to the Gulf of Mexico (Figure 9.5).

Spearheading the second period of Auto Alley investment were the two German-owned luxury car companies, BMW and Daimler-Benz. Both companies opened assembly plants in the United States during the 1990s to produce sport utility vehicles specifically aimed at the American market. BMW became the first carmaker to assemble vehicles in South Carolina, a state that had already attracted a number of major

Figure 9.5 Light Vehicle Assembly Plants in the United States and Canada, 2009

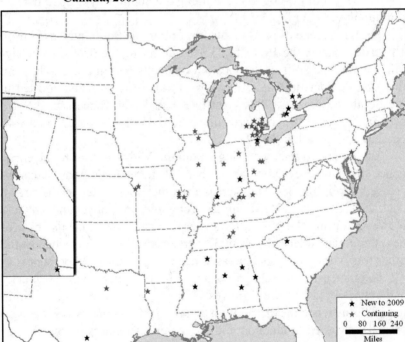

NOTE: Black stars represent new plants that opened or were scheduled to be opened between 1990 and 2009; replacement plants are not shown as new. Projections made to 2009 are based on manufacturers' announced plant openings and closings as of March 2008.

SOURCE: Adapted by the authors from the *Ward's Automotive Yearbook* database.

European suppliers. In the big picture, though, BMW's Greer, South Carolina, plant remained on the edge of Auto Alley investment.

The Mercedes-Benz plant, on the other hand, was the first of what would prove to be a stampede into the Heart of Dixie. When it selected a plant site in rural Vance, near Tuscaloosa, Alabama, in 1993, Mercedes-Benz was regarded as having made a questionable decision. The company would be entrusting its luxury brand to a state with one of the poorest and least skilled workforces, in a location well south of what was then the southern end of Auto Alley in central Tennessee.

Following Mercedes-Benz in short order into Alabama were Honda and Hyundai. Kia went a few miles east across the state line into Georgia. Nissan and Toyota located just to the west in Mississippi.

For their part, the Detroit 3 no longer built new assembly plants, except to replace older ones in nearby communities. Closures continued to be aimed at coastal plants that had escaped the first round of cutbacks a decade earlier. As it happens, Ford and GM both pulled out of Georgia not long before Kia announced plans to enter the state.

The southern end of Auto Alley received 30 percent of new parts plants during the 1990s, a further increase from the 1980s. The northern end continued its decline, attracting 52 percent, slightly less than during the 1980s (Table 9.1). Within the South, Kentucky and Tennessee continued to increase their share of all new parts plants, to 17 percent of the national total. Within the Midwest, Michigan increased its share of new parts plants from 20 percent during the 1980s to 23 percent during the 1990s, whereas the other four states declined from 35 percent of the national share to 28 percent. The gradual change in supplier plant geography observed since 1970 changed drastically in the first few years of the twenty-first century. While Table 9.1 only shows 83 plant openings between 2000 and 2006, 61 percent of them occurred in the South, with the Midwest garnering only 27 percent. Nearly half of all plants opened south of Tennessee.[4]

Infilling within Auto Alley

The extension of Auto Alley into the Deep South in the last years of the twentieth century left site selection officials of international carmakers and suppliers struggling to identify fresh sites in the twenty-first century. Should they pick sites rejected in earlier site selections or explore outside Auto Alley? Rejected sites had risky flaws, but abandoning Auto Alley could add punishing charges to the logistics bill.

Through most of the first two periods of investment in Auto Alley, the rule of thumb had been one international assembly plant per state. In order of opening, Honda picked Ohio, Nissan Tennessee, NUMMI California, Mazda Michigan, Mitsubishi Illinois, Toyota Kentucky, Subaru Indiana, BMW South Carolina, and Mercedes-Benz Alabama.

The state "captured" by a carmaker influenced the location of key suppliers. For example, Toyota suppliers clustered in Kentucky even though the carmaker's Georgetown assembly plant could be easily reached from southern Ohio. What Kentucky gained on its north side, it lost on the south side, as Nissan suppliers stayed on the Tennessee side of the state line rather than stray into southern Kentucky.

The one-international-plant-per-state pattern had a logical basis. International carmakers were reluctant to compete with each other for qualified workers, subsidies, tax breaks, and training programs. It was also politically astute: each time international carmakers entered a new state, they expanded the list of public officials sympathetic to their distinctive needs and priorities.

But by the late 1990s, international carmakers had run out of states in Auto Alley. Yet they still had some fresh states to pick off: Nissan went to Mississippi, Kia to Georgia, and Toyota to Texas. The two remaining unclaimed states—Arkansas and Louisiana—were both branded as having unattractive political climates, and into the twenty-first century Louisiana carried the added burden of the bungled response to Hurricane Katrina. Consequently, international carmakers were forced to look for sites in states already occupied by a competitor.

The principal objective when entering a previously selected state was to avoid competing for labor. The supply of qualified labor is relatively scarce in Auto Alley, especially the southern end, a function of both low population density and average educational attainment. Furthermore, carmakers have discovered that their workers are willing to commute longer than the national average of 24 minutes to obtain good, high-paying jobs in the final assembly plants; one-hour commutes are not uncommon at plants in the rural portions of Auto Alley.

To locate potential plant sites within Auto Alley, carmakers therefore start by eliminating sites within two hours of existing assembly plants. Two hours represents the sum of the one-hour commuting range of the proposed plant plus the one hour from the existing one. Carmakers then calculate if the proposed site has a sufficiently large pool of labor surrounding it. A total population of 200,000 within the one-hour radius has been the minimum for carmakers to consider.

Toyota's consideration in 2007 of sites for an assembly plant illustrated the process of infilling within Auto Alley. According to press reports, Toyota was considering five sites: Marion, Arkansas; somewhere in western North Carolina; Alamo and Chattanooga, Tennessee; and a fifth unnamed site (Shirouzo 2007). A map of Auto Alley shows that all four named finalists were outside a 50-mile radius—corresponding to the one-hour commuting range—surrounding all of the existing assembly plants (Figure 9.6).

In the end, Toyota selected Tupelo, Mississippi, perhaps the fifth unnamed site. Tupelo was also beyond a 50-mile radius of existing as-

Figure 9.6 Labor Markets around Assembly Plants

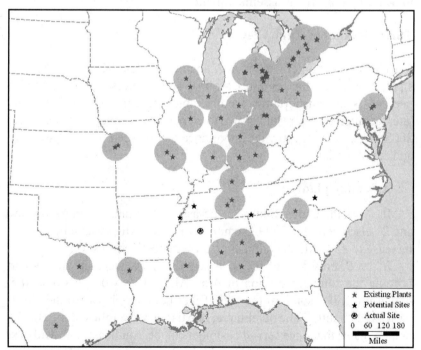

SOURCE: Adapted by the authors from the *Ward's Automotive Yearbook* database.

sembly plants (Figure 9.6), including the one already operated by Nissan in Canton, Mississippi.

Toyota and Honda also located new assembly plants in portions of Indiana beyond the labor market area of the existing international plant operated by Subaru in Lafayette. Toyota went to the far southwestern corner of the state and Honda to the far southeastern corner. Honda and Hyundai also selected sites in Alabama, a state first staked out by Daimler.

The other location strategy, to look outside Auto Alley, had been employed only once as of 2007. That was Toyota's decision to build an assembly plant near San Antonio, Texas. A quarter-century earlier, GM had considered sites in Texas for its Saturn plant but rejected them after calculating that freight charges would be $400–$500 higher, primarily because haul-away drivers would have to stop overnight more often (Rubenstein 1992). Toyota justified the choice on the basis of Texas being the world's largest market for full-sized pickup trucks, which were to be built at the Texas assembly plant.

Three Decades of Auto Alley

The seven southern states of Alabama, Georgia, Kentucky, Mississippi, North Carolina, South Carolina, and Tennessee together had 7 percent of all transportation sector employment in 1972. Thirty years later, the region's share had grown to 16 percent (Cooney and Yacobucci 2005). The South's growing importance can be seen in both assembly and supplier plants.

Assembly plants

In 1979, the United States had 55 assembly plants, 34 in Auto Alley and 21 elsewhere. By 2009, the number in Auto Alley was scheduled to increase to 43 while the number elsewhere declined to seven.

In 1979, only five of the 55 assembly plants were in what would become the southern portion of Auto Alley. Two were in Louisville, only a few miles south of the Ohio River boundary between the "Midwest" and "South." The other three, in Atlanta, were relics of the Big 3's branch plants that once served customers in the Southeast. The Midwest portion of Auto Alley (including the St. Louis area) had 29 assembly plants.

Twenty-one of the 55 assembly plants were outside Auto Alley in 1979. Ten were in the Northeast, five in California, and six elsewhere in the interior of the country, including three in Kansas City. Of the 48 final assembly plants scheduled to operate in the United States in 2009, only 8 were outside Auto Alley (Figure 9.5). The Northeast declined from 10 to 1 assembly plant, and California declined from 5 to 1. Interior locations outside Auto Alley had the remaining five, two each in Texas and the Kansas City area and one in Louisiana—all relatively close locations to Auto Alley.

Within Auto Alley, the number of assembly plants in the South increased from 5 to 13 between 1979 and 2009. The number in the Midwest increased by 1 to 30.

Supplier plants

The South's rise in importance can also be seen in parts plants (Figure 9.7). At the time of this study, 67 percent of the parts plants in the South were new (i.e., they opened between 1980 and 2006), compared with only 40 percent in the Midwest and 39 percent in the rest of the United States. Conversely, only 19 percent of the parts plants in the South in operation in 2006 had opened before 1970, compared with 45 percent of those in the Midwest and elsewhere in the United States.

Parts plants have headed south in part to be with their customers, the final assembly plants. The distribution of final assembly plants within the United States has changed sharply since the 1970s, and so has the distribution of parts plants.

The southerly drift observed for final assembly plants does not necessarily mean that parts plants were expected to locate in similar fashion. Chapter 6 showed that three-fourths of parts plants are located within one-day delivery of their customers, but only 5 percent are located within one hour. The cost advantage in shipping assembled vehicles to the national market enjoyed by Auto Alley compared with the rest of the United States applies to most locations within Auto Alley. From Toledo to Huntsville, at opposite ends of Auto Alley, most assembly plants can be reached within a one-day drive. So why have parts plants headed south? Some have followed their customers, but many parts plants have been moving south for their own reasons.

Figure 9.7 Distribution of Motor Vehicle Parts Plants Opened

(a) Before 1980 and   **(b) Since 1980**

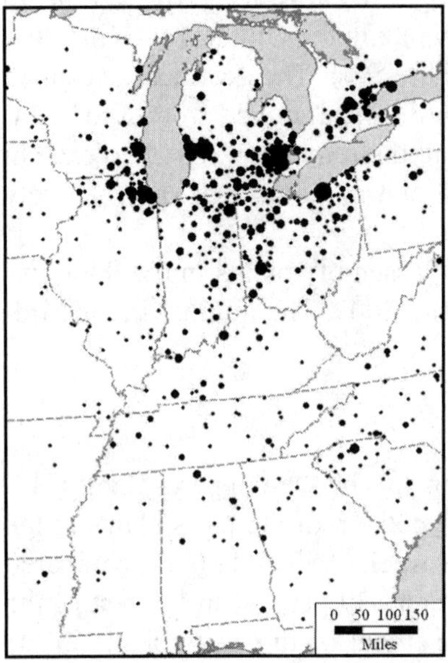

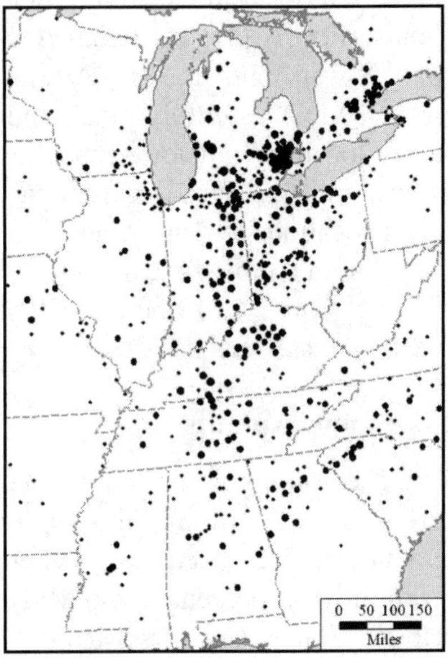

SOURCE: Adapted by the authors from the ELM International database and other sources.

Nationality of southern suppliers

Leading the move southward within Auto Alley have been foreign-owned parts suppliers. In the Midwest, 76 percent of the parts plants were owned by U.S.-based companies and 24 percent by foreign-based companies. In the South, only 57 percent of the parts plants were U.S.-owned and 44 percent were foreign owned. Foreign ownership was especially high in South Carolina and Kentucky.

Otherwise stated, the Midwest had 58 percent of U.S.-owned plants and only 44 percent of foreign-owned ones. The South had 36 percent of foreign-owned ones and only 20 percent of U.S.-owned plants.

A map of Auto Alley shows the north–south split between U.S.-owned and foreign-owned plants opened in the United States between 1980 and 2006. U.S.-owned plants cluster in the Midwest and foreign-owned ones in the South. The two groups overlap in southern Ohio and Indiana (see Figure 9.8).

Figure 9.8 Ownership of Parts Plants, 2006

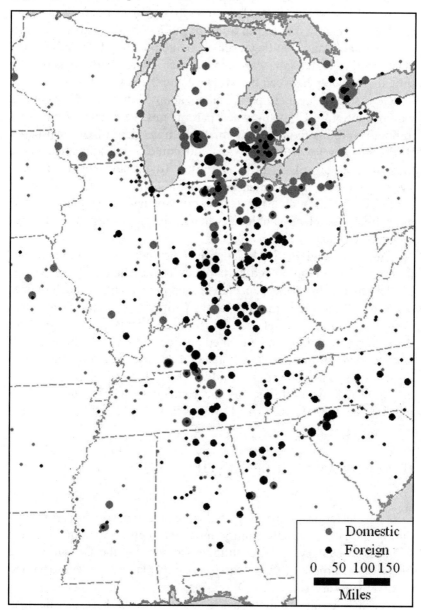

SOURCE: Adapted by the authors from the ELM International database and other
sources.

Parts makers based in Germany and Japan were responsible for most of the southern drift. Companies based in Germany and Japan each owned nearly one-fourth of all of the foreign-owned parts plants in the United States, but they each accounted for two-fifths of all parts plants in the South. Japanese- and German-owned parts makers both split about evenly between the Midwest and the South.

German and Japanese parts makers adopted different distributions within the South. German-owned parts plants were heavily clustered in South Carolina, home to the final assembly plant of German-based BMW. Japanese-owned plants favored Kentucky and Tennessee, home to final assembly plants of Japan-based Toyota and Nissan, respectively. Japanese- and German-owned parts plants also favored different locations within the Midwest. German-owned companies were far more likely to select Michigan, whereas Japanese-owned companies preferred Indiana.

Canadian- and British-based firms together owned another one-fourth of the foreign-owned parts plants in the United States. Michigan had two-fifths of the Canadian-owned parts plants, a much greater concentration in the home state of the "American" auto industry than even U.S.-owned parts plants. British-owned firms were more likely than other nationalities to be located outside Auto Alley. One-fourth of British-owned firms were in Michigan, a level comparable with U.S.-owned firms, but the rest of the Midwest had a lower than average number of British-owned firms, and the percentage in the South was not much higher than it was for U.S.-owned firms.

OUTLOOK AND UNCERTAINTIES

The clustering of the U.S. motor vehicle industry in Auto Alley during the late twentieth century appeared likely to continue into the twenty-first century. In their struggles to survive, the Detroit 3 were likely to shed more of their excess capacity, placing the last surviving coastal plants at risk.

As the Detroit 3 pulled back to their Midwest base in Michigan and adjacent Midwest states at the northern end of Auto Alley, foreign-owned carmakers were set to continue their expansion, primarily in the southern end of Auto Alley. The result was likely to be a greater rift within Auto Alley between a growing foreign-dominated south and a declining Detroit 3–dominated north.

Notes

1. Andreas Renschler, Mercedes-Benz U.S. International CEO, quoted in Chappell (1998).
2. In addition to the seven branch assembly plants, GM also maintained "home" plants for the exclusive assembly of Buick in Flint, Oldsmobile in Lansing, and Pontiac in Pontiac, a relic of the origin of these divisions as independent carmakers during the first decade of the twentieth century (Rubenstein 1992).
3. U.S. Senate Automobile Marketing Practices. Washington: Congressional documents, 1956, p. 895, cited in Rubenstein (1992, pp. 87–88).
4. Klier and McMillen (2008) show that the supplier plants that opened in the southern end of Auto Alley tend to follow a location pattern similar to the plants that have preceded them in the region. They find location choices of auto supplier plants to be well explained by a small set of variables: good highway access and proximity to Detroit and to assembly plants.

10

Abandoning Ohio:
A Tale of Two Cities

It appears likely that the center of the country's automotive production will remain near Toledo, and that a considerable portion of the community's industrial function will continue to follow the trends of this industry.(Ballert 1947)

Ohio has long been the second-leading motor vehicle production state behind Michigan. The state has accounted for about 15 percent of total U.S. motor vehicle employment, parts plants, and final assembly plants. Unlike its Great Lakes neighbor to the north, Ohio increased (at least slightly) its share of the national totals during the late twentieth and early twenty-first centuries.

Ohio's second-place position has partly been a legacy of Detroit 3 investment. As discussed in Part 1 of the book, the Detroit 3 built numerous powertrain and stamping facilities in Ohio, especially after World War II. Despite cutbacks and closures, the Detroit 3 combined still directly employed 42,298 in 22 Ohio facilities in 2006 (Ohio Department of Development Office of Strategic Research 2006).

The Detroit 3 decline has been largely offset in Ohio by growth in Japanese-owned production facilities. Honda of America employed 12,200 at its two assembly plants and three powertrain plants in Ohio in 2006 and another 3,174 at seven joint ventures with Japanese parts makers. The Ohio Department of Development identified another 55 Japanese-owned motor vehicle firms that together employed 22,785 in the state in 2006 (Ohio Department of Development Office of Strategic Research 2006).

Ohio's initial ascendancy in motor vehicle production came prior to the emergence of the Detroit 3, let alone Japanese carmakers. During the 1890s, the state had its share of pioneer carmakers, such as Alexander Winton, Henry Joy, and William Packard. Had venture capital been as readily available in Ohio in 1900 as it was in Detroit, Cleveland or

Cincinnati could have emerged as the center of automotive production (Rubenstein 1992, p. 41; Smith 1970, p. 31; Wager 1975, p. xiii).

Instead, Ohio became the center for production of two key parts: tires and glass. U.S. tire production concentrated in the northeastern Ohio city of Akron and glass in the northwestern city of Toledo. Just as Detroit became known as Motor City, Akron became Rubber City and Toledo became Glass City.

Tires and glass have shared similar positions in the auto industry:

- They are the two largest and most visible parts not made of metal.
- Applications and key technology breakthroughs predated the auto industry.
- Tires and glass are relatively self-contained and freestanding portions of the vehicle and are less integrated with other parts.
- They have been regarded by carmakers as not essential to their core competency.
- They have consistently been outsourced to independent suppliers, even at the height of vertical integration (with the exception of Ford, which once made glass).

The U.S. motor vehicle industry continues to depend on U.S.-made tires and glass in the twenty-first century. Neither of these large, bulky, low value-added parts is amenable to overseas outsourcing. But few tire and glass facilities remain in Ohio. As with Detroit, heavy dependence on one industry left both Akron and Toledo vulnerable to global shifts, especially globalization of ownership.

RISE AND FALL OF RUBBER CITY

Tire manufacturers may be the best-known suppliers among the broader public. Alone among suppliers, the tire maker emblazons its name in four places on the exterior of the vehicle, often in much bolder lettering than the name of the vehicle itself. Because of heavy advertising, the Michelin Man and the Goodyear Blimp are familiar icons even to people with no interest in motor vehicles.

Consumers typically purchase new sets of tires several times during the lives of their motor vehicles and replace flat ones periodically (although much less frequently than in the past). Above all, the purpose of the round rubber tire is understandable to even the most mechanically challenged individuals who have no comprehension of how the rest of a motor vehicle operates.

Hundreds of companies made tires in the United States during the 1910s and 1920s. As the tire became a low-cost, high-quality, long-lasting commodity, with little differentiation among competitors, suppliers succumbed to global consolidation during the late twentieth century. In the early twenty-first century, two-thirds of the world's original equipment tires were supplied by just four firms: Bridgestone/Firestone Inc.; Continental AG; Goodyear Tire & Rubber Co.; and Michelin Tire & Rubber Co. (Deutsch 1999; Miller 1996).

The variety of tires produced by the four large companies has proliferated as each company has tried to match the precise performance needs of the carmakers' wider variety of vehicle offerings. The big four tire companies have retained brand names of acquired companies that were already familiar to consumers. Brand names have also been used to distinguish between "premium" and "standard" tires, as well as between original equipment and aftermarket tires. Premium tires typically are first to get such innovations as run-flat capability.

Reflecting the globalization of the tire industry, Bridgestone/Firestone had its headquarters in Japan, Continental in Germany, Goodyear in the United States, and Michelin in France. Goodyear held about one-third of the North American original equipment tire market, and Michelin had one-fourth. Within the United States, all four produce at facilities that are clustered in the South.

Tires: Where the Rubber Meets the Road

The word "rubber" first became a popular term in England in the late eighteenth century to refer to a substance used to erase or rub out something written with a lead pencil, what Americans later called an eraser. Europeans called the substance *caoutchouc*, adapted from words heard by explorers in the Western Hemisphere, possibly from the Maïnas in Peru or the Tupi in Brazil.

Charles Goodyear, a bankrupt Philadelphia hardware merchant, is said to have become obsessed with rubber experiments during the 1830s. Rubber—the distinctive gummy elastic material isolated from the milky fluid or latex of various plants—was known in the West Indies and Central America at least since 1600 BCE, and rubber balls were seen by the earliest European explorers of the region.

Goodyear mixed raw rubber with sulfur to create an elastic substance resistant to heat and cold. The process was later called vulcanization, named for the Roman god of fire and metalworking. Until then, rubber's usefulness had been severely limited by its tendency to melt in summer heat and become brittle in winter cold. Goodyear had tried mixing latex with various drying agents such as magnesia, quicklime, and nitric acid, before stumbling by accident in 1839 on the successful combination.

British histories of rubber allocate partial credit for successful vulcanization experiments to Thomas Hancock. Given samples of Goodyear's vulcanized rubber in 1842, Hancock was able to replicate the process in a masticator machine he had invented to mix rubber with other materials. More importantly, Hancock made a commercial success of rubber, whereas Goodyear's rubber obsession left him broke and frequently in jail for inability to repay debts. He died in 1860, $200,000 in debt, having failed to either defend his vulcanization patent from pirates or invest in successful manufacturing applications.

With the rapid growth of the motor vehicle industry into the twentieth century, the tire became the principal use for natural rubber. Sixty percent of rubber was used to make tires in 2000, the remainder for components in motor vehicles, as well as in aircraft, appliances, medical equipment, and electrical and electronic devices. Synthetic rubber, developed in the 1930s, accounted for 50 percent of the rubber content in tires in 1950 and 60 percent in 2000.

Tire Production Clusters in Akron

Five companies were the leaders in U.S. tire production for much of the twentieth century: U.S. Rubber, Goodrich, Goodyear, Firestone, and General. All but the first of these were based in Akron.

U.S. Rubber

U.S. Rubber Company was founded in Naugatuck, Connecticut, in 1892 by Charles R. Flint and held three-fourths of the U.S. market for rubber boots and shoes during the 1890s. As motor vehicle production expanded, the company was the early market leader because it owned a patent on a "clincher," in which rubber beads held in place by air pressure "clinched" the rim (Epstein 1928). The Clincher Tire Association, controlled by U.S. Rubber, required tire makers to pay for a license to use the "clincher," which was the most common method of attaching the tire to the rim.

This monopoly had the beneficial effect of forcing standardization of tire sizes in the United States. But it kept tire prices high in the early years of motoring. Consumers in 1910 paid $30 to replace each tire on a small car like the Ford Model T, $50 per tire for a medium-sized car, and $80 per tire for a large car. Because tires lasted less than 3,000 miles, owners were paying more for replacement tires than for the car itself.

U.S. Rubber lost its dominant position when the Akron-based companies developed better methods of securing the tire to the rim. The use of cord increased the life of a tire to 13,000 miles in 1920 and reduced the price of a tire to $15. U.S. Rubber remained the largest tire maker outside Akron and GM's principal tire supplier during the 1920s and 1930s. Not by coincidence, controlling interest in both U.S. Rubber and GM was owned at the time by du Pont (Bernstein 1970).

Goodrich

B.F. Goodrich was the first rubber maker to locate in Akron, in fact the first to locate west of the Appalachians. Philadelphia physician Benjamin Franklin Goodrich and John P. Morris were friends and business associates involved in real estate. Goodrich became president of one of their joint acquisitions, the Hudson Rubber Co. After the business failed twice, Morris refused to invest further in it unless Goodrich moved the operation west, away from competitors.

Goodrich's search for a suitable location brought him to Akron, where he found enthusiastic investors, so he opened a rubber factory in Akron in 1871. Goodrich began supplying pneumatic tires in 1896 to Cleveland-based Alexander Winton, maker of one of the best-selling cars before 1900. On the advice of his doctor because of tuberculosis, Dr. Goodrich himself moved from Akron to Arizona in 1888.

Goodyear

The Goodyear Tire & Rubber Co. was founded in 1898 by Frank A. Seiberling, the son of an Akron businessman. Seiberling selected the name to honor the inventor of vulcanization, but Charles Goodyear had no connection with the company named for him nearly 40 years after his death. Goodyear Tire initially produced bicycle and carriage tires, made its first motor vehicle tire in 1899, and passed U.S. Rubber as the world's largest tire maker during the 1910s.

Early tires were made of stiff woven fabric glued to the wooden wheel rim. The ride was much too jarring for passengers, and the wheel broke frequently. Goodyear employee P.W. Litchfield applied for a patent in 1903 covering the two principal elements of the contemporary tire: an outer portion made of rubber called the tread and an inner casing made of belts (bands of cords or plies) wrapped around a bead (steel wire shaped in a hoop). Litchfield, a chemical engineer, worked at Goodyear for more than a half-century, including as president (1926–1930) and chairman (1930–1956).

The smooth rubber tread on early car tires provided little traction. Goodyear Tire was credited with first cutting grooves in the hard tread surface to improve traction in 1908. The concept of wrapping cords around a bead evolved from a process to stretch fabric invented for the clothing industry by New York businessman Alexander Strauss in 1894. In 1911 Philip Strauss, treasurer of the Hardman Tire & Rubber Co., applied his father's process to making a tire by reinforcing a hardened rubber tube with fabric. Cords were originally made of cotton, and synthetic fibers such as nylon and rayon were introduced during World War II.

Overextended in the recession that followed World War I, Frank Seiberling lost control of Goodyear in 1921 to New York bankers Dillon, Read and Co., which also took over Dodge at about the same time. Forced out of Goodyear, Seiberling started the Seiberling Rubber Company in 1922 in Barberton, Ohio, near Akron, and it became the country's seventh-largest tire maker. He remained its chairman until retiring in 1950 at the age of 90.

Goodyear's well-known symbol, the blimp, derived from a company interest in aviation dating back to the 1920s. It gained patents from the German company Zeppelin in 1924 to build airships in the United States and built its first (the Pilgrim) in 1925. Goodyear painted its name on the side of the blimp and flew it around the country to promote aviation as well as the tire brand. Goodyear built 300 airships, mostly during the 1940s and 1950s for military surveillance and aerial photography, and sold the Aerospace division in 1986.

Firestone

Harvey S. Firestone sold buggies in Columbus, Ohio, from 1890 to 1895, manufactured rubber tires in Chicago from 1896 to 1900, and moved production to Akron in 1900. Firestone Tire's success was linked unusually closely to that of the Ford Motor Co. Harvey Firestone and Henry Ford met during the 1890s when Firestone persuaded Ford to buy four carriage tires. The two men became close friends. For most of the twentieth century, Ford bought most of its tires from Firestone, making it Firestone's largest customer.

Ford and Firestone were both fighting their respective industry associations during the first decade of the twentieth century. The Association of Licensed Automobile Manufacturers rejected Ford's application for a license to build cars, and the Clincher Tire Association rejected Firestone's application to make tires. Instead of clinchers, Firestone secured the tire tightly to the wheel by riveting plates and bolts. Ford tested Firestone tires, decided they were superior to the clincher, and placed what in 1906 was the auto industry's largest single tire order to date, 2,000 sets at $55 each. Members of the Clincher Tire Association monopoly had all quoted Ford the same price of $70 per set.

General

General Tire was founded in Akron in 1915 by William F. O'Neil and Winfred E. Fouse, originally to produce premium replacement tires. O'Neil sold Firestone tires in Denver and Kansas City before setting up General with financial support from his father, owner of Northeast Ohio's leading department store chain.

General was more diversified than Akron's other leading tire makers, with interests in radios, aviation, plastics, and chemicals. The company began producing original equipment tires in 1955, primarily for GM.

Impact on Akron

Propelled by booming tire production, Akron was the fastest-growing city in the United States during the 1910s. It grew from an isolated Midwestern town of 69,067 (eighty-first largest in the United States) in 1910, best known as a manufacturing center for Quaker Oats, to the Rubber Capital of the World, with a population of 208,435 (thirty-second largest) in 1920.

At its peak in 1920, Akron had 60,000 workers employed in the tire plants, and it was home to the four of the five largest tire suppliers: Goodyear, Goodrich, Firestone, and General. Akron was more dominated by a single industry than any other large city in the country, even Detroit, which "merely" doubled in population from 1910 to 1920.

The founders of the major tire companies—Firestone, Goodrich, O'Neil, and Seiberling—were known as Akron's "rubber barons." They built or bequeathed the city's parks, museums, and hospitals, as well as neighborhoods for their workers with such names as Goodyear Heights and Firestone Park. Seiberling was probably the "rubber baron" with the most impact on Akron, in part because he outlived the others. After his death, Seiberling's home (Stan Hywet Hall) became Akron's leading tourist attraction.

Tire Makers Abandon Akron

Akron's decline as the center of U.S. tire production came in two waves. First, Akron's Big 4 tire makers opened factories elsewhere in the United States, especially during the 1960s. The location decisions were motivated by labor cost considerations; the tire makers were in the vanguard of looking south for cheaper labor. Three of Akron's four leading tire makers were then sold to foreign companies during the 1980s.

When General closed its last tire plant in Akron in 1982, the city that had been synonymous with rubber and tire production through the twentieth century was left without any active tire plants.

France's tire competitor: Michelin

U.S. Rubber and B.F. Goodrich merged in 1986 to form Uniroyal Goodrich; the merged company was sold four years later to Michelin. The acquisition made French-based Michelin the second-largest U.S. tire supplier behind Goodyear.

Brothers Edouard and André Michelin founded the company bearing their name in Clermont-Ferrand, France, in 1889. The company entered the tire business two years later when a cyclist asked for help in repairing an English-made tire that was glued to the wheel rim. Michelin started making tires for bicycles in 1891, for horse-drawn carriages in 1894, and for motor vehicles in 1895.

Michelin made two particularly important contributions to tire technology. First was the demountable tire, which Michelin patented in 1891. The practicality of an easy-to-change tire was quickly established when the winner of the 1891 Paris–Brest–Paris bicycle race, Charles Thery, was the only competitor to use it. Michelin's other important innovation during the 1890s was the pneumatic tire. However, it did not perform well in early races, so it was not adopted by carmakers until the 1910s.

The pneumatic tire—an air-filled rubber "balloon" or tube placed between the fabric and the rim—had been originally patented by a Scottish engineer, Robert W. Thomson, in 1845, only a few years after vulcanization. But no practical ideas existed at the time for actually using it, and the patent expired. Another Scot, John B. Dunlop, living in Belfast, Ireland, equipped his son's tricycle with tires made by pumping air into thin rubber sheets covered with fabric. Dunlop secured a patent for this version of the pneumatic tire in 1888, and it was quickly adopted for most bicycles. Dunlop himself had no connection to the tire maker bearing his name because he sold the idea of making pneumatic tires to Harvey du Cross Jr., who founded Dunlop Tyres in 1888.

Michelin's domination of the French tire market was solidified by distinctive marketing. To promote motoring, in 1900 the company compiled and gave away a Red Guide that rated hotels in France and provided street plans for many towns that were so detailed and accurate that they helped the Allied army during World War II. During the 1920s, the Red Guide dropped advertising, added restaurant reviews, and was sold in bookstores rather than given away. The company produced road maps beginning in 1910 and sightseeing information guides beginning in 1926, which became known as Green Guides beginning in 1938. Bibendum, better known in the United States as the Michelin Man, first appeared in 1898.

Michelin patented the radial tire in 1946. Most tires at the time were bias-ply, with body or carcass cords arranged diagonally to the center line of the tread. Better quality bias tires also wrapped around the diagonal body cords an outer layer of belt or crown cords arranged in a herringbone pattern. Radial tires also had belt cords arranged in a herringbone pattern, but the inner body cords were arranged at right angles to the center line of the treads rather than diagonally.

The radial tire provided better handling than the bias-ply tire, especially at high speeds and around corners. By placing the body cords at right angles, the sidewalls on radial tires could flex, whereas they remained stiff on bias-ply tires. As a result, the radial tire tread maintained a larger surface contact with the road during turns.

Radials were popular in Europe by the 1960s, but they faced resistance in the United States because they produced a stiffer and noisier ride. However, the energy crisis of the 1970s stimulated the use of radials in the United States because they yielded higher gas mileage than bias-ply tires. When U.S. firms were slow to introduce competitive radial tires during the 1970s, Michelin grabbed a much larger share of the U.S. market.

Michelin opened four tire plants in South Carolina and one in Alabama during the late 1970s and early 1980s. The company also retained five plants inherited from Uniroyal, including two in Alabama and one each in Indiana, Oklahoma, and Virginia.

Japan's tire competitor: Bridgestone

In 1988 Firestone was sold to Japanese-based Bridgestone, which outbid Italian tire maker Pirelli for it. The Firestone acquisition made Bridgestone the world's largest tire maker.

Bridgestone Tire Co. was Japan's first tire company, founded in 1931 by Shojiro Ishibashi, who had been producing traditional rubber-soled footwear known as *tabi* since 1923. Ishibashi called the tire company Bridgestone, because his own surname literally meant stonebridge in Japanese. He transposed the syllables to produce a corporate name similar to Firestone, which he admired. Bridgestone became Japan's largest tire maker in 1953.

Although Ford Motor Co. bought some of its tires from other suppliers, and Firestone sold some of its tires to other carmakers, the two companies conducted a disproportionately high percentage of business with each other throughout the twentieth century. After all of the mergers and acquisitions of the 1980s and 1990s, Bridgestone/Firestone still provided Ford with 40 percent of its tires in 2000. Bridgestone/Firestone supplied one-third of Honda's tires and one-fifth of those purchased by GM, Nissan, and Toyota.

Firestone's downfall in the United States followed its inability to compete in the radial tire market. The National Highway & Traffic Safety Administration implicated Firestone "500" radial tires in 41 fatalities. Although Firestone never agreed that the tires were defective, it agreed to recall 14.5 million of them in 1978 due to tread separation.

The century-long close relationship between Ford and Firestone came to an end in 2001, when Ford Explorers equipped with Firestone Wilderness AT tires rolled over following tread separation, resulting in 271 deaths. Bridgestone argued that the Explorer's design made it prone to rollovers because Explorers had a tire failure rate 10 times higher than other Ford vehicles equipped with Firestones. Ford countered that it had 1,183 tread separation claims involving Firestone tires and only two involving Goodyear tires.

The dispute damaged both parties. Sales of Firestone replacement tires declined 40 percent in the year after the dispute (*Akron Beacon Journal* 2000). For its part, Ford offered to replace the 6.5 million tires on all of its vehicles. Still, Explorer sales dropped rapidly from their peak in 2000—as did Ford stock. With the overall quality of tires generally very high, the Ford Explorer's problem with Firestone Wilderness tires was especially devastating.

Through the merger, Bridgestone inherited Firestone plants in Decatur, Illinois; Wilson, North Carolina; Oklahoma City, Oklahoma; and LaVergne, Tennessee. Under Bridgestone leadership, the only northern plant, Decatur, was closed, whereas new southern facilities were added in Graniteville, South Carolina, and Morrison, Tennessee. Only a token facility was retained in Akron to produce a handful of tires for race cars.

Germany's tire competitor: Continental AG

General Tire was sold to German-based Continental in 1987. Continental's early history in Germany was similar to that of Michelin in nearby France. Continental-Caoutchouc und Gutta-Percha Compagnie was founded in 1871 in Hanover, Germany, to produce solid tires for carriages and bicycles, as well as other rubber products. Continental was the first German company to manufacture pneumatic tires for bicycles in 1892, then for motor vehicles in 1898. The company even emulated Michelin by publishing a popular road atlas in German, beginning in 1907.

Continental's tire products evolved through the familiar pattern: the world's first tire with patterned tread in 1904, the world's first detachable rim in 1908, the first German cord tire in 1921, the German patent for tubeless tires in 1943, and the first German radial tire in 1960. Continental took over small German rubber companies during the 1920s, Uniroyal's European operations in 1979, and then tire makers elsewhere in Europe, including Austria, Czech Republic, Slovakia, and Sweden, during the 1980s and 1990s.

Continental held a small share of the U.S. market until 1987, when it acquired General Tire, the third-largest U.S. tire maker. The combined company held 14 percent of the U.S. tire market in 2000. Continental General's most important customer in the United States was Nissan, which bought about half of its tires from the German company. Continental General also supplied Ford and GM with about one-fifth of their tires.

The U.S. survivor: Goodyear

Goodyear was the world's largest tire and rubber company from the 1920s until overtaken by competitors' mergers during the 1980s. Goodyear purchased Kelly-Springfield Tire Co. in 1935 in order to offer a lower-priced replacement tire brand. But when other leading U.S.-owned tire makers were sold during the 1980s, Goodyear was struggling financially and unable to buy any of them. British-French financier James Goldsmith had acquired 11.5 percent of Goodyear in 1986 in an unsuccessful takeover attempt; to fend off the effort, the company made a tender offer for the shares the following year that strapped it financially and compelled it to sell noncore divisions and close plants.

Goodyear reclaimed the title of world's largest tire producer in 1999 by acquiring a controlling interest in Sumitomo Rubber Industries, Japan's second-largest and the world's fifth-largest tire maker. The alliance gave Goodyear the right to use the Dunlop name, which Sumitomo had acquired in 1986.

The company's major tire-making facilities were in Gadsden, Alabama; Topeka, Kansas; Lawton, Oklahoma; Statesville, North Carolina; Union City, Tennessee; and Danville, Virginia. The Gadsden plant was one of the first parts-making facilities in Alabama when it opened in 1929. Corporate headquarters and research facilities were retained in Akron but not production facilities.

Faced with the loss of the rubber plants, Akron attracted 400 companies involved in polymer research and production during the late 1990s. With 35,000 employees, the polymer plants did not completely replace all of the jobs lost in the rubber plants, but the new jobs were better paid and demanded more skills than the old jobs. A key to attracting firms involved in polymer technology was creation of the Edison Polymer Innovation Corporation in 1984 and a School of Polymer Science and Engineering at the University of Akron.

RISE AND FALL OF GLASS CITY

Glassmaking is an ancient art—Egypt became a center of glass production in the second millennium BCE, and knowledge of glassmaking diffused through Europe during the Roman Empire. Glass was blown, pressed, and drawn into many shapes, primarily household objects such as plates, bowls, goblets, and bottles. Venice, the center of glassmaking in medieval Europe, specialized in decorative glass as well as household objects.

Rolling molten glass into thin flat sheets was a difficult craft, limiting the use of windows prior to the nineteenth century. Because windows were expensive, the number found in a house was a good indicator of the owner's wealth. The square footage of windows in a house was a common measure for calculating property taxes, so to lower their taxes, homeowners reduced the size of their windows. Large expanses of windows were limited to important public structures, notably churches, where (tax exempt) brightly colored stained glass windows were installed.

Early motor vehicles were open carriages without windshields. Wearing goggles was the driver's principal protection against dirt and mud. A glass windshield was introduced as an extra-cost option on luxury vehicles in 1904. The first windshields consisted of two horizontal panes of glass connected by hinges. The top half could be tipped open for an unobstructed view when the bottom half was completely splattered.

The surface area of glass increased rapidly during the 1920s, when the enclosed compartment replaced the open carriage as the predominant body style. Glass was now needed for the rear and side windows of the passenger compartment, not just for the front windshield. Consumer acceptance of closed body vehicles had been slowed by fear of being injured in an accident from shattered glass. The introduction of laminated safety glass for motor vehicles helped consumers to overcome that fear.

French scientist Edouard Benedictus discovered in 1903 that a glass flask coated with an adhesive film made of nitrocellulose (a liquid plastic) did not shatter when he accidentally dropped it. British inventor John C. Wood introduced Triplex in 1905, a "sandwich" that prevented shattering by cementing a layer of celluloid between two pieces of glass. Two decades later, the process was applied to motor vehicle glass.

Toledo's Glassmakers

Glass manufacturers clustered in Toledo during the late nineteenth century, a decade before the start of commercial motor vehicle production. Glassmakers were first attracted to Toledo by proximity to critical inputs. They solidified their leadership through proximity to the increasingly important customer base in Detroit, only 50 miles to the north.

Three materials account for 99 percent of inputs into glassmaking: silica sand, soda ash, and limestone (dolomite). Glass manufacturers did not wish to incur the expense of long-distance shipping of a ubiquitous resource like sand, and in the nineteenth century, the sandy soil of northwest Ohio seemed to offer an abundant source of silica, which is the most important of the three inputs. But "impurities made this source unsatisfactory shortly after the turn of the century," so Toledo glassmakers instead brought in silica from Ottawa, Illinois, by rail. Soda ash was obtained from northeastern Michigan. Only limestone was mined locally in northwestern Ohio (Ballert 1947, p. 190).

As glassmaking was transformed from a handicraft to an industrial process in the late nineteenth century, access to low-cost energy became especially important. Toledo sat atop what at the time appeared to be an unlimited field of natural gas—the largest in the northeastern United States. "A survey of fifty [Toledo] glass plants [published in 1937] showed twenty-three indicating fuel as the most important factor for locating their industries" (Lezius 1937, cited in Ballert 1947, p. 188). Compared with coal, the principal energy source at the time, natural gas proved to be a more efficient, lower-cost means of providing the heat needed to keep glass molten. "By the end of the [nineteenth] century, this supply largely was exhausted and many glass factories in the smaller communities south of Toledo moved to new sources of fuel. Toledo, however, retained her glass industry, though natural gas had to be piped from increasingly distant fields" (Ballert 1947, p. 188).

Toledo's three leading glass-making firms in 1900 were Libbey Glass Company (originally New England Glass Company), Toledo Glass Company, and Edward Ford Plate Glass Company.

New England Glass was founded in East Cambridge, Massachusetts, in 1818, to produce blown, pressed glass for household products, as well as engraved glass. Edward Drummond Libbey (1854–1925), who had succeeded his father William L. Libbey as manager in 1883, relocated the business to Toledo in 1888, along with 100 workers, to escape labor unrest. The company name was changed to Libbey Glass in 1892. Into the twentieth century, Libbey was the leading producer of glass tableware.

Toledo Glass was incorporated in 1895 by Michael J. Owens (1859–1923), who had been one of the first hired at the new Libbey plant in 1888 and was promoted after three months to supervisor. In 1899 Owens created a glass-blowing machine that made mass production of glass bottles possible. Through growth and acquisitions, Owens was the world's largest glass company in 1929.

Recognizing the growing market for windows, Owens and Libbey together organized a firm in 1916 to make flat glass. Libbey-Owens Sheet Glass Company ("Sheet" was later dropped from the name) began production in 1917 in a plant in Charleston, West Virginia, near Owens's birthplace in Mason County.

Toledo's other major late-nineteenth-century glassmaker, Edward Ford Plate Glass Company, also had out-of-town origins. The Star Glass Works was founded in 1867 in New Albany, Indiana, on the Ohio River, near Louisville, Kentucky, by John Baptiste Ford (1811–1903), his sons Edward (1843–1920) and Emory, and his cousin Washington C. DePauw. When the New Albany venture failed, the Fords started New York Plate Glass Company in Creighton, Pennsylvania, 18 miles up the Allegheny River from downtown Pittsburgh, in 1880. The Fords left the Creighton firm in 1897 because of a dispute over distributorships. Edward headed west for Toledo, where he started construction on a plant in 1898 and began production in 1899.

Ford built the flat glass plant in Rossford, on the opposite bank of the Maumee River from Toledo. Rossford became a company town for the glass company, with housing and services for the workers, as well as the factory.

Toledo's glassmakers came together during the Great Depression. The two leading flat glass producers, Libbey-Owens and Edward Ford, merged in 1930 to form Libbey-Owens-Ford (L-O-F). Flat glass production was consolidated at Edward Ford's Rossford complex. On the houseware side, Owens acquired Libbey in 1935.

> Toledo's important function in the glass industry has brought it the title of "Glass Capital of America" and "Glass Center of the World." Such illustrious phrases rightfully are deserved, although in terms of actual production the word "capital" perhaps is better chosen than is "center," for although four of the country's leaders in the glass industry have their executive offices and research laboratories in Toledo [in 1947], two of the group have all of their production elsewhere. (Ballert 1947, p. 187)

The Big 3 in World Glass

Toledo still calls itself the Glass City, and the city's football stadium is named the Glass Bowl. But most of the automotive glass production has moved elsewhere. As in Akron, globalization hit Toledo in the 1980s; L-O-F was acquired by the British glassmaker Pilkington in 1985, leaving none of the surviving U.S.-owned glassmakers based in Toledo.

Two trends have favored globalization of the glass industry. First, demand for auto glass has grown relatively rapidly, not only because of increased worldwide vehicle production but also because the amount of glass per vehicle has increased. Glass usage has increased as a means of reducing vehicle weight and as a styling trend. In a typical vehicle, roughly 3 percent of weight is now devoted to glass, compared to 2 percent in the 1970s. The best-selling midsized sedans had 20 percent more glass in 2006 than they did 20 years earlier (NSG/Pilkington 2006, p. 28).

Second, carmakers have increasingly demanded complete "glazing systems" rather than pieces of glass. Glazing systems "use innovative finishing technologies, such as encapsulation or extrusion, which enhance the vehicle's styling and in certain cases, aerodynamics, as well as adding functionality . . ." (NSG/Pilkington 2006, p. 28). Much of the value added in glazing systems is to integrate tinting that reduces solar glare (NSG/Pilkington 2006, p. 29). Glass suppliers also have responsibility for design and assembly of modules such as tailgates that include wipers, latches, and hinges, as well as glass (NSG/Pilkington 2006, p. 28).

Motor vehicles consume about 10 percent of the world's flat glass. Windows for buildings account for 70 percent of demand, and interior applications such as mirrors account for the remaining 20 percent.

World production of automotive glass into the twenty-first century was dominated by three companies based in Europe and Japan: Asahi Glass Company, Saint-Gobain Group, and NSG/Pilkington. The three held 65 percent of the world automotive glass market in 2006, up from 49 percent in 1992 and 63 percent in 1998 (NSG/Pilkington 2006, p. 25).

Asahi

Asahi, Japan's largest glassmaker, was founded in 1907 by Toshiya Iwasaki, the second son of the second president of the original Mitsubishi Corporation. The company started supplying the auto industry in 1956, and it ranked as the world's largest auto glass supplier into the twenty-first century.

Asahi started U.S. production in 1985 through AGC Automotive (originally AP Technoglass), a joint venture with PPG Industries. The two companies had already come together in 1966 in a joint venture (Asahi Penn Chemical Company) to make chlorine products.

Saint-Gobain

Saint-Gobain, Europe's largest glass supplier, was founded in 1692 on the site of Saint-Gobain château near Soissons, France. The company combined in 1695 with the Mirror Glass Factory, established even earlier, in 1665, by Jean-Baptiste Colbert (1619–1683), Louis XIV's powerful contrôleur général. The combined company, known simply as the Glass Factory, produced mirrors for the Royal Court at Versailles and pioneered innovative industrial processes that enabled it to dominate European glass production for several hundred years.

Saint-Gobain began to make automotive glass for French cars during the 1930s, and it entered the U.S. market as a GM supplier during the 1990s. The company was better known in the United States for supplying glass to the rail industry, including the Acela high-speed northeast corridor trains, the New York City subway, and the Las Vegas monorail. Saint-Gobain also supplied the glass for the pyramid designed by I.M. Pei as the entry into the Louvre museum in Paris. Half of the company's revenues come from materials other than glass, including insulation, building materials, pipes, containers, ceramics, and abrasives.

NSG/Pilkington

Pilkington's origins date from efforts orchestrated by the British government to reduce Saint-Gobain's domination of the European market. The British Cast Plate Glass Company was established in 1773 with financial backing from the British government. The company constructed a large factory at Ravenhead, where it started producing Britain's first plate glass in 1786.

A competitor, St. Helens Crown Glass Company, was founded near Ravenhead in 1826, financed by three local families—William and Richard Pilkington, Peter Greenall, and James Bromilow. The company was renamed Greenall & Pilkington in 1829, then Pilkington Brothers when the one family became the sole investor in 1849.

Pilkington entered the twentieth century as Britain's sole producer of flat glass after acquiring its competitors, including the Ravenhead facility in 1901. Pilkington remained a privately held firm until 1970, and a family member ran the company until 1992.

Pilkington's operations were merged in 2007 with those of Nippon Sheet Glass Co., the second-largest Japanese glassmaker behind Asahi. Nippon acquired 10 percent of Pilkington in 2000 and increased its stake to a controlling interest in 2006. Completing the circle to Toledo, when Nippon was established in 1918, it produced glass with technology from Libbey-Owens-Ford.

Leading U.S. Glass Suppliers

Four companies together held more than three-quarters of the U.S. auto glass market in 2007. Two of the four market leaders were NSG/ Pilkington and Asahi. The other two leading U.S. glass suppliers, Ford Motor Company and PPG, were both sold in 2007 to private investors Glass Products and Platinum, respectively, and both faced uncertain futures (NSG/Pilkington 2006).

Glass Products (Ford Motor Company)

Glass Products was formed in 2007 through acquisition of Ford Motor Company's glass plants. That ended Ford's involvement in making glass, an activity that had began with the company's founder. Henry Ford's obsession with controlling raw materials played a major role in the decision, especially when glass proved expensive and hard to obtain during and after World War I (Nevins and Hill 1957, p. 230). Even at the height of vertical integration, Ford was the only automaker producing its own glass.

Ford spent more than a decade trying to sell its glass facilities. After several failed attempts, Ford finally found a buyer in 2007, a new company called Glass Products formed by private investor Robert Price (*Automotive News* 2007b). Price was described in Ford's press release as "a Tulsa-based private investor and experienced business leader with a strong record of success in the natural gas industry, logistics, and medical facility management" (Ford Motor Company 2007).

Platinum (PPG)

Before he left New York Plate Glass Company, John Ford had changed its name to the Pittsburgh Plate Glass Company (PPG) in 1883. PPG was the first commercially successful producer of plate glass in the United States and became the leading independent supplier outside Toledo during the early twentieth century. PPG was the second-leading supplier of glass to the U.S. auto industry in 2007, although glass accounted for only one-fourth of revenues; more than half came from paint and coatings (see Chapter 4).

In 2007, PPG sold its glass business to Platinum Equity, a private equity group. PPG chose to focus on its coatings sector, which it considered to have better earnings prospects than glass (Nussel 2007).

As for Toledo, NSG/Pilkington continued to operate the Toledo-area glass plant at Rossford, but other than that, the four leading U.S. glass suppliers were firmly entrenched elsewhere in Auto Alley:

- Asahi's first U.S. plant was opened in 1986 at Bellefontaine, Ohio, to supply windshields to Honda's Marysville assembly plant 20 miles away, and a second plant was opened in 1989 at Elizabethtown, Kentucky, 75 miles from Toyota's Georgetown assembly plant. Until 1989, the plants were operated as a joint venture with PPG.

- Glass Products had plants in Tulsa, Oklahoma, and Nashville, Tennessee, built by Ford after World War II.

- Platinum produced OEM glass at five U.S. facilities in Evansville, Indiana; Evart, Michigan; Crestline, Ohio; and Creighton and Tipton, Pennsylvania.

- NSG/Pilkington had facilities in Lathrop, California; Ottawa, Illinois; and Laurinburg, North Carolina; as well as Rossford, Ohio.

OUTLOOK AND UNCERTAINTIES

Ballert's 1947 dissertation concluded that Toledo would remain at the center of the country's motor vehicle production. Among the reasons for this conclusion were the following four (Ballert 1947, p. 184):

1) The automobile companies and the producers of parts and equipment are mutually dependent upon one another, and this provides a deterrent to the dispersion of the industry.

2) The ubiquitous unionism in the automotive industry nullifies any reason for moving to obtain cheaper labor.

3) There is continued availability of skilled and semiskilled labor.

4) Toledo has a central position with respect to assembling raw materials and distributing the goods produced.

The future of Toledo's motor vehicle glass production seemed especially assured in 1947. "Continued prominence in the glass industry appears to be assured for Toledo, both from the standpoint of production and administration . . . Transportation costs are important for these bulky items, and Toledo is located excellently with respect to the market for such products, especially safety glass for automobiles." When this was written in 1947, Libbey-Owens-Ford was the sole supplier of glass to GM and, along with PPG, supplied 85 percent of the safety glass in the United States (Kennedy 1941, cited in Ballert 1947).

Toledo has in fact remained an important center for motor vehicle production. Sixty parts suppliers are located in northwest Ohio, including 16 in Lucas County where Toledo is located. Motor vehicles have been assembled in Toledo since the nineteenth century, most recently at an assembly plant opened for Jeep production in 2001. Toledo is even attempting to reinvent itself by leveraging its deep roots in the glass industry in light of rising demand for alternative energies (Carlton 2007).

On the other hand, Summit County, where Akron is located, had only two remaining suppliers in 2007, one making wheels and the other plastic parts. Akron has moved on to become a center for polymer production.

The experiences of Toledo and Akron show that communities at the northern end of Auto Alley face an increasing challenge in retaining suppliers. Locations further south offer greater proximity to the plants of growing carmakers as well as lower costs of doing business, without sacrificing equally good access to national markets and raw materials.

11
Chassis Suppliers Move
South in Auto Alley

When kids draw airplanes, they draw wings; cars, they draw wheels.[1]

The chassis makes a vehicle safe to drive and provides passengers with a comfortable ride. Because the undercarriage of the vehicle is largely invisible, motorists generally don't know who has made the components, and they generally don't care. Unlike the powertrain, chassis performance rarely influences buying decisions. And unlike the interior and exterior, chassis styling rarely influences buying decisions. Encouraged by the "invisibility" of the chassis, carmakers have long outsourced key chassis components to strong independent suppliers.

Major chassis modules include brakes, driveline, fuel handling, steering, suspension, and wheels. The wheels are connected to the powertrain by the driveline and to the operator of the vehicle by the steering. In the absence of a suspension system, every rough spot in the road would transmit an intense shock through the car, making the ride unpleasant at low speed and intolerable at high speed.

Although the various chassis modules must fit together and function harmoniously, they do not have to be produced in the same place. The chassis has been the main "battleground" system in the twenty-first century over the future geography of the U.S. auto industry. Overall, 56 percent of chassis plants were in the Midwest in 2006, a smaller percentage than any other system except electronics. But not every chassis supplier has been equally likely to leave the Midwest. The regional distribution has varied both among types of chassis modules and among leading suppliers within each chassis module.

One-fourth of all chassis parts were made within 158 miles of Detroit, one-half within 366 miles, and three-fourths within 642 miles (Figure 11.1). These distances are larger than those of all other systems except electronics (see Chapter 14). The makers of parts such as

Figure 11.1 Location of Chassis Components Plants

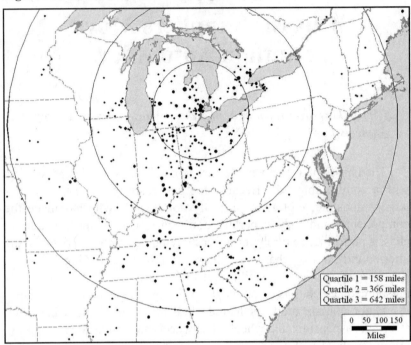

SOURCE: Adapted by the authors from the ELM International database and other sources.

wheels, brakes, and suspensions have been sensitive to price pressures and have relocated production to places with lower labor costs. Imports of chassis parts have risen especially rapidly (see Chapter 13).

The six major chassis modules could be placed into three groups based on geographic distribution (Table 11.1). More than 60 percent of the plants making driveline and steering parts were still in the Midwest in 2006. On the other hand, suppliers of wheel and fuel handling parts were most likely to move southward in Auto Alley. Between these two were brake and suspension suppliers.

The probability of production remaining in the Midwest or moving to the southern end of Auto Alley has been influenced in part by the nature of the part. Relatively bulky and fragile parts have been more likely to remain in the Midwest, whereas low-cost commodities have moved south in Auto Alley. The probability of the Midwest retaining or losing production has also been influenced by competitive pressures among leading suppliers of particular modules.

HANGING ON IN THE MIDWEST

Nearly two-thirds of plants making driveline and steering parts were located in the Midwest in 2006. The driveline and steering modules are closely linked to the powertrain modules, which are produced primarily in the Midwest, as described in Chapter 3. The Midwest has also remained the center for producing these parts because the leading suppliers have been U.S.-owned firms with roots in the region.

Driveline Parts Suppliers

Key driveline components are the axles and drive shaft (or propeller shaft). The axles hold the wheels in place and drive them forward or backward. The drive shaft, which connects the transmission output shaft with the axles, permits the axles and wheels to move up and down on an uneven surface while the transmission remains fixed to the vehicle frame.

The drive shaft is a hollow steel tube that absorbs the vertical movement of the axle at one end without affecting the rigid transmission output shaft at the other end. Early motor vehicles transferred power from the engine to the axles by a chain-and-sprocket arrangement adapted from bicycles. The chains were noisy and hard to lubricate, and broke frequently. Several nineteenth-century experimental French vehicles replaced the chains and sprockets with a drive shaft; the 1901 Autocar may have been the first American car with a drive shaft.

Axles transmit engine power to the wheels. Most U.S. vehicles were rear-wheel drive until the 1970s. The rear wheels had responsibility for power while the front wheels had responsibility for steering and braking. Sending most of the weight to the rear made early cars more stable and easier to control.

In the wake of the 1970s energy crisis, front-wheel-drive vehicles became popular and accounted for about 70 percent of U.S. vehicles into the twenty-first century. A major advantage of front-wheel drive

Table 11.1 Chassis Parts Plants in the Midwest

Chassis parts	Number of plants	% in Midwest
Driveline	192	63.0
Axles	57	66.7
CV and universal joints, yokes	40	57.5
Drive shafts and torque converters	46	63.0
Other driveline parts	49	60.8
Steering	257	61.5
Columns	26	65.4
Steering gears and knuckle	40	62.5
Steering hoses	11	45.5
Linkages and tie rods	17	58.8
Power steering systems	27	92.6
Steering wheels and shafts	34	41.2
Other steering parts	102	60.8
Wheels and related parts	158	46.1
Wheel bearings and bushings	15	46.7
Hubs and related parts	67	67.2
Wheels	47	31.9
Other wheel-related parts	29	55.2
Fuel handling	355	51.0
Carburetors	17	58.8
Air cleaners and filters	31	64.5
Fuel filters	29	48.3
Hoses, tubes, and fuel lines	52	61.5
Fuel injection systems	60	41.7
Fuel pumps	35	48.6
Fuel system sensors	42	26.2
Fuel tanks	25	68.0
Other fuel-related parts	64	54.7
Brakes	358	58.1
ABS	26	53.8
Calipers, master cylinders, rotors	49	63.3
Hoses, tubes, brake lines	54	57.4
Drum brakes	20	75.0
Parking brakes	19	42.1
Hydraulic pumps	14	92.9

Table 11.1 (continued)

Chassis parts	Number of plants	% in Midwest
Brakes (continued)		
Disc brakes	34	44.1
Other brake parts	142	57.0
Suspension	229	56.3
Springs	37	56.8
Struts and stabilizers	40	57.5
Shock absorbers	31	58.1
Control arms	29	69.0
Other suspension parts	92	51.1
Total chassis	1,549	56.8

SOURCE: Adapted by the authors from the ELM International database.

was elimination of the long drive shaft between the transmission and rear axle. The shorter distance from the transmission to the front wheels meant fewer parts and less weight, and therefore higher gas mileage and a lower price. Front-wheel drive also had the advantage of increasing interior passenger space by eliminating the large hump on the floor to accommodate the drive shaft connection to the rear axle. Putting the weight of the engine directly over the drive axle also improved traction in slippery conditions.

On front-wheel-drive vehicles, the transmission and axle form a module called a transaxle. The axle is in two halves, each attached to a wheel at the outer end. The two wheels on the driving axle must be interconnected in order to receive power from the same source, the driveshaft.

Given the close link between axles and transmissions in contemporary vehicles, it is no surprise that axle production is as highly clustered in the Midwest as is transmission production. The two leading axle producers—American Axle & Manufacturing (AAM) and ArvinMeritor—had 15 U.S. axle plants in 2007; 6 were in Michigan and 3 each were in Ohio, New York, and the South.

American Axle and Manufacturing

During the height of vertical integration, the Detroit 3 produced most axles for cars in-house, but GM sold its axle-making facilities to

AAM, which was easily the most successful of the suppliers spun off from GM during the 1990s. The company took over old plants that many regarded as unsalvageable yet prospered thanks to the SUV boom.

Much of the credit for AAM's early success was given to Richard E. Dauch, its founder, first CEO, and first chairman of the board. AAM has borne the imprint of this single individual as much as any of the very large suppliers. Even the AAM corporate office in Detroit was located at 1 Dauch Drive.

However, AAM's prospects were ominously tied to those of GM. More than four-fifths of sales went to GM, primarily light truck axles. GM selected AAM as its Tier 1 integrator for the driveline system for full-sized pickups and large sport utilities. AAM would be responsible for both axles as well as the driveshaft, brake components, suspension parts, and design and sourcing of the driveline system (Sherefkin 2002a).

ArvinMeritor

The leading supplier of heavy truck axles has been ArvinMeritor, created through the merger of exhaust specialist Arvin Industries with Meritor Automotive. Meritor had been spun off as an independent company only two years before the 1999 merger. Prior to then, Meritor had been a division of Rockwell International.

Rockwell International's predecessor Timken-Detroit Axle Co. was established in 1909 to make truck axles. Its founder Henry Timken (1831–1909) was better known for making roller bearings. The company, renamed Rockwell Spring & Axle Co. in 1953 in honor of its first president Willard Rockwell, entered the aviation and defense business when it merged with North American Aviation in 1967.

As a division of Rockwell International, Rockwell Automotive was ripe to be spun off. Although the automotive division ranked among the largest suppliers in the 1990s, its parts sales of $2 billion per year accounted for less than one-fourth of total sales at Rockwell. Of more importance, the automotive division was contributing only 10 percent to Rockwell's corporate earnings.

Dana Corp.

Early drive shafts shattered easily because they were held in a fixed rather than a flexible position. Inventing an effective way to make a drive shaft flexible was the basis for the success of Dana Corp. While an engineering student at Cornell University's Sibley College in 1903, Clarence W. Spicer patented the solution—a universal or U-joint attached to either end of the drive shaft. U-joints allow the drive shaft to change angle without breaking as the axle moves up and down.

Spicer Universal Joint was rescued from financial difficulties in 1914 when New York lawyer, politician, and entrepreneur Charles Dana (1881–1975) purchased controlling interest. Dana was company president from 1914 to 1958 and chairman from 1948 to 1966, the longest period under a single leader of any of the major motor vehicle suppliers and possibly of any multibillion-dollar firm in the United States.

Dana reorganized Spicer Universal Joint and moved its headquarters and production facilities to Toledo in 1929, where it joined Willys-Overland and Libbey-Owens-Ford as part of Toledo's growing automotive production complex. In recognition of Charles Dana's first 32 years of service, the company was renamed for him in 1946. However, the Spicer name was retained for the company's drivetrain products.

Dana filed for bankruptcy protection in 2006. Declining sales to Detroit 3 carmakers and increased cost of raw materials, especially steel, were blamed for the financial difficulties. The company sold many of its plants to other suppliers, restructured its labor contracts, and established trusts for retiree health care obligations. Dana received a substantial infusion of capital from Centerbridge Capital Partners in 2007. In 2008 it emerged from Chapter 11 as Dana Holding Corporation.

GKN Automotive

Spicer's U-joint had one notable flaw: it caused the drive shaft to rotate at a variable speed. As long as rear-wheel-drive vehicles predominated, the variability was not a problem. But on a front-wheel-drive vehicle, the drive shaft's variable rotation caused hard steering, slippage, and uneven tire wear when turning corners.

In the 1920s, Spicer engineer Alfred H. Rzeppa invented a major improvement to the U-joint, the constant velocity joint (CVJ), which eliminated the variable drive shaft speed. But Dana ceded leadership in supplying drive shafts and CVJs to the British firm GKN Automotive Inc. during the late twentieth century.

Guest, Keen and Nettlefolds Ltd. (shortened to the acronym GKN in 1986) was formed in the early twentieth century through merger of several venerable British firms. Dowlais Iron Company, established in 1759 in the South Wales village of Dowlais, was the world's largest ironworks in the late eighteenth century and the world's largest steel mill for much of the nineteenth century. John Guest and his descendants controlled Dowlais for more than a century until selling it in 1900 to Arthur Keen, who merged it with Patent Nut and Bolt Company, which he had established in 1856. In 1902, Keen acquired Nettlefolds Ltd., one of the world's largest manufacturers of nuts, bolts, screws, and nails.

GKN was nationalized in 1951 by Britain's Labour government, privatized later that year by the newly elected Conservative government, nationalized a second time by Labour in 1967, and again privatized by the Conservatives in 1973. With its core products of steel and nails under pressure from lower cost overseas competitors, GKN was an unlikely survivor of the 1970s-era bankruptcies, closures, and mergers. The company halted steel production altogether in the early 1980s and lost most of its nail market.

The constant velocity joint proved to be the savior of GKN. In 1966 GKN had acquired a share in Hardy Spicer Ltd., which held patents on a CVJ for front-wheel-drive cars. After interest in front-wheel-drive transmissions increased in reaction to the 1970s energy crisis, GKN emerged as the leading CVJ producer, holding one-third of the world market by the 1990s. Acquisition of the CVJ facilities of Fiat, GM, and Nissan boosted GKN's share to 43 percent of world production in 2002 (GKN 2007).

Steering

The principal interface between the driver and chassis is through the steering system. For a car to turn smoothly, each wheel must follow a different circle. Since the inside wheel is following a circle with a smaller radius, it makes a tighter turn than the outside wheel. The steering linkage makes the inside wheel turn more than the outside wheel.

Nineteenth-century vehicles were steered by a tiller that pivoted the entire front axle. This was possible because most of the weight of early vehicles was distributed to the rear. The tiller was generally positioned in the middle so that the driver could sit on either side. When the engine was moved to the front, a more elaborate steering system was needed to get the wheels to turn. A mix of tillers and steering wheels were offered through the first decade of the twentieth century, until the steering wheel became standard.

Two types of steering gears have been widely used: recirculating ball and rack-and-pinion. The recirculating ball system predominated for most of the twentieth century and is still used on many trucks and SUVs, whereas rack-and-pinion steering has become most common on cars.

The recirculating ball system has a steering shaft connected at one end to the steering wheel and at the other end to a block with a hole in the middle and gears on the outside. The end of the steering shaft has a worm gear, similar to a bolt, which fits in the hole in the metal block, similar to a nut. With rack-and-pinion steering, the end of the steering shaft is fashioned into a pinion gear rather than a worm gear. Rack-and-pinion steering was confined to racing cars and sports cars until it was adopted on smaller European cars during the 1960s. The rapid expansion of foreign car sales during the 1970s introduced many Americans to rack-and-pinion steering.

Nearly all power steering parts were made in the Midwest in 2006, along with two-thirds of steering columns and gears. Hoses, shafts, and steering wheels were less likely to be made in the Midwest.

TRW

The leading supplier of steering gears in the United States was TRW Automotive Inc. TRW was formed through the merger of Thompson Products and Ramo-Wooldridge Corp. in 1958. The acronym TRW was adopted in 1965.

TRW's motor vehicle parts heritage came through Thompson, which was originally known as the Cleveland Cap Screw Co. and established in 1901 to make fasteners, including the eponymous cap screw, a large heavy-duty bolt with cap and stem welded together. An adaptation of the cap screw became Cleveland Cap Screw's first motor vehicle part, an engine valve stem. Impressed with the part, Cleveland-based pioneer motor vehicle producer Alexander Winton purchased the company in 1904 and installed the welder who created the valve, Charles E. Thompson, as general manager. The company's name was changed in 1926 to honor Thompson.

The company's first steering product, introduced in 1914, was a steering reach rod, also known as a drag link, a long, hollow tube with a ball-and-socket attachment at each end that connected the steering column with the front wheels (Dyer 1998, p. 42). The company introduced the first rack-and-pinion steering gear in the United States in 1972.

Thompson's valves were also used in aircraft engines. The company's involvement in the aviation industry induced it to invest in a new company founded in 1953 by two former California Institute of Technology classmates and Hughes Aircraft Co. engineers, Simon Ramo and Dean Wooldridge. Ramo-Wooldridge grew rapidly after being named systems engineer and technical adviser to the Air Force for the Intercontinental Ballistic Missile program in 1955. The combined Thompson-Ramo-Wooldridge company became a major military and aviation supplier.

TRW Automotive was spun off from the aviation portion of the firm in 2003 and acquired by the Blackstone Group L.P. Shares were sold to the public in 2004, although Blackstone retained control. Steering gears and other chassis products accounted for two-thirds of TRW's revenues in 2004, occupant safety components one-fourth, and valves and other powertrain components the remainder (Dyer 1998).

TRW's steering gear plants were split between northern and southern locations. Three newer plants were in Tennessee and three older ones were in Indiana, Michigan, and Ohio.

CHASSIS PARTS PRODUCTION MOVES SOUTH

The two chassis modules that have most aggressively moved out of the Midwest have been wheels and fuel handling. Only 46 percent of wheel parts and 51 percent of fuel-handling parts were still made in the Midwest in 2006.

The wheel has been buffeted by contradictory trends. On one hand, it has been transformed from a purely functional component into an important design element. At the same time, it has been subject to intense pricing pressures through increased competition. As a result, the wheel has become a low-cost commodity in the vanguard of outsourcing to cheap-labor locations, including China.

Fuel handling includes three sets of components: the line to move the fuel from the tank to the engine, the control system to push the fuel into the engine, and the tank to store the fuel. Fuel line production has been especially likely to remain in the Midwest, whereas the other two have been less tied to the Midwest.

Wheels: Ugly Duckling No More

The wheel is mounted to the axle with the brake drum or disc on one side and the tire on the other. The central part of the wheel through which the axle passes is the hub.

Nineteenth-century vehicles rode on enormous four-foot-diameter wheels inherited from buggies and bicycles. Long spindly wooden spokes—typically 12 or 14—radiated from a central hub to a wooden rim. As motor vehicle production increased after 1900, and vehicles acquired their contemporary appearance, wheels shrunk to about 2 feet in diameter.

The wooden wheel was replaced during the 1920s by a flat pressed-steel disk wheel painted the same color as the body. The steel wheel was later reshaped to include a drop center, in which the diameter on the outside of the wheel was smaller, to facilitate installation and removal of the tire. The tire was mounted on the wheel by threading four to six lug nuts through holes in the tire hub onto bolts in the center of the wheel. The drop-center steel wheel with a roughly one-foot diameter on the outside became the industry standard during the 1930s and changed little over the next 60 years.

Beginning in the 1930s, the unattractive drop-center wheel was hidden by a cover, commonly known as a hubcap. The wheel cover was pressed from steel into elaborate fluted patterns and plated with a shiny finish. The covers were thought to enhance a new vehicle's appearance, although they soon became tarnished, dented, misshapen, stolen, or dislodged by a bump in the road. Most hubs are made in the Midwest, but fewer than one-third of the wheels themselves are made in the Midwest.

262 Klier and Rubenstein

The veteran: Hayes

The leading supplier of wheels for most of the twentieth century was Hayes Wheels and its successors. Hayes's wheel production has been heavily centered in the Midwest.

The company founded by Clarence B. Hayes in 1908 captured two-thirds of the wooden wheel market during the 1910s. Most of the remainder was held by K.H. Wheel Co., which was founded in 1909 by John Kelsey and John Herbert and reorganized a year later as the Kelsey Wheel Co. As steel wheels replaced wooden ones, the two leading wheel-making firms merged in 1927 to form Kelsey-Hayes Wheel Corp. When it invented the drop-center wheel in 1934, Kelsey-Hayes solidified its position as the country's dominant producer of steel wheels.

Kelsey-Hayes experienced multiple takeovers during the late twentieth century. Fruehauf Corp., a semitrailer manufacturer, acquired it in 1973 and sold it in 1989 to Varity Corp., formerly known as Massey-Ferguson. Varity spun off Hayes Wheels International as a separate company in 1992, while retaining Kelsey-Hayes's other capabilities, notably brake components, which is discussed later. Varity announced its intention to buy back Hayes in 1995 but withdrew the offer a year later. Hayes then merged with Motor Wheel Corp., the second-largest steel-wheel producer. In 1997, Hayes acquired 77 percent of the German company Lemmerz Holding GmbH to form Hayes Lemmerz International, Inc.

Competition from both domestic and international wheel makers drove Hayes Lemmerz into Chapter 11 bankruptcy in 2001 from which it emerged two years later. The company has since sold most of the plants that made parts other than wheels. It also expanded wheel production in Mexico and India while closing some of its midwestern plants.

The upstart: Superior

Superior Industries International Inc., founded in California in 1957 as an aftermarket supplier, successfully challenged Hayes's stranglehold on the original equipment market beginning in the early 1970s. Key to Superior's success was aluminum wheels. In contrast to Michigan-based Hayes, four of Superior's seven U.S. plants were located in Arkansas.

Like much of the automotive industry, long-standing wheel preferences were first shaken by the energy crisis of the 1970s. Looking to shed weight from vehicles in the wake of the energy crisis, wheel suppliers looked for alternatives to steel. A wheel made of aluminum was only half the weight of a steel one; the savings of 60 pounds per vehicle more than offset a four-times-higher price for aluminum than for steel. The share of the market held by aluminum wheels increased from 7 percent in 1983 to 40 percent in 1993 and 56 percent in 2000.

Hayes had been a pioneer in the use of aluminum, but it stumbled when demand for aluminum wheels soared during the 1980s. Its sales declined from more than 22 million wheels in 1999 to fewer than 10 million in 2004 (Chappell 2004e). Superior's big break came in the late 1980s, when Hayes lost several large GM contracts because of quality problems. Its share of GM's aluminum wheel purchases fell from 45 percent in 1989 to 12 percent in 1994, while Superior's rose from virtually nothing to 53 percent. However, Superior also struggled because it was deriving three-fourths of its sales from Ford and GM.

The boutique wheel

The ugly duckling twentieth-century drop-center wheel was transformed into an attractive component in the twenty-first century. "Wheels are what set autos apart from every other product out there."[2] The wheel became an important element in designing a distinctive appearance for a brand of vehicle. "In the evolution of the design of a vehicle, we look at wheel design on Day One."[3] Wheel diameters grew by 50 percent during the 1990s. "A big wheel and big tires make vehicles look more confident."[4]

The wheel was especially vulnerable to imports from low-cost countries, such as China. Wheels made in China gained a strong position in the aftermarket: "The aftermarket often leads the way on product innovations, since small suppliers need to respond fast to mercurial consumer tastes. Wheels are an example. Aftermarket companies capitalized on the demand for oversized wheels and high-end rims long before the automakers did" (Chappell 2005e). Original equipment suppliers were challenged as well, especially by GM, which started purchasing aluminum wheels in China, thanks to a favorable contract arranged by the Chinese government (Andersson 2006).

Hayes tried to reclaim its lost dominance in wheel production by offering "corner" modules, consisting of wheels, brakes, and suspension parts. In 1999, it acquired CMI International Inc., a producer of aluminum suspension components, including control arms, knuckles, spindle arms, hub carriers, cross members, and engine cradles. Hayes claimed it was capable of supplying $1,100 worth of parts out of the $1,300 that carmakers typically spent to purchase components for "corners." The portion of the corner that Hayes was not able to offer was the brake, ironically a capability that the company possessed until the convoluted restructuring of the 1990s.

Going into the twenty-first century, it was still unsettled as to what the optimal strategy for a wheel maker was: Hayes's effort to build modular capability or Superior's concentration on one component. Carmakers were not rushing to purchase entire modules from Hayes, preferring to continue to deal separately with the well-established suppliers of the other components. When Hayes was forced to reorganize under Chapter 11 bankruptcy protection, Superior's strategy appeared superior, at least in the short run.

Fuel Handling

The geographic distribution of fuel-handling parts has been mixed. Air filters, hoses, and tanks have been more likely to be produced in the Midwest, whereas fuel filters, injection systems, and pumps have been more likely to be located in the South. Overall, only one-half of the plants making fuel-handling parts were located in the Midwest in 2006.

The southward drift of fuel-handling production may have been a function of the dominance of foreign-owned suppliers. European suppliers have been especially important in this sector.

Fuel lines: TI Automotive

The leading supplier of fuel lines, as well as other fluid-delivery lines, has been British-based TI Automotive Ltd. (*Automotive News Europe* 1999). TI's predecessor, Tube Investments Ltd., founded in 1919 in Birmingham, England, became a major U.S. supplier in 1987 through the acquisition of Bundy Group, then the world leader in fuel and brake-fluid delivery. "Bundy supplies either the complete brake line or complete fuel line, or the two in combination. Carmakers increasingly favor combined systems. These are efficient because a rigid steel fuel system supports the sometimes flexible brake fluid system. The combined unit is more easily added to the car's underbody on the assembly line" (Chew 1997).

In 1999, TI acquired Walbro Corp., which had been founded in 1950 by Walter E. Walpole in Fenton, Michigan, to manufacture carburetors. TI combined Bundy's fuel lines with Walbro's fuel storage and delivery technology to create fully integrated fuel storage and delivery systems. Eight of the company's nine U.S. plants that made fuel-handling components in 2007 were located in the Midwest, including six in Michigan.

Fuel injection: Robert Bosch

The fuel control system includes fuel injectors to inject fuel into the intake air flow, throttle bodies to control air flow, an intake manifold to distribute air flow from the throttle bodies to engine cylinders, and a pump to push the fuel out of the tank. Increasingly popular is a common-rail injection system that stores fuel in a central rail and delivers it to the individual electronically controlled injector valves.

Several of the world's largest automotive parts suppliers have been leaders in producing fuel control systems. Robert Bosch Corp., the world's largest supplier in 2007, was also the largest supplier of fuel control systems for gasoline engines. Delphi, Denso, and Continental were the other leading suppliers of fuel injection systems and common-rail systems (Lewin 2005).

Bosch introduced electronic fuel injection in 1967 and was supplying nearly all European vehicles in the 1980s. Electronic fuel injection was less wasteful than a mechanical system using a carburetor because motorists no longer had to pump the accelerator or pull the choke knob to get a steady stream of fuel to the engine. Sensors measured airflow and air temperature to adjust the amount of fuel being delivered (Armstrong 2004c). Bosch has supplied the U.S. market with fuel injectors primarily from overseas facilities.

Fuel injection: Keihin

The leading Japanese supplier of fuel injection modules has been Keihin Corp., a Honda keiretsu. Keihin was formed in 1997 through the merger of Keihin Seiki Manufacturing Co. with two Honda captives, Hadsys and Denshigiken. Honda controlled nearly one-half of company shares. Fuel control systems accounted for one-third of the company's worldwide revenues in 2004, air conditioning one-fourth, and electronic control units and motorcycle fuel systems one-fifth each. The half-dozen fuel injection plants in the United States in 2007 were divided between three in Indiana and three in the Carolinas.

Fuel tanks: Inergy

The leading supplier of fuel tanks, with about one-third of the U.S. market, has been French-based Inergy Automotive Systems. Inergy was a 50–50 joint venture between two of Europe's leading plastics producers, Plastic Omnium and Solvay S.A., and was formed in 2000. Plastic Omnium, a French company established after World War II by chemical engineer Pierre Burelle, was an early European-based innovator in plastic parts and has become a leading supplier of bumpers (see Chapter 4). Solvay, a Belgian company founded in 1863 by Ernest Solvay, was the leading producer of sodium carbonate, made through combining ammonia with salt, carbon dioxide, and lime. The company ventured into plastics production during the 1950s, beginning with polyvinyl chloride (PVC).

Inergy became the world leader in fuel tanks by making them out of plastic (e.g., high-density polyethylene or HDPE). These tanks are lighter and less prone to corrosion than those made of metal (Chew 2002, 2004a) and are relatively easy to transport. Inergy's U.S. plant locations in 2007 included one each in the Midwest and South.

NORTH–SOUTH BATTLEGROUND

The brake may be the best example of part production being pulled toward the two ends of Auto Alley in the early twenty-first century.

Cutthroat competition, induced by rapid technological change and price drops, favored southern, low-cost locations.

Suspension production has been divided between the Midwest and the South for different reasons. Assembled suspension modules, especially control arms, are especially difficult and fragile to transport, thus favoring locations further north. At the same time, individual suspension parts, such as springs and shocks, can be transported easily, so the production of those parts is more likely to head south.

Brakes: Supplier Turmoil

Nineteenth-century vehicles were slowed by putting a long stick with a weight on the end in a front wheel, similar to the practice with a horse-drawn carriage. The first automotive brakes were placed only on rear wheels. Four-wheel brakes did not become standard on production vehicles until the 1920s.

Early automotive engineers believed that brakes on all four wheels would be dangerous because in a sudden stop the wheels could lock, causing the car to roll over and passengers to be thrown forward against the instrument panel (seat belts and other passenger restraint devices had not yet been invented). Four-wheel brakes were limited during the early twentieth century to racing cars, which were traveling too fast for two-wheel brakes to be effective. The percentage of vehicles with brakes on all four wheels increased quickly during the 1920s, from 2 percent in 1923 to 36 percent in 1925 and 91 percent in 1927 (Epstein 1928). Early brakes were mostly drum brakes. A strip or lining of friction material was fastened to a steel shoe or block shaped to fit snugly inside a drum attached to the wheel. When the brake pedal was depressed, the curved brake shoe was pushed outward to make contact with the rotating drum.

Introduced in the 1950s were disc brakes, which consisted of heavy discs or rotors bolted to the wheel hubs. When the brake pedal was depressed, both sides of the disc were pressed by brake shoes or friction pads; two shoes were used to keep the wheel more stable. Because they initially required more pedal pressure than drum brakes, disc brakes were shunned by consumers until power assistance was added during the 1960s.

With power brakes, most of the work involved in pushing the pedal was done by vacuum pressure. Depressing the brake pedal exerted a force on a piston inside a master cylinder, made stronger through opening and closing of vacuum control valves. The force was transferred from the master cylinder piston to cylinders located at each wheel. Pistons in each of these wheel cylinders were then moved, causing the brake shoes to come into contact with the revolving disc.

Antilock brake systems (ABS) appeared during the 1980s. With ABS, a computer controlled the movement of the brake shoes when the brake pedal was pressed, enabling the shoes to press against and then release the discs or drums many times per second. ABS prevented wheels from locking up, thereby increasing the ability of drivers to maintain control of their vehicles. The percentage of U.S. vehicles with ABS increased from 0.7 percent in 1986 and 4 percent in 1989 to 44 percent 1993 and 56 percent in 1994.

Drum brakes were more likely to be made in the Midwest, whereas disc and ABS brakes were more likely to be made in the South. Other brake-related parts were also likely to be made in the Midwest.

Rapid diffusion of low-cost ABS brought chaos to brake suppliers. The price of a state-of-the-art brake declined during the 1990s from $1,000 to $100 per vehicle. What was a high-tech component back in 1990 had become a generic commodity by 2000. Of the four companies responsible for nearly all U.S. brakes in 1994—AlliedSignal Automotive, GM, ITT Automotive, and Kelsey-Hayes Co.—not one was still supplying brakes five years later:

- AlliedSignal sold its Bendix brake division to Robert Bosch in 1996.
- GM's brake operations were spun off in 1999 as part of Delphi, which in turn put it up for sale in 2007.
- ITT sold its automotive brakes and chassis unit in 1998 to Continental AG, which placed it in its Alfred Teves group.
- Kelsey-Hayes was sold in 1989 to Varity Corp., which merged in 1996 with a British firm, Lucas Industries. LucasVarity in turn was sold to TRW in 1999.

As was the case with wheels, the market share losers among brake competitors into the twenty-first century were firms based in the North, whereas the suppliers based in the South were gaining. Nationality also played a role. The two brake suppliers with most of their plants in the North, Delphi and TRW, were U.S.-owned, whereas the two with most of their plants in the South, Robert Bosch and Continental, were German-owned.

Robert Bosch

Robert Bosch gained its strong position in the brake market as the ABS pioneer. The company built the first ABS in 1978 and provided the luxury German cars with it beginning in the 1980s. For the U.S. market, Bosch opened ABS plants in the South during the 1980s, including two in Tennessee and one in South Carolina. Bosch became a leader in the U.S. brake market by acquiring Bendix in 1996.

When four-wheel drum brakes became standard equipment during the 1920s, Bendix was the leading supplier. Because the company was already supplying 90 percent of electric starters, company founder Vincent Bendix was called "The King of Stop and Go" (Crain Communications 1996).

Bendix had close relations with both Ford and GM that extended deeper than supplying parts. GM bought 24 percent of Bendix in 1929. GM's interest was not brakes, but rather Bendix's growing involvement in aviation. GM officials believed that personal flying machines might someday replace terrestrial motor vehicles. "During the 1920s, it became steadily clearer that aviation was to be one of the great American growth industries" (Sloan 1964, p. 362). GM also bought 40 percent of the Fokker Aircraft Corporation of America and 100 percent of the Allison Engineering Company in 1929. With the prospect of personal flying vehicles clearly unrealistic, GM sold its Bendix shares in 1948.

Meanwhile, Bendix officials were instrumental in leading Ford's modernization and turnaround after World War II. Bendix president Ernest R. Breech became executive vice president of Ford in 1946 and chairman from 1955 to 1960. He was credited with hiring a team of energetic young executives known as the Whiz Kids. Lewis D. Crusoe, also a former Bendix official, set up Ford's first cost-accounting system during the 1950s.

Bendix was acquired in 1983 by Allied Corp., which had been founded in 1920 through the merger of five chemical companies. Allied merged in 1985 with Signal Companies, which had started producing gasoline from natural gas in 1922. A decade later AlliedSignal sold its brake division to Bosch.

Continental

The principal competition for Bosch's leadership in ABS came from another German firm, Continental, which is discussed in Chapter 10 as a leading tire supplier and in Chapter 14 as an interior electronics supplier. Continental, like its fellow German brake supplier, set up U.S. brake plants in the South, including three in North Carolina and one across the state line in Virginia.

Continental gained its leadership position in brake production by acquiring U.S.-owned ITT Automotive in 1998. Completing the international circle, ITT in turn had become a major brake supplier by acquiring German-owned Alfred Teves in 1967. Teves had been founded in 1906 to produce brakes for German cars. ITT's Teves subsidiary supplied its first U.S. ABS in 1984, for Ford's Lincoln Continental.

ITT originated in 1925 as International Telephone & Telegraph when American Telephone & Telegraph spun off its overseas interests as separate company. ITT became one of the best examples of a large conglomerate with interests in numerous unrelated industries. During the 1990s ITT was one of the 10 largest parts suppliers in the United States, but the company chose to concentrate on sectors with higher rates of return, primarily defense electronics and water treatment.

TRW

TRW was the largest supplier focusing primarily on chassis components; its steering operations have already been discussed. Its brake production was acquired from Kelsey-Hayes. During the 1920s, Kelsey-Hayes, already described as the leading supplier of wheels, was also Bendix's chief competitor in producing drum brakes. One year after the company was formed through the merger of Kelsey Wheel and Hayes Wheel, Kelsey-Hayes produced its first brakes for Ford in 1928.

Kelsey-Hayes's brake operations fell behind the other brake suppliers during the 1990s; the company suffered from multiple takeovers and failed to stay competitive in the rapidly growing and ever-cheaper ABS market. TRW inherited plants clustered in the Midwest, including one in Michigan and two each in Minnesota, Ohio, and Wisconsin.

Delphi

The ABS price breakthrough came in the early 1990s from the unlikely source of General Motors. GM's Delco Products division had been building brakes in Dayton since 1934. The Delco Brake Division was organized in 1936, moved to the Moraine Products division in 1942, and renamed Delco Moraine in 1960 so that GM could use the Delco trade name on its brakes.

Delco Moraine's ABS system, while less sophisticated than Bosch's, cost only $300 per vehicle instead of $1,000 in the early 1990s, when GM made ABS standard even on its low-priced vehicles. Stung by Delco Moraine's low price, other brake manufacturers quickly introduced more advanced ABS at even lower prices. ABS designs soon became fairly standard, and since quality was comparable, pricing became the key to market share.

With the rapid conversion of ABS from an expensive option reserved for luxury cars to low-cost accessory for all vehicles, production of brakes lost its attraction for the long-time market leaders. Delphi gave up on brakes, along with compressors, fuel handling, ignition, interiors, and suspension. Plants making these parts were placed in the Automotive Holdings Group, pending sale or closure.

In 2007 Delphi sold its brake hose business to Marco Manufacturing LLC, its brake component machining assets to TRW, and its two Mexican brake plants to Bosch.

Suspension

When a vehicle is driven on uneven road surfaces, the suspension system stabilizes the vehicle and keeps its tires on the road. The suspension system also cushions passengers from uncomfortable bumps and vibrations. Suspension components were invented early in the history of the car to dampen the rough ride over poor roads.

The principal components in the suspension system include springs, bars, and shock absorbers. The Midwest share of suspension production was below average for all parts.

Shock absorbers dampen much of the up-and-down movement because, if the car were suspended only on springs, it would bounce and sway uncomfortably after each bump. They are mounted inside the front springs and in front of the rear springs, allowing the springs to compress fully and rebound slowly.

A shock absorber consists of one cylinder nestled inside another. When the wheel travels over a bump, the lower cylinder moves with the wheel and is telescoped into the upper cylinder, which is bolted to the frame. A piston attached to the upper cylinder eases this telescoping action. As the shock absorber rebounds after impact, the lower cylinder is pulled downward.

Monroe has been the leading supplier of shock absorbers in the United States and had a well-known brand name primarily because a large percentage of its sales has been in the aftermarket. Monroe's predecessor, Brisk Blast Manufacturing Co., produced the first modern shock absorber in 1926. Monroe was acquired in 1977 by Tenneco, which has split shock absorber production between northern and southern locations, with plants in Arkansas, Georgia, Indiana, Nebraska, and Ohio.

Suspension has attracted the interest of other chassis suppliers, including the major steering suppliers and all of the major wheel suppliers, because of the possibility of integration with other handling functions through electronics. Continuous damping control is an electronic system that can adjust the tension in a shock absorber to improve vehicle handling. Sensors in the suspension modules can detect the position of the body, movement of the wheels, pace of acceleration, and steering angle. However, it was unclear if that was going to happen. The leading wheel suppliers Hayes Lemmerz and Superior both exited the suspension business where the necessary capital investment was regarded as too large to make a profit (Sherefkin 2006c).

OUTLOOK AND UNCERTAINTIES

Where a parts plant locates within Auto Alley depends to a great extent on the type of part being made. Parts that are relatively expensive and fragile to ship are more likely to continue to be produced in the Midwest. The question of where to produce a part is also influenced by labor considerations. As discussed in the next chapter, some suppliers have been lured to the South by a nonunion, lower-wage labor environment. Except for electronics, chassis parts production is currently the most dispersed among the six major subsystems. Production of some chassis parts has been moved south within the auto corridor or out of the country, whereas other parts have stayed in the Midwest.

One possible impetus for moving the production of some chassis parts back to the Midwest would be the widespread diffusion of the so-called rolling chassis. The term refers to an integrated chassis that is rolled on its own tires to the position on the assembly line moments before needed. The roll-in chassis is particularly suitable for assembly of trucks that have bodies that are bolted to frames near the end of the assembly line.

In the mid-1990s, Chrysler contracted with Dana, which secured a trademark on the name "Rolling Chassis," to supply the rolling chassis as a single module at its Camp Largo, Brazil, truck assembly plant. Dana itself manufactured some of the components, including the driveshaft, axles, fuel lines, and brake hoses. The remainder, including tires, fuel tanks, and steering linkages, were purchased from 66 suppliers. Altogether, the chassis module contained 220 components, accounting for more than one-fourth of the truck's content (*Automotive News* 1999; Kisiel 1998).

Dana lost out unexpectedly in its first attempt to supply a rolling chassis in the United States. Korean supplier Mobis was awarded a contract in 2004 to supply rolling chassis to Chrysler's Jeep plant in Toledo—an especially stinging defeat because Toledo is Dana's hometown.

Mobis was already building rolling chassis for Kia at its plant in Hwasung, Korea. Mobis was part of the Hyundai chaebol through interlocking ownership. Hyundai owned 60 percent of Kia, which in turn owned 16.2 percent of Mobis, which in turn owned 13.2 percent of Hyundai. Mobis had no North American manufacturing operations when it won the Jeep contract. But Mobis expected to rank among the world's top 10 suppliers by 2010. In the cutthroat world of global parts supply, Dana was caught asleep at the switch in its own backyard (Chang and Chappell 2004).

However, even if the rolling chassis were to become an industry standard, it is unclear how it would affect the geography of chassis production because it involves a number of components that are currently characterized by a very different geography of production within Auto Alley. As this chapter has shown, the key subsystems of a rolling chassis are currently being produced at different locations within Auto Alley for reasons distinctive to the various subsystems.

Notes

1. Ed Golden, executive director of design at Ford, quoted in Garsten (2001).
2. Ed Golden, executive director of design at Ford, quoted in Garsten (2001).
3. Richard Aneiros, vice president of Jeep and truck design at DCX, quoted in Garsten (2001).
4. Ed Golden, executive director of design at Ford, quoted in Garsten (2001).

12
Working for Suppliers

Everything that has been negotiated by the UAW, that's what comes out to $65 [in total hourly compensation] . . . Roughly $20 is what we say is competitive.[1]

The auto industry has been moving south in Auto Alley primarily because of labor considerations. Wage rates have been lower in the South than in the Midwest, and union membership has been lower. As the auto industry has moved southward, it has been transformed in a generation from a high-wage to an average-wage industry, and rates of unionization have gone from high to low.

At first glance, labor conditions in the motor vehicle industry in the early twenty-first century would appear to be favorable to the workforce. The motor vehicle industry has been one of the highest-paid manufacturing sectors in the United States. Production workers earned $921 per week in motor vehicle plants in 2007, one-third more than the $705 in the average U.S. factory.

Not by coincidence, the motor vehicle industry has also been one of the most unionized sectors in the United States. Nearly one-half of motor vehicle production workers belonged to a union in 2007, compared to less than one-tenth of the total U.S. workforce.

This early twenty-first-century snapshot of a relatively well paid and highly unionized workforce masked sharp downward trends in these figures. As recently as the 1980s, 90 percent of production workers in the U.S. motor vehicle industry belonged to a union, and in nominal terms, their wages were on average 35 percent higher than manufacturing wages.

The decline was especially steep in the first decade of the twenty-first century. Wages were declining by 1 percent per year in the U.S. motor vehicle industry while, at the same time, rising 2 percent per year in manufacturing as a whole. Meanwhile, the percentage of unionized motor vehicle workers was declining by 2 percent per year.

Wage rates in the seven leading southern states of Auto Alley—Alabama, Georgia, Kentucky, Mississippi, North Carolina, South Carolina, and Tennessee—have been one-sixth lower than those in the five Midwest states of Indiana, Illinois, Michigan, Ohio, and Wisconsin. The median hourly wage for all manufacturing workers in 2006 was $12.31 in the South compared to $14.24 in the Midwest.

Similarly, the South has had a lower unionization rate. The five Midwest states had 3.4 million workers represented by a union in 2006, or 16.7 percent of all salaried and hourly workers in the region (excluding self-employed workers). In Michigan, 20.4 percent of the workforce was unionized. The states in the portion of Auto Alley lying south of the Ohio River had 1.1 million unionized workers in 2006, representing only 6.6 percent of the total workforce.

The opportunity to move south within Auto Alley has been provided by the structural changes that the motor vehicle industry has undergone. As responsibility has shifted from carmakers to suppliers, and as market share has shifted from the Detroit 3 to foreign-owned carmakers, production has shifted from higher wage unionized plants in the Midwest to lower wage nonunion plants in the South.

Outsourcing by carmakers has been most responsible for lower rates of pay and union membership. The final assembly plants and powertrain and stamping plants operated by the carmakers have had wage rates nearly twice as high as the parts plants owned by independent suppliers. Two-thirds of the workers at carmakers were union members in 2007, compared to less than one-fifth at suppliers.

Market shifts also have had an impact on wage rates because labor costs have been lower at foreign-owned carmakers than at the Detroit 3. In 2007, hourly labor costs, including wages, benefits, and pension obligations, were about $72 at the Detroit 3, compared to about $45 to $50 at Japanese-owned carmakers (Barkholtz 2007b). The impact of foreign-owned carmakers has been even greater on union membership because all foreign-owned assembly plants (with the exception of joint ventures with the Detroit 3) have been nonunion, and union membership rates have been much lower at foreign-owned suppliers than at U.S.-owned ones.

As a result of the shifts, parts once made by union members earning $70 an hour in wages and benefits at Detroit 3 facilities—most of which are in the Midwest—have been turned over to nonunion suppliers—increasingly located in the South—paying $20 an hour in wages and benefits.

RISE AND FALL OF AUTO UNIONS

According to the U.S. Bureau of Labor Statistics, the U.S. motor vehicle industry employed approximately 751,000 production workers in 2006. Approximately 162,000 of these production workers were employed at assembly plants (NAICS Code 33611) and 589,000 at parts plants (NAICS codes 336211 and 3363).

Our database of several thousand plants showed that, in 2006, 34.5 percent of employees at supplier plants had union representation and 65.5 percent did not. Applying these percentages to the total number of production workers, an estimated 203,000 workers at supplier plants belonged to a union and 386,000 did not.

A somewhat more precise count can be made of union workers at assembly plants. In 2006, approximately 122,000 production workers at assembly plants belonged to a union and 40,000 did not. Combining the figures for assembly plants and suppliers, we estimate that a total of 325,000 production workers (43.3 percent) belonged to a union in 2006 and 426,000 (56.7 percent) did not.

Profile of Union Decline

The principal auto-related union in the United States since 1937 has been the United Auto Workers (UAW), officially the United Automobile, Aerospace and Agricultural Implement Workers of America. At parts suppliers (excluding Detroit 3 facilities), though, other unions combined have represented more workers than the UAW.

UAW

The UAW had 538,446 members in 2006, according to the union's 2007 annual report. The "real" number at the time may have been as low as 500,000 and as high as 576,131 according to UAW officials.[2]

There was no uncertainty concerning the precipitous decline in UAW membership. From its peak of 1.5 million in 1979, the union

Figure 12.1 UAW Membership, 1979–2006

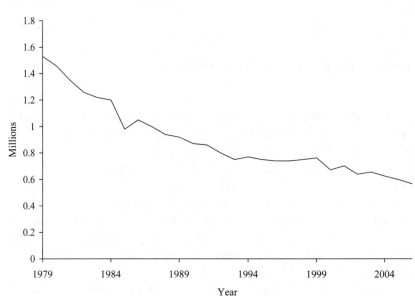

SOURCE: McAlinden (2007).

lost two-thirds of its members in three decades. And there is no end in sight in the early twenty-first century. The decline has been steady and continuous: 1,150,000 members in 1985, 850,000 in 1990, 750,000 in 1995, 650,000 in 2000, and 550,000 in 2005 (Figure 12.1).

We estimate that about 251,000 UAW members held production jobs in the motor vehicle industry in 2006. The other UAW members worked in aerospace and agricultural equipment factories, as recognized in the union's full name, as well as in casinos, hospitals, legal services, local government, and universities. UAW members also worked in nonproduction jobs in the motor vehicle industry, as well as for manufacturers of medium- and heavy-duty trucks that have not been included in this book. The 251,000 UAW members in the motor vehicle production jobs in 2006 included approximately 120,000 in final assembly plants and 131,000 in parts plants. The UAW represented production workers at every assembly plant operated by the Detroit 3, with one exception— GM's Moraine, Ohio, assembly plant—which recognized the International Union of Electronic, Electrical, Salaried, Machine and Furniture

Workers-Communications Workers of America (IUE-CWA). The IUE presence at Moraine was a legacy of the plant's original purpose of making refrigerators for Frigidaire, which GM owned until 1979.

The UAW also represented workers at three foreign-run assembly plants: AutoAlliance in Flat Rock, Michigan; Mitsubishi in Normal, Illinois; and NUMMI in Fremont, California. All three plants were originally established as joint ventures between Japanese and U.S. companies, Ford and Mazda at Flat Rock, Chrysler and Mitsubishi in Illinois, and GM and Toyota in California. Inclusion of the union was part of the joint-venture agreements.

The 131,000 parts workers represented by the UAW could be divided into two groups: about 67,000 in parts plants owned by the Detroit 3 and 64,000 in plants owned by suppliers.

UAW membership was heavily clustered in the Midwest portion of Auto Alley. The Midwest had one-half of all automotive parts workers in the United States, compared with two-thirds of all unionized parts workers and four-fifths of all UAW parts workers. Michigan, with one-fifth of all parts workers, had one-half of all UAW members. The southern portion of Auto Alley, on the other hand, with one-fourth of all parts workers, had only one-eighth of all unionized parts workers and one-fourteenth of all UAW parts workers.

Other auto industry unions

An estimated 72,000 parts workers belonged to a union other than the UAW in 2006. Roughly half of them were in the USW, a union that is derived from the United Steelworkers of America. The USW evolved from its steel-industry origins through numerous mergers. Most USW members in the motor vehicle industry arrived through a 1995 merger with the United Rubber Workers (URW), which had organized the tire factories. The second-largest group of USW members came through a 2004 merger with the Paper, Allied-Industrial, Chemical and Energy Workers International Union (PACE).

The third-largest auto-related union has been the IUE-CWA, which represented about 15,000 auto industry workers in 2006. Half were in former GM factories, especially in the Dayton area, that had been turned over to Delphi in 1999. As noted above, these factories originally produced electrical products, such as refrigerators and air conditioners. Two other unions with roughly 10,000 auto workers each in

2006 were the International Brotherhood of Teamsters and the Union of Needletrades, Industrial and Textile Employees (UNITE). With the exception of the cluster of IUE-CWA plants in the Dayton area, the pattern of representation of the various unions has been a result of the happenstance of local events.

Foreign-owned suppliers: Unions not welcome

The flip side of declining market share for the Detroit 3 and their suppliers has been an increasing market share for foreign-owned companies and their suppliers. As a result, unions lose in two ways: the Detroit 3 and their suppliers have cut union jobs, while foreign-owned companies and their suppliers have added nonunion jobs.

Union representation has been extremely low among foreign-owned suppliers in the United States. Roughly 15,000 of the 125,000 employees of Japanese-owned supplier plants belonged to a union in 2006, including only about 5,000 in the UAW. The two largest Japanese-owned suppliers in North America—Denso and Yazaki—had no union. At the largest German-owned supplier—Robert Bosch—only 7 percent of production workers were unionized.

Unions and companies agree that foreign-owned plants do not provide an environment conducive for collective bargaining, but they would describe the environment differently. The companies see an environment in which collective bargaining is unnecessary, whereas unions see an environment in which collective bargaining is suppressed.

Foreign-owned companies argue that a union is not needed in plants run according to Japanese-style flexible work rules and that most of their employees recognize and accept that fact. They view key elements of flexible production, especially reliance on teamwork and local-scale problem-solving, as inimical with union-imposed work rules.

At unionized motor vehicle plants, jobs were traditionally allocated to hundreds of classifications, and workers could not be moved from one classification to another without permission of the union. Jobs were assigned to individual members according to seniority. Unions defended the seniority system for allocating jobs. A 50-year-old should not be placed in a team with a 30-year-old and told to do the same job. The older worker should be assigned a less physically demanding job, and the seniority system was the way to accomplish that.

Unions have alleged that nonunion plants, especially Japanese-owned plants, have had substantially higher injury rates. U.S. Occupational Safety and Health Administration (OSHA) statistics used to support the charge have been vehemently disputed by the companies. The UAW has claimed that Honda's East Liberty, Ohio, assembly plant had annual injury rates exceeding 50 percent, a figure that Honda has denied, compared to less than 10 percent at Detroit 3 plants (Hakim 2002).

Unions and companies agree that automotive workers in union and nonunion plants alike have been prone to repetitive stress injuries, even if they disagree on the rates. The overall injury rate in the auto industry ranks third highest among all sectors, behind only shipbuilding and meatpacking. Unions argue that company treatment of injured workers varies between union and nonunion plants, and those differences ultimately contribute to the higher nonunion injury rates.

In a UAW plant, an injured worker with 10 years of service is assigned a less physically demanding job until the worker retires with maximum benefits, normally 30 years. In a flexible production plant, an injured worker can be returned to the same job that led to the repetitive stress injury in the first place. Rather than transfer to a less demanding job, a repeatedly injured worker in a nonunion plant may be offered a cash severance buy-out. An unproductive worker can thereby be removed years before the individual has qualified for the maximum pension, thus providing the company with a double financial savings.

To obtain employees capable of working under flexible work rules, factories hire people who pass through an elaborate process run by human resource specialists. Applicants are first tested for basic skills in reading, writing, arithmetic, and mechanical dexterity. Those with acceptable basic skills are placed in groups for a few hours of behavioral assessment. The groups are asked to work together to assemble a product or solve a problem. Applicants considered successful team players are interviewed to determine if they are trainable, reliable, and willing to try unfamiliar work.

Unions charge that the more elaborate hiring process under flexible production takes place at taxpayer expense. States routinely agree to do the initial screening and interviewing at their offices and to provide subsidies for training at community colleges. Unionized plants obtain new workers primarily through relatives or friends of people already working there. With sharp reductions in hiring at the Detroit 3 and unionized suppliers, opportunities had been meager for children and other relatives of long-time autoworkers to gain entry to the same generous wages and benefits enjoyed by the older generation.

In a union plant, an individual who has a job-related problem first meets with the union representative. If the union official considers the complaint justified, a formal grievance is filed with the company. Thousands of grievances can pile up in a plant and take months to resolve.

In contrast, under flexible rules, a worker is expected to look for solutions through direct consultations with team and group leaders. Suggestions for changing the immediate workplace environment are encouraged, reviewed, and often adopted. When the arrangement of machines on the factory floor needs to be changed, management first asks line workers how they think things should flow. When tooling changes take too long, management asks hourly workers rather than expensive outside consultants how to fix the problem.

The UAW has viewed its failure to organize foreign-owned plants to be caused not by better plant conditions but by more effective intimidation tactics by employers. Foreign-owned carmakers vigilantly guard against unionization at their suppliers as an outer line of defense against unionization attempts inside their facilities. Unions charge that international carmakers make explicit threats to drop a supplier that lets in the union.

Unions also suggest that they are benefiting workers in nonunion plants to the extent that they get a "free ride." Workers in nonunion plants freely admit that collective bargaining agreements elsewhere in the industry positively influence their wages and benefits. Given this reality, why go to the trouble of voting in the union and paying dues? The union may be providing informal services to the roughly one-third or so in a nonunion plant who signed union cards or voted for the union in a losing election.

Organizing Parts Plants during the 1930s

The key event in the successful organizing of the motor vehicle industry is usually identified as the 1937 sit-down strike at several GM plants in Flint, Michigan, which ended with the company recognizing the UAW. The 1937 GM strikes actually represented the culmination of a campaign that began three years earlier and 100 miles south of Flint in supplier plants.

"In 1934 labor erupted," wrote labor historian Irving Bernstein. "A number of these strikes were of unusual importance . . . Four were social upheavals [including] those of auto parts workers at the Electric Auto-Lite Company in Toledo . . ." (Bernstein 1970, p. 217). Bernstein's three other three defining events were strikes by truck drivers in Minneapolis, longshoremen in San Francisco, and cotton-textile workers in New England and the South.

Auto-Lite, the linchpin

Auto-Lite, now part of Honeywell, was one of the largest independent parts suppliers at the time of the 1934 strike. The company was founded in Toledo in 1911 to produce generators that were called "Auto-liters" and were sold as a power source for electric headlamps, which were then replacing gas-fired ones.

Founder Clement O. Miniger, a native of Fostoria, Ohio, near Toledo, had been a pharmaceutical salesman and so-called drug huckster among other professions and later would be a leading Toledo banker (Bernstein 1970, p. 219). Miniger sold Auto-Lite in 1914 to a friend, John Willys, owner of Willys-Overland Co., which was producing the country's second-best-selling car brand behind Ford. Miniger returned to Auto-Lite as president in 1918 and was chairman during the 1934 strike.

Like most parts suppliers—and half of all U.S. manufacturers at the time—Auto-Lite paid workers a specified sum for each piece produced rather than according to a preset hourly rate. Workers did not object to piece rate during prosperous times because the faster they worked, and the more they produced, the more pay they took home. But if the line stopped, workers were paid nothing.

Suppliers like Auto-Lite stayed in business during the Depression by slashing the piece rate. Piece rate workers had to stay in the plant as long as 14 hours a day to take home what they could have made in a few hours before the Depression. In reaction, workers formed a union in 1933 at Auto-Lite, as well as at other large Toledo plants, including Willys and Spicer Axle (which became part of Dana).

When demands to grant union recognition, seniority privileges, and a 10 percent wage increase were rejected, a strike was called on February 23, 1934. It ended five days later, when federal mediators convinced the employers to offer a 5 percent wage increase and to agree to "set up machinery for future negotiations . . . on all other issues." The union understood "future negotiations" to mean that a settlement would be reached by April 1 (Bernstein 1970, p. 220). When Auto-Lite again refused to negotiate, the union called a second strike for April 12. This time, only one-fourth of the workers went out on strike. The company hired strikebreakers and kept the plant open.

At this point, the Lucas County Unemployed League, an affiliate of the Marxist American Workers Party, began mass picketing of the Auto-Lite plant with unemployed workers. Court orders limiting the number of picketers to 25 were defied. Although Party officials were repeatedly arrested, the number of picketers grew to 10,000. Fearing he did not have enough personnel to control the crowd, the sheriff deputized special police, who were paid by Auto-Lite. One of these deputies seized an elderly man in view of many in the crowd and started hitting him. "This triggered 'the Battle of Toledo'" (Bernstein 1970, p. 222).

Fighting between the picketers and police lasted for seven hours on May 23, 1934. The Ohio National Guard arrived the next morning to evacuate 1,500 strikebreakers trapped in the factory all night. Twice the picketers charged the Guard and were repelled with bayonets and tear gas. On the third charge, the Guard opened fire, killing two and wounding 15. A final charge was repelled by more rifle fire, with two more wounded.

Prominent Ohioan Charles P. Taft, son of President William Howard Taft and brother of long-time Senator Robert A. Taft, was brought in to mediate. He ordered closure of the Auto-Lite plant pending a settlement of the dispute. Because it had recently negotiated a large contract to supply Chrysler, Auto-Lite was anxious to settle, so it agreed to negotiate directly with the union. A settlement was quickly reached, and the plant reopened June 5. The company recognized the union, rehired strikers, raised wages 5¢ per hour, and set a minimum wage of 35¢ per hour.

Organizing successes at other parts plants

The union's Auto-Lite victory in June 1934 came at a critical time for the U.S. labor movement, which was split between the American Federation of Labor's (AFL) entrenched craft-based unions and advocates of industry-wide unions for autoworkers and other mass production industries. The AFL chartered the United Automobile Workers of America in 1935 but permitted it to try to organize only workers on the final assembly lines, excluding parts makers and other workers at final assembly plants such as cleaners. The union was suspended a year later when members refused to accept the AFL's choice of leadership.

The unwillingness of the AFL's craft-based unions to vigorously organize unskilled mass production workers led disaffected UAW members and other unions to create the Committee of Industrial Organizations (CIO) in 1935. The initial purpose of the CIO was to work for AFL acceptance of industrial unionism, but when the AFL suspended the UAW and nine other unions in 1936, CIO leaders transformed the organization into an independent federation, which was renamed Congress of Industrial Organizations in 1938. The CIO and AFL remained rival organizations until merging in 1955.

Unable to make inroads at the Detroit 3, the UAW turned next to organizing suppliers. Its first use of the sit-down strike came at a Bendix brake plant in South Bend, Indiana, beginning November 17, 1936. The plant was occupied by 1,500 of the 2,600 workers to forestall an attempted lockout—the company had ordered all workers to assemble outside the plant. After a nine-day strike, the company agreed to honor a contract negotiated with the union five months earlier.

The day after settling at Bendix, the UAW brought the sit-down tactic to Detroit supplier plants. First, Midland Steel's 1,200 Detroit-area production workers went on strike on November 27, 1936, to demand union recognition, a wage increase, and an end to piecework. The strike ended December 4, when Midland agreed to all demands. Six days later, 500 of Kelsey-Hayes's 5,000 workers occupied the company's Detroit factory to protest a line speedup. The company settled on December 24, offering higher wages and overtime pay, seniority protection, and a 20 percent reduction in the line's speed.

The Midland and Kelsey strikes were both settled on terms favorable to the union in large measure because of pressure on the companies from the Detroit 3. Midland was a major supplier of frames to Chrysler and Ford, and Kelsey was a major supplier of wheels and brake drums to Ford. Once their final assembly lines were forced to halt because of parts shortages, Chrysler and Ford threatened to move their business to other suppliers.

The UAW's penultimate strike against GM was also aimed at parts production rather than final assembly. A sit-down strike began at GM's Fisher Body plant in Cleveland with 7,000 workers on December 28, 1936. Strikes spread to the Fisher One and Two plants in Flint on December 30; to the Chevrolet transmission and Guide Lamp plants in Norwood, Ohio, and Anderson, Indiana, respectively, on December 31; to the Chevrolet transmission plant in Toledo on January 4; and to the Fisher Body plant in Janesville, Wisconsin, on January 5. Only then did the strike finally reach assembly plants, beginning with Chevrolet's Janesville plant on January 5 and Cadillac's Detroit plant on January 7. Strikes at parts plants produced enough shortages to force GM to shut production everywhere until the strike was settled on February 11.

GM's recognition of the UAW in 1937 was followed quickly by agreements at Chrysler, as well as at smaller independents such as Hudson, Packard, and Studebaker. Several large parts makers also reached an agreement with the UAW, including Bohn Aluminum, Briggs Body, Motor Products, Murray Body, Timken-Detroit Axle, and L.A. Young Spring & Wire. Ford held out until 1941. By the time the United States entered World War II, the UAW had successfully organized nearly the entire motor vehicle industry, both final assembly and parts.

The URW used a somewhat different form of the sit-down strike in the Akron tire plants. Hundreds of "quickie" sit-down strikes occurred in the tire plants beginning in 1934, ranging from a few minutes to a few days to protest job insecurity, lower wages, and line speedup. The URW won its first contract with one of the four major tire makers, Firestone, in 1937, after an eight-week strike. B.F. Goodrich and U.S. Rubber signed contracts in 1938 without strikes; the last of the Goodyear plants held out until 1941.

Pattern bargaining

With most automotive production workers in a union, and with most production in the hands of only three companies, the motor vehicle industry in the years after World War II adopted a distinctive form of negotiations called pattern bargaining. Pattern bargaining was instrumental in securing high wages for Detroit 3 automotive workers compared to production workers in other manufacturing sectors.

UAW contracts with the Detroit 3 expired on the same date. Shortly before the expiration, the union would select one of the companies for intense negotiations. After the union and the targeted company reached an agreement, the pattern set in that contract became the basis for negotiating with the other two carmakers. The contract covered workers in the Detroit 3 parts plants as well as final assembly plants.

The UAW selected as its target the company considered most likely to accede to the union's principal demand. In general, the UAW targeted Ford when it sought acceptance of innovative concepts, such as annual improvement factor (AIF), cost of living adjustment (COLA), and supplemental unemployment benefits (SUB). When its principal goal was a higher wage rate, the UAW targeted GM—known as "Generous Motors" in those days. Chrysler was targeted if preliminary negotiations indicated that it would balk at proposals accepted by its two larger competitors.

The UAW also targeted the company considered most vulnerable to a strike for competitive reasons. If an agreement were not reached, the union struck only that company, leaving the other two companies to continue operating at full capacity. The targeted company was pressured to settle the strike quickly because customers were buying cars from the other two companies. Instead of annual contracts, the UAW agreed to sign multiyear contracts so that the companies could plan investment and product development over several years free from the uncertainty of possible work stoppages. The typical length was three years during the second half of the twentieth century and four years into the twenty-first century.

Pattern bargaining spilled over to the other auto-related unions after World War II. The URW negotiated the same wage increase with all four major tire companies beginning in 1946, rather than continue to bargain on an individual plant and company basis. U.S. Rubber signed a master agreement that applied uniformly to all 19 of its plants in 1947, and the other three large tire makers followed suit within a year.

In 1960, when pattern bargaining was new, Detroit 3 wages were 16 percent higher than the average of all U.S. manufacturing workers, $2.63 per hour compared to $2.26. After several decades of pattern bargaining, the $25.95 average hourly rate for Detroit 3 workers in 2002 was 69 percent higher than the $15.36 average for all U.S. manufacturing workers (McAlinden 2007).

STATE OF THE UNION IN THE TWENTY-FIRST CENTURY

With the precipitous decline in employment at the Detroit 3, the UAW has recognized that its future viability depends on organizing independent parts suppliers. A sign of its importance was the appointment for the first time of a vice president with responsibility for organizing and representing supplier plants. In the past, the UAW had allocated the assignment to lower level officials.

Subsequently the 2003 national agreement stated that the Detroit 3 would inform their suppliers of their "positive and constructive relationship" with the UAW and of their belief that all employers should respect the right of employees to seek union representation (Hudson 2003). All things being equal, the Detroit 3 would award contracts to union suppliers, but that left the UAW with the challenge of actually demonstrating that productivity in the union plant was comparable to that of a nonunion competitor. Achieving competitive productivity in a union plant inevitably meant reducing wages, reducing workforce, or reducing both.

Some Recent Organizing Successes

The UAW lacked the resources to attempt to organize several thousand parts suppliers. So it identified the group of suppliers with the brightest organizing prospects. This turned out to be Tier 1 interior parts producers.

Organizing interior suppliers

Several factors have pointed to UAW organizers toward interior suppliers. First, interior suppliers—especially final seat assemblers—have been relatively constrained by geography, specifically the need to locate immediately adjacent to final assembly plants for just-in-time delivery. Because seat suppliers must locate next door to a final assembly plant, they cannot run away from a union organizing campaign.

Second, wages in the interior sector have been near the average for all suppliers. Average hourly wages for production workers ranged from a high of $18.14 at engine parts suppliers to a low of $12.93 at stamping suppliers in 2003, a gap of 40 percent, according to the Center for Automotive Research. Between the two, workers earned an average of $14.07 at electrical parts suppliers, $14.15 at chassis parts suppliers, and $16.51 at interior parts suppliers (McAlinden 2004, p. 41). The best prospects for expanding union membership seemed to be among workers in the middle categories.

The most important reason for targeting interior suppliers was the extreme consolidation of production at three very large suppliers—JCI, Lear, and Magna—incidentally, each with very different labor relations histories. As the UAW began to target the interior sector, nearly all of Lear's production workers were union members in 2000, compared to only 2 percent at Magna and about half at JCI. The UAW was able to leverage its strong position at Lear to increase representation at JCI and Magna.

Lear's high unionization rate stemmed in part from its acquisition during the 1990s of Ford and GM seating plants that already had UAW representation. Subsequently Lear proactively decided to turn this legacy of labor relations into a strategic asset. The UAW was invited to organize Lear's nonunion plants, most notably the 5,000 production workers making headliners and instrument panels at plants acquired from UT Automotive in 1999. In part because of its employee relations, Lear was judged the most admired company in the United States in the motor vehicle parts industry in *Fortune* magazine's 2004 survey of corporate reputation.

At JCI, the UAW represented workers at 20 of its 32 plants in 2004, compared with only 10 of 28 plants a decade earlier. Gains were made in part at plants that JCI had acquired from Chrysler and in part through successful organizing campaigns. The focus of conflict between the UAW and JCI during the late 1990s was a plant in Oberlin, Ohio, that supplied Econoline seats for Ford's Lorain assembly plant, as well as one in Plymouth, Michigan, that supplied Expedition seats for Ford's Wayne assembly plant.

In 1995, the UAW threatened to strike Ford after it sourced seats to nonunion JCI plants in Oberlin and Plymouth. The strike against Ford was averted when JCI agreed to recognize the union in 1996 at the two plants, as well as at a third one in Strongville, Ohio, without an election, after the UAW had collected enough cards to force an election at Oberlin. Two years later the JCI plants in Oberlin and Plymouth were struck. The workers demanded wages comparable to those paid by Lear to its UAW-represented workers. The strike could have quickly brought Ford's production of the Econoline and Expedition to a standstill. In turn, JCI offered to supply Ford with seats from its nonunion plants, but Ford refused. Instead, Ford moved to obtain seats from Lear and Visteon. Ford's move forced JCI to the bargaining table, and the strike was settled on terms comparable to those at Lear.

JCI management has since reached the conclusion that antiunion activities and practices viewed as unfair by the union were not in the company's strategic interest in attracting and retaining Detroit 3 business. Consequently, in 2002 JCI gave the UAW an opportunity to organize 8,000 workers at the company's 26 plants that supplied the Detroit 3. Not all JCI plants immediately adopted more conciliatory attitudes. At three plants where the union had been recognized—Earth City, Missouri; Shreveport, Louisiana; and Oklahoma City, Oklahoma—contracts were signed in 2002 only after a two-day strike.

The UAW has secured JCI's tacit agreement not to oppose organizing efforts at plants supplying the Detroit 3, and the union in turn has tacitly agreed not to attempt to organize JCI plants supplying international carmakers. Although it has consistently trailed competitor Lear in total world and North American sales, JCI has become the dominant supplier of seats to Japanese transplants in the United States, one of the few U.S.-owned suppliers to achieve such a market position.

Japanese-owned assembly plants have been eager to have nonunion seat suppliers because of close links between the two: seats are put together very close to the final assembly plant and are delivered frequently. A unionized seat plant could encourage organizing activities at other nearby suppliers, not to mention the final assembly plant itself. The ability to keep the union away from foreign-owned assembly plants is a significant component of JCI's strong market position with them.

Unions have also made progress organizing the other leading seat supplier, Magna, which had staked out an especially aggressive antiunion stance. Magna's Windsor, Ontario, seat plant, a Chrysler supplier, became the company's first plant to recognize the Canadian Auto Workers (CAW) union in 2001. In 2007, Magna and the CAW agreed on a landmark deal that ended years of adversarial relations. The union could organize Magna's Canadian plants in exchange for a no-strike pledge and more flexible work rules (Sherefkin and Barkholz 2007a).

In the United States, Magna and the UAW negotiated an arrangement similar to the one in Canada (Sherefkin and Barkholz 2007b). As Magna became Chrysler's leading seat maker and largest overall supplier, union recognition was inevitable given the attitudes of competitors Lear and JCI.

As a result of the UAW's organizing success at JCI and Magna, wages for seat production workers coalesced in the first decade of the twenty-first century at about $17 per hour, about $30 including benefits. Given the extreme demand for just-in-time delivery and sector consolidation, an orderly labor market proved especially critical in the rationalization of the interior sector of the supplier industry.

Other UAW organizing successes

Beyond seats, UAW organizing was also directed at selected chassis and powertrain suppliers. The principal successes in the first few years of the twenty-first century came at Dana and Eagle-Picher.

Toledo-based Dana, initially known as Spicer Axle, was one of the first parts suppliers to be organized during the early 1930s, along with Auto-Lite. The company was also one of the first to negotiate a master agreement with the UAW, in 1955. The UAW negotiated a neutrality letter with Dana in the late 1970s stating that the supplier would not communicate to its workers in an anti-UAW manner during organizing drives.

Nonetheless, Dana adopted aggressive antiunion policies. UAW-represented plants were closed and new nonunion ones were built, primarily in the South. Workers were threatened with job loss, questioned about voting intentions, forced to walk past antiunion management to get to work, and prohibited from wearing prounion shirts while the company supplied opponents with antiunion ones. Dana plant managers understood that they would lose their jobs if the union got in. The UAW took Dana to arbitration five times for violating the neutrality agreement and won each time. Into the twenty-first century, only 30 of Dana's 200 U.S. facilities were unionized, only 9 by the UAW.

The turning point in relations between Dana and the UAW came at a frame plant in Elizabethtown, Kentucky, the company's largest and possibly most profitable plant. After workers rejected the union by a vote of 670 to 320 in 2002, and two earlier campaigns failed to reach the voting stage, the UAW accused Dana management of intimidation and filed grievances with the National Labor Relations Board. Cards were signed by 61 percent of Elizabethtown's production workers asking for another vote.

Stepping into the picture at this critical juncture was Elizabethtown's customer, Ford. Elizabethtown was supplying frames for the Explorer sport utility, assembled at nearby Louisville, and Ford wanted no disruption in production of what was then a very popular—and profitable—model. Around the same time Dana lost its Jeep axle contract, the historic core of its business. The loss of that business was poignant because both Dana's headquarters and the Jeep assembly plant were based in Toledo.

Dana was then also facing a hostile takeover by ArvinMeritor. In its axle business Dana's major competitor was Eaton Corp., a company with an impeccable prounion stance. All Eaton plants had been unionized between 1937 and 1941. Founder J.O. Eaton, a New Deal supporter, raised wages of all employees by between 20 and 35 percent in 1933 in the depth of the Depression. Eaton declared that the subsistence income for a family of four was $25 a week, and anyone earning less would receive the difference as a loan. Eaton reasoned that the company could borrow money but people could not. He loaned his workers $300,000, and all but $300 was ultimately repaid (Eaton Corporation 1985, p. 14).

Faced with a threat to its Detroit 3 business, Dana suddenly changed its long-standing antiunion stance in 2003. The company and union quickly struck a "partnership agreement" in which Dana agreed to stop opposing organizing efforts at its Detroit 3 supplier plants. "Good labor relations is a competitive advantage," said Dana spokesman Gary Corrigan (Butters 2004).

Only a few hours after announcing the agreement, it was explained to workers at Elizabethtown by Dana managers and Bob King, then UAW vice president in charge of organizing suppliers. This was the first time a union official had been allowed inside the plant. Dana recognized the union at Elizabethtown on the basis of a majority of workers having already signed cards requesting an election—normally only 30 percent of workers need to sign cards to hold an election. Dana also agreed to recognize the union at other Detroit 3 supplier plants on the same basis, beginning with two plants in Virginia, Buena Vista and Bristol. The company had been charged with 36 violations of federal law after the union lost an election by eight votes at Bristol in 2002.

The UAW also made organizing gains at Eagle Picher, a Cincinnati-based supplier of gaskets and dampers. The union had only 17 members at Eagle Picher in 1999, at a gasket plant in Inkster, Michigan, but it was able to organize another 1,200 workers at three plants in 2000 and 2001. The UAW won an election at Eagle Picher's Hillsdale, Michigan, plant in 2000, after two previous failures in 1992 and 1998. The National Labor Relations Board had overturned the 1999 election and ordered another vote because of management threats and harassment.

Further union election victories in 2001 came at Eagle Picher plants in Blacksburg, Virginia, and Traverse City, Michigan. Workers voted for the union in an attempt to halt erosion of wages, medical benefits, and working conditions. The Traverse City vote was especially significant because it represented the third major organizing victory in that northwestern Michigan community far from the union's core support in southeastern Michigan. The other two were a Tower Automotive plant and a Lear plant acquired from United Technologies Automotive. In addition to Traverse City, the UAW also organized a Tower plant in Clinton Township, Michigan.

A Time to Fold

Poker players know that there is a time to hold and a time to fold. For the UAW, the time to fold came early in the twenty-first century, as the carmaker-owned parts plants could not keep up with competition from independent parts producers. At the heart of the issue was the fact that the carmakers paid workers in their parts plants according to the assembly wage schedule. As the competitive position of the Detroit 3 continued to erode rather quickly in the late 1990s, issues like the uncompetitive nature of in-house parts operations came to the forefront. Continuing to pay $70 an hour in wages and benefits for work that could be done by competing unionized suppliers for $20 an hour was not sustainable.

That issue first came to a head at a former Chrysler drivetrain parts plant in New Castle, Indiana. The New Castle plant was one of the oldest in the country, having opened in 1907 as a Maxwell-Briscoe assembly plant. When Walter Chrysler acquired Maxwell-Briscoe in 1925 and renamed the company after himself, New Castle was one of six original facilities. Rather than final assembly, Chrysler used the New Castle plant to make drivetrain parts.

Metaldyne

When Chrysler put several of its parts plants up for sale, the future of the New Castle one was grim. Metaldyne agreed to purchase a 60 percent stake in the plant and to run it for one year, 2003, to see if it could be made profitable. Metaldyne was willing to keep the union in the plant but said it couldn't run it profitably unless a new labor contract was negotiated. The union was faced with a stark choice: keep the plant open, with fewer jobs at lower wages, or let the plant close.

Under Metaldyne's management, a new contract was successfully negotiated with the UAW. According to the agreement, average hourly wages were reduced from $26 to $16, and new hires started at a lower wage tier of $12 an hour. The contract also introduced flexible work rules (Sherefkin 2002b). The 1,200 Chrysler employees at New Castle were given three choices: early retirement, transfer to Chrysler plants in other cities, or work for Metaldyne at lower wages. Those remaining at Metaldyne with at least 10 years' service would receive a $10,000 bonus for each year of service. Only 200 stayed. Subsequently Metaldyne hired 550 new workers for the plant.

Metaldyne has considered the New Castle plant to be a success. In the first year, sales increased from $400 million to $500 million and productivity increased 30 percent. The UAW has also considered the Metaldyne story a success, as it has signaled that it would be willing to entertain similar restructuring at other endangered parts plants.

Former Detroit 3 suppliers

Suppliers spun off by GM during the 1990s, such as American Axle, DelcoRemy, and Guide, also inherited high-wage assembly labor contracts. In 2004 the UAW and Guide agreed to a five-year contract with a two-tier wage structure of $22.95 per hour for existing workers and $12.50 for new ones (Armstrong 2004d). However, this was of little relevance in the short run because few new hires were anticipated for many years. The new contract represented the erosion of a wage structure that had become unsustainable.

A one-day strike at American Axle in February 2004 produced an agreement that permitted two-tier wages of $17 per hour for new hires and $25 for existing workers. In exchange for the two-tier wages, the company agreed not to close any plants during the four-year term of the contract. It had wanted to close a forge plant in Detroit and an axle plant in Buffalo. To gain ratification of the contract, American Axle threw in a signing bonus of $5,000 plus 2 percent of wages for each worker, as well as $1,000 annual Christmas bonuses. In 2008, the UAW struck American Axle again. This strike was over the company's intent to substantially cut wages and benefits. It severely disrupted its principal customer, GM.

By far, however, the greatest challenge that the UAW faced in salvaging former Detroit 3 parts plants came with Visteon and Delphi. When it was spun off in 1999, Delphi became the largest supplier in the United States and in the world, the largest supplier for GM, and the largest unionized supplier. Similarly, Visteon was turned into an independent company by Ford in 2000. It instantly became the second-largest supplier in the United States and in the world, as well as Ford's largest supplier. Likewise, it also instantly became the second-largest unionized supplier. The UAW represented 50 percent of Visteon's 24,000 workers and 90 percent of Delphi's 44,000 workers, and other unions represented the rest.

However, Delphi and Visteon found themselves paying Detroit 3 wages while trying to compete for business with suppliers—unionized and nonunion—paying much lower wages. This was clearly an unsustainable position for Delphi and Visteon, and the UAW understood that. But instantly slashing wages in half to become competitive was just as untenable—even if the UAW permitted it, the company would face a crippling morale problem.

The UAW agreed to a two-tiered wage structure at Visteon, with starting wage for new hires set at $14, compared with $24 for former Ford workers.[3] Yet even a mere two-tier wage structure didn't satisfy former Ford workers, who were to be treated as indistinguishable from other Ford workers even though they were now at a parts supplier. They received Ford checks and Ford pensions, and they could exercise seniority rights to transfer to facilities still owned by Ford. The expectation was that as job openings occurred at Ford, they would be filled by Ford employees "assigned" to Visteon. Still, Visteon's high costs continued to cause "considerable tensions with Ford" (Sedgwick 2003).

The arrangement at Ford lasted less than five years. Having lost money each year of its existence, Visteon faced bankruptcy unless drastic action was taken. As a result, half of Visteon's plants were "given" back to Ford because Visteon couldn't operate them profitably even with $15-an-hour labor. Like the children's card game old maid, Visteon hoped to survive by having Ford extract the "losers" from its hand. Visteon would drop from the second- to the ninth-largest supplier in the United States by shedding half of its business and workforce (see Chapter 2).

The principal way to address Delphi's uncompetitive wage bill in a manner agreeable to the UAW in the short term was a sharp reduction in the size of the workforce, accelerated through buyout programs. The number of UAW employees at Delphi declined from 22,000 in 2006 to 4,000 in 2008 (*International Herald Tribune* 2007; *USA Today* 2006). Wages were cut from about $27 per hour to between $14 and $18.50 an hour. To make the cuts more palatable, 4,000 long-term employees received a bonus of $105,000 to be paid over three years (Barkholtz 2007c; Stoll and McCracken 2007).

OUTLOOK AND UNCERTAINTIES

The restructuring of the auto industry in the twenty-first century has made and lost the fortunes of investors and the careers of executives, but it has been the rank and file workers who have been most buffeted by the changes. Wages have been lowered, benefits slashed, job classifications eliminated, work rules modified, and jobs cut altogether.

Between 2000 and 2006, the number of production jobs in the U.S. motor vehicle industry declined from 948,000 to 751,000. Production jobs declined from 207,000 to 162,000 at assembly plants and from 741,000 to 589,000 at parts plants. The vast majority of the 197,000 production jobs lost between 2000 and 2006 were held by unionized workers. On the assembly side, the loss of 45,000 production workers masked an even larger decline in union members; employment at Detroit 3 assembly plants was reduced by more than 45,000 between

2000 and 2006, whereas employment at nonunionized foreign-owned assembly plants actually increased.

On the parts side, about 64,000 of the 153,000 decline in employment between 2000 and 2006 came at Delphi and Visteon, where most production workers were represented by a union. The share of unionized workers among the other 89,000 production jobs lost at parts plants between 2000 and 2006 cannot be determined from our data, but we believe it to have been a substantial percentage.

Two issues have shaped the changing labor agreements in the auto supplier sector in the early twenty-first century. By paying the relatively high levels of wages and benefits typical of assembly plants, the Detroit 3's parts operations had become woefully uncompetitive compared to their domestic competition. Furthermore, continuing erosion of the Detroit 3's market share in combination with the southern movement of assembly and parts plants has contributed to a transformation of labor relations in the U.S. auto sector.

The higher wage rates at Detroit 3 parts plants have dominated the drive for increased outsourcing to independent suppliers. Contracts negotiated in unionized supplier plants were substantially lower than those in the Detroit 3 plants. In 2002 the average hourly wage in the UAW contract with 25 suppliers covering 19,379 workers was $15.76, only 3 percent higher than the average for all U.S. manufacturing (McAlinden 2004). Wages paid in nonunion plants have been even lower.

A key to restructuring labor relations has been the southern movement of assembly and parts plants. Auto alley has become the heart of U.S. motor vehicle production, its southern end having experienced rapid growth as most new assembly plants and parts plants have been opened there. The attraction of the South has been its nonunion environment.

As the downward spiral of market share loss and job loss ran its course, inevitably the Detroit 3 and unions have blamed each other. Companies have blamed excessive wage and benefit obligations, and unions have blamed poor management and products. Corporate executives have reassured jittery shareholders that investments would be protected, while democratically elected union leaders have reassured jittery members that jobs would be protected. Neither could deliver on their promises.

The precipitous decline in auto union representation showed no signs of slowing in the early twenty-first century. The percentage of union workers in the U.S. auto industry in the twenty-first century was the lowest since the 1930s. At the current rate of decline, in a quarter century, the union would no longer have any auto workers to represent. Reversing that trend is the main challenge of automotive unions going forward.

The UAW leadership has held many discreet meetings with the Detroit 3, parts makers, government officials, and even Toyota. Asking current members to choose between unemployment and wage cuts has been politically impossible for UAW leadership, a surefire recipe for being voted out of office. Instead, the UAW has negotiated lower wages and employment levels for the future while protecting the status of current members. When current employees retire, they are either not replaced or are replaced by new employees at lower wage rates.

In moments of detached analysis, the UAW and the Detroit 3 recognize that the survival of one depends on the survival of the other. Yet after nearly a century of bitter conflict between them, the biggest challenge facing both parties is bringing themselves to acknowledge explicitly that they must transform the existing antagonist labor–management paradigm.[4] The 2007 labor agreement between the UAW and the Detroit 3 offered promise of such a transformation. It improved the competitiveness of the Detroit 3 by establishing a lower wage structure and independent trusts to manage retiree health care liabilities. The agreement seemed based on a recognition by both the UAW and the Detroit 3 that their fates are inseparably linked (Howes 2007b; Simon 2007a).

Notes

1. Delphi chairman and CEO Robert S. Miller, quoted in *The Washington Post* (2005).
2. The lower number is from Congressional testimony presented in March 2007 by UAW president Ron Gettelfinger. The higher number is from an unnamed UAW source in Shepardson (2007).
3. The rationale was that a growing Visteon would get labor cost relief by being able to hire new workers at substantially lower wages.
4. See, for example, *Detroit News* columnist Daniel Howes, "Change or Die: It's Our Choice" (Howes 2007a).

Part 4

The Endangered U.S. Supplier

On paper, the U.S. auto industry looks set to prosper in the twenty-first century. New vehicle sales in the United States remained at historically high levels through the 1990s and the first decade of the twenty-first century. Despite globalization of the industry, most vehicles sold in the United States in the early twenty-first century were still being assembled in the United States from parts made mostly in the United States.

The supplier sector of the industry is expected to prosper as well. As this book has shown, suppliers are responsible for adding more than two-thirds of the value added to cars. And the supplier's share is expected to increase. Having been given more responsibility by carmakers, suppliers have evolved into providers of complex manufacturing tasks based on their own research and development.

Despite all of these favorable trends, U.S.-owned parts suppliers face an uncertain future. The number of U.S.-based Tier 1 suppliers is declining rapidly. As discussed in this section of the book, two factors account for this decline.

First, the U.S. auto parts industry has seen an increase in international competition, which manifests itself through an increase in both the percentage of imported parts as well as the number of U.S.-based suppliers owned by foreign companies. As a result, less than one-half of the parts in vehicles assembled in the United States were made in the United States by U.S. companies in the first decade of the twenty-first century. The endangered status of U.S. parts makers can also be attributed to decisions by vehicle assemblers to streamline their supply chains by sharply reducing their numbers of Tier 1 suppliers. GM reduced its Tier 1 suppliers from 3,700 in 2001 to 3,200 in 2005, and Ford from 2,500 to 800. The international carmakers have set up assembly operations in the United States with only a few hundred Tier 1 suppliers.

Even more vulnerable have been smaller Tier 2 suppliers, as surviving Tier 1 suppliers have reduced the number of their own suppliers in turn. Valeo went from 4,500 Tier 2 suppliers in 2002 to 3,000 in 2004, ArvinMeritor from 1,850 in 2000 to 1,000 in 2005, and Faurecia from 2,800 in 2003 to 1,500 in 2006.

13
The Rising Tide of Imports

Just about all electronic subcomponents now originate in China or Korea or Singapore . . . You are more aware and you buy better when you are where the action is.[1]

The national origin of the parts installed on vehicles assembled in the United States can be divided into three portions: parts made in the United States at factories owned by U.S.-based companies, parts made in the United States in foreign-owned factories, and parts imported from other countries. This chapter examines the magnitude of imports and exports, the specific types of parts that are being imported into and out of the United States, and the countries of origin and destination.

Imported parts captured one-fourth of the U.S. new vehicle market in the early twenty-first century, and foreign-owned factories in the United States another one-fourth. That left U.S.-owned factories in the United States with the remaining one-half. But with the domestic share declining by several percent per year, the three sources were positioned to hold approximately equal shares of the market by 2010.

At the same time, some of the parts produced in U.S. plants have been exported to other countries. Exports and imports expanded at about the same level during the 1990s, but after 2000, imports of parts into the United States continued to increase rapidly whereas exports stagnated. As a result, the United States opened up a substantial trade deficit in car parts in the twenty-first century.

The changing fortunes of carmakers in the United States have been responsible for the widening trade gap. The principal exporters have been the Detroit 3 carmakers, which ship parts to their final assembly plants in Canada and Mexico. As the Detroit 3 have lost market share, their assembly plants in these countries have needed fewer U.S.-made parts.

Meanwhile, foreign-owned carmakers have been meeting increased demand for their vehicles primarily through assembling more vehicles in the United States. Although a growing share of their parts has come from U.S. suppliers, foreign-owned carmakers continue to import a higher percentage of parts than the Detroit 3 (Figure 13.1). For their part, the Detroit 3 have relied more on foreign-made parts to reduce their costs as they try to compete with the foreign-based carmakers (Klier and Rubenstein 2007).

NATIONALITY OF LARGEST SUPPLIERS

Consumers have long since recognized the blurred national origin of vehicles sold in the United States. Foreign-owned companies have been selling some vehicles classified by the U.S. government as foreign and some classified as made in the United States. At the same time, some of the vehicles that Chrysler, Ford, and GM sell in the United States are classified as domestic, but they have actually been assembled in Canada and Mexico.

Figure 13.1 Production-Weighted Domestic Content of Light Vehicles

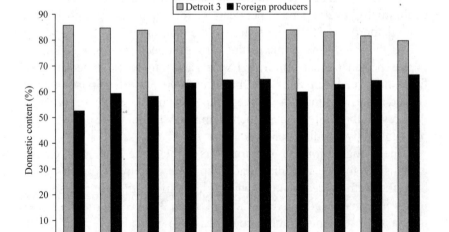

SOURCE: Adapted by authors from the National Highway and Traffic Safety Administration and Ward's AutoInfobank.

Distinguishing between U.S. and foreign origins has in some re-spects been easier for parts than for finished vehicles. Ultimately, each individual part has been manufactured either in the United States or in another country, whereas every assembled vehicle is a blend of thou-sands of parts made in many countries.

In reality, classifying national origin of parts is a complex task be-cause of the sheer magnitude of individual parts and companies that must be tracked and because of limitations on the sources of data. Each of the thousands of individual parts in a motor vehicle could be made by a U.S.-owned company in a factory it operates in the United States or in a factory it operates abroad, or it may be made by a foreign-owned company either in the United States or abroad.

Canadian analyst Dennis DesRosiers has estimated that 41 percent of parts used in the United States in 2005 for both original equipment and aftermarket were made in the United States by U.S.-owned sup-pliers, 30 percent were made in the United States by foreign-owned companies, and 29 percent were imported into the United States. The share held by U.S.-owned firms has declined rapidly, according to Des-Rosiers. In 1997, 68 percent of parts came from U.S.-owned firms, 12 percent from foreign-owned plants in the United States, and 20 percent from abroad. Thus, the share of parts made in the United States by U.S.-owned firms was declining by about 3.5 percent per year in the early twenty-first century (DesRosiers 2006).

The changing nationality of the largest suppliers operating in the United States can be tracked. In 1994, the first year that *Automotive News* listed the 150 largest suppliers of original equipment in North America, 108 of them, or 72 percent, were U.S.-owned companies. These 108 companies accounted for 83 percent of the combined sales of the 150 largest suppliers. Little more than a decade later, in 2006, only 59 U.S.-owned suppliers remained among the 150 largest. For-eign-owned companies included in the top-150 list more than doubled from 42 to 91, and their share of sales increased from 18 percent to 48 percent (Table 13.1). Seventy-three of the 108 U.S.-owned firms among the top 150 in 1994 disappeared during the next decade. Thirty-three stayed in business but were no longer in the top 150, and four were removed following changes in the definition for inclusion on the list. Thirty-six of the 73 were sold to competitors, including 21 U.S.-owned suppliers and 15 foreign ones. British companies bought five of them,

Table 13.1 Top 150 Parts Suppliers by Nationality and Sales

Nationality	Number of firms		North American OEM sales ($, billions)	
	1994	2006	1994	2006
Australia		1		0.4
Austria	1		0.4	
Belgium	1		0.2	
Brazil	1		0.1	
Canada	4	8	2.6	16.5
China		1		0.2
France	3	6	1.6	5.8
Germany	10	18	5.4	22.6
Germany/Japan JV	1	2	0.5	0.9
Italy		2		0.8
Japan	13	38	7.2	36.5
Japan/U.S. JV	1		0.2	
Korea		1		0.2
Mexico	3	1	0.3	1.1
Netherlands		2		0.5
Spain		1		0.4
Sweden		4		2.8
Switzerland		1		0.5
United Kingdom	4	5	1.3	3.5
United States	108	59	96.4	101.2
Total	150	150	116.2	193.9

NOTE: JV denotes joint venture.
SOURCE: *Automotive News* (1995, 2007a).

Canadian and German three each, Swedish two, and French and Japanese one each.

The dramatic increase in Japanese representation among the largest suppliers from 13 to 38 thus did not result from acquiring American competitors. Instead, new Japanese companies entered the U.S. market during the decade, especially to serve the rapidly growing electronics sector.

WHICH TYPES OF PARTS ARE IMPORTED?

The widespread belief in Detroit is that most imports are price-sensitive generic parts that can only be produced competitively in low-wage countries. "The giant sucking noise in Detroit is the sound of parts production being pulled into Mexico, or China"—or words to that effect reflect American perceptions. In reality, a large and increasing share of imports arriving at U.S. final assembly plants actually consists of engines and transmissions made by highly skilled workers in wealthy countries like Canada and Japan.

Sources of Trade Data

Every good that moves in and out of the United States, as well as other leading trading countries, is assigned a four-digit Harmonized Commodity Description and Coding System (HS) number by the World Customs Organization in Brussels. "Parts and accessories of motor vehicles" has been assigned HS code 8708, but car parts are scattered among two dozen other four-digit codes as well, such as 9401 for vehicle seats. Customs officials in participating countries use the HS code to determine the duties, taxes, and regulations that apply to each imported and exported good.

The Bureau of Customs and Border Protection in the Department of Homeland Security is responsible for setting and reporting the value of each good imported into the United States. The Customs Bureau generally sets the value of an imported good as the price paid for the merchandise minus import duties, freight, insurance, and other charges associated with the transfer.

The World Customs Organization subdivides four-digit HS codes into six-digit codes that are also standardized around the world. Code 8708, for example, is divided into 15 six-digit codes, such as 870829 for body parts. Individual countries are permitted to create their own eight- and 10-digit codes, as long as the more detailed levels are consistent with the internationally mandated six-digit HS code. In the United States, the 1988 Trade Act created the Harmonized Tariff System (HTS), which authorized eight-digit and 10-digit codes for imports.

The International Trade Commission, an independent quasi-judicial federal agency, maintains and publishes the HTS for U.S. imports. The Trade Commission also investigates allegations of unfair trade practices, provides legal and technical assistance concerning remedies available under U.S. trade laws, forecasts impacts of proposed tariff and duty changes on specific products, and maintains an extensive library of trade-related information.

Ninety-one eight-digit HTS codes have covered motor-vehicle parts. The top four codes together accounted for almost one-third of the value of all parts imported into the United States in 2006, and the top 10 codes together more than one-half. Each of the top four was responsible for at least 5 percent of all parts imports, and each of the top 10 for at least 3 percent.

These four codes each exceeded $4 billion in imports in 2006:

1) 87082950 Parts and accessories of bodies for motor vehicles.

2) 87089980 Parts and accessories not elsewhere classified.

3) 85443000 Insulated ignition wiring sets and other wiring sets of a kind used in vehicles, aircraft, or ships.

4) 84073448 Spark-ignition reciprocating piston engines for vehicles, cylinder capacity over 2000 cc.

Another six codes exceeded $2 billion in imports 2006:

1) 87084020 Parts and accessories of motor vehicles—gear boxes.

2) 87089967 Parts and accessories for powertrains not elsewhere classified.

3) 40111010 New pneumatic radial tires, of rubber, of a kind used on motor cars.

4) 94019010 Parts of seats of a kind used for motor vehicles not elsewhere classified.

5) 84099150 Parts not elsewhere classified used solely or principally with spark-ignition internal-combustion piston engines.

6) 87083950 Parts and accessories of motor vehicles—brakes and servo-brakes and parts thereof.

While the Trade Commission has had the responsibility for coding imports into the United States, the Census Bureau has had the responsibility for coding exports. Each exporter is required to report the value of the goods according to a code, known as Schedule B, assigned with the assistance of the Census Bureau's Foreign Trade Division. To make trade figures consistent with its other economic reports, the Census Bureau reclassifies export and import data into NAICS codes.

Not surprisingly, having two agencies publish trade data means that two differing sets of figures are being circulated. The Trade Commission and Census Bureau may start with the same raw data, but they process the data in different ways that are consistent with the distinct missions of the two agencies. The Trade Commission is concerned with trade practices, whereas the Census Bureau is concerned with the role of trade in the overall U.S. economy. The Trade Commission Web site has a translation wizard to reconcile HTS and NAICS codes. For example, NAICS 336340, which covers steering and suspension components, corresponds to a combination of five HTS codes: 87088030 for McPherson struts; 87088045 for shock absorbers; 887089450 for steering wheels, columns, and boxes; 87089970 for other suspension parts; and 87089973 for other steering parts.

THE BIG PICTURE IN TRADE

According to the Trade Commission, the United States imported $87 billion of motor vehicle parts in 2007. These imports accounted for 27 percent of all shipments of vehicle components in the United States in 2002, according to the Census Bureau. Both the Trade Commission and the Census Bureau combined original equipment with aftermarket parts, so it was not possible to determine the precise share of each. In compiling the data we only counted original equipment parts destined for cars and light trucks wherever possible.

The value of all imported parts more than doubled in a decade, from $37 billion in 1996 to $87 billion in 2007, according to Trade Commission data (Figure 13.2). Through most of the 1990s, exports of motor vehicle parts were roughly equivalent to imports. Were it possible to split out original equipment from aftermarket parts in the trade data,

Figure 13.2 U.S. Motor Vehicle Parts Imports, Exports, and Trade Balance

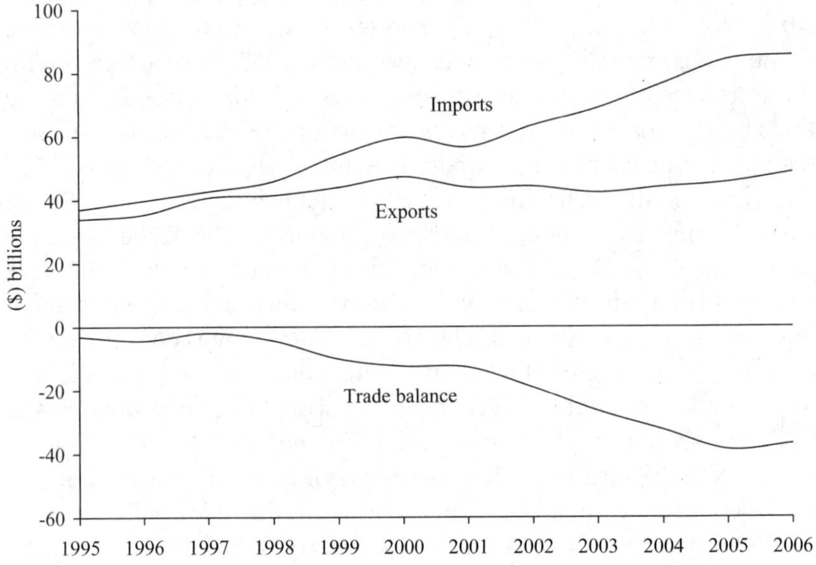

SOURCE: International Trade Commission, dataweb, and authors' calculations.

original equipment exports may have actually exceeded imports in the 1990s.

Of the major vehicle systems—chassis, electronics, exterior, interior, and powertrain—the expectation may have been that electronics would have the largest amount of imports. Although the percentage of electronics imported is high (see Chapter 14), the system with by far the largest value of imports has been the powertrain (Table 13.2).

Powertrain Imports

Vehicles assembled in the United States contained $28 billion worth of imported powertrain parts in 2006, an increase from $10 billion a decade earlier. Powertrain imports included $5 billion worth of complete engines, $4 billion worth of complete transmissions, $8 billion worth of drivetrain components, $6 billion worth of engine components, and $5 billion worth of air- and fluid-handling components.

Table 13.2 Value of Imports and Exports by System, 1995 and 2006

	Imports ($, billions)		Exports ($, billions)	
System	1995	2006	1995	2006
Powertrain	10	28	8	13
Chassis	6	18	6	8
Body	4	12	8	11
Interior	2	5	1	2
Electrical	9	16	3	3
Other	6	8	9	11

SOURCE: International Trade Commission and authors' calculations.

Assembly plants in the United States installed about one-half million engines manufactured in Canada and one-quarter million each made in Mexico, Japan, and Germany in 2006. Ford has been the primary producer of engines in Canada for export to U.S. assembly plants. Chrysler has been especially reliant on importing engines into the United States from Mexico (see Chapter 3 for the location of the Detroit 3 engine plants).

The Japanese-owned assembly plants in the United States have received most of their engines from North America. Honda, Nissan, Subaru, and Toyota have all built engines in the United States although they have imported about one-fifth or their engines from Japan (Chappell 2005f). Other Japanese carmakers imported their engines. Germany became a major source of engines after BMW and Mercedes-Benz began assembly operations in the United States during the 1990s.

The increase in transmission imports came especially from Japan. Toyota receives about one-third of its transmissions from Aisin's Durham, North Carolina, plant, one-third from its own Buffalo, West Virginia, plant, and one-third from Japan. "Transmissions may be the greatest bottleneck facing Toyota" (Chappell 2005f). Nissan similarly received a minority of transmissions from its plant in Decherd, Tennessee, and the remainder from Japan. The smaller Japanese-owned U.S. assembly plants also imported transmissions from Japan.

About $6 billion worth of engine components were imported for use in engines assembled in the United States. Leading components included $660 million worth of filters, $660 million worth of cylinder heads, and $330 million worth of camshafts and crankshafts.

Air- and fluid-handling components accounted for $5 billion worth of imports in 2006. Passenger air conditioning, engine cooling, and fuel and exhaust line components each accounted for about one-third of the total. Import levels were relatively low for fuel and exhaust lines because they are especially fragile and must be packed in elaborate individual coffinlike containers that are expensive to transport over long distances. Most air- and fluid-handling components imported into the United States originated in Mexico.

Chassis Imports

The chassis has been the system where imports have made the greatest percentage gains since the 1990s, primarily because the starting base was so low. Imports may hold a larger market share in electronics-related components, and powertrain imports may be more valuable, but the chassis has become the principal "battleground" system between domestic and imported sources.

Chassis imports grew rapidly in this period because major components in the system—especially brakes, steering, and suspension—underwent "commodification." Engineering advances have transformed these chassis components from high-cost products requiring skilled labor and careful handling to low-cost, easy-to-ship "generic" items that are highly sensitive to labor-cost savings.

Despite commodification, most chassis imports originated in high-wage countries in 2006. Canada was the leading foreign source for four of the five major chassis systems, with the exception of steering. Japan was the leading supplier of steering and was second to Canada in brakes, tires, and suspension systems.

Among major chassis components, tires had the highest levels of imports, with $5 billion in 2006. Brakes had $4 billion, suspensions had $3 billion, and steering, wheels, and bearings each contributed about $2 billion to the import total.

Brakes have been viewed as especially vulnerable to outsourcing from cheap-labor countries. Antilock brakes that once cost thousands of dollars can be produced for under a hundred. Most brake imports were components such as drums, discs, linings, and pads, rather than complete modules.

Imports of wheels have increased relatively rapidly, from $0.5 billion in 1995 to more than $2 billion in 2006. The wheel has been the chassis component most susceptible to outsourcing from low-wage countries. Canada was the leading source of wheels until it was passed by Mexico in 2002. Wheel producers in China, as well as other low-cost Asian countries such as South Korea and Taiwan, tripled their factory capacity during the first years of the twenty-first century, from 10 million to 30 million wheels per year. At first, wheels from Asia were destined primarily for the aftermarket, but OEM sales were likely to grow as well (Chappell 2004e).

One of the oddities in the trade and census data was the import of $120 million of steering components from the tiny country of the Principality of Liechtenstein. These components originate at ThyssenKrupp Automotive's Presta subsidiary, which produced steering systems in Eschen. Exports from that plant have dominated Liechtenstein's overall trade picture.

Exterior Imports

The major exterior components, such as stamped body panels and bumpers, are among the least likely of all components to be imported. Bulky and fragile to ship, these major body components have traditionally been produced near the final assembly plants.

Although large stamped body components are unlikely to be imported, small body parts are. Mirrors, door handles, trim, and other body parts rank among the highest percentage of the U.S. market held by imports. In contrast with panels and bumpers, small body parts are easy to ship and regarded as akin to generic bin parts. Nearly all of the growth in the miscellaneous body parts market has been captured by imports. Canada was the source of one-half of the small miscellaneous body parts during the 1990s, but Mexico has been gaining share and had one-fourth of the market in 2006.

Interior Imports

The leading interior suppliers rarely import finished seats. The combination of bulkiness and short delivery notice makes it especially imperative for seat suppliers to locate facilities near final assembly plants.

The interior manufacturers have not placed the same demand for proximity on facilities producing seat parts, such as foam, frames, and covers. Along with electronics, plants producing seating parts have long been established in Mexico.

Lear has been one of the largest employers in Mexico, with 30,000 employees in 26 plants, 14 of which were in the state of Chihuahua. Into the twenty-first century, Mexican plants have been responsible for producing two-thirds of the parts used to put together seats in the United States. However, Mexico has been losing share to Canada, whose share increased from one-fourth to one-third of the market in the early twenty-first century.

Electronics Imports

Import of electrical and electronics components increased relatively modestly, from $8 billion in 1995 to $16 billion in 2006. At first glance, this modest increase may seem counterintuitive because electronics content has been increasing rapidly, and it has long been regarded as the quintessential candidate for outsourcing from low-cost labor countries.

The relatively modest growth in electronics imports in the twenty-first century is partly a legacy of high growth during the 1980s, at a time when imports of others components were still limited. Wiring accounted for the largest share of electrical imports, and 80 percent of wiring imports came from Mexico, which became the dominant producer of wiring harnesses in the 1980s as the centerpiece of the *maquiladora* program (see below). Relatively labor intensive and easy to ship, wiring was the first major component to be shipped in large batches from foreign production sites.

The four leading importers of wiring harnesses from Mexico in 2003 were Delphi, Alcoa, Yazaki, and Lear. Delphi's Alambrados y Circuitos Electricos, Packard, and Rio Bravo Electricos divisions employed 26,000 workers at 18 Mexican plants in 2003 according to ELM. Alcoa employed 18,000 in Mexico in 2003, according to ELM, half at its Arneses y Accesorios de Mexico subsidiary and half at Areneses de Juarez, Cableados del Norte, and Maquilados Fronterizos joint ventures with Fujikura. Yazaki had 14,000 employees in two Mexican subsidiaries, Autopartes y Arneses de Mexico in Ciudad Juarez and Nuevo Casas and AXA in Saltillo. Lear Corporation's Electrical and Electronics Division employed 9,000 in 2003 in Chihuahua and Ciudad Juarez, producing wiring harnesses for seat recliners, track adjusters, and other power-assisted interior components.

Radio components have also been imported primarily from Mexico. However, the overall value of radio imports has declined from a peak of $3.6 billion in 2000 to $2.8 billion in 2006. As with other electrical components, the quantity and percentage of imports may be increasing, but because of rapidly declining prices, the value has decreased. Mexico has been losing market share in the early twenty-first century, in this case to China. The value of radios imported from Mexico declined from a peak of $2 billion in 2001 to $1.3 billion in 2006, whereas radios imported from China increased from $300 million to almost $700 million during those five years.

Imports have accounted for more than $1 billion, or 30 percent of the total U.S. market for vehicle lighting. Mexico and Taiwan have replaced Japan as the leading suppliers of lighting equipment. Apodaca has been the center of vehicle lighting production in Mexico, with large facilities operated by Visteon and Guide. Robert Bosch produces lighting components in Juarez, Valeo in San Luis Potosi and Queretaro, and Visteon in Hermosillo.

Electronics imports from China are set to increase. Within a few days of each other in 2006, GM and Visteon both announced a shift of worldwide electronics purchasing from Michigan to Shanghai. Shanghai is "at the hub of China's electronics industry . . . and China is widely viewed as the world's new hub for consumer electronics" (Sherefkin and LaReau 2006). However, because China is "GM's largest growth market . . . much of the electronics that GM buys in China are destined for its Asian assembly lines, not U.S. shores" (Sherefkin and LaReau 2006).

NATIONAL ORIGIN OF IMPORTS

Canada, Japan, and Mexico were the countries of origin for 68 percent of the parts imported into the United States in 2007. Imports in 2006 totaled $27 billion from Mexico, $19 billion from Canada, and $13 billion from Japan. That is down noticeably from 1996, when the same three countries also accounted for 78 percent of total imports. Canada was the country of origin for $12 billion in parts in 1996, Mexico $11 billion, and Japan $8 billion. China and Germany were in fourth and fifth place in 2007, far behind the lead held by the top three with $7 billion and $5 billion, respectively.

Canada was the leading source of parts in 1995, followed closely by Mexico and Japan (Figure 13.3). Canada and Mexico both gained market share at the expense of Japan during the mid 1990s. Implementation of the North American Free Trade Agreement (NAFTA) and the high yen–dollar exchange rates contributed to Japan's decline during the period. Mexico passed Canada as the leading source of imports for the first time in 2002, and the gap widened in subsequent years.

Canada lost market share after 1997, slipping from 31 percent to 22 percent in 2007, whereas the share of imports from Japan and Mexico changed little. Meanwhile, China gained 7 percent during the 12-year period, passing Germany as the fourth-largest source of inputs, and the rest of the world gained the remainder.

Figure 13.3 Auto Parts Imports by Country

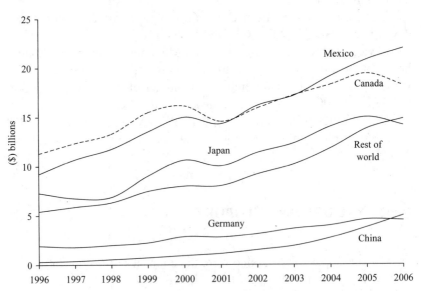

SOURCE: International Trade Commission, dataweb, and authors' calculations.

Figure 13.4 Auto Parts Imports by System from Canada, Mexico, and Japan, 2006

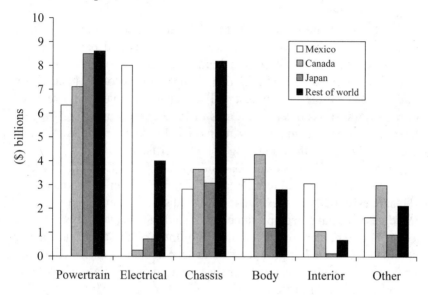

NOTE: Powertrain comprises: engine, engine parts, fluid and air, and drivetrain.
SOURCE: International Trade Commission, dataweb, and authors' calculations.

Canada, Japan, and Mexico have specialized in importing different types of parts (Figure 13.4). Canada has been the leading source of exterior and chassis components, which are bulky metal structures that have traditionally been built close to final assembly plants. Japan has been the leading source of powertrain components, which are closely tied to Japanese carmakers in the United States through keiretsu relationships. Mexico has been the dominant source of electrical and interior components that are especially sensitive to labor costs.

Imports from Canada

Canada's distinctive contribution to the U.S. parts industry is a legacy of policies from the 1960s that were designed to integrate the two countries' vehicle production. Prior to that time, Canada's motor vehicle industry was organized separately from that of the United States. Canada placed tariffs of 17.5 percent on vehicles and 25 percent on parts imported from the United States and required that at least 60 percent of content in domestically built cars be sourced from the British Commonwealth.

A Royal Commission headed by Vincent Bladen reported in 1961 that the Canadian motor vehicle assembly plants and parts suppliers would become increasingly uncompetitive because of the small size of the domestic market. The Bladen Commission recommended closer integration with the U.S. industry. The Canadian government reduced tariffs on transmissions and engines in 1962 and on other parts a year later. The 1965 Canada–U.S. Automotive Products Trade Agreement eliminated most of the remaining vehicle tariffs.

In a series of letters of understanding sent to the Canadian government, U.S. firms agreed to maintain a minimum level of production in Canada, essentially at a level that exceeded sales in Canada. As a result, more vehicles have been produced than sold in Canada each year since 1964. With 9 percent of the population of the United States and Canada combined, Canada has produced about 15 percent of the two countries' vehicles, thus well above its "fair share" based on population and sales. Canada also had 11 percent of the two countries' parts plants, according to ELM International.

Canada's disproportionately large contribution to North American vehicle assembly also stemmed from the country's lower health care costs for employers. Because of national health insurance, final assembly costs as recently as 2002 were about $500 lower per vehicle in Canada. "We do have a cost advantage here in Canada versus our production, for example, in the United States. Health care costs probably contribute just a little under half of that advantage," according to GM Canada president Mike Grimaldi in 2002 (*Automotive News* 2002a). According to Canadian Auto Workers president Buzz Hargrove (English 2002), Canada held a $16-per-hour wage advantage over the United States in 2002, when health care costs, productivity, and the value of the Canadian dollar were taken into consideration. By 2008, a rising Canadian dollar in combination with wage concessions agreed to by the UAW in 2007 had essentially eliminated that cost advantage.

Exterior parts have been especially prominent in Canada's supplier industry. Five of the six leading suppliers based in Canada specialize in exterior parts. The leading supplier has been Magna International, with 10,000 employees in 30-some production facilities across Ontario. Magna's largest division specialized in what the company calls "exterior vehicle appearance systems," such as plastic bumpers, fascias, body panels, liftgates, and sealants. Other leading Canadian exterior suppliers included ABC Group, Multimatic, SKD Automotive Group, and AGS Automotive.

Chassis parts have also been important for Canada's suppliers. Magna's second-largest unit has produced metal chassis and body components such as cross members, floor pans, suspension systems, and other support structures. Canada's second-largest parts maker, Linamar, with 3,000 employees at two dozen plants, mostly in Guelph, produced brake drums and powertrain components such as cylinder blocks, heads, camshafts, and crankshafts.

Canada's parts industry, clustered in Ontario between Windsor and Toronto, is within a one-day drive of U.S. vehicle production centers, and plants in Windsor are only minutes from Detroit's assembly plants. But Canada's advantageous proximity has been threatened by the drift of U.S. final assembly plants southward from Michigan. Newer plants opened in the southern United States are beyond a one-day driving range from the southern Ontario production center. Ontario's auto industry is tied more closely to the fate of Michigan than to the United States as a whole, and more to the Big 3 than to the international transplants (see Chapter 6 on border issues).

Imports from Japan

Canada's parts industry has relied heavily on JIT delivery for and by the Detroit 3. Japan's import record, in contrast, has been heavily influenced by the changing needs of Japanese-owned assembly plants in the United States.

When they opened assembly plants in the United States, Japanese carmakers ordered their major suppliers to start producing parts in the United States as well. "[U.S.-owned] large tier ones pressed [Presidents] Bush and Clinton to press Japanese carmakers to buy more U.S. content" (Chappell 2005g). Once they started producing in the United States, many of these Japanese parts makers also became major suppliers to Detroit 3 and European carmakers. By forcing their key suppliers to build in the United States, Japanese carmakers caused parts imports from Japan to grow at a much lower level than would otherwise be expected from their increasing share of the U.S. light vehicle market.

Drivetrain components emerged as the leading imports to the United States from Japan after 2000. Complete transmissions have been shipped from Japan to transplants in the United States, as well as components for producing transmissions in the United States. Toyota in particular has been a major importer of transmissions into the United States rather than depending primarily on U.S.-based suppliers. Meanwhile, the value of engines exported from Japan to the United States declined from a peak of $1.5 billion to less than $0.5 billion in 2006.

Powertrain imports are often for low-volume or newly established products, for which production in the United States is not justified at the time, and may never be. In other cases, importing is a temporary expediency pending construction of another U.S. plant or redeployment of an existing one. Reliance on high-value imported powertrain components is a major reason why transplants have had a lower impact on the local economy than was predicted by development officials and promised by politicians.

Competing with Mexico or even Canada on price is difficult for parts makers in Japan. Japanese suppliers face much higher production costs than Mexican competitors, and much higher shipping costs than Canadian competitors. Consequently, Japan's market share of parts imports is small for bulky just-in-time body and interior components, and it is declining for most price-sensitive chassis components.

Imports from Mexico

Mexico's parts supplier industry has a profile that is very different from those of Canada and Japan. Dominating production are electrical and interior components, both of which take advantage of hourly wage rates of less than $2 in Mexico in 2005.

The leading suppliers of electrical and interior components from Mexico have been foreign-owned maquiladora plants. The term maquiladora derives from the Spanish verb *maquilar*, which means to take measure of payment for grinding or processing. The miller who did the grinding would be compensated with a portion of the grain known as the *maquila*, which was also the name of a colonial tax.

Mexico's Border Industrialization Program (BIP), established in 1965, permitted foreign companies to import materials from the United States, assemble them in maquiladora plants, and export them back to the United States without having to pay duty on the raw materials brought into Mexico, the equipment in the maquiladora plants, or the subassemblies shipped back to the United States. Antonio J. Bermudez, first head of the BIP, is credited with developing the idea as a way to generate economic development in his hometown of Ciudad Juarez. RCA was the first large American company to open a maquiladora plant in Ciudad Juarez in 1968.

It took another decade before U.S. auto parts makers started taking advantage of the maquiladora laws. GM's Packard Electric Division, now part of Delphi, established Conductores y Componentes Electricos to make wire harnesses in Ciudad Juarez in 1978. Electrical components dominated Mexican early maquiladora production, accounting for twice as many imports as all other systems combined into the 1990s.

GM's Inland Division, now also part of Delphi, arrived in Ciudad Juarez in 1978 to make seat covers and interior trim. Production of seat components expanded rapidly into the twenty-first century as the three large assemblers of complete seats—Lear, JCI, and Magna—relocated production of some individual components to Mexico and purchased more individual seat parts from Mexican-based lower tier suppliers.

Maquiladora plants are strung out in Mexican cities along the U.S. border, especially (from east to west) in Matamoros (across the border from Brownsville, Texas), Reynosa (across from McAllen), Nuevo Laredo (across from Laredo), Ciudad Juarez (across from El Paso), and Tijuana (across from San Diego). The more easterly cities have attracted most of the auto parts maquiladoras because of their relative proximity to Auto Alley, whereas Tijuana has more clothing and textile plants. Auto-related maquiladora production is also clustered in larger northern Mexican cities 100 miles or so south of the border, such as Nuevo Leon, Monterrey, Chihuahua, and Hermosillo.

NAFTA authorized Mexicans to drive trucks filled with car parts and other goods into the United States. However, U.S. and Mexican government regulations blocked free cross-border truck movement for several years after implementation of NAFTA. Administrative red tape required trucks to be unloaded at warehouses in U.S. border towns and driven into the interior of the United States on U.S.-registered trucks by American drivers. U.S. restrictions were ruled illegal in 2000, but Mexican restrictions remained in effect. Mexican officials have refused to permit U.S. officials to conduct security inspections required of importers since the September 11, 2001, attacks. Fear of security-driven border delays has forced major U.S.-owned maquiladoras to expand inventory being held in the U.S. border towns, essentially adding to the cost of producing in Mexico.

According to the México Maquila Information Center, 24 of the 100 largest maquiladoras in 2006 were motor vehicle suppliers. The three largest maquiladoras on the list were motor-vehicle suppliers—Delphi, Lear, and Yazaki. The 24 auto-related maquiladoras together employed 216,696 workers in Mexico in 2006, including 66,000 at Delphi in Mexico, 34,000 at Lear, and 33,400 at Yazaki (México Maquila Information Center 2006).

The number of maquiladora plants—most of which were not automotive related—increased from 600 in 1982 to 1,000 in 1986, 1,800 in 1989, and a peak of 3,630 in 2001. Employment in maquiladoras increased from 70,000 in 1982 to 360,000 in 1988, and a peak of 1.3 million in 2000. In the first years of the twenty-first century, the number of maquiladoras declined slightly from the 2000 peak. Mexican officials have feared that border plants will continue to decline in the face of competition from lower-wage countries, notably China (México Maquila Information Center 2007).

Further fanning fears for the future of the border plants, the growth in the value of auto parts imported into the United States from Mexico has been outpaced by the growth of imports from China for every year since 1996.

The China Factor

China's contribution to the U.S. parts market in the early twenty-first century could be seen in two ways. On one hand, China was playing an insignificant role that barely registered in the statistical tables. Only 5 percent of all imports and only 2 percent of the total U.S. auto parts market came from China in 2006. Balanced against the statistical record and geographic constraints was the universal assumption that China would inevitably play a major role in all facets of the world's motor vehicle industry, including original equipment parts production.

China's impressive compound annual growth rate of 58 percent between 1996 and 2006 was calculated from a very low starting base. Otherwise stated, China accounted for 12 percent of the $45 billion growth in imports from all countries during the decade. Imports from China increased by $4.5 billion between 1996 and 2006, from $0.5 billion to $5 billion, but during the same decade, imports increased by much greater dollar values from other countries, including $12 billion more from Mexico, $6 billion more from Canada, and $6 billion more from Japan.

Chassis and electrical components accounted for almost two-thirds of all imports from China in 2006. China's first major impact in the U.S. import market came through chassis components, which increased from $142 million in 1995 to $2.55 billion in 2006 (Table 13.3). Among major chassis components, imports from China increased during the

Table 13.3 Parts Imports from China by Major Subsystem, 2006

System	Value ($, millions)	% of total
Chassis	2,552	41.9
Wheels	877	14.4
Tires	843	13.8
Brakes	550	9.0
Bearings	162	2.7
Other chassis	120	2.0
Electrical	1,314	21.6
Radios	676	11.1
Other electrical	638	10.5
Engine	542	8.8
Components	253	4.1
Fluid & air	289	4.7
Generic	496	8.1
Body	474	7.8
Interior	347	5.7
Child's seats	233	3.8
Other interior	114	1.9
Drivetrain	379	6.2
Total	6,104	

SOURCE: Adapted by the authors from the ELM International database.

decade from $9 million to $877 million for wheels, from $5 million to $843 million for tires, and from $51 million to $550 million for brakes. The aftermarket was the destination for most of these imports, but not all of them, especially after 2001. "It's a scary prospect right now to see the Chinese gearing up for this [OEM wheel production]. Anybody in the wheel business who thinks this won't matter is about to have their head served to them on a platter."[2]

Imports of electronic components such as radios also increased rapidly from China after 2000. Shanghai has become the center of manufacturing motor vehicle electronics in China. General Motors has moved its global electronics purchasing office, and Visteon has moved its global electronics group to that city.

Does Mexico have reason to fear competition from China? Imports of radios from Mexico, which had increased from $1 billion to $2 billion between 1995 and 2001, declined to $1.3 billion in 2006. Similarly, the total of all radio imports into the United States, which had increased from $2.5 billion in 1995 to $3.4 billion in 2001, also declined by $600 million to $2.8 billion in 2006. Meanwhile, imports of radios from China increased from $319 million to $676 million between 2001 and 2006. Thus, as the cost of the average radio declined sharply in the early twenty-first century, China nearly tripled its share of imports from 9 to almost 25 percent in five years. China has started to make a dent in Mexico's dominance of electronics imports.

However, the growth in Chinese imports has not come without some problems. "Lured by promises of long-term, high-volume contracts from their major customers—and sometimes encouraged at gunpoint, metaphorically speaking—auto suppliers are finding plenty of justification for their early caution about committing to the Chinese market" (*Automotive News Europe* 2005). As in other newly industrializing countries, China has faced quality control issues.

> International parts makers in China are learning that a local supplier-development program is a must. Patience is also a must since it often takes as long as two years for a Chinese supplier to meet international quality standards. Only 15 percent of Chinese suppliers can meet those standards, says [manufacturing consultant Frank] Ogden, who is vice president of global supplier development for the PAC Group, a Shanghai consulting company. Problems range from not knowing how to meet a customer's deadlines

to inadequate testing of raw materials. "You can't just walk into a company and expect to buy off the shelf," [TRW senior manager for Asia Pacific supplier development Clive] Woodward says. "You have to be willing to work beside them and bring them up to your quality level." (Webb 2005)

Again, as in other newly industrializing countries, however, China has seen rapidly improving quality. GM's defect rate for parts in China declined from 2,197 per million in 1999 and 1,397 per million in 2000 to only 23 per million in 2003. In comparison, GM's worldwide defect rate in 2003 was much higher (35 per million) and only slightly lower (22 per million) in the United States (Armstrong 2004e). GM "expects to increase its parts purchases from China 20-fold in six years—from $200 million in 2003 to $4 billion in 2009—while spending about $5 billion on sourcing for its China production" (*Automotive News Europe* 2005). "We will see a shift into more electronics, air conditioning, and also chassis parts, brake parts, steering parts . . ." (Lan 2007).

Though China's quality control issues may fade over time, parts destined for assembly plants in the United States cannot avoid the 6,500-mile journey across the Pacific Ocean and the 2,500 mile journey from the West Coast to Auto Alley. For all but the most labor-intensive components, the obvious attraction of low-cost labor in the manufacturing process would continue to be offset by the high costs of maintaining a trans-Pacific supply chain.

WHICH TYPES OF PARTS ARE EXPORTED?

Exports have performed differently than imports in the twenty-first century. Imports and exports increased at the same rate during the 1990s, but imports accelerated after 2000 while exports stagnated. The combination of increasing of imports and stagnating exports has produced a widening trade imbalance in the United States.

Canada and Mexico have been on the receiving end of three-fourths of the parts exported from the United States (Figure 13.5). In 2007, 55 percent of exports went to Canada and 20 percent to Mexico. A decade earlier, the percentages were virtually the same.

Figure 13.5 Value of U.S. Parts Exports by Country

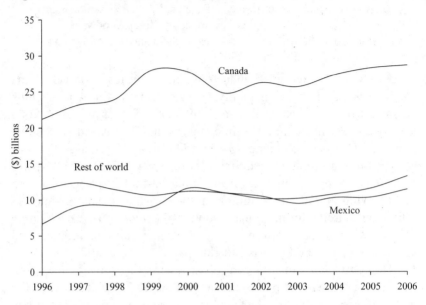

SOURCE: International Trade Commission, dataweb, and authors' calculations.

Mexico and Canada play a more dominant role in exports from the United States than they do with imports. With imports, Japanese- and German-owned assembly plants in the United States have depended on parts from their home countries, and other U.S.-based producers have been scouring the world for low-cost suppliers. With exports, final assembly plants in Canada and Mexico have been virtually the only markets for original equipment parts made in the United States.

This pattern is a function of integration of parts-making and final assembly operations within the NAFTA zone during the 1990s. Final assembly plants in Canada and Mexico make heavy and increasing use of parts made in the United States, just as U.S. final assembly plants make heavy and increasing use of parts made by suppliers based in Canada and Mexico.

The export pattern has varied by type of system. The overwhelming majority of powertrain components and body stampings exported from the United States are destined for Canadian assembly plants (Figure

Figure 13.6 U.S. Exports by System to Canada and Mexico, 2006

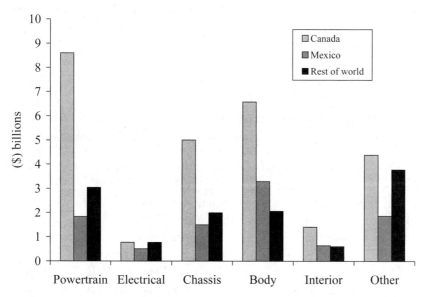

SOURCE: International Trade Commission, dataweb, and authors' calculations.

13.6). These parts are much less likely to be exported anywhere else, in part because they are bulky and fragile to ship long distances.

Export of powertrain components accounted for much of the increase in exports during the 1990s, especially engines and complete transmissions destined for final assembly plants in Canada and Mexico. Exports of exterior components have hovered around $10 billion: stampings have generated $1.5 billion worth of exports, lighting more than $0.5 billion, and bumpers, glass, and wipers between $0.25 and $0.5 billion each. The principal chassis export has been axles, with more than $1 billion sent to other countries in 2006. Exports of interior components have fluctuated between $2 and $3 billion; the leading interior export has been seat parts for use at seat assembly plants located near final assembly plants.

As recently as the late 1990s, only electronics had a substantial trade deficit, reflecting the importance by that time of Mexico's maquiladoras. Exterior and drivetrain components showed trade surpluses in the United States during the 1990s, and chassis, engine, and interior components had annual trade deficits in the $1 to $2 billion range. During the early twenty-first century, imports increased faster than exports by $1.5 billion per year for powertrains, $1 billion for interior parts, and $0.5 billion each for electronics and exterior components.

OUTLOOK AND UNCERTAINTIES

Are any sectors of the U.S. parts industry impervious to foreign competition? The short answer is no. As the auto sector becomes more international, foreign competition manifests itself in more ways than one. Domestic carmakers and their parts suppliers face competition from imported vehicles (that include mostly parts produced abroad) as well as from foreign carmakers and parts makers based in North America. In fact the low exchange rate of the U.S. dollar is expected to drive a fair amount of inbound foreign investment over the next few years. Finally, trade in motor vehicle parts has been growing faster than domestic production for many years. Yet, not all sectors are equally exposed to foreign competition.

Of the five major systems, the body is the least vulnerable to import competition. Large body panels have always been stamped out near final assembly plants, and that trend is likely to continue. They are too bulky and fragile to ship long distance safely and efficiently. Similarly, seats are too bulky to ship long distance and are designed to arrive at the final assembly ready for installation within hours of being built. Nevertheless, large body and interior suppliers have been able to identify individual parts that can be produced in low-wage countries and shipped to trim and seat plants in the United States for finishing before being sent on to final assembly plants in integrated modules.

Similarly, engines and transmissions will continue to be assembled primarily in the United States, but they will contain a number of individual parts that are manufactured overseas. Powertrain components will continue to account for more imports than bodies and seats because, to some extent, complete engines and transmissions will be imported, such as small-displacement engines from Mexico and small-batch engines and transmissions from Japan.

At the beginning of the twenty-first century, the main battleground between domestic and foreign production was the chassis. The principal chassis modules—brakes, suspension, steering, wheels, and tires—were all vulnerable to outsourcing to lower cost producers. In general, the chassis is the system that is least difficult to ship and least affected by just-in-time delivery pressures. Innovations have reduced chassis prices quickly, adding pressure to relocate production to low-wage countries.

"There are some advantages when you go to low-cost countries. But on the flip side, you can't ignore the costs of freight, duty, the cost of inventory, the 45 days or whatever it is in the pipeline. Those are all true costs. What we look at is the total delivered cost."[3]

Notes

1. Unnamed GM source, quoted in Sherefkin and LaReau (2006).
2. Dick Lilley, president of Lilley Associates Inc., which tracks the original-equipment wheel industry, quoted in Chappell (2004e).
3. Chip McClure, ArvinMeritor CEO, quoted in *Automotive News* (2005c).

14

The Driving Force:
Electronics Suppliers

*Historically, mechanical engineers controlled the destiny of
the vehicle. Now it is the electrical engineer.*[1]

A 1960 vehicle needed electrical power to operate little more than
the lights, radio, heater motor, and wipers. The availability of ever
cheaper and faster microprocessors has spawned a tremendous amount
of control systems applications in the automotive industry in the last
two decades. From engine and transmission systems, to virtually all
chassis subsystems, some level of computer control is present. A car is
now actually a network of computers (*The Economist* 2007). As electronics have become increasingly prominent features of motor vehicles,
motorists have seen their service mechanics transformed into electrical
diagnosticians (Couretas 2000).

"Automotive electronics are major criteria of differentiation in the
automotive market. Car manufacturers use chips in increasing numbers to develop powerful electronic systems for driver information and
communication, in-car entertainment electronics, power train and body
control electronics, as well as automotive safety and convenience electronics" (Gupta 2005).

According to our database, 15 percent of all parts plants in the United States made an electronic part in 2006. Our figure is a little lower
than the average of four other studies: 11 percent according to the Center for Automotive Research, 18 percent according to Merrill Lynch, 21
percent according to the U.S. Census of Manufactures, and 25 percent
according to Roland Berger Strategy Consultants (Armstrong 2004f;
Couretas 2000; Gupta 2005; Guyer 2004; Riches 2005). The dispar-
ity comes from classification challenges. Is the temperature regulator
counted as electronics or as part of the air conditioner? Is the seat ad-
juster counted as electronics or part of the interior?

Regardless of magnitude, the value of electronics has clearly increased more rapidly than the value of the overall vehicle content. The

value of the electronics content rose 8.3 percent in 2004, for example, compared with only 2 percent for all content (Riches 2005). The world market for motor vehicle electronics was expected to increase from $36 billion in 2004 to $58 billion in 2012, with most of the increase coming from the interior system (Table 14.1). "If I'm going to grow in a flat market, where is the growth? It's in electronics."[2]

The increasing importance of electronics is reflected in the changing composition of the largest suppliers. Only six of the top 150 suppliers in 1994 listed electronics as a capability, compared to 41 in 2006, including eight of the nine largest (*Automotive News* 1995, 2007a). Some of these 41 suppliers were electronics specialists, but most combined electronics with capabilities in chassis, exteriors, interiors, and powertrains.

In our database, 39 percent of plants making electronics parts could not be allocated to a particular system. These parts included switches, sensors, actuators, circuit boards, relays, and miscellaneous electronics parts. Excluding these plants, 42 percent of electronics plants made a part for the interior, 30 percent for the powertrain, 18 percent for the exterior, and 10 percent for the chassis.

Given the large percentage of electronics parts that are not attributable to a specific system, this chapter is organized around the three principal purposes of electronics: performance, safety, and convenience. Performance-oriented electronics are found primarily but not exclusively in the powertrain; safety-oriented parts are found in the interior,

Table 14.1 World Automotive Electronics Market and Anticipated Growth by System

System	2004 ($, billions)	2012 ($, billions anticipated)
Powertrain	11.4	16.9
Chassis	4.2	6.7
Exterior	8.6	13.2
Security	1.8	2.4
Body	6.8	1-0.8
Interior	11.5	21.0
Driver information	6.8	11.0
Safety	4.7	10.0
Total	35.7	57.8

SOURCE: Riches (2005).

Figure 14.1 Location of Electronics Parts Plants

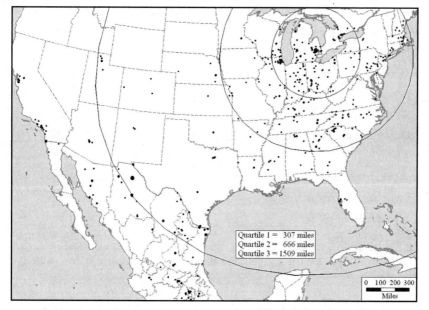

Quartile 1 = 307 miles
Quartile 2 = 666 miles
Quartile 3 = 1509 miles

0 100 200 300
Miles

SOURCE: Adapted by the authors from the ELM International database and other sources.

exterior, and chassis; and convenience-oriented electronics are found in the interior.

Most electronics parts are being made outside the United States, as discussed in the previous chapter. Of those produced in the United States, less than half have come from plants in the Midwest (Figure 14.1, Table 14.2). Two-thirds of plants producing electronics for the exterior were in the Midwest, compared to only one-third of plants producing parts for the interior.

PERFORMANCE: GETTING POWER FROM THE ENGINE TO THE ACCESSORIES

Motor vehicles contain dozens of microprocessors, tiny computers known as electronic control units (ECUs). Information in microproces-

Table 14.2 Electronic Parts Plants in the Midwest

Electronic part	Number of plants	% in Midwest
Powertrain (engine management)	205	47.3
Chassis (wiring)	65	50.8
Exterior (lighting)	123	63.4
Interior	282	36.2
Safety	128	40.6
Driver information	112	28.6
Audio	42	42.9
Other electronics	432	46.8
Switches, sensors, actuators	282	43.3
Miscellaneous	150	53.0
Total electronics	1,107	46.2

SOURCE: Adapted by the authors from the ELM International database and other sources.

sors is stored on semiconductors made from silicon chips. First-generation ECUs each performed one function, but electronics specialists were able to combine multiple functions in ECUs, thereby reducing the number needed.

ECUs collect, store, and display information about vehicle performance, such as speed, oil pressure, engine temperature, distance traveled, and operator behavior. Information is collected through sensors embedded in key components. Based on information from sensors, ECUs determine optimum settings for actuators that operate specific functions, such as opening a window or regulating the flow of heat into the passenger compartment. ECUs can be regarded as the brain of the system, sensors as the eyes and ears, and actuators as the hands.

Suppliers of ECU Components

Manufacture of semiconductors for the world's motor vehicles was an $18 billion business in 2005, accounting for nearly half of the total electronics market (Gupta 2005). One-third of the semiconductors were used in interior systems, one-fourth each in powertrain and exterior systems, and one-sixth in chassis systems (Table 14.3).

**Table 14.3   Global Automotive Semiconductor Sales by System, 2005
and 2006**

System	Global sales 2006 ($, billions)	% change 2005–06
Powertrain	4.7	6.2
Chassis	2.7	9.7
Exterior	4.8	14.1
Body	3.8	14.8
Security	1.0	11.3
Interior	5.8	11.7
Safety	2.5	20.2
Driver information	1.6	8.9
Audio	1.7	3.5
Total	18.1	10.5

SOURCE: Webber (2005b, 2006b).

The semiconductor market has been one of the most highly frag-
mented in the motor vehicle industry. According to Hansen (2003):

> The automotive semiconductor industry has too many suppliers
> . . . Yearly price cuts are guaranteed and pressures to cut prices
> further when industry margins are already thin or nonexistent are
> greater now than they have been in the last 15 years. While there
> are plenty of new electronics features on the horizon, it can take
> three to five years following the development of a new component
> before it goes into volume production . . .

> What still attracts semiconductor suppliers to the auto industry and
> could bring in new players, is its relative stability. In 2001, when
> the worldwide semiconductor market dropped 32 percent, the auto
> semiconductor market dropped only 1 percent.

The three leading companies together held 29 percent of the market
in 2003, the top five had 43 percent, the top seven had 50 percent, and
the top 30 had 80 percent (Hansen 2003). Only one of the seven largest
made the list of *Automotive News* top 150 suppliers—Robert Bosch,
the world's largest parts supplier overall and the sixth-largest automotive semiconductor supplier in 2006. The fifth- and seventh-largest—
NEC and Toshiba—were more familiar as small consumer electronics
producers than as motor vehicle suppliers.[3] The four largest semiconductor suppliers—Freescale, Infineon, STMicroelectronics, and Rene-

sas—were unfamiliar names to most consumers and auto workers alike (Webber 2006a). All four, though, were spin-offs or mergers of well-known firms between 1999 and 2004.

Freescale

Freescale, the largest semiconductor supplier, was the only U.S.-based firm among the top seven. It was created in 2004 when Motorola spun off its semiconductor products business. In 2006, Freescale was acquired by the private equity firm Blackstone Group. Motorola had originated in 1928 as the Galvin Manufacturing Corp., when brothers Paul V. and Joseph E. Galvin took over a battery eliminator business. The battery eliminator enabled radios to operate on household current instead of batteries. The company produced one of the first commercially successful car radios in 1930 (see below). The radio was sold under the brand name Motorola, said to have been invented by Paul Galvin by adding the suffix "ola," which means sound, to the word "motor." The company's name was changed to Motorola in 1947, the year it started to sell televisions.

Motorola was a pioneer in development of semiconductors, setting up a research center in 1949 in Phoenix, Arizona, one of the few parts suppliers to locate a major production facility in that state. Its first mass-produced semiconductor, for use in car radios, came in 1957. In 1961 Motorola had its other major automotive-related breakthrough, the silicon rectifier, which was critical to manufacturing an attractively priced alternator and was the basis for the company's leading position among suppliers in engine-related electronics (HowardForums 2006). The first major application of Motorola microprocessors was an ECU for motor vehicles in 1980.

Infineon

Second to Freescale was German-based Infineon Technologies AG. Like Freescale, Infineon was spun off from one of the world's largest electronics firms, in this case Siemens AG, in 1999 (Floerecke 2005).

Siemens's predecessor Telegraphen-Bauanstalt von Siemens & Halske was founded in 1847 by Prussian inventor Werner von Siemens and mechanical engineer Johann Georg Halske to erect Europe's first telegraph line between Berlin and Frankfurt, using equipment patented by Siemens. Siemens became one of the world's largest companies in the twentieth century through generation of electrical power and telecommunications.

The motor vehicle industry was not a significant component of the Siemens empire until the rapid rise in electronics content in the late twentieth century. Siemens set up an automotive engineering business unit in 1989, and spun it off as the independent Siemens Automotive AG in 2000. Although it was one of the world's 10 largest parts suppliers, with worldwide sales of $12 billion in 2004, Siemens generated only one-eighth of its total 2004 worldwide revenues of $95 billion from the motor vehicle industry.

STMicroelectronics

Unlike the other three of the four largest semiconductor suppliers, STMicroelectronics (ST) did not trace its roots to the motor vehicle industry. It was a product of a 1987 merger between Italy's Micro-elettronica and France's Thomson Semiconducteurs and was known as SGS-Thomson Microelectronics until 1998.

Although it was the third-largest motor vehicle supplier of electronics, ST derived only 15 percent of its revenues from that industry in 2006. Communications, consumer products, and computers were the largest segments at ST.

Renesas

Renesas, the fourth-place semiconductor company with 7 percent of the market and the leading microcontroller supplier, was spun off from prominent parts suppliers. Renesas was established in 2003 as Japan's largest semiconductor supplier through a joint venture between Hitachi, which owned 55 percent, and Mitsubishi Electric Corp., which owned the other 45 percent.

Founded in 1910 by Namihei Odaira as an electrical repair shop, Hitachi—the name combined Japanese words for sun ("hi") and rise ("tachi")—produced its first automotive product in 1930, a generator. Hitachi Automotive Products, set up as a separate division in 1985, was only one of 10 U.S. subsidiaries and accounted for one-sixth of U.S. sales.

The name Mitsubishi was first applied in 1874 to a shipping company originally called Tsukumo Shokai, launched in 1870 by Yataro Iwasaki on the island of Shikoku. The company started out with three steamships chartered from a powerful local clan called Tosa. Yataro's son Hisaya expanded into banking, real estate, marketing, and administration into the twentieth century. After World War II, the company was split into 139 companies, most of which abandoned the name Mitsubishi. Motor vehicle parts production originated in 1934 at the predecessor of Mitsubishi Heavy Industries. Motor vehicle electronics production originated at the predecessor of Mitsubishi Electric Corp., founded in 1921 to produce electric fans.

Engine Management

The most powerful computer on most cars is the engine control unit, referred to here as "engine ECU" to avoid confusion with the electronic control unit, which is also abbreviated "ECU." The engine ECU is a special-purpose computer that manages such engine functions as fuel injection, idle speed, and ignition timing. The engine ECU fires the spark plugs, opens and closes the fuel injectors, and turns the cooling fan on and off.

The engine ECU makes decisions through processing information, for example, engine coolant temperature and amount of oxygen in the exhaust, that it receives from sensors embedded in key engine components. Based on information from input sensors, the computer determines optimum settings for actuators that operate engine functions. By accounting for many variables and compensating for behavior of individual drivers, the engine ECU reduces engine emissions and fuel consumption and extends engine life.

The principal incentive for electronic engine management has probably been stricter emissions laws. Controls were needed to regulate the mixture of air and fuel so that the catalytic converter could remove pollutants from the exhaust. Also driving growth in powertrain electronics has been the replacement of mechanical power steering and throttles with sensors and wires. Electronic throttle control uses sensors and wires to control the throttle based on the pressure the driver puts on the accelerator.

Rather than engine ECU specialists, engine electronics have been integrated into production of mechanical components by large Tier 1 suppliers. Continental, Delphi, Denso, Robert Bosch, TRW, Valeo, and Visteon have been major players in engine management electronics.

Wiring Suppliers

Electrical components get their power from a battery. Six-volt batteries were sufficient to generate the electricity needed to run the handful of electrical components found in motor vehicles during the first half of the twentieth century. Twelve-volt batteries became standard during the 1950s to handle the increasing number of power accessories appearing in vehicles then.

As power consumption continued to increase by 5 percent per year, conventional wisdom proclaimed during the 1990s that the twelve-volt battery would soon be obsolete, to be replaced with a 42-volt battery. Carmakers started announcing the imminent arrival of the 42-volt battery and ordered suppliers to plan accordingly. However, the 42-volt battery was shelved because engineers figured out how to make the 12-volt battery more efficient (Truett 2004).

The leading supplier of batteries has been Johnson Control (JCI), already described as one of the two leading interior suppliers (see Chapter 7). JCI entered the battery market through acquisition of Globe-Union Inc. in 1978. The company sold 80 percent of its batteries to the aftermarket (JCI 2006). In 2006, JCI formed a joint venture with Saft, a French company specializing in the design and manufacture of high-tech batteries. The venture combined Saft's capabilities in lithium ion technology with JCI's automotive electronics capability in order to produce lithium ion battery packs and control systems for gasoline-electric hybrid vehicles. Its first manufacturing facility, located in France, was up and running by early 2008. The venture also operates a battery technical development center in Milwaukee (Truett 2007b).

Power is carried from the battery to the components through the vehicle's wiring. Because of growing complexity of wiring, carmakers have increased their sourcing of a platform's complete wiring system from a single supplier (Chew 2004b). Wiring suppliers have been asked to design a complete system three years in advance of a vehicle launch. The average entry-level vehicle had $315 worth of wiring in 2004, and high-end models had \$757 (Chew 2004b). Although the amount of wiring has increased rapidly in vehicles, prices have declined sharply.

The amount of wiring needed to connect all the convenience equipment would be excessive. Inside the door, for example, wires would be needed to connect power-window, mirror, lock, and seat controls. To address the challenge of fitting more wiring into a fixed amount of space, suppliers have used coaxial cable and developed flat wire. A vehicle's wiring is put together into a so-called wiring harness at a dedicated supplier plant. The vast majority of wiring harnesses that end up in vehicles made in North America have been produced in Mexico (see Chapter 13). Vehicles may contain some two dozen modules, including a central module called the body controller. For example, the driver's door contains a module that monitors all of the switches. Pressing the window switch causes the door module to close a relay that provides power to the window motor. "OEMs have packaging needs in headliners, dashboards and in the doors and mirrors, where traditional wiring solutions won't allow you to package."[4]

The two leading suppliers of wiring in North America have been Yazaki North America and Sumitomo. Both are Japanese owned.

Yazaki North America

Yazaki North America was the leading Japanese-owned electronics supplier and second-largest of all Japanese-owned suppliers in the United States, behind Denso. The company claimed to have invented harnesses in 1929 to bundle together the large amount of otherwise chaotic wires that thread through motor vehicles and has been the world's leading supplier of wiring harnesses, with one-fourth of the world market. Yazaki started selling harnesses in the United States in 1966 and gained production capability through acquiring Circuit Controls Corp. in Petoskey, Michigan, in 1987, and Elcom, Inc. and EWD Limited Liability Co., both in El Paso, Texas, in 1988.

Sumitomo

Sumitomo Electric Industries was part of one of Japan's largest enterprises, with interests in aerospace, chemicals, coal, finance, forestry, insurance, metals, real estate, and transportation, as well as electronics. The company's roots may go back further than those of any other parts supplier, possibly to 1590, when Kyoto medicine and book shop owner Masatomo Sumitomo is said to have opened an establishment to produce and sell copper items. The wiring operation began in 1897.

SAFETY SYSTEMS

A mid-twentieth-century auto industry "truth" was that safety didn't sell. GM president Alfred P. Sloan argued against installing safety glass. "I do not feel that it is equitable to charge the General Motors stockholders with the cost of it [safety glass] if the public shows it is not interested to pay a reasonable extra for it," Sloan told shareholders in 1932. "And so far they have not evidenced that willingness" (Cray 1980, pp. 270–271).

In 1956 Ford heavily promoted "Lifeguard Design," a package of safety features that included seat belts, deep-dish steering wheel, and sun visors. Ford's safety campaign was an abject failure: Ford trailed Chevrolet by 67,000 vehicles in 1955 and outsold it by 37,000 in 1957, but in the safety campaign year of 1956, Chevrolet outsold Ford by 190,000.

Stung by consumer resistance, carmakers tried to make interiors safer in ways that did not remind motorists of the dangers of driving or require them to modify their behavior. Padded instrument panels, softer edged trim, and blunter control buttons were marketed as comfort and appearance features rather than for safety and did not require motorists to change their behavior. The principal exception was seat belts, which required drivers and passengers to take the action of clicking them into position. With the increased diffusion of electronics, key safety innovations in the late twentieth and early twenty-first century have included airbags in the interior, lighting in the exterior, and stability control in the chassis.

Interior Safety

The interior safety system received the most improvements during the twentieth century. The two principal interior safety features have been seat belts and airbags.

Seat belts

The first automotive customers for seat belts were drivers of race cars and other vehicles used in dangerous stunts and competitions. Irvin Air Chute is said to have manufactured the first automotive seat belts for Barney Oldfield's Indianapolis 500 race car during the 1920s.

Dozens of suppliers began to make seat belts in response to Ford's 1956 safety campaign. Seat belts were already being made for aircraft, so early manufacturers of automotive seat belts included aviation suppliers, such as Davis Aircraft and American Safety Equipment, as well as Irvin. Brown Automotive and Superior Industries were also early automotive seat belt manufacturers. After the campaign failed, seat belt manufacturers turned to the aftermarket, where they were sold for as low as $1 with private labels of such retailers as NAPA, Shell Oil, Sears, and Pure Oil.

An intensive education campaign to promote the use of seat belts was undertaken during the 1960s by the National Safety Council and the Advertising Council, as well as by the American Seat Belt Council (ASBC), a manufacturers' association formed in 1961. The U.S. Department of Transportation mandated seat belts in all cars beginning in 1968. Once seat belts were installed in all new cars, the aftermarket disappeared, leading to a consolidation into a handful of original equipment manufacturers.

Despite the national seat-belt campaign, as well as intrusive warning bells and buzzers, few motorists bothered to use them. It took another generation of driver education to make buckling up an unreflective habit. Seat belt use increased from 12 percent in 1986 to 58 percent in 1994 and 82 percent in 2005 (Glassbrenner 2005).

Airbags

Officially known by the more prosaic "Supplemental Restraint System" (SRS), airbags were developed during the 1960s, first installed in luxury vehicles during the 1970s, and required in all cars in 1998 (and in other light vehicles in 1999). A crash sensor located in the front of the vehicle detects rapid deceleration and sends a signal to activate the inflator in 25 to 55 milliseconds.

When first made available, the airbag was viewed with suspicion by safety advocates because motorists did not have to do anything to activate it. The ASBC-led seat-belt lobby feared that airbags would be counterproductive to its campaign to promote universal use of seat belts: motorists might incorrectly view the airbag as a substitute for the seat belt. Once the major suppliers of seat belts also became the major suppliers of airbags, the dispute dissipated. The ASBC expanded its mission to include all forms of automotive occupant restraints and was renamed the Automotive Occupants Restraint Council in 1988.

Suppliers of safety systems have consolidated into three major providers that together hold about three-fourths of the $3 billion North American airbag market. Autoliv was the leading supplier of airbags in 2005 with two-fifths of the North American market, followed by TK and TRW, each with one-sixth of the market. Delphi, Key, and Toyoda Gosei split most of the remainder of the airbag market. TRW was first and Autoliv second in seat belts.

Autoliv. Autoliv pioneered seat-belt technology in Europe in 1956, and it started selling seat belts in the United States in 1993 and airbags a year later. As Europe's leading safety supplier, Swedish-based Autoliv had played a major role in establishing the reputation for safety of its fellow Swedish firm, Volvo.

Autoliv became the U.S. leader when it acquired Morton International's Automotive Safety Products division in 1997. Morton was well known to U.S. consumers as the best-selling table salt. Expansion into other products came through development of specialty chemicals, adhesives, and coatings. Morton's airbag research began in 1968 as an extension of interest in chemicals, and it produced the first commercially successful airbag system in 1980.

Autoliv further expanded its share of the safety restraint market through acquisitions, including the seat-belt operations of the Japanese company NSK in 2000 and the Restraint Electronics operations of Visteon in 2002. Airbags accounted for about one-half of Autoliv's sales and seat belts for about one-third in 2003. It held about 30 percent of the U.S. market for airbags in 2002, down from 44 percent in 1997, and 10 percent of seat belts.

TRW. TRW started producing seat belts in 1962 and airbags in 1989. It got into the seat-belt business through the acquisition of industry pioneer Hamill Manufacturing from Firestone. Its airbag business was strengthened in 1996 through acquisition of Magna International's operations. TRW held about one-third of the airbag market in 1997 and a higher share of the seat-belt market.

TK. Founded in 1933 by Takezo Takada to make textiles, TK started making seat belts in Japan in 1960 and in the United States in 1984. Airbags were produced in Japan beginning in 1983 and in the United States in 1992. TK Holdings had about one-fifth of the U.S. market in both seat belts and airbags.

Exterior Safety

Safety features added to the exterior have been far less controversial than those in the interior. Lighting enabled the driver to see an otherwise dark road and others to see an otherwise dark vehicle.

Oil lamps were first attached to vehicles around 1902, and they were replaced by acetylene gas lamps about four years later. Electric headlamps were introduced during the 1910s; filaments were made initially of carbon, then tungsten. The electric lamps were the first headlamps that were useful for illuminating dark roads. Hella introduced rear lights in 1915, a red one for illumination and a yellow one for braking. Lamps with sealed beams became the dominant design from around 1941 until 1983.

As nighttime driving became more common and roads more crowded, motorists complained that they were being blinded by oncoming headlights. In response, manufacturers inserted a second filament in the lamp during the 1920s. The illumination of both filaments was known at the time as "driving or country beam." When another car approached, the driver used only the filament projected lower and to the right, a position then known as "passing beam."

Exterior lighting is an important design element because it is a highly visible component. During the 1950s, the twin filament headlamp was replaced with dual headlamps, one of which was always used ("low beam") and the other only on dark roads with no other vehicles in sight ("high beam"). Meanwhile, rear lamps were integrated into the tailfins of the era.

After spending much of the twentieth century developing uniform lighting standards, manufacturers have replaced interchangeable round headlamps with individualized styles and shapes. Unique irregularly shaped exterior lights have given each vehicle a distinctive look, but they are more expensive to replace than the uniform headlamps of the past.

Into the twenty-first century, exterior lighting suppliers faced two particular issues. The first was competition between halogen and xenon headlamps. Halogen lamps, introduced in the 1960s, were cheaper and easier to produce, but newer xenon lamps were more durable, brighter, and color adjustable. It was generally assumed that xenon headlamps would follow the traditional model of appearing on more expensive models first and eventually diffusing to lower priced models. However, xenon headlamps cast a bluish light whose acceptance among consumers was not assured.

The second distinctive issue faced by exterior lighting suppliers was an adaptive front lighting system. On a curve, headlamps swiveled up to 15 degrees in the same direction that the steering wheel was turned. Two types of adaptive lighting have been developed. One housed additional bulbs in specially engineered reflectors within the headlight lens assembly. The other used motors and projector lenses to pivot the headlamps. Swiveling headlamps diffused more rapidly in Europe, where roads are more winding, while they remained illegal in the United States.

Three independent suppliers were the leading producers of headlamps in the United States between the 1920s and 1970s. Two were the country's dominant electricity pioneers, Westinghouse Electric Co. and General Electric Co. Neither has remained a supplier of automotive headlamps, although GE produced other components into the 1990s. The third independent supplier, TungSol, stopped making automotive light bulbs before World War II.[5]

During the height of vertical integration, Ford and GM produced most of their own headlamps. Responsibility for making Ford's headlamps passed to Visteon in the 1990s. GM obtained headlamps from its subsidiary Guide Lamp, started in 1906 by Hugh J. Monson, William F. Persons, and William Bunce in Cleveland, a center for manufacturing automotive accessories, because no other lamp makers were there. General Motors acquired Guide in 1928 and relocated lamp production to Anderson, Indiana, a year later. A second Guide plant was opened in Monroe, Louisiana, during the 1960s.

Guide was especially buffeted by GM's late twentieth century re-structuring. GM merged Guide with Fisher Body in 1986 and with In-land in 1990, then sold it in 1998 to Palladium Equity Partners L.L.C., a New York leveraged-buyout fund management firm. Guide then passed to B.N. Bahadur, founder and principal of BBK, a Southfield, Michigan, consulting firm to troubled suppliers (Armstrong 2004d). Guide filed for Chapter 11 protection and disappeared as a major parts supplier.

German and Japanese companies have become the leading suppli-ers of exterior lighting in the United States.

Osram Sylvania

The largest exterior lighting supplier, German-owned Osram Syl-vania, with one-third of the world market, was created in 1993 when Siemens's Osram division acquired GTE's Sylvania division. Osram Sylvania has supplied the U.S. market primarily through imports. Its major production facility in the United States was a 50–50 joint venture with Valeo in Seymour, Indiana.

The word "osram" was coined in 1906 as a combination of "osmi-um" (a metal) and "Wolfram" (German for tungsten). Siemens & Hal-ske AG (now Siemens AG) gained control of Osram through a merger with Osram's original owner Auer-Gesellschaft and AEG in 1919. Wer-ner von Siemens had been the first German to produce a light bulb in 1880, one year after Edison.

Sylvania Products Co. was formed as a spin-off of Nilco Lamp Works in 1924 to make radio tubes. Nilco (an acronym for Novelty Incandescent Lamp Co.) had been established in 1906 to make nov-elty lights as well as to recycle old light bulbs by cutting off the glass tips, replacing the filaments, and resealing the bulbs. Nilco merged with Hygrade Incandescent Lamp Co. in 1931. Hygrade made carbon-fila-ment light bulbs beginning in 1909 and tungsten filament light bulbs beginning in 1911. The combined company, called Hygrade Sylvania Corp., sold lamps under the Hygrade brand and radio tubes under the Sylvania brand. The company changed its name to Sylvania Electric Products, Inc. in 1942, merged with General Telephone in 1959, and became known as General Telephone & Electronics, later GTE.

Stanley Electric

The leading supplier of exterior lighting to Japanese-owned assembly plants was Stanley Electric. Stanley Electric, founded in 1920, was named by its founder Takaharu Kitano for Sir Henry Morton Stanley, the nineteenth-century African explorer famous for rescuing Dr. Livingston. Stanley has constructed two plants in Ohio to supply Honda.

North American Lighting

North American Lighting was a joint venture created in 1983 to supply Toyota and other Japanese-owned North American plants. It was originally owned 50 percent by Hella, 40 percent by Koito Manufacturing Co., and 10 percent by Ichikoh. Hella sold its shares to Koito in 1998.

Hella

Hella was founded in Germany in 1899 by Sally Windmuller to make lanterns and bulb horns (cornets) for carriages and bicycles, as well as cars. The "Hella" brand name was first used in 1908 for acetylene gas headlamps. Hella opened its first U.S. plant in 1980 in Flora, Illinois, to serve Volkswagen's Westmoreland plant that had opened two years earlier. A second plant was opened in Detroit in 1983 to supply relays and electronic control modules.

Stability Control

Electronics suppliers specializing in the chassis have focused on electronic stability control (ESC), which uses sensors to work with the brakes, steering, and suspension to make sure a vehicle keeps going in the direction a driver intends and does not spin out of control (Lewin 2007). ESC compares the vehicle's trajectory with what sensors say the driver intended. If they differ, brakes are applied to one or more of the wheels to reposition the vehicle back to the course intended by the driver. The system uses two sets of sensors. One set measures the motion of the vehicle, including acceleration and wheel and turning speeds. The other set measures driver behavior, including steering angle and accelerator and brake pressure (*Automotive News* 2007c). "Electronic stability control is mostly a software add-on for cars with antilock brakes because it uses the same sensors and actuators" (Lewin 2007).

In 2005, 40 percent of vehicles in Europe and 72 percent in Germany had ESC. The U.S. market share was only 25 percent, although it was expected to rise to 70 percent in 2010. The growth was expected because of a 2006 U.S. National Highway Traffic Safety Administration recommendation that electronic stability control be mandatory for all light vehicles sold in the United States starting with the 2009 model year (Wernle 2006). "With one less CD player in the car and more ESC, we might have several thousand fewer people killed on the roads."[6]

The North American stability control market was, not surprisingly, dominated by German companies. Continental had 40 percent of the North American stability control market in 2005, Bosch 37 percent, and TRW 7 percent.

Continental is one of the companies currently developing a brake-by-wire system that it intends to introduce by 2010. According to the company, the new system will be 30 pounds lighter than a hydraulic brake system. Bernd Gombert, who developed the system for the company, said, "[W]e are concerned with intelligent electronics, but we don't want to build brake components" (Floerecke 2007).

INTERIOR CONVENIENCE COMPONENTS

Convenience was far down the to-do list for nineteenth-century motor vehicles. In the absence of enclosed passenger compartments and windshields, the top convenience items were sturdy outerwear and goggles.

Gauges and controls made vehicles more convenient to use into the twentieth century. A speedometer, an odometer, a fuel level gauge, and a clock became common during the 1910s. Gauges were soon added to show oil pressure, engine temperature, and battery amperage. Controls also proliferated, beginning with the starter, lights, and ventilation. These gauges and controls at first were bolted to the body almost as afterthoughts, but during the 1910s they were integrated into the design of the interior.

With the essential operating equipment set in place and standardized by the 1920s, carmakers started loading up the interior with features that enhanced comfort and convenience rather than performance. The most notable addition during the 1920s was the nation's brand-new medium of popular entertainment, the radio. Another burst of convenience features appeared after World War II, most prominently power assists for windows, door locks, and seat adjusters.

Carmakers have struggled to find entirely new realms of comfort and convenience beyond the entertainment and power assists of earlier generations, but they have continually refined the details of the features. The most significant change, especially during the 1980s, was replacement of large clunky motors with electronics, enabling more features to be packed into the limited interior space.

The Control Center: Cockpit

Across the front of the passenger compartment, beneath the windshield, is a plate, known for most of the twentieth century as the dashboard. The dashboard—originally stamped from steel and more recently molded from plastic—contains cutouts so that other parts can be inserted. A cluster of gauges and switches, known as an instrument panel, is mounted on the driver's side of the dashboard.

"Instrument panel" and "dashboard" sound too old-fashioned to describe twenty-first-century interiors. Carmakers and suppliers prefer to use the term "cockpit," following a long tradition of trying to closely align the driving experience with piloting an airplane. "Instrument panel" lingers as a term for the portion of the cockpit in front of the driver, but many of the "cockpit" controls are actually housed in the center console or driver's door.

Electronics contribute an estimated 44 percent of the value of the cockpit. The instrument panel monitors a communications bus that sends updated information, such as speed and temperature, several times a second to the appropriate gauge. One-half of the vehicle's total wiring is packed into the cockpit. The molded plastic housing of the dashboard comprises only about 3 percent of the value of a cockpit. Heating and cooling systems contribute an estimated 23 percent of the value of a cockpit, trim 21 percent, and safety restraints 9 percent (*CSM Insights* 2001).

Like seats, instrument panels and dashboards were traditionally put together on the final assembly line from a large collection of individual parts. "Outsourcing a module such as the cockpit would mean major changes for Nissan's supply base. Currently [1999], Nissan itself is the gathering point for the dozens of subcomponents that go into the cockpit."[7] One-fourth of cockpits were being delivered in 2005 by outside suppliers as complete modules ready for installation. These cockpit modules integrated so-called infotainment components with HVAC components in the center or "mid-console" part of the instrument panel.

As with other modules, final assembly is made more efficient by replacing dozens of individual components with a single installation. In addition to gauges and panels, a cockpit module may also include the heating and cooling system, safety restraints, and the audio equipment. More importantly, though, the cockpit replaces components that were among the most difficult to install, because they went in places difficult for final assembly workers to reach.

Speedometers. Early motor vehicles were capable of moving much faster than the pedestrians, horse-drawn carriages, streetcars, and assorted chickens, dogs, and pigs then filling the roads. Taking advantage of that capability, early motorists—often selfish rich young men inexperienced at driving—often plowed through the teeming throngs at high speed, frightening and scattering them.

To facilitate sharing of the increasingly crowded roads, many U.S. localities enacted speed limit laws during the first decade of the twentieth century, and European countries updated nineteenth-century laws. To obey speed limits, motorists needed a device to show how fast their vehicles were moving. Credit for inventing the speedometer is disputed. Numerous Web sites carry the following identically worded paragraph. "The Chinese invented the speedometer. In 1027, Lu Taolung presented the Emperor Jen Chung with a cart that could measure the distances it spanned by means of a mechanism with eight wheels and two moving arms. One arm struck a drum each time a 'li' (about a third of a mile) was covered. Another rang a bell every 10 li."

Nice story, but that sounds like an odometer, not a speedometer, and the odometer is said by the *Encyclopaedia Britannica* to have been invented by Roman architect and engineer Vitruvius in about 15 BCE. Vitruvius is said to have attached to a wheel of known circumference a wheelbarrow-like frame that automatically dropped a pebble into a container upon each revolution of the wheel. The odometer may be the third-oldest car part, following the wheel and the seat.

As for the disputed speedometer, Warner Electric Co., part of Altra Industrial Motion, credits its founder, Arthur Pratt Warner (1870–1957), with the invention. Warner is said to have invented the speedometer that became "the industry standard" while serving as vice president and general manager of Warner Electric between 1903 and 1912. Overland is said to be the first U.S. car to have a speedometer as standard equipment in 1908. Warner, based in Beloit, Wisconsin, became the largest U.S. manufacturer of speedometers. Reorganized in 1912 as the Stewart-Warner Manufacturing Co., the company, now known as Stewart Warner Performance, specializes in industrial clutch and brake technology rather than car parts (Warner Electric 2005; Wisconsin Historical Society 2007).

Electrical engineer Nikola Tesla (1856–1943) is also credited with inventing the speedometer. Tesla, best known for inventing alternating current, is said by a number of sources to have invented the speedometer in 1916 (e.g., Autotech 2004; DASH Electronics and Speedometer n.d.; Electroherbalism 2007; U-S-History.com 2005). No information is given in these Web sites that Tesla ever manufactured or sold his invention.

Meanwhile on the other side of the Atlantic, Continental company history suggests that the speedometer was patented in 1902 by Otto Schulze, an engineer from Strasbourg, now in France, then in Germany. The date is earlier than the Warner and Tesla claims, but the production predecessor of Continental did not start manufacturing speedometers until the 1920s, two decades after Warner.

Schulze's "eddy current" speedometer had a shaft attached to a wheel at one end and a magnet at the other end. As the shaft revolved at a particular speed, a metal disc close to but not touching the magnet also turned, but only by a few degrees because a spring prevented it from rotating the full 360 degrees. A pointer attached to the metal disc indicated the speed. Production of the Schulze eddy current speedometer began in Germany in 1905. The speed of the wheel's rotation was transmitted to the speedometer by means of an electric signal across a wire beginning in the 1950s, and electronically via a computer chip beginning in the 1980s (Siemens VDO 2002).

Continental

Regardless of the speedometer's origin, the leading supplier of cockpit modules into the twenty-first century was Continental AG, Germany's second-largest parts maker behind Robert Bosch. Continental gained its leadership position by acquiring Siemens VDO in 2007. Siemens VDO in turn was formed through a 2001 merger between Siemens Automotive AG and Mannesmann VDO.

Speedometer expertise came through VDO. VDO's predecessor Otto Schulze Autometer (OSA), established in 1920 by Adolf Schindling, Georg Häußler, and Heinrich Lang, started making speedometers in 1923. OSA (known after 1925 as OTA) merged in 1928 with another speedometer specialist, Deuta Werke, to form VDO Tachometer AG— an acronym for Vereinigte Deuta OTA (union of Deuta and OTA). Mannesmann AG gained majority control of VDO in 1991 and completed the takeover in 1994.

Competitors in supplying cockpit modules were the two downsized former captive suppliers Delphi and Visteon, as well as major interior suppliers JCI and Lear. A joint venture of Valeo SA and Textron Automotive formed in 2000 was also a major cockpit supplier. Textron provided the instrument panel and trim and Valeo the electronics and air conditioning (Miel 2000).

Infotainment Center: Not Just a Radio Anymore

By the Roaring Twenties, with vehicles mechanically sound and reasonably reliable, motorists were ready for more creature comforts. Passenger compartments were enclosed, and outfitted with sofalike seating. Vehicle interiors were ripe for marriage with the new medium of mass entertainment then sweeping America, the radio.

Like the speedometer, the car radio also has a disputed origin. Motorola, produced by Galvin Manufacturing Corporation, has been most commonly cited as the first practical car radio, meaning affordably priced for most motorists, in 1928. Philadelphia Storage Battery Corporation, generally known as Philco, sold a radio called Transitone for use in a car two years earlier. As noted in Chapter 2, Bill Lear claimed to have made the first car radio back in 1922, before assigning the rights to Motorola.

No matter who created it, the car radio diffused quickly, essentially simultaneously with the spread of radio for home entertainment. A radio was an option on most new cars during the early 1930s, despite costing more than $100, and by the time automotive production was halted for World War II, radios were being installed in all but the cheapest models.

Additions to the basic prewar AM radio included push buttons for tuning in favorite stations during the 1950s, FM band during the 1960s, stereo speakers during the 1970s, tape decks during the 1980s, CD players during the 1990s, and satellite receivers during the 2000s. Through all of these technological updates, audio equipment has retained the prominent position accorded to it in the center of the dashboard.

Audio systems have been integrated with information services, a combination now known as infotainment or telematics. Telematics systems combine radio with navigation devices, DVDs, GPS systems, traffic reports, voice-activated cellular phones, and MP3 players.

Early radios were made by independent suppliers, including Radio Corporation of America (RCA) and Zenith Corporation, as well as Philco and Galvin (the company name was changed to Motorola in 1947). To make its own radios, Ford acquired Philco in 1961, but sold it in 1974 to GTE-Sylvania, now part of Philips. GM's Delco Radio Division made radios at a plant in Kokomo, Indiana, acquired from Crosley Manufacturing Co. in 1936. The division's successor, Delco Electronics System, became part of Delphi.

The car radio business is still dominated by Ford and GM's spun-off parts divisions, Visteon and Delphi. Chrysler also used to make its own radios but sold its plant in Huntsville, Alabama, to Siemens VDO in 2004. The acquisition gave Siemens VDO 6 percent of the U.S. radio market and made it the largest supplier of electronics to Chrysler.

Panasonic

Panasonic, a division of Matsushita Electric Industrial Co. (MEI), was the leading automotive audio equipment supplier in North America, especially to international carmakers. MEI, founded in Japan in 1918, first used the brand name Panasonic in 1955 to market radios in North America. In 2003, MEI applied the Panasonic name to a division that consolidated the development, manufacturing, and sales functions of five Japanese electronics firms: Automotive Multimedia Co., AVC Co.

Automotive Systems, Kyushu Matsushita Electric Co., Ltd. (KME), Matsushita Communication Industrial Co. (MCI), and MEI Automotive Electronics Business Promotion Center and Corporate Automotive Electronics Marketing Division.

Continental

Discussed earlier in the chapter as the leading supplier of cockpits, Continental acquired Motorola's automotive electronics business for $1 billion in 2006. The acquisition gave Continental additional capabilities in electronics for powertrain and chassis systems and made it the leading telematics producer worldwide. Continental was the main supplier for GM's OnStar technology, and it developed a telematics product for Ford, called "Ford SYNC." Continental designed and manufactured the hardware, and Microsoft designed the software (Snavely 2007b).

OUTLOOK AND UNCERTAINTIES: WILL THE TAIL WAG THE DOG?

The increasing importance of electronics in future motor vehicles is a given. What is up for grabs is control over the provision of the electronics. A four-way battle is being waged among vehicle producers, parts producers, hardware producers, and software producers. Along the way we are observing some interesting combinations of different players. A case in point was the Ford SYNC system, which linked telephones, MP3 players, and other devices to car electronics. The major contributors were Microsoft, which provided the operating system, Continental, which provided the electronic hardware, and Ford, which provided the automotive technology (*Automotive News* 2007d).

Vehicle producers have traditionally played the dominant role in the production process. Carmakers that took the early lead in providing electronics, notably German luxury brands Mercedes-Benz and BMW, stamped their own names on elaborate driver information centers. However, these driver information centers proved too complex for most drivers and dragged down quality ratings. BMW's iDrive "is so complicated that even BMW's own executives have had trouble learning how to use it" (Teich's Tech Tidbit 2003). To change the radio, "Tug the controller back, rotate it clockwise two clicks, depress it, rotate it clockwise two more clicks, depress it again and then, finally, rotate the knob to your desired station. Got it? That's six steps—assuming you know the right path—all while looking at the display instead of the road ahead" (Bornhop 2002). The question, then, is not if electronics will play an increasingly important role but whether carmakers can success-fully integrate the electronics functions.

Traditional vehicle parts suppliers have played an increasing role in provision of all systems, including electronics. The in-dash radio has long carried the brand name of the parts maker, as have navigation de-vices and cell phones more recently. Roland Berger forecast in 2000, "Because only a few electronics suppliers will be able to shoulder the huge capital investments required to develop new products, OEMs will have to source most of their electronics from only a few key suppliers. And as the value of outsourced electronics increases, the value of OEM content will decline, increasing the suppliers' bargaining power" (Crain 2000).

Martin Anderson of Babson College predicted in 1997, "'We will see the Hewlett-Packards and IBMs of the world among the major auto-motive suppliers. And we will see a power struggle between carmakers and software suppliers over who owns the software architecture of the car . . . If you can update an engine's performance by downloading a new software program,' Anderson asked, 'whose engine is it?'" (Chap-pell 1997). We might also ask, will the consumer be aware of such link-ages? The computer on which this book was written features a label that states "Intel inside," but motor vehicle cockpits do not yet announce "Infineon" or "Freescale" inside.

IBM predicted in 2005 that, by 2010, "almost all cars will have essentially the same mechanical systems. What will make the cars dif-ferent will be software that operates the systems in ways specific to the brand of car" (Moran 2005). The world's dominant software provider, Microsoft, gained its first visibility in motor vehicles with a deal to brand Fiat's driver information center. Microsoft is counting on driv-ers increasingly insisting on connectivity with their computers, most of which prominently display the Microsoft name. "What we are looking at really is the car as a mobile PC . . . It is about the digital lifestyle and integration between the car, office and home."[8]

Which suppliers will become the major providers of electronics going forward is not obvious. At stake are not merely the billions of dollars in manufacturing contracts, but even more important, the electronics provider's visibility to the consumer, and ultimately its brand recognition.

Notes

1. Martin Anderson, director of supply chain programs, Babson College, quoted in Chappell (1997).
2. Dave Royce, Siemens VDO Automotive Corporation North American corporate strategy head, quoted in Kosdrosky and Snavely (2004).
3. The top seven in 2004 in terms of world share were Freescale Semiconductor (12 percent), Infineon (9 percent), STMicroelectronics (8 percent), Renesas (7 percent), NEC (6 percent), Bosch, and Toshiba (Webber 2005a).
4. James Spencer, president, Delphi Packard Electric Systems, quoted in Chew (2004b).
5. Letter from David R. Dayton, a lamp engineering consultant for incandescent and halogen lamps, to the U.S. Department of Transportation Document Management Section, October 17, 2001, accessed at http://dmses.dot.gov/docimages/pdf75/147722_web.pdf.
6. Manfred Wennemer, CEO Continental, quoted in Landler (2005).
7. Emil Hassan, Nissan North America senior vice president, quoted in Chappell (1999).
8. Manuel Simas, Microsoft European automotive business development manager, quoted in Mackintosh (2006).

15
Conclusion: Surviving the Car Wars

*[Consumers and investors] are looking at Detroit and say-
ing . . . get real . . . quit your crying, work together to fix your
problems or get out of the way.*[1]

This book was written to shed light on the manufacturers of motor
vehicle parts. Parts suppliers employ far more people and add much
more value to the vehicle than do carmakers. Yet our understanding of
the parts makers is quite limited.

We know much more about the identity and struggles of the companies whose names are on the vehicles. Much is written about the histories of the companies and their leaders, the features of their brands,
and the distinctive assets and the challenges of each. But vehicles are
made of thousands of parts about which we know relatively little. Who
are the companies that made all of these parts? How do they relate to
one another and to their customers, the carmakers? And where are these
parts made?

The U.S. auto industry through most of the twentieth century consisted of three major carmakers responsible for making most of their
own components, supplemented by thousands of mostly small parts
suppliers. In the twenty-first century, the number of major carmakers
competing in the United States has increased with the addition of foreign-owned carmakers, and many suppliers have become major players
in the vehicle production process.

Thus, the relationship between carmakers and suppliers has been
transformed from a hierarchical one, with a steep pyramid shape, to
a complex Venn diagram of interrelations among many competitive
carmakers and many competitive suppliers. "Those are very difficult
relationships to manage . . . People within the OEMs just are not trained
to manage these relationships" (McKinsey & Company Automotive &
Assembly Extranet 2005, p. 4).

355

The role of parts makers has evolved as substantial changes have occurred in the motor vehicle industry as a whole. Some of the most important changes include

- a shift from in-house production of parts by carmakers to outsourcing to independent suppliers;

- a smaller number of Tier 1 suppliers working directly with the carmakers;

- a complex supply chain of Tier 2 suppliers working with Tier 1 suppliers, Tier 3 suppliers working with Tier 2 suppliers, and so forth;

- an increase in the demand for just-in-time delivery of parts to the final assembly plant; and

- a quickening pace of technological change, especially in areas of energy conservation, reduced emissions, and enhanced safety, partly driven by regulatory requirements.

"'Relentless' and 'brutal' are the two words most often used to describe competitive pressure in the automotive supply chain. Battered by global over-capacity, shorter model lifecycles and seemingly permanent rebates of up to $5,000 per car, automakers are passing the pain—with interest—on to their suppliers" (Murphy 2004). Given these competitive pressures, a good relationship with its supply base represents one of the most significant competitive advantages a carmaker can have.

A good relationship with suppliers is a central element of the competitive advantage in the U.S. market held by Japanese carmakers, especially Toyota. Most succinctly, SupplierBusiness.com cites two basic models for carmaker–supplier relationships: the command and control contract (or adversarial) model preferred by the Detroit 3 and the collaborative (or partnership) model preferred by Japanese automakers (Snyder 2005).

Time and time again during the course of this study, suppliers have repeated in private that relations with the Detroit 3 are poor, especially in comparison with their Japanese customers. Supplying the Detroit 3 calls for "testosterone games to see who can squeeze more, pay more slowly, or demand extortion—uh, excuse me, productivity."[2]

The Detroit 3 model of supplier relationships has been one of "exit" and the Japanese model one of "voice," according to economists Susan

Helper and John Paul MacDuffie. The Detroit 3's exit model has been characterized by "short-term relationships, limited amounts of collabo-ration, and the willingness of either party to 'exit' the relationship for short-term gain." The Japanese model has been characterized by "lots of collaboration (with supplier 'voices' being heard)" (McKinsey & Company Automotive & Assembly Extranet 2005, p. 1).

Differences in quality and efficiency between Japanese and U.S. carmakers observed in the twentieth century have narrowed if not dis-appeared altogether in the twenty-first century. The principal measure where the gap between Japanese and U.S. carmakers has widened in the twenty-first century is in supplier relations.

SUMMARY OF FINDINGS

This book set out to document the existing structure of the North American motor vehicle parts industry. The key to the analysis was creating a database that allowed us to describe and analyze the industry at an unprecedented level of detail. The ability to draw on a database of 4,268 individual parts-making plants in North America, including plant-level geography and product information, allowed us to analyze a little-known industry at a rich level of detail. We have identified several major trends currently shaping this industry.

- **Role of the Midwest.** Most parts for motor vehicles were once made in and near southeastern Michigan. The area has lost its dominance in parts production, but it is still home to the largest number of plants. Most of the parts for the powertrain and ex-terior continue to be made in the Midwest because the parts are relatively bulky and are most efficiently produced near sources of both inputs (especially steel) and customers.

- **Carmaker–Supplier Networks.** Most parts need to be produced within a one-day delivery radius of the customer in order to ensure arrival at the final assembly plant on a just-in-time basis. Only a handful of parts, though, need to be produced right next door to the final assembly plant. The seat is the single most prominent example of a major module that is invariably made within one hour of the final assembly plant. Carmakers and suppliers depend on logistics specialists to coordinate the flow of information and goods within a network.

- **Auto Alley.** The U.S. motor vehicle industry is still highly clustered, but it is now located in a narrow north–south corridor known as Auto Alley. The industry's traditional Midwest core now forms the northern end of Auto Alley. It is still home to most facilities operated by the Detroit 3 carmakers. But newer plants have headed south within Auto Alley, especially those operated by foreign-owned companies. The primary reason for selecting a southern location within Auto Alley has been to minimize the likelihood of a unionized workforce. Southern plants have somewhat lower wage scales, but the principal benefits have been much lower benefit packages and more flexible work rules.

- **Global Shifts.** The percentages of parts made outside the United States and inside the United States by foreign-owned companies have increased. Production of relatively bulky, low-value interior and exterior systems has been less likely to leave the United States. Instead, motor vehicle parts imports have grown for both high-value powertrain modules (e.g., complete engines and transmissions) and low-value, high-labor-content routine electronics parts.

OUTLOOK AND UNCERTAINTIES FOR PARTS SUPPLIERS

On paper, the U.S. auto industry looked set to prosper in the twenty-first century. New vehicle sales in the United States remained at historically high levels through the 1990s and into the twenty-first century. Despite globalization of the industry, most vehicles sold in the United States were still being assembled in the United States from parts made mostly in the United States. In 2008, news stories suggested that a Chinese automaker is planning to assemble cars in North America (Ying 2008).

The supplier sector of the industry looked to be prospering as well. As this book has shown, suppliers were already responsible for adding two-thirds of the value to vehicles in the early twenty-first century, and the share was expected to rise. Having been given more responsibility by carmakers, suppliers have evolved into providers of complex manufacturing tasks that required their own research and development.

Buffeting Headwinds

Though the overall industry conditions appear favorable for parts producers, in reality individual motor vehicle parts producers had to navigate a challenging course to survive in a competitive environment. The parts industry based in North America has been buffeted by what billionaire investor Wilbur Ross (2006) has called "the perfect storm." Key elements of what could be more modestly described meteorologically as strong headwinds include:

- **Shifting Market Shares.** Parts suppliers live and die by the fortunes of the carmakers. Suppliers dependent for their business primarily on the Detroit 3 carmakers have had to quickly adjust to a sharp decline in volume, more than 3 percent annually in the first decade of the twenty-first century. Conversely, suppliers dependent on foreign-owned carmakers have had to quickly respond to a corresponding increase in volume.

- **Globalization of Supply Chains.** Suppliers producing commodity or generic parts are facing increased competition from producers located in low-wage countries such as China. On the other hand, suppliers producing high-tech and research-intensive parts face increased competition from European and Japanese suppliers with close ties to foreign-owned carmakers.

- **High Cost of Inputs.** The motor vehicle industry is the major manufacturing destination for steel, glass, aluminum, rubber, and a host of other materials, not to mention petroleum. Rising costs for these materials have been borne primarily by suppliers. As carmakers expect suppliers to lower the price of their product annually over the life of the contract, passing on cost increases to carmakers is next to impossible.

- **Technological Changes.** In many instances technological changes are driven by regulatory requirements, such as safety and emission standards. Some technological improvements, such as more efficient internal combustion engines, are incremental and are being pursued by existing suppliers. New technologies, such as hybrids, electric, fuel-cell, and other alternative-fuel vehicles, are potentially much more disruptive to the existing supply chain. New suppliers will compete to provide new technology. A technological breakthrough can therefore have major implications for Auto Alley because it is not certain that new suppliers will feel compelled to locate in the traditional production region.

Supplier Restructuring

The consequences of Ross's "perfect storm" have been severe for some parts suppliers.

Bankruptcy

Twenty-five suppliers ranked among the 150 largest filed for Chapter 11 bankruptcy protection between 1999 and early 2008. Suppliers dependent on the Detroit 3 have been especially vulnerable. "As Detroit's auto makers struggle with slowing sales, a slew of the parts manufacturers who depend on them have skidded into financial trouble. Several already have sought bankruptcy protection and others are racing to fix debt-laden balance sheets" (Pacelle 2005). "The lenders are very leery of people in the automotive parts business. They think the car companies are killing the suppliers."[3] Filing for Chapter 11 can serve as a backstop for a beleaguered company, providing some breathing room for its restructuring. In the case of Dana, it worked out that way. The case of Collins & Aikman illustrates, however, that restructurings can't always be pulled off. Having filed for bankruptcy and unable to emerge with a workable business plan, the company went out of business.

Private equity investment

Equity investment firms owned 25 percent of industry revenues in 2007, according to management consultancy firm AT Kearney, and the figure was expected to rise to 36 percent in 2010 (Simon 2007b). Major players have included Blackstone Group LP, Carlyle Group, Cerberus Capital Management, Heartland Industrial Partners, and Questor Management Group. They have specialized in applying state-of-the-art management practices to struggling undervalued and underperforming suppliers. Capital is provided to fix these struggling parts makers, usually in order to generate quick profits. In some cases, the massive investment is designed to be recovered by a public sale of shares to investors. "The growth of control by investment firms is bound to raise concern at the Detroit 3, which have traditionally been uneasy with such deals. Automakers worry that financial returns for these owners will take priority over quality and delivery, said a spokesman for one car company" (Sherefkin 2001).

Restructuring labor contracts

With a rising share of motor vehicle production undertaken by non-union labor, both at home and abroad, owners of unionized plants have argued that their labor costs need to be reduced. For their part, union leaders have accepted the argument that protecting jobs and pensions required them to offer concessions. Suppliers have introduced two-tier wage structures, placing newly hired employees on a lower scale than veterans. Buyouts have been offered to entice voluntary retirement by long-term employees. Especially intractable has been the desire of employers to reduce their legacy costs, that is, their responsibility for retiree health-care and long-term disability benefits. Establishing a union-managed voluntary employees' beneficiary association (VEBA) was one way to shift responsibility from the company to separate management, such as the UAW.[4]

Survival Strategies

Successful suppliers are adopting one of three business models: systems integrator, high-tech module developer, or low-cost parts provider. "Trying to combine all three in one corporate structure will be futile."[5] Two of these three business models are typical of many industries: companies often choose between trying to be the most efficient low-cost producer or the most advanced high-tech producer. In the auto industry, carmakers have also opened the door to the systems integrator.

Systems integration

Systems integrators benefit from having relatively low manufacturing and research and development costs. As they bring together modules and components provided by other suppliers, they add value through efficient management and cost control. Magna International, an especially exuberant proponent of systems integration, started calling itself a Tier 0.5 supplier, and even trademarked the term Tier 0.5. Ignoring Magna's trademark, other suppliers began to call themselves Tier 0.5 to promote their ability to design and manufacture entire vehicle systems (Chappell 2002).

Becoming a systems integrator has attracted many suppliers, who have been encouraged by carmakers wishing to deal with fewer larger suppliers, but some financial analysts have questioned the model's logic. A study by Booz Allen Hamilton compared the returns on investment of highly specialized suppliers and broad-based system suppliers with the industry average. For many companies, the time and effort invested in becoming a system supplier failed to produce the desired effect. "All too often, activities are merely transferred from automaker to supplier with no gain in efficiency. In fact, some tasks of system integration can be handled far more efficiently by the automaker. The automaker, after all, is responsible for the vehicle concept" (Ziebart 2002).

High-tech suppliers

The second survival approach for suppliers is to develop unique technologies. Especially attracted to this business model are technology-oriented suppliers. Increased electronics content is especially important to high-tech suppliers. "Companies that develop features their customers will pay a premium price for will win. For example, there are more and more sensors and actuators. The whole market in the developed countries has gone nuts relative to driver features such as power sliding doors in minivans. You've got this huge motors market."[6]

Examples of high-tech module specialists are Autoliv and Freudenberg-NOK. Freudenberg-NOK was the largest supplier of engine seals and the world's largest producer of molded rubber products other than tires. The company prides itself on its "laser-sharp focus on the core competencies of sealing, vibration control and elastomeric technologies" (Freudenberg-NOK 2007). Autoliv was the leading supplier of airbags in the United States and worldwide. Their first product was located inside the steering wheel to protect the driver. Additional airbags have been located in the instrument panel in front of the passenger, at a lower level to protect knees, and as "curtains" along the sides of the interior. Each successive airbag system developed has generated revenue for Autoliv and its competitors. "[D]river and passenger airbags have become a commodity. But extra airbags, such as side curtains or knee bolsters, are promoting growth for companies such as Autoliv Inc."[7]

Low-cost suppliers

Meanwhile, some contrarian suppliers are finding success by following the industry's traditional model of producing generic parts and components. "It's hard for a supplier to survive just building to the automaker's design. There's nothing setting you apart. You're just competing on price, and that's really hard."[8] Even though it is "really hard," the strategy is working for some suppliers. They gain contracts through low-price bids, build revenues through large-volume production of specific parts and components, and earn profits through lean management and efficient operations. Suppliers with revenues between $50 and $200 million "are poised to emerge as industry stars" (Kosdrosky and Snavely 2005).

Many of the parts makers adhering to the "efficiency" model have moved down the supply chain to lower tiers. A thriving practitioner of this model, Illinois Tool Works, made door handles, seat latches, and hundreds of generic "bin" parts for motor vehicles, as well as a wide variety of parts for consumer and industrial applications. The company has earned a profit through efficient management practices, notably decentralizing operations to several hundred autonomous business units while maintaining an exceptionally lean central staff.

OUTLOOK AND UNCERTAINTIES FOR COMMUNITIES

The twenty-first-century auto parts industry in the United States is concentrated in a region known as Auto Alley, a 700-mile-long north–south corridor through the interior of the United States between the Great Lakes and the Gulf of Mexico, with extensions into Canada and Mexico. This book presents the contemporary Auto Alley as the sum of a complex web of relationships between carmakers and their suppliers.

Changing Shape of Auto Alley

Within Auto Alley are situated most of the country's final assembly plants, but the shape of Auto Alley has been evolving in the twenty-first century.

Traditional clustering in Michigan

For most of the twentieth century, the motor vehicle industry was highly clustered in and near southeastern Michigan. The area's preeminence in the auto industry derived from the emergence of Ford, GM, and Chrysler, which were all based there. For most of the twentieth century, the Detroit 3 produced nearly all of their parts in and near southeastern Michigan, although they assembled most of their vehicles elsewhere. Thus, the preponderance of Michigan's Detroit 3 auto jobs have traditionally been in parts-making facilities.

Geographical implications of market shifts

Into the twenty-first century, the declining fortunes of the Big 3—now more modestly known as the Detroit 3—have brought declining fortunes to Michigan's economy. Michigan was losing 6 percent of its auto industry jobs annually in the first years of the twenty-first century. During the twentieth century, Michigan's motor vehicle employment frequently declined, but with very few exceptions, these were all temporary or cyclical declines: workers were laid off during slow-selling years and hired back during boom years. In contrast, Michigan's job losses in the early twenty-first century were structural in nature. Because of the changes discussed in this book, the jobs lost during this time period were not going to return. This represented a stunning reversal of the late 1990s during which the auto industry was booming. Michigan had to adjust to this harsh new reality. Its implications for future vehicle employment in the state have been difficult for Michigan's citizens and policymakers to recognize and accept.

Management and technical operations have remained in the Detroit area, but the growth in production employment has been further south in Auto Alley. Ironically, as the Detroit 3 made the necessary capacity reductions at plants at the periphery of their footprint, they were more concentrated at the northern end of Auto Alley at the beginning of the twenty-first century than they had been for many decades.

Carmaker–supplier networks

The tightness of an assembly plant's network of suppliers determines that plant's regional economic footprint. Surrounding each of these assembly plants is a supplier network extending, for the most part, to within a one-day shipping distance as a result of widespread adoption of just-in-time delivery. However, just-in-time does not mean that suppliers must be located immediately next door to final assembly plants. In fact, most of the supplier networks extend far beyond the immediate vicinity of an assembly plant.

Location by type of part

Just-in-time doesn't mean the same geographical arrangement for each type of part. Rather, the specific geography of the supplier relationship is heavily influenced by the nature of the part being produced. Parts can be classified as those that need to be made within an hour or so of the final assembly plant, those that need to be within a one-day drive, and those that can be made further away. Seats are nearly always produced within an hour of an assembly plant. Sequencing and kitting operations are also located in a very close vicinity. At the other end of the distance spectrum, most electronics parts are produced outside the United States.

Attracting New Plants

States within Auto Alley have provided incentives to entice carmakers to locate in one of their communities. Financial incentives have included tax breaks, training programs, and site improvements.[9]

To attract Toyota, the state of Kentucky agreed in 1985 to provide $147 million in incentives. The package included $10.3 million for land acquisition, $20 million for site preparation, $10.3 million for water and gas lines, $7.2 million for a training facility, $12.2 million for a wastewater treatment facility, $32 million for highway improvements, and $55 million for training and education. The state also took on an obligation estimated at $168 million to assist in paying interest on debts that Toyota could incur in conjunction with plant construction.

Kentucky's commitment of at least $147 million to Toyota represented a substantial escalation in the subsidies being offered to international carmakers at the time. Less than a year earlier, Illinois had attracted Mitsubishi with subsidies totaling only $86 million, and $86 million was sufficient to entice Subaru to Indiana a year later. Honda, the first Japanese carmaker to build an assembly plant in the United States, received only $24 million from Ohio five years earlier (Molot 2003; Rubenstein 1992).

The University of Kentucky concluded that the Georgetown plant would generate $632.6 million in property, sales, and income taxes during its first 20 years. Other economists offered differing views on what benefits to measure and how to measure them. For example, economist Larry Ledebur calculated expected benefits to be only $267.5 million and therefore concluded that Kentucky had overpaid for Toyota (Fiordalisi 1989).

In hindsight, Kentucky may have paid more than its neighbors for an assembly plant during the 1980s, but the Bluegrass State appreciates thoroughbreds, and in Toyota it backed the company that subsequently proved to be the Triple Crown winner in the global automotive industry competition. For its $147 million subsidies, Toyota promised Kentucky in 1985 that it would spend $800 million to build and operate the Georgetown facility and employ 3,000 workers with a $90 million annual payroll in order to assemble 200,000 vehicles per year. All figures soon climbed to substantially higher levels than Toyota had promised. In 1997, Toyota's investment in the plant had reached $4.5 billion, 7,689 workers were employed, 435,000 vehicles were assembled, and payroll was $470.4 million (CanagaRetna 2004).

> Between 1986 and 2005, [a 1998 University of Kentucky Gaton College of Business and Economics] study noted that Kentucky would collect over and above the costs of the incentive package, approximately $1.2 billion in tax revenues, attributable to the direct and indirect effects of Toyota's operations in the commonwealth.
>
> In terms of state revenue collections, discounted cash flow analysis in 1985 indicated an annual rate of return of 8.5 percent from increased revenue collections attributable to the direct and indirect effects of the plant's operations. A 1992 economic impact study, also carried out by the University of Kentucky, revealed that the projected rate of return had increased to 16.8 percent per annum. These projections were revised upward again in the 1998 study which indicated that the updated annual rate of return stood at 36.8 percent. (CanagaRetna 2004, p. 74)

A generation later, the lesson other states seemed to have learned from Kentucky was the value of subsidizing assembly plants. During the 1990s, incentives averaged about $100 million per assembly plant. Incentives increased because carmakers "learned to bargain" (Molot 2003). That Kentucky had backed a winner was the real point. States that had subsidized also-rans were getting much less value for their money. Earlier subsidies paled in comparison with the $409 million package provided to Kia by the state of Georgia in 2005. To attract an assembly plant projected to employ 2,900, Georgia offered Kia a whopping $141,000 per worker. How could such a figure be justified?

> The stakes are high. West Georgia badly needs Kia's jobs as the textile industry has flagged in recent years.
>
> Georgia's prestige as an economic center is on the line, too. Car factories in neighboring states like Alabama are churning out paychecks by the thousands, while the Peach State stands to lose its only plants, Ford's and General Motors'. (Woods 2006)

It was not just that Kia's assembly plant would arrive. Georgia officials argued that an assembly plant always brings along supplier plants.

As we documented earlier in this book, "just-in-time" does not translate into "right next door." Many suppliers only need to be within one day's drive of an assembly plant. In Kia's case, Georgia was unlikely to see many supplier plants materialize because much of Kia's supplier base had already built plants within the one-day radius of the Georgia site to support the nearby Hyundai plant in Alabama. "Hyundai (Kia's corporate parent) is supported by 78 suppliers in the U.S. and Mexico, 35 of them located in Alabama. Kia has promised Georgia there will be at least five suppliers in the state" (*Columbus Ledger-Enquirer* 2006).

The spatial characteristics of assembler–supplier networks presented in this book call into question the logic of providing enormous subsidies to carmakers. States have been providing generous subsidies, especially to final assembly plants, in part not because of jobs generated inside these plants but primarily because of the multiplier effect, that is, the number of supplier jobs that are expected to come along with final assembly. The number of suppliers within close range of the assembly plant rarely exceeds 30, suggesting that the supply chain of an individual assembly plant is regional in nature. Furthermore, within a given supplier network, many supplier operations count among their customers more than that one assembly plant.

Consider the fate of the Greensburg, Indiana, site of an assembly plant opened by Honda in 2008. Greensburg has seen the arrival of several thousand new jobs at the Honda plant as well as in such services as grocery stores and restaurants. The community, though, has not seen a boom in parts makers other than the inevitable seat plant plus a few trim producers. Southeastern Indiana is strategically placed between the southern end of the traditional auto production region centered in the Great Lakes and the northern end of the recent growth in Kentucky and points south. Most suppliers to Honda are already capable of delivering to Greensburg within one day from existing sites in Auto Alley.

Greensburg also demonstrated the strategy of infilling within Auto Alley. As Auto Alley has extended fully between the Great Lakes and the Gulf of Mexico, manufacturers have been taking a second look at sites that were passed over during the push south in the late twentieth century. Trying to avoid competition for labor with existing plants will increasingly take precedence in selecting specific sites within Auto Alley.

CONCLUSION

The analysis presented in this book is intended to provide a framework that helps put in context ongoing developments in the motor vehicle parts industry. We demonstrated that underneath the robust cluster that characterizes this industry in North America lies a complex web of very dynamic relationships. We suggest that it is at that level of detail one has to assess the impact of ongoing changes, be they in trade or technology.

Based on our analysis, we believe that the fundamental geography of auto assembly in North America is not likely to change anytime soon: most vehicles sold in North America will continue to be assembled in North America. But more parts will be coming from elsewhere in the world. And the parts made in North America and vehicles assembled in North America will increasingly be produced by corporations with global headquarters outside North America.

All of this means that there will be more turmoil ahead for suppliers. Surviving companies will have picked a winning strategy of either low-cost supplier, high-value supplier, or systems integrator. Survivors will have selected winning customers, those that are gaining market share, while reducing exposure to those that are losing market share. Surviving suppliers will also have selected a winning global strategy.

Notes

1. Tim Leuliette, chairman, president, and CEO of Metaldyne Corporation, in a speech to the Federal Reserve Bank of Chicago (2006).
2. Tim Leuliette, CEO of Metaldyne, quoted in Sherefkin and Wilson (2003).
3. John Doddridge, Intermet CEO, quoted in *Automotive News* (2002b).
4. In their 2007 labor contract, the union and each of the Detroit 3 agreed to establish a VEBA.
5. Michael Heidingsfelder, Roland Berger managing partner, quoted in Guilford (2002).
6. Jim Gillette, CSM Worldwide analyst, quoted in Wernle (2005c).
7. Jim Gillette, CSM Worldwide analyst, quoted in Wernle (2005c).
8. Greg Salchow, director of investor and public relations at Noble International Ltd., supplier of laser welding, quoted in Kosdrosky and Snavely (2005).
9. For a comprehensive discussion of state and local economic development policies, see Bartik (1991).

References

Akron Beacon Journal. 2000. "Firestone Tires Take a Plunge in Sales." November 11. http://infoweb.newsbank.com/iw-search/we/InfoWeb?p_ action=doc&p_docid=0EB6D69F81BA9A1D&p_docnum=4&p_ queryname=4&p_product=NewsBank&p_theme=aggregated4&p_nbid= M45A4EHCMTE5NDAxNTM4MS4yMTczODoxOjEzOjEzNC41My41N y4xODg (accessed November 2, 2007).

AK Steel. 2006. *Annual Report and 10-K Form 2006.* Middletown, OH: AK Steel. http://www.aksteel.com/data/financial_stmts/51402_011_Web.pdf (accessed October 15, 2007).

American Iron and Steel Institute. 2005. "High-Strength Steel Quietly Makes Major Automotive Gains." Detroit: American Iron and Steel Institute. http://www.autosteel.org/AM/Template.cfm?Section=Auto_Articles1& TEMPLATE=/CM/ContentDisplay.cfm&CONTENTID=6964 (accessed October 15, 2007).

———. 2007. "A I S I Market Development Progress 2006–2007. http://www .steel.org/md/md_2007_progrep_auto.pdf (accessed October 18, 2007).

Andel, Tom. 2007. "18th Annual State of Logistics Report: The New State of Interdependence." *Logistics Management,* July 1. http://www.logisticsmgmt .com/article/CA6457606.html (accessed October 19, 2007).

Andersson, Bo. 2006. "GM's Global Supply Footprint." Presented at the Detroit branch of the Federal Reserve Bank of Chicago conference "The Supplier Industry in Transition: The New Geography of Auto Production," held in Detroit, April 18–19. http://www.chicagofed.org/news_and_conferences/ conferences_and_events/2006_auto_agenda.cfm (accessed October 15, 2007).

Andrea, David. 2007. "Turmoil to Triumph: Is 2007 the Tipping Point for Suppliers?" Presented at the Detroit branch of the Federal Reserve Bank of Chicago's "Fourteenth Annual Automotive Outlook Symposium," held in Detroit, May 31–June 1. http://www.chicagofed.org/news_and_conferences/ conferences_and_events/files/2007_aos_andrea.pdf (accessed December 6, 2007).

Andrea, David, Mark Everett, and Dan Luria. 1988. "Automobile Company Parts Sourcing: Implications for Michigan Suppliers." Excerpts published in *AIM Newsletter* 3(2): 1–8.

Armbruster, William. 2002a. "Third-Party Logistics Producers Are Well-Established; Now Lead Logistics Providers Are Springing Up to Manage Them." *JoC Week,* June 24–30.

———. 2002b. "4PL Logistics Producers Are Well-Established." *JoC Week* June: 24–30.

Armstrong, Julie. 2004a. "New Magna Strategy Was Pre-Hogan." *Automotive News*, November 11, p. 1.

———. 2004b. "Rieter Says It Will Miss Revenue Goals: Supplier Expects Improvement with Acoustics Product." *Automotive News,* July 19. http://www.autonews.com/apps/pbcs.dll/article?AID=/20040719/SUB/407190722 (accessed November 23, 2007).

———. 2004c. "Bosch's Fuel Injection Transformed the Engine." *Automotive News,* August 9, p. 36B.

———. 2004d. "Supplier Pact Will Phase Out Top-Paying Jobs." *Automotive News,* April 5, p. 8.

———. 2004e. "GM Raises Goal for China Parts." *Automotive News,* January 19, p. 1.

———. 2004f. "Electronics Spark Supplier Growth." *Automotive News,* June 28, p. 16.

Armstrong, Richard, and Thomas Foster. 2007. "Movable Feast of Top 25 Global Third-Party Logistics Providers." *Global Logistics & Supply Chain Strategies* 28(May): 28–53.

Arnold, Horace L., and Fay Leone Faurote. 1919. *Ford Methods and the Ford Shops.* New York: Engineering Magazine Co.

Australia Department for Environment and Heritage. 2002. "Environmental Impact of End-of-Life Vehicles: An Information Paper." Adelaide, South Australia: Australia Department for Environment and Heritage. http://www.environment.gov.au/settlements/publications/waste/elv/impact-2002/chapter4.html (accessed October 16, 2007).

Automotive Aftermarket Suppliers Association. 2007. "Automotive Aftermarket Suppliers Top 100." Research Triangle Park, NC: Automotive Aftermarket Suppliers Association. http://www.aftermarketnews.com/files/top100_07.pdf (accessed October 15, 2007).

Automotive Logistics. 2004. "Auto Logistics Global Conference Report." January/February, p. 15.

Automotive News. 1995. "Top 150 Suppliers to North America." *Automotive News Market Data Book,* pp. 106–111.

———. 1997. "Systematically, Now You Know." April 28, p. 2.

———. 1999. "Dana Rolls Forward with Modules." March 29, p. 24J.

———. 2002a. "Canadian Auto Sector Urges Renewed Health Spending." September 12. http://www.autonews.com/news.cms?newsId=3264 (accessed November 23, 2007).

———. 2002b. "Getting a Little Better." August 5, p. 17i.

———. 2004. "2004 Car Cutaways." July 5, p. 10. http://www.autonews.com/assets/PDF/CA38821213.pdf (accessed November 23, 2007).

———. 2005a. "Opinion: Bashing Suppliers Damages Big 3's Market Position." January 3, p. 12.

———. 2005b. "Lousy Relations with Suppliers Penalize Big 3." June 6, p. 12.

———. 2005c. "Price Pressures Weigh on ArvinMeritor Chief." May 9, p. 24J.

———. 2006. "Suppliers to the 2007 Toyota Camry." February 27, p. 28D.

———. 2007a. "Top 150 Suppliers." April 30. http://www.autonews.com/apps/pbcs.dll/article?AID=/20070430/DATACENTER/70427085/1056&title=2006%20Top%20150%20North%20America%20Suppliers (accessed October 16, 2007).

———. 2007b. "Ford Motor Finds Buyer for Glass Unit." April 23, p. 69.

———. 2007c. "How Electronic Stability Works." February 26, p. 32B.

———. 2007d. "Continental Gets Future in Sync with Ford, Microsoft." June 25, p. 22F.

Automotive News Europe. 1999. "TI Gains Complete Fuel Systems Capability." August 2. http://europe.autonews.com/article.cms?articleId=43538 (accessed November 23, 2007).

———. 2005. "2005 Guide to China's Auto Market." p. 25.

Autotech. 2004. "Quick History of the Speedometer." Tucson, AZ: Autotech. http://www.speedometers.com/Speedometers.html (accessed October 15, 2007).

Baily, Martin Neil, Diana Farrell, Ezra Greenberg, Jan-Dirk Henrich, Naoko Jinjo, Maya Jolles, and Jaana Remes. 2005. *Increasing Global Competition and Labor Productivity: Lessons from the US Automotive Industry.* San Francisco: McKinsey and Company.

Ballert, Albert George. 1947. *The Primary Functions of Toledo, Ohio.* PhD diss., University of Chicago.

Barkholz, David. 2006. "Dundee Engine Plant Seeks Title: Plant Seeks to Be No. 1 in Productivity." *Automotive News*, August 7. http://www.autonews.com/apps/pbcs.dll/article?AID=/20060807/SUB/60807015&SearchID=73276260264144 (accessed November 23, 2007).

———. 2007a. "Parts Mogul Ross Hunts for Ford Gem in Mexico." *Automotive News*, June 18, p. 4.

———. 2007b. "Detroit 3: Labor Costs Must Shrink So We Can Compete." *Automotive News*, June 18, p. 4.

———. 2007c. "UAW Workers at Delphi OK Wage Cuts, Plant Closings." *Automotive News*, June 29, p. 1.

Bartik, Timothy. 1991. *Who Benefits from State and Local Economic Devel-*

opment Policies? Kalamazoo, MI: W.E. Upjohn Institute for Employment Research.

Becker, M.N. 1999. "Aluminum: New Challenges in Downstream Activities." *JOM* 51(11): 26–38.

Bernstein, Irving. 1970. *Turbulent Years: A History of the American Worker 1933–1941.* Boston: Houghton Mifflin.

Bornholdt, Oscar C. 1926. "Interview with Oscar C. Bornholdt, Factory Manager of Wills St. Claire, Inc., Marysville, MI, July 26, 1926, by Franklin D. Jones, 1926." Accession 96, Box 2, Archives and Library. Dearborn, MI: Henry Ford Museum and Greenfield Village.

Bornhop, Andrew. 2002. "BMW 745i: iDrive? No, You Drive While I Fiddle with the Controller." *Road & Track,* June. http://www.roadandtrack.com/article.asp?section_id=3&article_id=210 (accessed November 23, 2007).

Bowens, Greg, and David Sedgwick. 2005. "GM Takes Interior Work In-House." *Automotive News,* July 4, p. 1.

Bowman, Robert J. 2000. "Delphi: A Piecemeal Approach to Marriage." *Global Logistics & Supply Chain Strategies*, July. http://www.glscs.com/archives/07.00.delphi.htm?adcode=5 (accessed November 23, 2007).

Broge, Jean L. 2002. "Tech Briefs: Brose Door Modules for Ford." *Automotive Engineering International On-Line,* December. http://www.sae.org/automag/techbriefs/12-2002/page3.htm (accessed November 1, 2007).

Buick Club of America. 2007. Photo Gallery. Columbus, OH: Buick Club of America. http://www.buickclub.org/PhotoGallery/Photogallery.html (accessed November 19, 2007).

Bumstead, Jon, and Kempton Cannons. 2002. "From 4PL to Managed Supply-Chain Operations." *Logistics & Transport Focus* (May): 19.

Bureau of Labor Statistics. n.d. http://data.bls.gov/PDQ/outside.jsp?survey=CE (accessed March 14, 2008).

Buss, Dale. 2004. "Shared Release." *Automotive Logistics*, January/February. http://www.ryder.com/pdf/rn_autolog_shared.pdf (accessed October 19, 2007).

Butters, Jamie. 2004. "UAW Organizes at Dana to Shore Up Membership." *Detroit Free Press,* January 29. http://www.freep.com/money/autonews/uaw29_20040129.htm (accessed November 23, 2007).

CalsonicKansei. 2004. *Annual Report 2004*. Tokyo: CalsonicKansei. http://www.calsonickansei.co.jp/english/ir/annual_report/2004.html (accessed October 15, 2007).

CanagaRetna, Sujit M. 2004. *The Drive to Move South: The Growing Role of the Automobile Industry in the SLC Economies.* A Special Series Report. Atlanta: Southern Legislative Conference. http://www.slcatlanta.org/Publications/

EconDev/AutoSouth/TheDriveToMoveSouth.pdf (accessed November 4, 2007).

Carlton, Jim. 2007. "Toledo Finds the Energy to Reinvent Itself." *Wall Street Journal*, December 18, B:1.

Carson, Iain, and Vijay Vaitheeswaran. 2007. *The Global Race to Fuel the Car of the Future*. New York: Twelve.

Chang, Peter, and Lindsay Chappell. 2004. "Hyundai Mobis Snatches Jeep Chassis Contract." *Automotive News,* August 9. http://www.autonews.com/apps/pbcs.dll/article?AID=/20040809/SUB/408090766 (accessed November 23, 2007).

Chappell, Lindsay. 1997. "Electronics Firms Dominate Supplier List." *Automotive News,* July 21, p. 1.

————. 1998. "Suppliers Growth with M-B in U.S." *Automotive News,* May 4, p. 28.

————. 1999. "Outsourcing Buzz Stirs Transplants." *Automotive News,* August 9. http://www.autonews.com/article.cms?articleId=9872 (accessed November 23, 2007).

————. 2001. "Two Minority Suppliers Break the Tier 1 Ranks." *Automotive News*, November 26. http://www.autonews.com/apps/pbcs.dll/article?AID=/20011126/FREE/111260708 (accessed October 19, 2007).

————. 2002. "Bigger Is Not Necessarily Better." *Automotive News,* August 5, p. 28i.

————. 2004a. "Big 3 Pay Price for Bad Supplier Relations." *Automotive News,* December 27, p. 1.

————. 2004b. "Gulf Widens between Big 3, Suppliers." *Automotive News,* August 2, p. 4.

————. 2004c. "Honda Seeks to Improve Parts Shipping to Ala. Plant." *Automotive News*, November 1, p. 26.

————. 2004d. "Honda's Ga. Plant Won't Draw Suppliers." *Automotive News,* November 22, p. 20.

————. 2004e. "Asians Chase N.A. Wheel Market." *Automotive News,* December 20, p. 4.

————. 2004f. "Siemens' Plan: Injecting Simplicity." *Automotive News,* May 3, p. 22.

————. 2005a. "Boosting M-Class Quality Is Taylor's Biggest Challenge." *Automotive News,* June 13, p. 24D.

————. 2005b. "Toyota Aims to Satisfy Its Suppliers." *Automotive News,* February 21, p. 10.

————. 2005c. "Visteon Scores Big Win with Honda." *Automotive News*, July 25, p. 3.

————. 2005d. "Honda Considers On-site Suppliers." *Automotive News,* October 3, p. 22.

————. 2005e. "Nissan Courts Aftermarket Suppliers, Innovations." *Automotive News,* June 6, p. 22.

————. 2005f. "Toyota on the Prowl for 4th N.A. Engine Plant." *Automotive News,* November 21, p. 39.

————. 2005g. "A New Wave of Suppliers Pursues Transplant Work." *Automotive News,* June 13, p. 32J.

————. 2006a. "Haden's a Mystery, but Jeep's on Track." *Automotive News,* February 13, p. 1.

————. 2006b. "Chrysler Scrambles After Paint Vendor Skips." *Automotive News,* April 10, p. 36.

————. 2006c. "Magna Steyr: Big Changes Are Needed." *Automotive News,* September 4. http://www.autonews.com/apps/pbcs.dll/article?AID=/20060904/ANE/60831017&SearchID=73285957225144 (accessed November 23, 2007).

————. 2006d. "Kia's New U.S. Plant Is No Windfall for U.S. Suppliers." *Automotive News,* April 3, p. 1.

Chew, Edmund. 1997. "Systems Move Bundy into Customer Plants." *Automotive News Europe,* April 28. http://europe.autonews.com/article.cms?articleId=47714 (accessed November 23, 2007).

————. 2002. "SUPPLIER INNOVATION: Inergy; Being Bigger Breeds Innovation." *Automotive News Europe,* July 29. http://europe.autonews.com/article.cms?articleId=51520 (accessed November 23, 2007).

————. 2003. "Exterior Supplier Moves to Modules." *Automotive News Europe,* March 24. http://www.autonews.com/article.cms?articleId=42959 (accessed November 23, 2007).

————. 2004a. "Automakers Rely on Suppliers for More Key Parts" *Automotive News,* April 19. http://www.autonews.com/article.cms?articleId=47955 (accessed November 23, 2007).

————. 2004b. "Demands on Electrical Systems Intensify." *Automotive News,* January 26, p. 24D.

————. 2005. "Bosch Will Be Hybrid Player." *Automotive News,* June 20. http://www.autonews.com/apps/pbcs.dll/article?AID=/20050620/SUB/506200702&SearchID=73230774117989 (accessed November 23, 2007).

Child, Charles. 1996. "GM Will Streamline Stamping." *Automotive News,* May 27, p. 10. http://www.autonews.com/apps.pbcs.dll/article?AID=/20080128/ANA06/801280359 (accessed March 14, 2008).

————. 2008. "We Call It: Toyota Topped GM in '07." *Automotive News,* January 27.

Chrysler, Walter P. 1937. *Life of an American Workman.* New York: Dodd, Mead.

Clarion Ledger. 2008. "Delphi's Overhaul Conditionally OK'd." January 23.   http://www.clarionledger.com/apps/pbcs.dll/article?Aid=/20080123/ Biz/801230363/1005/biz (accessed March 14, 2008).

Colby, Charles C., and Alice Foster. 1940. *Economic Geography.* Boston: Ginn and Co.

Columbus Ledger-Enquirer. 2006. "Kia Asks for Patience in Construction of Georgia Auto Plant." March 28. http://www.motortrend.com/features/auto_ news/2006/112_news20 (accessed October 15, 2007).

Connelly, Mary. 2004. "Zetsche: Haden Looks Like Partner in Toledo." *Automotive News,* October 11. http://www.autonews.com/apps/pbcs.dll/ article?AID=/20041011/SUB/410110719&SearchID=73254552601177 (accessed November 23, 2007).

Cooney, Stephen. 2005. "Comparing Automotive and Steel Industry Legacy Costs." Washington, DC: Congressional Research Service. http://www .chicagofed.org/news_and_conferences/conferences_and_events/files/ 2006_auto_cooney2.pdf (accessed December 10, 2007).

Cooney, Stephen, and Brent D. Yacobucci. 2005. "U.S. Automotive Industry: Policy Overview and Recent History." CRS Report for Congress. Washington, DC: Congressional Research Service.

Cottrill, Ken. 2000. "General Motors: A New Joint Venture Aims to Streamline Logistics." *Traffic World,* December 26. http://www.ebusinessforum.com/ index.asp?layout=printer_friendly&doc_id=1796 (accessed November 23, 2007).

Couretas, John. 2000. "Electronics' Role to Surge, Study Says." *Automotive News,* January 10, p. 18.

Crain Communications. 1996. "AlliedSignal Reveres King of Stop and Go." In *America at the Wheel: 100 Years of the Automobile in America.* Detroit: Crain Communications, p. 84.

Crain, Keith. 2000. "OEM's Dilemma." *Automotive News,* January 10. http:// www.autonews.com/article.cms?articleId=7991&a=a&bt=bargaining+ power+Roland+Berger (accessed November 23, 2007).

Cray, Ed. 1980. *Chrome Colossus.* New York: McGraw-Hill.

CSM Insights. 2001. "Electronics Lead Cockpit Content Value." Fall, p. 7.

Cullen, Thomas James. 2002. "Automakers Are Divided on Supplier Parks." *Automotive News,* October 7, p. 22G.

DASH Electronics and Speedometer. n.d. "History of the Speedometer." Troy, MI: DASH Electronics and Speedometer. http://www.dashusa.com/history _of_the_speedo.htm (accessed October 15, 2007).

Davey, Monica. 2007. "A Bridge's Private Ownership Raises Concerns on Security." *New York Times*, October 12, A:14.

De Koker, Neil. 2006. "Supplier-Carmaker Relationships and Networks: Challenges for Suppliers." Presented at the Detroit branch of the Federal Reserve Bank of Chicago conference "The Supplier Industry in Transition: The New Geography of Auto Production," held in Detroit, April 18–19. http://www .chicagofed.org/news_and_conferences/conferences_and_events/2006_ auto_agenda.cfm (accessed November 23, 2007).

Denso Corporation. 2007. *Annual Report*. Tokyo: Denso Corporation.

DesRosiers, Dennis. 2005. *Death by a Thousand Cuts*. Toronto: DesRosiers Automotive Consultants.

———. 2006. "Implications of the Globalization of the Supplier Industry: The Road Ahead." Presented at the Detroit branch of the Federal Reserve Bank of Chicago conference "The Supplier Industry in Transition: The New Geography of Auto Production," held in Detroit, April 18–19. http://www .chicagofed.org/news_and_conferences/conferences_and_events/2006_ auto_agenda.cfm (acessed November 23, 2007).

Detroit City Plan Commission. 1944. *Economic Base of Detroit*. Detroit: City Plan Commission, p. 5.

Detroit News. 2005. "Text of Remarks by Delphi's Steve Miller." October 29. http://www.detnews.com/2005/autosinsider/0510/29/biz-364915.htm (accessed November 2, 2007).

Deutsch, Claudia H. 1999. "Deal Reached by Goodyear and Sumitomo." *New York Times*, February 4, C:5.

Dodge et al. v. Commissioner of Internal Revenue. 1927. "Petitioners' Statement of Facts." April 18. Accession 96, Box 3, Archives and Library. Dearborn, MI: Henry Ford Museum and Greenfield Village.

Durant, William C. n.d. "The True Story of General Motors." Autobiographical notes. D74-2.1a and D74-2.1b. Flint, MI: Kettering/GMI Alumni Foundation Collection of Industrial History.

Dyer, Davis. 1998. *TRW: Pioneering Technology and Innovation since 1900*. Cambridge, MA: Harvard Business School Press.

Dyer, Jeffrey H. 2000. *Collaborative Advantage: Winning through Extended Supplier Networks*. New York: Oxford University Press.

Dyer, Jeffrey H., and Kentaro Nobeoka. 2000. "Creating and Managing a High-Performance Knowledge-Sharing Network: The Toyota Case." *Strategic Management Journal* 21(3): 345–367.

Eaton Corporation. 1985. *The History of Eaton Corporation 1911–1985*. Cleveland: Eaton Corporation.

The Economist. 2007. "Something New under the Sun." A Special Report on Innovation. October 13, p. 7.

———. 2008. "A Fence in the North, Too." March 1, pp. 40–41.

Electrocoat Association. 2007. Electrocoat.org: The Online Home of the Electrocoat Association. Cincinnati, OH: Electrocoat Association. http://www.electrocoat.org/# (accessed October 18, 2007).

Electroherbalism. 2007. "Tesla versus Edison." Electroherbalism.com. http://www.electroherbalism.com/Bioelectronics/Tesla/TeslaversusEdison.htm (accessed October 31, 2007).

Ellison, Glenn, and Edward L. Glaeser. 1997. "Geographic Concentration in U.S. Manufacturing Industries: A Dartboard Approach." *Journal of Political Economy* 105(5): 889–927.

English, Bob. 2002. "CAW Seeks Aid to Stem Job Losses." *Automotive News,* May 20. http://www.autonews.com/apps/pbcs.dll/article?AID=/20020520/REG/205200765 (accessed December 11, 2007).

Epstein, Ralph C. 1928. *The Automobile Industry: Its Economic and Commercial Development.* Chicago: A.W. Shaw Co.

European 4PL Research Club. n.d. "Background 4PL." Hamburg, Germany: European 4PL Research Club. http://www.e4plrc.com/4pl.htm (accessed October 19, 2007).

Fiordalisi, G. 1989. "Did Kentucky Overpay for Toyota?" *Automotive News,* July 7, p. 18.

Flanagan, Maureen. 2001. "Plastech Engineered Products Contracts with Top Automotive Supplier." News release, November 27. Bethesda, MD: American Capital Strategies, Inc. http://www.americancapital.com/news/newsreleases/2001/pr20011127a.html (accessed October 18, 2007).

Floerecke, Klaus-Dieter. 2005. "Infineon's Goal: Be the Top Semiconductor Supplier." *Automotive News,* October 31, p. 22JJ.

———. 2007. "Siemens VDO to Offer Electronic Brakes by 2010." *Automotive News*, April 16, p. 43.

Ford Motor Company. 2007. "Ford and Glass Products Reach MOU for Automotive Components Holdings Glass Business." News release, April 18. http://news.thomasnet.com/companystory/516709/rss (accessed November 23, 2007).

Foster, Thomas A., and Richard Armstrong. 2004. "Top 25 Third-Party Logistics Providers Extend Their Global Reach." *Global Logistics & Supply Chain Strategies,* May. http://www.supplychainbrain.com/content/headline-news/single-article/article/top-25-third-party-logistics-providers-extend-their-global-reach-1/ (accessed December 5, 2007).

Freudenberg-NOK. 2007. "Business Imperatives." Plymouth, MI: Freudenberg-NOK. http://www.freudenberg-nok.com/philosophy/business.htm (accessed November 4, 2007).

Fung, Walter, and Mike Hardcastle. 2001. *Textiles in Automotive Engineering.* Abington, England: Woodhead Publishing.

Gardner, Greg. 1996. "JCI Buys Itself a Prince." *Ward's Auto World*, August 1. http://waw.wardsauto.com/ar/auto_jci_buys_itself/ (accessed October 15, 2007).

Garsten, Ed. 2001. "Big Wheels Keep on Turning." *Automotive News,* June 18, p. 20B.

GKN. 2007. "The History of GKN." Worcesterhire, England: GKN PLC. http://www.gkn.com/Groupoverview/History.asp (accessed October 22, 2007).

Glassbrenner, Donna. 2005. "Safety Belt Use in 2005—Overall Results." Traffic Safety Facts Research Note DOT HS 809 932, August. Washington, DC: National Center for Statistics and Analysis, National Highway Traffic Safety Administration. http://usgovinfo.about.com/gi/dynamic/offsite .htm?site=http://www.nhtsa.dot.gov/people/NCSA (accessed November 23, 2007).

Global Engine Manufacturing Alliance (GEMA). 2007. "Why Dundee?" Dundee, MI: GEMA. http://www.gemaengine.com/why.htm (accessed October 15, 2007).

Goodenough, L.W. 1925. "Statement on Behalf of Messrs. David and Paul Gray, and Philip Gray, Deceased before the Solicitory of Internal Revenue in Re: Valuation of Ford Motor Company Stock as of March 1st, 1913." Accession 84, Box 2, Archives and Library, pp. 165–184. Dearborn, MI: Henry Ford Museum and Greenfield Village.

Guilford, Dave. 2002. "Study: Suppliers Must Specialize, Avoid Tech Mergers." *Automotive News,* October 28, p. 21.

———. 2004. "GM Pushes Pushrods—and Reaps Savings." *Automotive News,* April 5, p. 4.

Gupta, B.L. 2005. "World Automotive Semiconductor Markets." *BCC Report* SMC054A, May, Wellesley. MA: BCC Research.

Gustin, Lawrence R. 1993. "Buick Motor Division: A Brief History." Columbus, OH: Buick Club of America. http://www.buickclub.org/Misc/history .htm (accessed October 15, 2007).

Guyer, Lillie. 2004. "Suppliers' 2005 Challenge: Develop More Vehicle with Less Money." *Automotive News,* December 27, p. 22B.

Haight, Brent. 2004. "A Plan for Every Part: Manufacturers Fine-tune Just-in-Time Delivery to Better Serve an Evolving Supply Chain." *Automotive Industries,* August. http://www.findarticles.com/p/articles/mi_m3012/is_8_ 184/ai_n6173990 (accessed October 15, 2007).

Hakim, Danny. 2002. "Auto Union and Honda Dispute Safety Record at Plants in Ohio." *New York Times,* June 26, C:1.

———. 2004. "Coloring America Hopeful." *New York Times*, January 25, 9.1.

http://query.nytimes.com/gst/fullpage.html?res=9906E0DB1E39F936A15 752C0A9629C8B63 (accessed December 6, 2007).

Halberstam, David. 1986. *The Reckoning.* New York: William Morrow and Co.

Hansen, Paul. 2003. "Too Many Auto Semi Suppliers–Electronics–Automotive Semiconductor Industry." *Automotive Industries*, August. http://findarticles .com/p/articles/mi_m3012/is_8_183/ai_106733126 (accessed October 15, 2007).

Harrington, Lisa. 2007. "Change Drivers: Navigating the New Auto Supply Chain." *Inbound Logistics*, February. http://www.inboundlogistics.com/articles/features/0207_feature02.shtml (accessed October 15, 2007).

Helper, Susan, and Mari Sako. 1995. "Supplier Relations in Japan and the United States: Are They Converging?" *Sloan Management Review* 36(3): 77–84.

Henrickson, G.R. 1951. *Trends in the Geographic Distribution of Suppliers of Some Basically Important Materials Used at the Buick Motor Division, Flint, Michigan.* Ann Arbor, MI: University of Michigan Institute for Human Adjustment.

Hill, Kim. 2005. "Contribution of Toyota to the Economies of Fourteen States and the United States in 2003." Ann Arbor, MI: Center for Automotive Research. http://www.cargroup.org/documents/Toyota.pdf (accessed October 15, 2007).

Hill, Kim, Debbi Menk, and Steven Szakaly. 2007. "Contribution of the Motor Vehicle Supplier Sector to the Economies of the United States and Its 50 States." Ann Arbor: Center for Automotive Research. http://www.cargroup .org/documents/MEMA-Final2-08-07.pdf (accessed October 15, 2007).

Hoffman, Kurt C. 2000. "Just What Is a 4PL Anyway?" *Global Logistics & Supply Chain Strategies*, August. http://www.glscs.com/archives/8.004pl .htm?adcode75 (accessed October 15, 2007).

HowardForums. 2006. "Motorola Company History." HowardForums.com. http://wiki.howardforums.com/index.php/Motorola_Company_History (accessed October 31, 2007).

Howes, Daniel. 2007a. "Change or Die: It's Our Choice." *The Detroit News*, May 23. http://www.detnews.com/apps/pbcs.dll/article?AID=/20070523/AUTO02/705230343/1322/OPINION0301 (accessed July 10, 2007).

———. 2007b. "UAW Gives Big Three Chance at Reinvention." *The Detroit News*, November 5. http://www.detnews.com/apps/pbcs.dll/article?AID=/20071105/OPINION03/711050349 (accessed November 5, 2007).

Hudson, Mike. 2003. "UAW Turns to Smaller Suppliers: Analysts Say Parts Shops Pressured to Accept Union to Keep Work from Detroit Automakers." *The Detroit News*, November 21, B:1.

Hyde, Charles K. 2005. *The Dodge Brothers: The Men, the Motor Cars, and the Legacy*. Detroit: Wayne State University Press.

International Automotive Components. 2007. "About Us." Dearborn, MI: International Automotive Components. http://www.iacna.com/aboutus.html (accessed November 1, 2007).

International Herald Tribune. 2007. "IUE-CWA Members Ratify New 4-Year Contract with Delphi." August 19. http://www.iht.com/articles/ap/2007/08/19/business/NA-FIN-US-Delphi-Unions.php (accessed March 14, 2008).

Jewett, Dale. 2004. "LaSorda: Toledo Plant Is a Prototype." *Automotive News*, August 5. http://www.autonews.com/apps/pbcs.dll/article?AID=/20040805/SUB/408050704&SearchID=73254552914478 (accessed November 23, 2007).

Johnson Controls, Inc. (JCI). 2006. *2006 Form 10-K*. Milwaukee, WI: JCI. http://www.johnsoncontrols.com/publish/us/en/sustainability/sustainability_reporting/2006_business_review.-CenterPar-000111-DownloadFile.tmp/2006_Form_10-k.pdf (accessed November 23, 2007).

Kachadourian, Gail. 2000. "Ford Plans Supplier Campus in Chicago." *Automotive News,* October 9, p. 24D.

Keenan, Greg. 2006. "The Story behind Martinrea's Purchase of Thyssen-Krupp." *Globe and Mail*, October 20. http://www.theglobeandmail.com/servlet/story/RTGAM.20061020.wdecision21/BNStory/Business (accessed October 15, 2007).

Kelkar, Anish, Richard Roth, and Joel Clark. 2001. "Automobile Bodies: Can Aluminum Be an Economical Alternative to Steel?" *JOM* 53(8): 28–32.

Kennedy, E.D. 1941. *The Automobile Industry*. New York: Reynal & Hitchcock.

Kisiel, Ralph. 1996. "Snazzy New Look Ahead for Headliners." *Automotive News,* December 23, p. 14.

———. 1998. "New Dakota Plant Gets Dana Roll-in Chassis." *Automotive News,* July 13, p. 3.

Klier, Thomas. 1995. "The Geography of Lean Manufacturing, Recent Evidence from the U.S. Auto Industry." *Federal Reserve Bank of Chicago, Economic Perspectives* 19(6): 2–16.

———. 2000. "Does 'Just-in-Time' Mean 'Right-Next-Door'? Evidence from the Auto Industry on the Spatial Concentration of Supplier Networks." *The Journal of Regional Analysis and Policy* 30(1): 43–60.

Klier, Thomas, and Dan McMillen. 2008. "Evolving Agglomeration of the U.S. Auto Supplier Industry." *Journal of Regional Science* 48(1): 245–267.

Klier, Thomas, and James Rubenstein. 2007. "Whose Part Is It? Measuring Domestic Content of Vehicles." *Chicago Fed Letter* 243, October.

Knudsen, William S. 1926. "Memorandum of Interview with Wm S Knudsen, President of Chevrolet Motor Co, by Mr. Sidney T. Miller and Mr. F. D. Jones. June 25, 1926."Accession 96, Box 11, Archives and Library. Dearborn, MI: Henry Ford Museum and Greenfield Village.

Konicki, Steve. 2001. "Ryder's Movin' On." *Informationweek.com*, June 25. http://www.informationweek.com/story/showArticle.jhtml?articleID=6506956 (accessed October 19, 2007).

Korth, Kim. 2007. "Key Issues for Suppliers: Navigating a Challenging Landscape." Presentation at OESA Chicago Regional Meeting, May 22. http://www.oesa.org/presentations/index.php (accessed November 7, 2007).

Kosdrosky, Terry, and Brent Snavely. 2004. "Suppliers Sense Profit in Electronics Growth." *Automotive News,* October 18, p. 24F.

———. 2005. "Suppliers Thrive 'Under the Radar.'" *Automotive News,* June 27, p. 24B.

Krebs, Michelle.1997. "Moods of 5 Decades, Color by Color." *New York Times,* October 16, D:34.

Lan, Lan. 2007. "GM Plans Rapid Growth of Purchasing in China." *Automotive News*, December 17, p. 6.

Landler, Mark. 2005. "A German Auto Supplier Delphi Might Envy." *New York Times,* November 24, C:1.

LaReau, Jamie. 2007. "GM's Hurdle: Create a Supply Base for Volt." *Automotive News*, April 30, p. 4.

Lear Corporation. 2006. "Form 10-K." Southfield, MI: Lear Corporation. http://ir.lear.com/downloads/10KLEAR.pdf (accessed October 19, 2007).

Leuliette, Tim. 2006. "Successfully Maintaining Production in the Midwest: The Automobile Producers, Suppliers, and the Economic Model." Presented at the Detroit branch of the Federal Reserve Bank of Chicago conference "The Supplier Industry in Transition: The New Geography of Auto Production," held in Detroit, April 18–19. http://www.chicagofed.org/news_and_conferences/conferences_and_events/2006_auto_agenda.cfm (accessed November 23, 2007).

Lewin, Tony. 2005. "Denso Targets French Automakers." *Automotive News,* October 31, p. 22HH.

———. 2007. "Rule Changes Could Trigger Stability Control Boom." *Automotive News*, February 26, p. 32B.

Lezius, Walter G. 1937. "Geography of Glass Manufacture at Toledo, Ohio." *Economic Geography* 13(4): 402–412.

Liker, Jeffrey K. 2004. *The Toyota Way.* New York: McGraw-Hill.

Liker, Jeffrey K., and Thomas Y. Choi. 2004. "Building Deep Supplier Relationships." *Harvard Business Review* 82(12): 104–113.

Liker, Jeffrey, and Yen-Chun Wu. 2000. "Japanese Automakers, U.S. Suppliers and Supply-Chain Superiority." *Sloan Management Review* 42(1): 81–93.

Logistics List. 2006. "Definition of Third Party Logistics." http://www .logisticslist.com/2006/02/definition-of-third-party-logistics_06.html (accessed October 19, 2007).

Logistics World. 2008. "What Is Logistics?" Hampton, VA: LogisticsWorld. http://www.logisticsworld.com/logistics.htm (accessed March 13, 2008).

Mackintosh, James. 2004. "Cars Worth More Than the Sum of Their Shared Parts." *Financial Times,* January 28, p. 16.

———. 2006. "Microsoft Gets Behind the Wheel." *Financial Times*, March 8, p. 10.

Magna International. 2007. "Magna's Corporate Constitution." Aurora, Ontario: Magna International. http://www.magna.com/magna/en/responsibility/constitution/viewconstitution.aspx (accessed November 4, 2007).

Maj, Andreas, Antonio Benecchi, and Wim van Acker. 2004. *The Odyssey of the Auto Industry: Suppliers Changing Manufacturing Footprint.* Detroit: Roland Berger Strategy Consultants.

Marshall, Alfred. 1920. *Principles of Economics.* London: Macmillan.

Masten, Scott E., James W. Mehan Jr., and Edward Snyder. 1989. "Vertical Integration in the U.S. Auto Industry: A Note on the Influence of Transaction Specific Assets." *Journal of Economic Behavior and Organization* 12(2): 265–273.

Maynard, Micheline. 2003. *The End of Detroit.* New York: Currency Books.

Mayne, Eric. 2002. "UAW in Talks with Ford Park Suppliers." *Ward's Automotive Reports*, May 20, p. 5.

McAlinden, Sean P. 2004. *The Meaning of the 2003 UAW-Automotive Pattern Agreement.* Ann Arbor, MI: Center for Automotive Research. http://www .cargroup.org/pdfs/LaborPaperFinal.PDF (accessed October 15, 2007).

———. 2006. "There's No Place Like Home: Geography of Automotive Production." Presented at the Detroit branch of the Federal Reserve Bank of Chicago conference "The Supplier Industry in Transition: The New Geography of Auto Production," held in Detroit, April 18–19. http://www .chicagofed.org/news_and_conferences/conferences_and_events/2006_ auto_agenda.cfm (accessed November 23, 2007).

———. 2007. "The Big Leave: The Future of Automotive Labor Relations." Presented at the Center for Automotive Research Breakfast Briefing, held in Ypsilanti, Michigan, February 20.

McAlinden, Sean P., and David J. Andrea. 2002. *Estimating the New Automotive Value Chain.* Ann Arbor, MI: Center for Automotive Research. http://cargroup.org/pdfs/CAR2002_7.pdf (accessed November 23, 2007).

McCracken, Jeffrey. 2008. "Car-Industry Woes Push Key Supplier to Financial Brink." *Wall Street Journal*, January 31, B:1.

McKee, Keith E. 2004a. "Does the Universe Revolve around the Earth?" *Logistics Frontiers* (Winter): 2–3.

———. 2004b. "Wow! That's a Lot of Space." *Logistics Frontiers* (Winter): 12. http://www.intm.iit.edu/frontiers/LogisticsFrontiersWinter04.pdf (accessed October 19, 2007).

McKinsey & Company Automotive & Assembly Extranet. 2005. "Points of View: Meet the Leaders of the Automotive Industry, Interview with Dr. Susan Helper." McKinsey & Company Automotive & Assembly Extranet, September. http://autoassembly.mckinsey.com/html/home/home.asp?logout (accessed December 10, 2007).

Meiners, Jens. 2007. "Former CEO Returns to Magna Steyr." *Automotive News,* March 26, p. 20B.

Merrill Lynch. 2006. "Energy Security & Climate Change: Alternatives for the Clean Car Evolution." *Merrill Lynch Industry Overview*, November 6. New York: Merrill Lynch.

———. 2007. "Who Makes the Car—2007." *Merrill Lynch Industry Overview*, May 29. New York: Merrill Lynch.

Metaldyne. 2006. *Annual Report.* Plymouth, MI: Metaldyne. http://www.sec.gov/Archives/edgar/data/745448/000110465906021795/a06-7690_210k.htm (accessed October 15, 2007).

México Maquila Information Center. 2006. "100 Top Maquilas." http://www.maquilaportal.com/cgi-bin/top100/top100.pl (accessed October 26, 2007).

———. 2007. "Maquila Overview." http://www.maquilaportal.com/Visitors_Site/nav21.htm (accessed October 26, 2007).

Miel, Rhoda. 2000. "Valeo, Textron Announce Cockpit Tie-up." *Automotive News Europe*, August 14. http://www.autonews.com/apps/pbcs.dll/article?AID=/20000814/FREE/8140791 (accessed November 1, 2007).

———. 2002. "Bye-bye Paint Shops?" *Automotive News,* October 7, p. 1.

Milgrom, Paul, and John Roberts. 1990. "The Economics of Modern Manufacturing: Technology, Strategy and Organization." *American Economic Review* 80(3): 515–528.

Miller, Joe. 1996. "Big 3 Pick Tires on Price, Performance." *Automotive News*, September 16, p. 24B.

Miller, Rick. 2005. "Carmakers Eye Plastic Panels." *Automotive News,* December 5, p. 26L.

Model T Automotive Heritage Complex. 2007. "History of the Model T Factory: Building History." Detroit: Model T Automotive Heritage Complex. http://www.tplex.org/2_buildingconst.html (accessed November 2, 2007).

Model T Ford Club of America. 2007. *How the Ford Motor Company was*

Established. Centreville, IN: Model T Club of America. http://www.mtfca
.com/encyclo/begin.htm (accessed November 23, 2007).

Molot, Maureen Appel. 2003. "Location Incentives: The Cost of Attracting Auto
Investment or 'The New Normal'?" Presented at the Detroit branch of the
Federal Reserve Bank of Chicago conference "Geography of Auto Production—Will Detroit Continue to Be the Industry's Hub?" held in Detroit, November 3. http://www.chicagofed.org/news_and_conferences/conferences_
and_events/files/geography_of_auto_production_role_of_plant_location_
incentives.pdf (accessed November 5, 2007).

Monteverde, Kirk, and David J. Teece. 1982. "Supplier Switching Costs and
Vertical Integration in the Automobile Industry." *Bell Journal of Economics*
13(1): 206–213.

Moore, Thomas Gale. 2002. "Trucking Deregulation." *The Concise Encyclope-
dia of Economics*. Indianapolis, IN: Liberty Fund, Inc. Library of Economics and Liberty. http://www.econlib.org/library/Enc/TruckingDeregulation
.html (accessed October 15, 2007).

Moran, Tim. 2005. "What's Bugging the High-Tech Car?" *The New York Times,*
February 6. http://sss.nytimes.com/2005/02/06/automobiles/06AUTO
.html?_r=l&oref=slogin (accessed December 6, 2007).

Motor & Equipment Manufacturers Association. 2007. *Motor Vehicle Suppliers: The Foundation of U.S. Manufacturing*. Research Triangle Park, NC:
Motor & Equipment Manufacturers Association.

Mudambi, Ram, and Susan Helper. 1998. "The 'Close but Adversarial' Model
of Supplier Relations in the U.S. Auto Industry." *Strategic Management
Journal* 19(8): 775–792.

Murphy, Jean V. 2004. "The Automotive Supply Chain: Where Only the Best
and the Tough Survive." *Global Logistics & Supply Chain Strategies*,
September. http://www.supplychainbrain.com/archives/09.04.automotive
.htm?adcode=90 (accessed October 15, 2007).

Nevins, Allan. 1954. *Ford: The Times, the Man, the Company*. New York:
Charles Scribner's Sons.

Nevins, Allan, and Frank Ernest Hill. 1957. *Ford: Expansion and Challenge,
1915–1933*. New York: Charles Scribner's Sons.

———. 1962. *Ford: Decline and Rebirth, 1933–1962*. New York: Charles
Scribner's Sons.

Nice, Karim. 2007. "How Bearings Work." Atlanta, GA: HowStuffWorks
.com. http://science.howstuffworks.com/bearing.htm (accessed October 15,
2007).

Nice, Karim, and Jonathan Strickland. 2007. "How Fuel Cells Work." Atlanta,
GA: HowStuffWorks.com. http://science.howstuffworks.com/fuel-cell3
.htm (accessed October 15, 2007).

NSG/Pilkington. 2006. "Pilkington and the Flat Glass Industry." Merseyside, Wales: Pilkington Group Limited. http://www.pilkington.com/resources/ pfgi2006.pdf (accessed October 20, 2007).

NTN Bearing Corporation. 2007. "A Commemorative History." Mississauga, Ontario: NTN Bearing Corporation. http://www.ntn.ca/corporate_history .htm (accessed October 18, 2007).

Nussel, Philip. 2006. "Paint Shop Operator Withdraws from Toledo Jeep Plant." *Automotive News,* February 6. http://www.autonews.com/apps/pbcs .dll/article?AID=/20060206/REG/60205001&SearchID=73254554515983.

————. 2007. "PPG Will Sell Auto Glass Business." *Automotive News*, September 17. http://www.autonews.com/apps/pbcs.dll/article?AID=/20070917/ SUB/70914072 (accessed October 20, 2007).

Office of Aerospace and Automotive Industries. 2007. *U.S. Automotive Parts Industry Annual Assessment.* Washington, DC: U.S. Department of Commerce.

Ohio Department of Development Office of Strategic Research. 2006. "Ohio's Motor Vehicle Industry." Columbus, OH: Ohio Department of Development Office of Strategic Research.

O'Reilly, Joseph. 2006. "3PL Perspectives: *Inbound Logistics* Exclusive 3PL Market Insight Survey." *Inbound Logistics* 26(7). http://www.inboundlogistics .com/articles/features/0706_feature01b.shtml (accessed October 15, 2007).

Original Equipment Suppliers Association (OESA). 2006. *2006–2007 OE Industry Report.* Troy, MI: OESA.

Pacelle, Mitchell. 2005. "Detroit Woes Keep Suppliers in a Pinch." *Wall Street Journal,* April 12, C:1.

Parlin, Charles Coolidge, and Henry Sherwood Youker. 1914. "Automobiles Volume 1B. Gasoline Pleasure Cars. Report of Investigation: Curtis Publishing Co." Accession 96, Box 3, Archives and Library. Dearborn, MI: Henry Ford Museum and Greenfield Village.

Penske Logistics. 2007. "Ford Motor Company: Six Sigma Initiatives Streamline Operations." Reading, PA: Penske Logistics. http://www.penskelogistics .com/casestudies/ford.html (accessed October 15, 2007).

Pescon, F.A. 2001. "Achieving Superior On-Time Performance." *Advanced Manufacturing* 3(March): 36.

Phillips, David. 2007. "Getrag Plans Ind. Factory with Chrysler." *Automotive News,* June 18, p. 40.

Phillips, David, and Bradford Wernle. 2007. "Chrysler-Getrag Deal Signals More Partnerships: Dual-Clutch Transmissions Key to Future Product." *Automotive News*, June 25, p. 3.

Planning Perspectives Inc. (PPI). 2005. "Strained Relationships with Suppliers Costing GM and Ford." News release, May 31. Birmingham, MI: PPI. http://www.ppi1.com/news/?image=news (accessed October 15, 2007).

———. 2007. "Annual Study Shows Suppliers Still Prefer Toyota, Honda, but General Motors Shows Dramatic Improvement." News release, June 4. Birmingham, MI: PPI. http://www.ppi1.com/news/?image=news (accessed October 17, 2007).

Polito, Tony, and Kevin Watson. 2006. "Just-in-Time Under Fire: The Five Major Constraints upon JIT Practice." *The Journal of American Academy of Business* 9(1): 8–13.

Pound, Arthur. 1934. *The Turning Wheel: The Story of General Motors through Twenty-Five Years 1908–1933.* Garden City, NY: Doubleday, Doran.

Powder Coating Institute. 2007. "The Benefits of Powder Coating." Alexandria, VA: Powder Coating Institute. http://www.powdercoating.org/benefits/ (accessed October 18, 2007).

Quaife, Milo M. 1950. *Life of John Wendell Anderson.* Detroit: Privately printed.

Riches, Ian. 2005. "Safety Systems Drive Automotive Electronics Growth." *Strategy Analytics*, August 22. http://www.strategyanalytics.net/default .aspx?mod=PressReleaseViewer&a0=2536 (accessed October 24, 2007).

Robinet, Michael. 2005. *Global Automotive Outlook: Increased Trade and Rationalization Drives Change.* Northville, MI: CSM Worldwide.

Ross, Wilbur L., Jr. 2006. "Prospects for Auto Suppliers." Presented at the Detroit branch of the Federal Reserve Bank of Chicago conference "The Supplier Industry in Transition: The New Geography of Auto Production," held in Detroit, April 18–19. http://www.chicagofed.org/news_and_conferences/ conferences_and_events/files/2006_auto_ross.pdf (accessed November 23, 2007).

Rubenstein, James. 1992. *The Changing U.S. Auto Industry: A Geographical Analysis.* London and New York: Routledge.

———. 2001. *Making and Selling Cars: Innovation and Change in the U.S. Automotive Industry.* Baltimore and London: The Johns Hopkins University Press.

Sako, Mari. 2004. "Supplier Development at Honda, Nissan and Toyota: Comparative Case Studies of Organizational Capability Enhancement." *Industrial and Corporate Change* 13(2): 281–308.

Sako, Mari, and Susan Helper. 1998. "Determinants of Trust in Supplier Relations: Evidence from the Automotive Industry in Japan and the United States." *Journal of Economic Behavior & Organization* 34(3): 387–417.

Sawyers, Arlena. 1993. "Automotive Color Tips Its Hat to the Fashion Runways of the World." In *America at the Wheel: 100 Years of the Automobile in America.* Detroit: Crain Communications, p. 56.

Scherer, Frederic M., and David Ross. 1990. *Industrial Market Structure and Economic Performance*. Third ed. Boston: Houghton Mifflin.

Schnatterly, John. n.d. "Steel Content of North American Vehicles." Washington, DC: American Iron and Steel Institute. http://www.autosteel.org/AM/Template.cfm?Section=PDFs&CONTENTFILEID=9286&TEMPLATE=/CM/ContentDisplay.cfm (accessed October 18, 2007).

Schoenberger, Erica. 1987. "Technological and Organizational Change in Automobile Production: Spatial Implications." *Regional Studies* 21(3): 199–214.

Schwartz, Ephraim. 2003. "Supply-Chain Logistics Handoff." *InfoWorld*, November 7. http://www.infoworld.com/article/03/11/07/44FElogic_1.html (accessed October 15, 2007).

Sedgwick, David. 2003. "UAW Aids Visteon Turnaround." *Automotive News*, September 22, p. 1.

Severstal. 2006. *Annual Report*. Moscow, Russia: Severstal. http://www.severstal.com/files/219/Annual%20report%202006_eng.pdf (accessed October 18, 2007).

Shea, John. 2001. "Optimizing Logistics: Automotive OEMs Are Increasingly Turning to Outside Companies—4PLs—to Help Them Get the Most Out of Every Shipment and Delivery." *Automotive Industries* 181(12): 24–25.

Shepardson, David. 2007. "UAW Ranks Fall to Post-WWII Low." *Detroit News*, March 31. http://detnews.com/apps/pbcs.dll/article?AID=/20070331/AUTO01/703310341 (accessed November 23, 2007).

———. 2008. "Visteon: 'We're Leaner and Smaller.'" *Automotive News*, January 7.

Sherefkin, Robert. 1999a. "Faurecia, AP Automotive Talks May Lead to Merger." *Automotive News*, November 15, p. 8.

———. 1999b. "GM Seat Deal Would Create a New Player." *Automotive News*, August 30, p. 1.

———. 2001. "Tier 2 Titan David Stockman, a Former White House Whiz Kid, Has a New Vision of the Supply Chain. And He's on a Buying Spree." *Automotive News*, February 19. http://www.autonews.com/apps/pbcs.dll/article?AID=/20010219/FREE/102190747 (accessed November 23, 2007).

———. 2002a. "American Axle Gets GM Boost." *Automotive News*, May 20, p. 8.

———. 2002b. "Metaldyne Won't Fight UAW Organizing Effort." *Automotive News*, December 2, p. 1.

———. 2004. "Should ArvinMeritor Shrink?" *Automotive News*, February 16, p. 8.

———. 2005. "Cloth Maker Closes; Carmakers Scramble." *Automotive News*, January 31, p. 4.

————. 2006a. "A Ton of Trouble." *Automotive News*, October 2, p.1.

————. 2006b. "Dura Chapter 11 Filing Shows Failing of Roll-Up Strategy." *Automotive News*, November 6, p. 10.

————. 2006c. "Suspension Parts Units on Sales Block." *Automotive News*, January 23, p. 8.

————. 2007a. "No More Bidders Emerge for Tower." *Automotive News*, June 21. http://www.autonews.com/apps/pbcs.dll/article?AID=/20070621/REG/70621032 (accessed April 23, 2008).

————. 2007b. "Magna Eyes More Vehicle Assembly." *Automotive News*, June 4, p. 3.

————. 2008. "Visteon: 'We're Leaner and Smaller.'" *Automotive News*, January 7.

Sherefkin, Robert, and David Barkholz. 2007a. "Magna Prepares to Offer an Olive Branch to UAW." *Automotive News*, November 7. http://www.autonews.com/apps/pbcs.dll/article?AID=/20071105/ANA03/711050349/1128&template=printart (accessed November 7, 2007).

————. 2007b. "UAW Wants Truce That Magna Gave CAW." *Automotive News*, October 22, p.3.

Sherefkin, Robert, and Jamie LaReau. 2006. "Purchasing Unit Moves from U.S. to Shanghai." *Automotive News*, February 27, p. 1.

Sherefkin, Robert, and Amy Wilson. 2003. "Why the Big 3 Can't Be Japanese." *Automotive News,* February 10, p. 1.

Shirouzo, Norihiko. 2007. "Toyota Revs Up Its Push in U.S." *Wall Street Journal*, January 4, A:3.

Shister, Neil. 2005. "Manufacturer of the Year for Global Supply Chain Excellence: Ford Motor Company." *World Trade Magazine*, May. http://www.worldtrademag.com/CDA/ArticleInformation/coverstory/BNPCoverStoryItem/0,3481,149794,00.html (accessed November 23, 2007).

Siemens VDO. 2002. "100 Years of Speedometers—The History of Driver Information." News release, November 7. Schwalbach, Germany: Siemens VDO. http://www.siemensvdo.com/press/releases/interior/2002/SV_200211_001_e.htm (accessed November 1, 2007).

Simon, Bernard. 2007a. "Detroit Discovers the Real World." *Financial Times*, November 5, p. 18.

————. 2007b. "Car Sector a 'Magnet' for Private Equity Deals." *Financial Times*, June 21, p. 16.

Sloan, Alfred P. 1964. *My Years with General Motors*. Garden City, NY: Doubleday.

Smith, P.H. 1970. *Wheels Within Wheels: A Short History of American Motor Car Manufacturing*. Second ed. New York: Funk & Wagnalls.

Snavely, Brent. 2007a. "Wilbur Ross' Interiors Biz Seeks Higher Profile. *Automotive News*, August 20, p. 24.

———. 2007b. "Hungry Continental Studies Acquisition Menu." *Automotive News,* June 25, p. 34.

Snyder, Jesse. 2005. "European Suppliers Play Favorites." *Automotive News,* May 16, p. 46.

Sorensen, Lorin. 2003. *Famous Ford Woodies.* Santa Rosa, CA: Silverado Publishing. http://www.vintagefords.com/woodiesample.htm (accessed November 23, 2007).

Stallkamp, Thomas T. 2005a. *SCORE!—A Better Way to Do Busine$$: Moving from Conflict to Collaboration.* Philadelphia: Wharton School Publishing.

———. 2005b. "How SCORE Bolsters Bottom Line." *Automotive News*, May 9. http://www.autonews.com/apps/pbcs.dll/article?AID=/20050509/SUB/505090751&SearchID=73234941847198 (accessed November 23, 2007).

Steinmetz, Jonathan. 2006. "Autos & Auto Parts Manufacturers. Presentation to the OESA." November 9. http://www.oesa.org/presentations/index.php (accessed November 7, 2007).

Stoll, John, and Jeffrey McCracken. 2007. "Delphi to Keep 4 UAW Plants." *Wall Street Journal*, June 25, A:11.

Strategy Analytics. 2006a. *Automotive Semiconductor Vendor 2006 Market Shares Study.* Boston: Strategy Analytics. http://www.strategyanalytics.net/default.aspx?mod=PressReleaseViewer&a0=3442 (accessed December 6, 2007).

———. 2006b. "Automotive Semiconductor Demand Forecast 2004–2013: Safety and Convenience Electronics Key to Growth." Quoted in "Automotive Semiconductor Market to Expand to $29 Billion by 2013." EDA Geek. http://edageek.com/2006/08/16/automotive-semiconductor-market (accessed December 6, 2006).

Strong, Michael. 2000. "Suppliers: Living Lean Keeps Them Healthy." *Automotive News*, December 4. http://www.autonews.com/apps/pbcs.dll/article?AID=/20001204/FREE/12040703&SearchID−73272756968817 (accessed November 23, 2007).

Sturgeon, Timothy, Johannes Van Biesebroeck, and Gary Gereffi. 2007. "Prospects for Canada in the NAFTA Automotive Industry: A Global Value Chain Analysis." Paper presented at the Industry Canada conference "Global Value Chains Conference: Creating Advantage through Policy Development" held in Ottawa, Ontario, September 25–26.

SupplierBusiness.com. 2004. "Modules and Systems." Stamford, England: Supplierbusiness. http://www.supplierbusiness.com/reports_endpoint.asp?id=26 (accessed October 17, 2007).

Taylor, Edward, and Mike Spector. 2008. "GM, Toyota Doubtful on Fuel Cells' Mass Use." *Wall Street Journal*, March 5, B:2.

Teich's Tech Tidbit. 2003. "BMW's 745i: Too Much Technology?" *Teich's Tech Tidbit*, January. http://www.alteich.com/tidbits/t010603.htm (accessed November 23, 2007).

Terreri, April. 2004. "Driving Efficiencies in Automotive Logistics." *Inbound Logistics*, January. http://www.inboundlogistics.com/articles/features/0104_feature02.shtml (accessed October 19, 2007).

Theobald, Mark. 2004. "C.R. & J.C. Wilson Carriage Co., 1873–1880s—C.R. Wilson Carriage Co., 1880s–1897—C.R. Wilson Body Co., 1897–1924—Detroit, Michigan." Coachbuilt.com. http://www.coachbuilt.com/bui/w/wilson_c_r/wilson_c_r.htm (accessed November 2, 2007).

Tomkins plc. 2004. *Tomkins Annual Review 2004*. London: Tomkins.

Toyota Boshoku. 2005. *Annual Report 2005*. Aichi, Japan: Toyota Boshoku. http://www.toyota-boshoku.co.jp/en/ir/annual/pdf/2005/Annual_Report_2005.pdf (accessed October 19, 2007).

Treece, James B. 2001. "Mitsubishi Trades Transmission Unit." *Automotive News*, October 8. http://www.autonews.com/apps/pbcs.dll/article?AID=/20011008/REG/110080755 (accessed December 11, 2007).

———. 2005. "Jatco Counts on CVTs to Fuel Growth." *Automotive News*, December 19, p. 28B.

Truett, Richard. 2004. "Electronics Boom Puts Heavier Workload on Alternators." *Automotive News*, August 9, p. 36B.

———. 2005. "Auto Experts Predict Strong Growth for Hybrids; European Uptake Will Be Slower Than in North America." *Automotive News*, February 7. http://www.autonews.com/apps/pbcs.dll/article?AID=/20050207/SUB/502070845&SearchID=73230774117989 (accessed November 23, 2007).

———. 2007a. "Consultant: Chrysler Powertrains Will Be Strong If Daimler Link Survives." *Automotive News*, May 14. http://www.autonews.com/apps/pbcs.dll/article?AID=/20070514/REG/70514010 (accessed November 23, 2007).

———. 2007b. "Hybrid Vet Leads Venture's Battery Project." *Automotive News*, June 25. http://www.autonews.com/apps/pbcs.dll/article?AID=/20070611/SUB/70606012 (accessed November 23).

USA Today. 2006. "Delphi Announces Deal with IUE-CWA, GM on Buyouts." June 17. http://www.usatoday.com/money/companies/2006-06-17-delphi_x.htm (accessed March 14, 2008).

U-S-History.com. 2005. "Nicola Tesla, 1856–1943." U-S-History.com. http://www.u-s-history.com/pages/h1619.html (accessed October 31, 2007).

Van Biesebroeck, Johannes. 2006. "The Canadian Automotive Market." In

Trade Policy Research 2006, D. Ciuriak, ed. Ottawa: Foreign Affairs and International Trade Canada, pp. 187–340.

Wager, R. 1975. *Golden Wheels: The Story of the Automobiles Made in Cleveland and Northeastern Ohio, 1892–1932.* Cleveland: Western Reserve Historical Society Publication.

Walsh, Tom. 2007. "Light at the End of the Tunnel: Novi Supplier on Path Out of Chapter 11." *Detroit Free Press*, April 16, A:1.

Ward's Automotive Group. 2001. *Ward's Automotive Yearbook.* Southfield, MI: Ward's Communications.

———. 2007. *Ward's Automotive Yearbook.* Southfield, MI: Ward's Communications.

Ward's Automotive Reports. 1997. "NUMMI Requires Returnables But No Deposit." *Ward's Automotive Reports,* October 27, p. 2.

Warner Electric. 2005. "History." South Beloit, IL: Warner Electric. http://www.warnernet.com/history.asp (accessed October 31, 2007).

The Washington Post. 2005. "Q&A: Delphi Chairman and Chief Executive Robert S. 'Steve' Miller." October 29. http://www.washingtonpost.com/wp-dyn/content/article/2005/10/29/AR2005102900700.html (accessed November 19, 2007).

Wasti, S. Nazli, and Jeffrey K. Liker. 1999. "Collaborating with Suppliers in Product Development: A U.S. and Japan Comparative Study." *IEEE Transactions on Engineering Management* 46(4): 444–461.

Webb, Alysha. 2005. "China Suppliers Often Need Nursing, U.S. Suppliers Learn." *Automotive News,* May 23, p. 4.

Webber, Chris. 2005a. "Strategy Analytics Announces Automotive Semiconductor Vendor Market Share Analysis." News release, June 30. Milton Keynes, UK: Strategy Analytics. http://www.strategyanalytics.net/default.aspx?mod=PressReleaseViewer&a0=2452 (accessed December 12, 2007).

———. 2005b. "Automotive Semiconductor Market Continues Steady Growth, Exceeding $16 Billion in 2005." News release, October 12. Milton Keynes, UK: Strategy Analytics. http://www.strategyanalytics.net/default.aspx?mod=PressReleaseViewer&a0=2585 (accessed December 12, 2007).

———. 2006a. "Automotive Semiconductor 2006 Vendor Market Shares." News release, May 25. Milton Keynes, UK: Strategy Analytics. http://www.strategyanalytics.net/default.aspx?mod=PressReleaseViewer&a0=3442 (accessed December 12, 2007).

———. 2006b. "Automotive Semiconductor Demand Forecast 2004–2013." News Release, August 16. Milton Keynes, UK: Strategy Analytics. http://www.strategyanalytics.net/default.aspx?mod=ReportAbstractViewer&a0=3035 (accessed December 12, 2007).

Wernle, Bradford. 2005a. "Bosch Boss: Stop Pointing Fingers." *Automotive News,* May 9, p. 8.

———. 2005b. "New Visteon Has Mexican Flavor." *Automotive News*, June 20, p. 3.

———. 2005c. "Big Suppliers Got Bigger in '04." *Automotive News,* June 27, p. 1.

———. 2006. "Continental Doubles Stability Control Business." *Automotive News,* January 23, p. 10.

White, Joseph B. 2007. "Toyota's Cautious Green Strategy." *The Wall Street Journal*, October 23, p. A12.

White, Lawrence. 1971. *The Automobile Industry since 1945.* Cambridge, MA: Harvard University Press.

Wilson, Amy. 2002a. "Less Noise Means More Sales. Quest for Quiet Ride Helps Rieter Grow." *Automotive News,* May 27. http://www.autonews.com/ apps/pbcs.dll/article?AID=/20020527/SUB/205270708 (accessed November 23, 2007).

———. 2002b. "Automakers See Payoffs in Supplier Parks." *Automotive News*, August 5, p. 34i.

Wilson, Rosalyn. 2007. *18th Annual State of Logistics Report.* Washington, DC: Council of Supply Chain Management Professionals. http://www.slu .edu/Documents/business/cscms/18StateLogisticsReport.pdf (accessed October 19, 2007).

Winter, Derek. 1996. "High-Tech Materials Not So New: Automakers Have Experimented with Them for Decades." *Ward's Auto World*, May. http:// waw.wardsauto.com/ar/auto_hightech_materials_not/ (accessed October 18, 2007).

Wisconsin Historical Society. 2007. "Dictionary of Wisconsin History." Madison, WI: Wisconsin Historical Society. http://www.wisconsinhistory.org/ dictionary/index.asp?action=view&term_id=1652&keyword=Warner+Ele ctric (accessed October 31, 2007).

Womack, James P., Daniel T. Jones, and Daniel Roos. 1990. *The Machine That Changed the World.* New York: Rawson.

Woods, Walter. 2006. "Another Delay Raises Concerns about Kia Plant." *Atlanta Journal-Constitution*, April 21. http://www.ajc.com/business/content/ business/stories/0421bizkia.html (accessed November 23, 2007).

Wortham, April. 2007a. "Automaker, Supplier Roles Blur." *Automotive News*, May 21, p. 42.

———. 2007b. "Faurecia Puts Brakes on Growth Plans for N.A." *Automotive News*, June 18, p. 17.

———. 2007c. "ThyssenKrupp Plans Ala. Steel Plant." *Automotive News*,

May 14. http://www.autonews.com/apps/pbcs.dll/article?AID=/20070514/MANUFACTURING/70511113 (accessed November 23, 2007).

Wright, Richard A. 1996. "The Free-Wheeling Gambler Who Created Conservative General Motors." *Detroit News*, July 30. http://info.detnews.com/history/story/index.cfm?id=100&category=business (accessed November 2, 2007).

Yanik, Anthony J. 1993. "Color Era Dawned with '24 Oakland True Blue Six." In *America at the Wheel: 100 Years of the Automobile in America*. Detroit: Crain Communications, p. 80.

Ying, Tian. 2008. "Changfeng Motors to Decide on North American Plant Plan by May." Bloomberg, March 7.

Ziebart, Wolfgang. 2002. "Building Systems Doesn't Always Build Profits." *Automotive News,* June 3, p. 10.

The Authors

Thomas Klier is a senior economist in the economic research department at the Federal Reserve Bank of Chicago. His research focuses on the effects of changes in manufacturing technology, the spatial distribution of economic activity, and regional economic development. Since joining the Chicago Fed in 1992, he has written widely on the evolving geography of the auto industry.

Dr. Klier's work has been published in scholarly journals, including the *Journal of Regional Studies,* the *Journal of Business and Economic Statistics, the Industrial Geographer, Economic Development Quarterly, the Review of Regional Studies, the Journal of Environmental Planning and Management,* and *Public Choice.*

Dr. Klier received an MBA from Friedrich-Alexander-Universitaet Erlangen-Nuernberg, Germany, and a PhD in economics from Michigan State University.

James Rubenstein is professor of geography at Miami University, Ohio, where he teaches courses on urban planning and urban and economic geography. He received an AB in public affairs from the University of Chicago, an MSc in city and regional planning from the London School of Economics, and a PhD in geography and environmental engineering from the Johns Hopkins University.

Dr. Rubenstein is the author of 35 chapters and articles, including 18 on the auto industry. He is also the author of five books: *The Cultural Landscape: An Introduction to Human Geography* (Prentice Hall, now in its ninth edition), *Making and Selling Cars: Innovation and Change in the U.S. Automotive Industry* (The Johns Hopkins University Press, 2001), *The Changing U.S. Auto Industry: A Geographical Analysis* (Routledge, 1992), *The French New Towns* (The Johns Hopkins University Press, 1978), and *An Introduction to Geography* (Prentice Hall, 1995, with William Renwick).

Index

The italic letters *f, n,* and *t* following a page number indicate that the subject information of the heading is within a figure, note, or table, respectively, on that page.

About the Institute

The W.E. Upjohn Institute for Employment Research is a nonprofit research organization devoted to finding and promoting solutions to employment-related problems at the national, state, and local levels. It is an activity of the W.E. Upjohn Unemployment Trustee Corporation, which was established in 1932 to administer a fund set aside by Dr. W.E. Upjohn, founder of The Upjohn Company, to seek ways to counteract the loss of employment income during economic downturns.

The Institute is funded largely by income from the W.E. Upjohn Unemployment Trust, supplemented by outside grants, contracts, and sales of publications. Activities of the Institute comprise the following elements: 1) a research program conducted by a resident staff of professional social scientists; 2) a competitive grant program, which expands and complements the internal research program by providing financial support to researchers outside the Institute; 3) a publications program, which provides the major vehicle for disseminating the research of staff and grantees, as well as other selected works in the field; and 4) an Employment Management Services division, which manages most of the publicly funded employment and training programs in the local area.

The broad objectives of the Institute's research, grant, and publication programs are to 1) promote scholarship and experimentation on issues of public and private employment and unemployment policy, and 2) make knowledge and scholarship relevant and useful to policymakers in their pursuit of solutions to employment and unemployment problems.

Current areas of concentration for these programs include causes, consequences, and measures to alleviate unemployment; social insurance and income maintenance programs; compensation; workforce quality; work arrangements; family labor issues; labor-management relations; and regional economic development and local labor markets.